Clive Haddon

Designing and Programming
CICS Applications

Designing and Programming CICS Applications

John Horswill and Members of the CICS
Development Team at IBM Hursley

O'REILLY®

Beijing · Cambridge · Farnham · Köln · Paris · Sebastopol · Taipei · Tokyo

Designing and Programming CICS Applications

by John Horswill and Members of the CICS Development Team at IBM Hursley

Published by O'Reilly & Associates, Inc., 101 Morris Street, Sebastopol, CA 95472.

Editor: Sue Miller

Production Editor: Maureen Dempsey

Cover Designer: Edie Freedman

Printing History:

July 2000:   First Edition.

Library of Congress Cataloging-in-Publication Data

Horswill, John.
    Designing and programming CICS applications/John Horswill and members of the CICS
        Development Team and IBM Hursley. p. cm.
    ISBN 1-56592-676-5
    1. Application software—development 2. CICS (Computer system) I. IBM United Kingdom.
        CICS Development Team. II. Title.
    QA76.76.D47 H69 2000
005.4'3—dc21   00-056535

ISBN: 1-56592-676-5

[M]

Table of Contents

Preface

This book explains how to write applications for CICS—the world's favorite transaction processing system. Customer Information Control System (CICS) systems have been running for more than 30 years and CICS has changed dramatically during that time, from being a basic transaction processing monitor to being an advanced distributed application server.

Throughout its evolution, CICS has preserved and enhanced its support for developing and running a very large application workload. This book teaches you the traditional CICS skills and techniques that have delivered results for over 30 years that are still just as relevant today for building high-speed transaction processing applications. It also teaches the modern CICS skills and techniques that exploit today's advanced technologies—Java™, Web, MQSeries, workstation tools—technologies that modern businesses need to exploit in order to stay competitive.

The Book's Audience

This book is for new and experienced CICS application developers; whether you're an undergraduate, a new employee, or an experienced CICS developer who wishes to update your skills, this book is aimed at you. Chapter 1, *Introduction*, should be particularly useful to business managers who need to know how they can use CICS to add to, and improve, their existing business systems. Chapter 2, *Designing Business Applications*, should be read by system architects, designers and programmers. It explains how to design the architecture for a modern transactional application, with a particular emphasis on the use of CICS. Chapter 3, *Introducing the Sample Application*, discusses the components of a business application, and how you should approach the development of these components.

From Chapter 4, *Designing the Business Logic*, onwards, we assume you're an application programmer needing to develop CICS applications. These chapters teach specific CICS skills such as developing programs in COBOL (the business logic), CICS Java, and Visual Basic, or integrating MQSeries with CICS. They contain guidance about designing, coding, and running the components of a typical CICS sample application.

We point you to various books in the CICS library that fill in any gaps because, in a book this size, we won't be able to tell you *all* about CICS. We discuss, and base our examples on, a subset of the full CICS facilities. This makes things easier for you because it means we won't have to keep referring you to other books in the CICS library while you're learning. These other books are listed in the bibliography, and are shown in the library diagram for your particular release of CICS. The subset of CICS commands we've chosen gives you a sound framework for your first application program and offers a logical starting point for more advanced work.

The main purpose of this book is to provide a friendly, straightforward, and modern approach to the writing of CICS application programs. It follows the development of a sample application, and at the end of each part you should be able to generate the relevant code and run the application.

Organization of the Book

The book describes a COBOL application that creates, reads, updates, and deletes records from a database with and without a locking mechanism. In addition, the COBOL program includes modules that browse, capture errors, and use the CICS Basic Mapping System (BMS) for data input and output to a traditional green screen. There are five additional parts that describe how you can use CICS to access your core COBOL application:

* Through a CICS Java application
* Through a web-based application using a CORBA
* By using the CICS Basic Mapping System for data input and output
* By using Visual Basic to design and implement a CICS Client application
* By integrating MQSeries with your CICS application

Each part describes the design of the component and how to write the code to implement the design.

Having written your application, you are guided through a step-by-step process to deploy your application into a CICS system. There is also advice on how to deal with the issues arising from large-scale deployment. Finally, there is a chapter describing some of the debugging facilities available in CICS.

About the CD-ROM

The CD-ROM accompanying this book contains the source code of the sample application that is discussed in this book. This can save you a lot of time by not having to enter the code. Some of the code has been compiled for use with CICS Transaction Server Version 1.3. If you want to use it with other CICS releases, you will have to re-compile the source code. Appendix A describes how to transfer the code from the CD-ROM to your OS/390 system, to install the files and programs, and configure your CICS region so that you can run the application. The remaining components of the application access and use the COBOL programs you install on your mainframe.

In addition to the sample code, the CD-ROM contains the entire CICS Transaction Server Version 1.3 library in Portable Document Format (PDF) format. Together with this is a copy of the Adobe Acrobat reader. Other software includes the Java Development Kit (JDK) Version 1.1.8.

Refer to Appendix B for detailed descriptions of the contents of the CD-ROM. The README files contains important information about running the sample application.

We've also made the code sample available on the O'Reilly web site:

http://www.oreilly.com/catalog/cics

Conventions in This Book

Throughout this book, we've used the following conventions:

Bold
> Indicates the code you need to edit within code examples.

UPPERCASE ITALIC
> Indicates CICS-supplied transactions, the Application Programming Interface (API) commands, and their command options.

Italics
> Indicates CICS command utilities, filenames, menu options, variable names, display text, examples and in-text references to syntax models. For example, if a procedure asks you to type *filename,* you must type the actual name of the file. Italics also indicates menu options as well as the first occurrence of a new term.

Indicates a tip, suggestion, or general note, For example, we'll tell you about some shortcuts or if an operation requires certain privileges.

 Indicates a warning or caution. For example, we'll tell you if you need to check your site's procedures before carrying out a particular action.

How to Contact Us

We have tested and verified the information in this book to the best of our ability, but you may find that features have changed (or even that we have made mistakes!). Please let us know about any errors you find, as well as your suggestions for future editions, by writing to:

> O'Reilly & Associates, Inc.
> 101 Morris Street
> Sebastopol, CA 95472
> (800) 998-9938 (in the U.S. or Canada)
> (707) 829-0515 (international/local)
> (707) 829-0104 (fax)

You can also send us messages electronically. To be put on the mailing list or request a catalog, send email to:

> *info@oreilly.com*

To ask technical questions or comment on the book, send email to:

> *bookquestions@oreilly.com*

We have a web site for the book, where we'll list examples, errata and any plans for future editions. You can access this page at:

> *http://www.oreilly.com/catalog/cics*

For more information about this book and others, see the O'Reilly web site:

> *http://www.oreilly.com*

Acknowledgments

This book is the product of the combined efforts of many individuals. A lot of the initial work was done by Ian McCallion and Bernard Swords. Phil Appleby developed the organization and structure that we have in the book today. Our thanks go to all three.

Part I was written largely by Ian McCallion but many people had a hand in its organization.

Andy Krasun and Peter Missen reviewed the book extensively. Our thanks to them for pointing out the inconsistencies and adding valuable details to the text. Andy, in particular, was able to add a lot of valuable information based on his extensive experience working with customers over many years.

The COBOL code on which Part II and Part V are based was developed by Jerry Ozaniec. Becca Dunleavey, Joanne Hodges and others revised and improved the application.

Part III and Part IV were written by Rob Breeds, who developed the application. He also spent a lot of time very patiently explaining things to Phil Appleby and myself. There must have been times when he despaired.

Part VI and Part VII were written by Mike Moynihan and Steve Young. Mike developed the Visual Basic component and persevered with the application when lesser mortals might have given in. Steve wrote the Java code for the MQSeries part of the book and helped us put the CD-ROM together.

Part VIII, written by Janet Righton, whose experience of debugging CICS programs is second to none!

Joyce Cousins spent a great deal of time ensuring that we had a mainframe application that worked. She also spent time with our graduates ensuring their tests worked.

Norman Bell has also been very helpful in ironing out the wrinkles in the application, and he helped us gain a much clearer understanding of the way that CICS works in an OS/390 environment.

Bob Yelavich always responded with copious comments, and gave us much valuable insight from his wealth of experience. We appreciate his commitment and support.

Finally, I have to thank the people from O'Reilly, including Frank Willison, who supported the original idea of producing this book, and Robert Denn, who followed through with the contract. Our thanks to our editor, Sue Miller, who kept us on the straight and narrow when we all wondered if this project would ever see the light of day. Our thanks to Steven Abrams for his patience in guiding me through the tools and formats and juggling the files and managing the external review. Our thanks go to Rob Romano for his work on the illustrations and to Maureen Dempsey for her role as production editor.

There are many others who have spent a lot of time reviewing and providing invaluable comments on this book, and I hope that I haven't omitted anyone.

I

Introduction to CICS

You may not be aware of it, but hardly a day goes by when something that you do has not involved a CICS application somewhere in the world—whether it is a trip to the supermarket, taking money from your bank account, having a package delivered to your house, managing your company's accounts, stock control or personnel records—CICS is involved. CICS is also involved in many manufacturing plants, providing feedback about the production processes and stock levels, and it may even be linked to suppliers so that stocks can be replenished when necessary. In short, CICS is likely to have played a part in much of the underlying software (often called middleware) that underpins all types of industry applications.

Part I looks at how CICS can help in the world of business applications. It contains the following chapters:

- Chapter 1, *Introduction*, describes the essentials of a business application, and the benefits of using CICS with business applications.

- Chapter 2, *Designing Business Applications*, looks at the key design elements in a business application, and the CICS facilities that support the application designer.

- Chapter 3, *Introducing the Sample Application*, describes the planning of a CICS application that uses existing COBOL business logic and a variety of presentation logic including Dynamic HyperText Markup Language (DHTML), CICS Java (JCICS), a Visual Basic front end using a CICS client, a Java frontend integrating MQSeries with CICS, as well as a traditional 3270 frontend.

In this chapter:
- *The Essentials of a Business Application*
- *Business Applications as Creators of Value*
- *Using CICS for Business Applications*

1

Introduction

Computer systems are used for many different purposes in business today. These range from keeping personal to-do lists to developing business-critical applications in banks. Applications are often categorized by their purpose. For example:

Personal productivity and groupware
> The use of Personal Computers (PCs) for word processing, electronic mail (email), and document sharing using a Local Area Network (LAN).

Design and development
> Computer-aided design and software development.

Manufacturing and production
> Monitoring and control applications in factories.

Business intelligence
> Data warehousing applications used to aid decision-making, arising from powerful, large-scale databases.

Business operations
> Business operations applications (sometimes called *line of business applications*) that "transact the business" of a company—in other words, they perform business transactions on behalf of the company. This is not limited to cash-for-goods transactions. It can include any buyer/supplier transaction that can be translated into a digital format, as well as internal business processes dealing with company resources. For example:
>
> — Credit card transactions
>
> — Cash transactions from a bank's Automatic Teller Machine (ATM) or supermarket cash dispenser
>
> — Stock market transactions for a stock exchange or brokerage

— Information transactions for collecting, collating, and distributing news—such as the results and medal tables for the Olympic Games

— Payroll transactions (essential for the smooth operation of any corporation)

— Logistics transactions, such as the scheduling of vehicles in a transportation company

— Voice application transactions ("Press 1 to enter your meter reading....") for a computer integrated telephony system

— Sales transactions for companies doing business through the Internet

Business applications are crucial to many large and medium-sized companies. For such companies, doing business without these applications would be unthinkable; a bank that lost its computerized account records would cease trading. Many, if not most, of the largest business applications around the world run on CICS.

The Essentials of a Business Application

Even though the computer is at its center, a business application is focused on people. It is a human system as much as a computer system. The purpose of a business application is to keep accurate, up-to-date, and secure operational business information and deliver it rapidly to the users of the application. There are a number of key features that any business application needs. They have to be fast, accurate, secure, and auditable. In addition, the information has to be up to date and available to multiple users across a company, its suppliers, customers, and business partners. A model of the relationship between computers and people is shown in Figure 1-1.

Division of Responsibilities

Accuracy (in the sense of adhering to the intent of the business) depends on the computer system being controlled appropriately; that is, having clear lines of responsibility and division of responsibilities. It is essential to have organizational responsibilities that the system itself monitors and enforces. To this end, business applications broadly separate system development, system operations, and system use with checks and balances. These may be as official as a system audit. There are, of course, many subdivisions of these roles; for example, system development may be subdivided into architecture, design, programming, and testing.

Division of responsibility ensures that different groups of people involved with an application are unable to take advantage of their situations. Consider a payroll application, it should be impossible for payroll clerks to update their own salaries without being monitored; programmers would have built into the program an

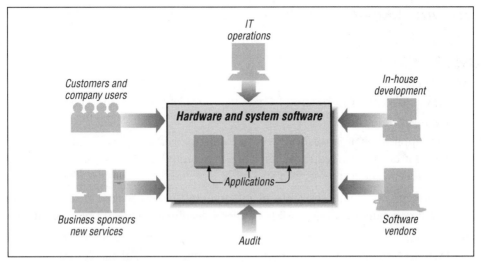

Figure 1-1. Business applications as people systems

audit log that is checked by the audit department. Similarly, the program should include a log of all software updates to ensure that system administrators are unable to make fraudulent changes to the program without trace.

Lifecycle Requirements

Business applications define the business rules that control the delivery and update of critical data; therefore, they require support throughout their lifecycle. The stages of a lifecycle include:

Design
Design user interfaces that meet users' needs; design for growth and extension; design to build complex applications with many features and capabilities.

Develop
Develop efficiently, using modern tools and techniques.

Test
Test thoroughly and efficiently to find problems and track down causes of problems.

Update
Update in such a way as not to disrupt the existing version when upgrading to a new version.

Technical Requirements

In addition to lifecycle requirements, business applications must also meet a set of general technical requirements:

Accessibility
> The application can be used from any appropriate place on the network.

Availability
> The application is available for use by authorized persons at all designated times; it does not need to be shut down for routine maintenance and can be upgraded without interruption.

Communication
> Rapid communication is possible between distributed parts of the application.

Manageability
> Systems administrators can monitor the application to detect problems, and can take corrective action *before* users complain.

Prioritized use of the hardware
> A management capability should be in place to determine how much the machines are used, so that the workload can be distributed evenly.

Rapid response
> The response time for end users is appropriate (which usually means short!).

Reliability
> The application is not expected to fail, but if it does, it provides diagnostic information to help identify the cause of the failure.

Recoverability
> The application restarts quickly after a failure, without loss of information or of data integrity.

Scaleability
> The application can support as many users as needed without slowing down excessively or requiring excessive resources.

Security
> The application includes the ability to control who can use it, and which actions the users can perform.

CICS was originally seen as a transaction processing system. Indeed behind the scenes this is a lot of what it is doing. But, like a lot of middleware, CICS comes to life by virtue of the many applications and operating systems that it supports. It not only provides an extensive Application Programming Interface (API), but it also controls the resources behind the applications; for example, security, databases, files, programs, transactions and so on, that the applications use. Hence, as

CICS has evolved, describing it as an application server gives a much truer picture of its role today. In Figure 1-1 we see a loose arrangement of applications, which largely function independently of each other. Figure 1-2, on the other hand, draws those applications together so that there can be, for example, shared resources distributed across a computer network. To support the division of responsibilities, lifecycle requirements, and general technical requirements, an application server is required to manage the business applications. This is where CICS fits in. IBM's product CICS is an application server.

If you have key applications that run 24 hours a day for 7 days a week and if your business requires that applications can be recovered completely after failure, you have good reason to move to CICS. If your business already uses CICS, extending your CICS system provides an integrated solution for your ever-increasing business requirements.

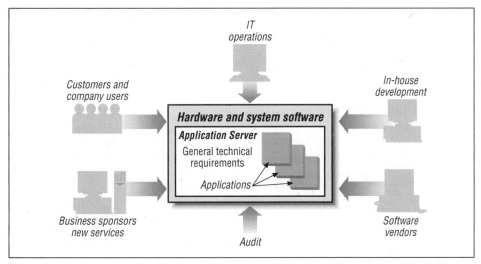

Figure 1-2. Application server supporting business applications

Business Applications as Creators of Value

Historically, companies adopted and became dependent upon business applications because of the reduced costs, improved accuracy, and timeliness of information achieved by transferring key operational data for their business onto computers. Today's business applications must enable rapid development of modern services and must be able to exploit new hardware and software technology for competitive advantage. The latest technology is, of course, the Internet.

Responsibility for developing and managing business applications has changed from being a separate business function to a central part of competitive strategy—from merely boosting operational efficiency to profoundly changing the nature of products, services, and business processes.

The ability to adapt and extend applications has become increasingly important when launching new products and services for maximum advantage. This applies when you're bringing your own ideas to market quickly, and bettering your competitor's offerings. Companies that are today maximizing the potential of Information Technology (IT) to create value are taking radical approaches to developing the systems necessary. The key features are:

- Use of cross-functional teams having responsibility to the business—especially between central and departmental IT groups—because command and control management needs to include all interested parties.

- Maximizing the amount of information held by IT networks.

- Maximizing connectivity to provide information where it is needed.

- Selective use of contracted skills—for example, in web design—rather than attempting to maintain in-house skills across the entire range of technologies.

At the heart of all successful implementations of this approach are the business applications that have been running the business for years—but expanded with more data, applications, processing power and connectivity, and augmented with technologies such as web servers and computer telephony integration. In Figure 1-2, we emphasized how CICS as an application server draws together the applications and resources of a computer system. Figure 1-3 shows application servers have to interact with other systems, both software, for example, web servers and firewalls, and hardware, for example, telephony. Interconnectivity between operating systems and hardware is critical. As a result, a modern business application looks something like that shown in Figure 1-3.

Using CICS for Business Applications

This book shows you how the CICS environment enables you to build a business application consisting of a varied set of components. By satisfying the essentials of a modern business application, CICS provides solutions for your business that improve efficiency, competitiveness, and productivity. Additionally, CICS can help your business implement an e-business strategy—competing in a global marketplace for worldwide customers who find you and trade with you electronically using the World Wide Web.

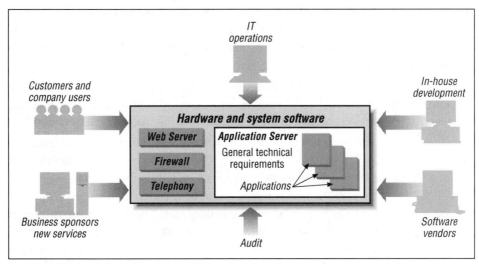

Figure 1-3. Structure of modern business applications

Examples of Business Applications That Use CICS

CICS is used in many different ways by many different businesses. Let's look at a few examples in which CICS is used to help businesses. These examples are based on real customers. For a much longer list of case studies, go to the CICS home page at *http://www.ibm.com/software/ts/cics/* and select case studies.

Financial services (banking, securities, investment services, and insurance)

Company A provides a wide range of services, from consumer banking to securities brokerage. Transaction processing is essential in providing these services. The company uses CICS to produce timely, accurate financial information, in the knowledge that if problems arise they can be resolved easily. Recovery of data is critical. There are a large number of vital CICS applications, written in COBOL many years ago, which Company A doesn't want to give up. But, at the same time, it wants to embrace the World Wide Web and spread some of its applications to workstations and Unix systems. The requirement is to retain the reliability and integrity of its mainframe-based systems while meeting the need from internal and external customers for more flexible, distributed processing.

With CICS, this is not a problem. The company's IT managers can use their existing COBOL programs, retaining all the existing CICS transactions. In addition, they decide to use their current files as their database and then use the CICS External Call Interface (ECI) as a gateway for non-CICS servers to gain access to their business data. This ensures that they extend their business to the distributed environment. Having done that, they are then able to implement a web-trading application very quickly. Six months later, they were processing 60,000 transactions per day in this environment, on top of a peak load of 1,200 CICS transactions per second. The key to their success was to build an infrastructure that enabled them to extend their mainframe processing to the distributed environment.

Bank B, which provides full banking sevices with 800 branches online connected with distributed CICS servers, processes 30 million transactions a day using all the business attributes of CICS: reliability, recoverability, scalability, security, and so on.

Retail

The distributed processing model can be extended to the retail market. Take the case of Company C, which runs a chain of pharmacies across the country. With the help of CICS, a data sharing system is set up for the processing of customer prescriptions. The system allows customers to input their information (name, address, specific allergies, and so on) and allows for detailed online checking to ensure that the drugs being dispensed are right for the customer. The information required to give the complete picture can be built up on the pharmacist's display in real time using CICS and DB2.

Distribution

The distributed processing model can also be used to track packages, from the time that they leave manufacturing to their final delivery. In Company D, drivers using hand-held devices record the delivery of the packages, and this information is sent to the server and made available to the anxious customer. The flexibility and variety of modes to input information—together with the ability to instantly deliver that information to the place it is wanted—are the true benefits of this real-time system.

News and information

At the Olympics, there is a huge amount of computer processing. Two of the main requirements are controlling the movements and providing adequate security for the competitors and officials, and dealing with the results from thousands of events.

During the games, more than 150,000 competitors and officials require access to 80 venues and facilities. Part of the process is a timely, accurate procedure for registering, authenticating, and badging the competitors and officials, and using those badges as a means to manage access to venues, thus ensuring the safety and security of the events. The badging process alone involves 5,000 complex transactions a day, together with background transactions involving 100–150 concurrent users, and emphasizes the need for a system that supports a high transaction throughput in a distributed environment.

The results system gathers, calculates, and tabulates information from the timing, scoring, and judging stations. The results are immediately sent out to the venue scoreboards and interactive touch screens, where they are checked by judges. They are then transferred to the mainframe for distribution to other venues, to printers and to the massed ranks of sports journalists. The Commentator Information System (CIS) communicates directly with the mainframe and PCs that run the results systems. A touch screen allows commentators to pull up information about different sports and participants, allowing a commentator in one venue to comment on several events taking place elsewhere. Altogether the data collection system contains over one million data fields of researched, validated historical results, 20,000 biographies and over 30,000 paragraphs of text—a total of 60 gigabytes of information.

CICS works as an integral part of both systems, people management and processing of results.

2

Designing Business Applications

In this chapter:
- *The Heart of a Business Application*
- *How CICS Can Help the Application Designer*
- *Developing the Components of a Business Application*
- *What's Next...*

Chapter 1, *Introduction*, looked at the essentials of a business application, and the advantages of using CICS to create and run business applications. It also described how many new types of applications, such as interactive web sites, involve an application server such as CICS. As well as having a long pedigree in supporting traditional business applications, CICS also has all of the characteristics needed to support the new types of applications. In this book we are going to develop a fictitious company called KanDoIT. They have been in business for a number of years and now want to expand their business and benefit from e-business opportunities either through the Web or by using message queuing technology or using clients to link to their CICS servers. Initially they have to set about gathering requirements from users and begin to develop an application that satisfies those needs. Much of the remainder of this book describes the design and the programming of the components of the KanDoIT company's application.

Before looking at the details of the application, this chapter gives you some more ideas about the facilities that you can exploit in CICS to make writing scalable transactions with integrity easier. It covers the following topics:

- The key design elements that you need to consider when developing general business requirements

- The CICS facilities that support the key design elements

- The process for developing the components of a business application

The Heart of a Business Application

There are three key aspects of a business application design that support the general business requirements outlined in Chapter 1:

- Components
- Transactions
- Error handling

These are described in more detail as follows.

Components

An important principle of business application design is to separate program code into components. Although this may sound obvious, this has not always been done and is such an important topic that we are going to spend some time on it.

Components are not the same things as objects, nor are they simply the *divide and conquer* aspect of implementing a large project. Components are about managing a complex IT environment, keeping it in step with the needs of the business, and about reuse—the ability to use large amounts of an existing application to build a new one. With good component design, you have the ability to enhance a business application rapidly in response to market needs or to exploit a newly-emerging technology with adherence to business rules assured and without loss of auditability.

There are three aspects that fundamentally differentiate the parts of a modern business application:

Different responsibilities within the overall application
> For example, in a bank application, one program might deal with personal accounts, and others with scheduled transactions or cash.

Different types of responsibility
> For example, one program may be dealing with presentation of data to users, another with interest rate calculations or credit to an account which results in the update of databases.

Different hardware and software platforms
> For example, you might have part of an application running in CICS Transaction Server, part running on another server platform, part running on a client workstation, and part running on a web server that presents static HTML and converts business data to dynamic HTML. Some are *server components*; others are *client components*.

> The advantage of server components is that they are (usually) installed in one place and shared by all users. Therefore they can be maintained easily. The

advantage of client components is that users get more predictable response times from the client code. However, because client code is installed in many places, it can be more difficult to maintain unless you employ methods that automatically update client code.

Where you place the function of a business application is determined by finding a balance between achieving good response times and maintainability.

There are also some practical differences; that is, the components may be:

- Run in different geographical locations
- Run on different types of hardware
- Written by different people (in different companies, different groups, or with different skills)
- Developed, tested, and deployed at different times
- Modified, retested, and redeployed at different times

These differences cannot be ignored. Instead, they must be taken into account when designing and developing an application. In other words, your application should be structured into components.

The key components of any business application are *business logic components* and *presentation logic components*. The business logic component is responsible for business calculations and updating databases. These components are the hardest to develop, the most critical to the operation of the business, and the most valuable to reuse. Get these right and everything falls into place. The presentation logic components and their component interfaces control the presentation of information to end users. The presentation logic components are represented in this book as the 3270 interface using COBOL, as a web interface using servlets and Java Server Pages (JSP), as a Graphical User Interface (GUI) using Visual Basic, and as a Java program using MQSeries to access data in our CICS application. In Figure 2-1 we show the 3270 frontend. Each of the three other frontends have a similar input screen and account display screen.

Business logic components

The individual functions of a business logic component should be designed to operate in a server environment. Business logic functions typically:

- Validate input data
- Search the database
- Cross-validate input data and database data
- Update data (including additions and deletions)
- Log activities

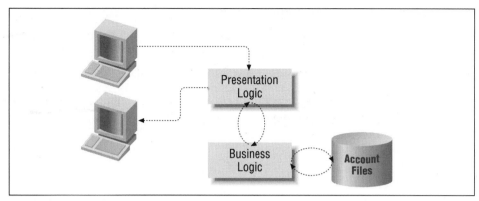

Figure 2-1. Initial outline of a 3270 application

Business logic components should do these things in a way that adheres to business rules and ensures their consistent implementation. For example, they should:

- Update a journal on a particular database containing sensitive material (such as a payroll) for an audit trail.

- Provide the one-and-only approved program that performs complex computations such as interest earned on a deposit account or discount granted on a customer order.

- Obey rules imposed by regulatory bodies.

- Ensure that consistency cannot be compromised. For example, critical updates that are inextricably linked should be done in the same program.

The criteria for grouping business logic functions into business logic components are pragmatic. Business logic components should:

- Encapsulate as much data as possible.

- Have an interface that can be tested independently.

- Be able to move to another server without affecting other components.

- Have a purpose and responsibility that can be discussed in a business context and should not have a purely technical definition such as *everything running on a server X*.

Presentation logic components

This is the code primarily concerned with the presentation of data to an end user and receipt of data from an end user. It should:

- Invoke the general-purpose presentation management code that controls the layout of data on a visual display screen or other output device.

- Validate input.

- Handle interactions in the correct sequence.

- Confirm completeness (that is, that all necessary information has been provided).

- Invoke one or more pieces of business logic, as needed.

Presentation logic may be designed to run on a client. For example, if the user sits at a personal computer, the presentation logic could be a Visual Basic application; if the user uses a web browser, the presentation logic could be a set of Java servlets running on a web server.

Component interfaces

Not all components have interfaces that can be invoked by other components. Those that have invocable variables must:

- Publish the interfaces for use when developing client components (which may not be programmed in the same language or run on the same type of machine).

- Be tested thoroughly against the interfaces.

- Protect the interfaces using security mechanisms.

- Make the interfaces available to any executing client, locally or remotely.

A note about traditional CICS applications

Many CICS applications written in the past combined presentation logic and business logic. Such applications are difficult to treat as components. As such, you would have to use the External Presentation Interface (EPI) to do many of the processes that are described in this book. For example, EPI allows a Java program to emulate a CICS 3270 terminal, and start CICS transactions on the server. The program sends and receives data as CICS terminal datastreams. Programming in EPI involves *screen-scraping*, where you must extract data from a screen-orientated buffer row by row and column by column. It is intended for use by CICS server programs that cannot be modified to be called by the External Call Interface (ECI) due to the tightly coupled presentation and business logic. See Chapter 12, *Designing the Visual Basic Component*, for more information about the ECI.

Transactions

In a business application, a *transaction* has the same meaning as it does in everyday English—a single event or item of business between two parties. Business application transactions should have the so-called ACID* (Atomicity, Consistency,

---

* The term "ACID properties of a transaction" was coined by Haerder and Reuter in 1983 and used by Jim Gray and Andreas Reuter. In CICS, ACID properties apply to a "unit of work" (see "CICS Transactions").

Isolation, and Durability) properties, which are described in more detail later on in this section. However, before explaining what ACID transactions are, consider the problems that can occur with transactions.

Imagine a component that operates on bank accounts. The component has three services that could be invoked by end users, one to add to an account, one to delete from an account, and one to move money between accounts.

The most difficult of these is to move money, because it must do everything necessary to ensure that all the accounts are updated and that the operation only proceeds when appropriate. Consider what would happen if things went wrong—if the server failed or if the database contained errors after some, but not all, of the updates had been done. One customer could have his money withdrawn, without the other customer receiving any money (providing an unintended bonus for the bank!). Or, even worse (for the bank at least!), both customers could receive money, resulting in an unintended loss for the bank.

Also, consider what could happen if two bank employees try to move money from the same account at the same time. If the component is designed to read the database to check whether there are sufficient funds and then update the database with the new balance, one of the updates could be lost.

To prevent problems such as these, we need to create ACID transactions:

"A" is for Atomicity

To be atomic, a transaction must execute completely or not at all. This means that every file, database, or queue operation within the transaction must execute without error. If any part of the operation fails, then the entire unit of work is terminated, which means that changes to the data are undone. There is no trace of the attempt to execute the transaction. The requirement may exist to log the start of a transaction for audit purposes. If all the operations execute successfully, the transaction can be committed, which means that the changes to the data are made permanent or durable.

"C" is for Consistency

This means that the transaction taken as a whole does not violate any of the integrity constraints associated with the state of the resources. Obviously, the program itself is the arbiter of consistency in a business sense. In our simple example, moving money should not alter the total amount of money in the accounts.

"I" is for Isolation

Isolation means that even though transactions execute concurrently, they appear to be serialized. In other words, it appears to each transaction that any other transaction executed either before it or after it, but not simultaneously.

Remember that we are developing a multi-user system accessing a shared database. When some but not all of the updates needed for consistency have been done, the database is inconsistent. When all the updates have been done but the transaction has still not yet committed, the transaction could back out. In either of these cases, allowing other transactions to see or update the records could result in errors in the database.

Isolation means that other transactions can be prevented from seeing or updating the same records. In other words, the data that a transaction accesses cannot affect or be affected by any other part of the system until the transaction is completed. If moving money was not isolated, an inconsistent view of the database would be possible—or worse, concurrent updates could corrupt the database. Complete isolation is logically equivalent to forcing serialization of all transactions against the database, only allowing concurrent transactions that do not affect each other in any way at all.

"D" is for Durability

This means that after a transaction completes successfully (that is, commits), its changed state survives failures. This normally requires that all the data changes made during the course of a unit of work must be written to some type of physical storage when the transaction is successfully completed.

Trying to implement the ACID properties by unique application code in every business application component would be difficult. It would totally obscure the business logic, making the code difficult to maintain and audit. The problem is that some things are not business issues but technical issues—things the technology should address in order to ensure the code is as easy to write as possible—so as to allow the business logic programmer to focus on the business issues. There is a clear difference between business exceptions, (such as, "the account does not have enough money in it") and technical exceptions (such as, "the account database has only accepted one of my updates"). Our system software, our middleware, should hide the messy realities of the machinery and present us with services that don't need us to solve this problem.

Using an application server such as CICS, you can obtain the ACID properties by defining groups of updates that must all be done together. As the transaction proceeds, the updates are done on a provisional basis, and logged. If they all work, you can commit (syncpoint) the changes, that is, make them permanent. But if there are problems you can cancel the changes, that is, back them out. If the system fails—say there is a power outage before you have issued the commit—the system automatically backs out the changes you made. Your program's responsibility has ended, though the client may need to resubmit the request once power is restored. You can concentrate on ensuring that business exceptions are handled, and you can safely leave the technical exceptions to the system.

Limitations of ACID transactions

Does the above sound too good to be true? You're right, it is! Here are the potential problems.

An ACID transaction should be "short," because it locks shared resources.

Here, "short" is a relative term. In a large system running hundreds of transactions per second, short would be less than a second. It is up to the designer to set a target for the duration of a transaction, but in almost all cases it is undesirable that human think-time be allowed to control the duration of an ACID transaction. This is important because it means the programs should not wait for user input in the middle of a transaction, however appealing it is to ask for user confirmation before committing. "Maintaining File Integrity: Using Locking" in Chapter 4 shows some of the practical ways to work around this issue.

ACID transactions should not be "big."

Here, "big" is also relative. For example, don't implement a transaction that runs through the entire database correcting telephone numbers due to changes in the national telephone numbering plan. It should not be logically necessary to do this atomically, that is, do one record or row at a time and commit the result before passing it on to the next, because otherwise it would effectively lock out all other users until completed.

Be aware that under certain conditions a state known as "deadlock" can occur.

This is where two or more transactions are trying to access the same set of resources and each ends up waiting for the others to complete. For example, program A has updated a record with key X and then wishes to update a record with key Y. Program B wishes to do the reverse. Neither can continue because invalid data would result. The system detects this and arbitrarily cancels one of the transactions which, since there is no actual error, should simply retry and start from the beginning.

Complete isolation may have intolerable throughput implications.

There are cases with adding or deleting records where complete isolation may not be recommended, in situations where, for example, all transactions are serialized. So typically, systems provide the ability to relax the isolation property, allowing improved concurrence while still preventing multiple concurrent updates to the same record.

Error Handling

It is a well known fact that in computing 80% of programming code deals with handling errors and/or exception conditions, that is, with knowing what is supposed to happen, checking that it has, and doing something about it if it has not!

Suppose a device error occurs on a disk—the data will not be available until the disk is replaced and the data restored. But suppose the application that was trying to read the disk failed to check that the operation succeeded and, as a result, wrote incorrect data to another file. Merely restoring the original data will no longer fix the problem, and finding out why the second file contained garbage could be very difficult.

Suppose a software bug in an infrequently used part of a program caused an undetected overwrite of stored data. Not only could subsequent uses of the program fail because some piece of memory is corrupted, but finding out why the problem occurred could be very difficult.

These examples show why handling errors is vitally important. Errors are a fact of life. In developing applications, it is best to remember these two maxims:

- "Anything that can happen will happen, usually at the worst possible time."

- "Absolutely *anything* can happen!"

Errors that disrupt business applications can stop a company doing business until the problem is fixed, so it is vital to detect errors early, clean up after the errors to allow operations to continue, and record diagnostic information so that problems can be fixed quickly.

The need for a methodical approach

In component-based applications, errors mostly occur in the interface between two components. It is therefore important to document and test the interfaces in a methodical way. Also, components are supposed to hide complexity from their users, so we want to notify errors in a simple way from the user's point of view.

How is that done? First, some definitions:

Fault
> Something going wrong, such as a LAN (Local Area Network) failure, software bug or unexpected data received.

Error
> The symptom of a fault, such as a parameter check failing.

Abend (Abnormal ending)
> The situation where program execution cannot continue normally, such as a storage violation.

Error notification
> The passing of information that an error has been detected from one component to another component. This can either be by return code or by executing an abort command.

Signalling component
> The component that notifies an error.

Receiving component
> The component to which notification of an error is given.

As for noticing an error, we need to decide if there is a fault causing it. Not all errors are the result of a fault; for example, a module issuing a database read command that returns a "record not found" error may regard the error as acceptable.

If there is a fault, you need to:

1. Record enough diagnostic information so that computer support staff can quickly determine what the fault is and correct it.

2. If possible, bypass the error so that no other components are affected by the problem.

3. If the error cannot be bypassed:

    a. Clean up as much as possible.

    b. Notify other components of the error.

    c. For presentation logic components, provide clear instructions to end users regarding who to inform about the error and what to do to continue working.

In practical terms, the above guidelines translate to the following:

During design:

- Always specify that component interfaces must have return codes.
- Consider what the end user should do when errors occur.

During development:

- Always check for return codes.
- Give meaningful return codes.
- Clean up before returning.
- Log errors.
- Include code for an abnormal end (abend) situation.
- Include error messages, explaining what needs to be done, in the end user interface.

You'll find more information about error handling in "Handling Errors" in Chapter 4, which looks at error handling in the COBOL business logic component of the sample application.

How CICS Can Help the Application Designer

A business application should incorporate the key design elements of components, transactions, and error handling. This section provides some more background to show how CICS supports the application designer to structure an application so that it meets the business requirements described in Chapter 1, and incorporates the key design elements. CICS provides the following facilities:

- An environment for executing presentation logic and business logic components
- Calls between components
- Efficient control of concurrently running application programs serving many online users
- Provision of ACID properties through management of the units of work (see the following section)
- Shared error handling
- System management

It's useful at this point to look at CICS transactions, and CICS programs and linking, in more detail. We'll also consider how CICS deals with critical activities such as error handling and security.

CICS Transactions

In a CICS application, a transaction is the processing initiated by a request, usually from an end user. A transaction starts, executes, and ends. A single business transaction (such as the enrollment of a new customer) may involve several CICS transactions.

 As well as referring to a single event, *transaction* can also refer to the class of similar events. Thus, we speak of adding Mary Smith to the payroll file with a (single) *add* transaction, but we also speak of the *add* transaction, meaning the class of additions to that particular file.

A CICS transaction may contain one or more Units of Work (UOW) where a UOW begins with the first action to alter a protected resource and ends with either an explicit or implicit syncpoint. To summarize, a business transaction involves one or more CICS transactions that, in turn, can involve one or more units of work.

When processing transactions, CICS accumulates performance statistics and monitors the resources used. This provides the information that enables user departments in your organization to be charged accordingly. It also allows you to find out which parts of CICS are being heavily or lightly used. This helps your systems managers to tune the system to improve its performance.

CICS Programs and Linking

A program is the smallest replaceable unit of an application. Programs are compiled, linked or bound, and turned into a single executable file which is then deployed. They can be written in many languages and run in many different environments. A component of a business application typically consists of multiple programs.

CICS provides a variety of ways for programs using CICS to invoke and be invoked by other programs running inside or outside CICS, for example on web servers or end-user workstations. Program calls can be:

Synchronous
> Control is not returned to the calling program until the call is complete.

Asynchronous
> The calling program continues executing while the call is performed. The access method informs the application program after the operation is completed.

Synchronous calling between programs

There are two main ways in which one program can invoke another program inside CICS. These are discussed in more detail in "Commands for Passing Program Control" in Chapter 5. For the time being suffice it to say that the CICS API consists of a number of commands that define resources, make calls to other programs and so on. In this book you will meet a wide range of these commands particularly in Part II and Part V. Two of these commands create links from one program to another. Figure 2-2 shows the linking process and relationship of one program to the next. The commands are:

EXEC CICS LINK
> Allows one program to transfer control to another in a synchronous manner and continue execution after the called program has returned. This also occurs by means of native programming language facilities such as a COBOL CALL statement."The LINK Command" in Chapter 5 gives more detail.

EXEC CICS XCTL
> Allows for one program to call another in a synchronous manner but unlike *LINK* will not receive control back when the called program returns. This has

no equivalent high-level language facility. It is particularly useful in error processing when an unexpected error is detected that implies that the program which trapped the error cannot continue. "The XCTL Command" in Chapter 5 gives more details.

In both cases a COMMAREA (for "communication area") is used to pass parameters and returned values. For more information about COMMAREAs see "Saving Data: Using a Scratchpad Facility" in Chapter 5.

The *LINK* and *XCTL* commands introduce the idea that different programs involved in the processing for a transaction can be executing at different logical levels. A program invoked directly by CICS is considered to be at the highest logical level of the task (level 1). If it then uses the *LINK* command to link to another program then the linked-to program is considered to be at a lower logical level (level 2). However, if the program detects an unexpected condition it can use *XCTL* to call an error handler which will be considered by CICS to be executing at the same logical level as the program issuing the *XCTL* request. Figure 2-2 illustrates this principle.

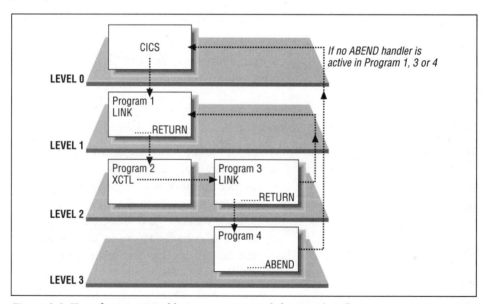

Figure 2-2. Transferring control between programs (after an Abend)

Asynchronous calling between programs

One CICS program can invoke another asynchronously passing data in the *FROM* area defined in the *EXEC CICS START* command. The program for which *START* has been issued is executed as logical level 1, independent of the level of program that issued the *START*. The *FROM* area can be accessed by executing a *RETRIEVE* command.

Alternatively you can use MQSeries. This is discussed in "Working with MQSeries," later in this chapter.

Calling CICS programs from non-CICS programs

CICS provides a number of ways in which non-CICS programs executing on a variety of hardware and software platforms can call CICS programs. In fact, there are more ways than we are able to describe in this book, but here are a few examples:

A software package known as the CICS Client provides the ECI and EPI facilities:

ECI (External Call Interface)
> Allows the calling program to call a CICS program as though it had been linked to (using the LINK command) by another CICS program. The ECI uses a COMMAREA.

EPI (External Presentation Interface)
> Allows the calling program to call a CICS program as though it had been invoked by a user at a 3270-type device.

The CICS Client is designed to run on end-user workstations and meet the needs of a single user running programs that invoke CICS programs. Our sample application makes use of the CICS Client ECI function call.

For programmers using the ECI or EPI, there are application tools that build some of the program calls automatically. One such tool is VisualAge Interspace. The sample application demonstrates the use of Interspace.

For server applications, a software package known as the CICS Transaction Gateway also supports the ECI and EPI. The CICS Transaction Gateway would be used, for example, by programs running under the control of a web server.

When the calling program is written in Java, there is a pure Java version of the ECI and EPI facilities that access the CICS Transaction Gateway using TCP/IP.

Finally, a CICS program written in Java can be invoked using the Internet Inter-ORB Protocol (IIOP); the sample program uses IIOP.

Defining resources

CICS has a set of resources that are grouped into categories, for example, File Control (FC), Temporary Storage (TS), and so on. These resources can be defined in batch using the DFHCSDUP utility program or online using the Resource Definition Online (RDO) transactions. A historical note: several years ago, many resources were assembled (sic) together into tables; so, for example, File Control resources were aggregated into a File Control Table (FCT).

Working with MQSeries

For asynchronous processing, you can achieve the greatest flexibility by using IBM's broad range of MQSeries products. Neither the calling program nor the called program needs to know anything at all about where or when the other program executes because MQSeries provides a common set of facilities for sending and receiving messages, takes responsibility for routing messages to the required location, and holds the message until the receiving program wants it. The sample application uses MQSeries to invoke a CICS program.

Error Handling Facilities

Error handling facilities are critical in any application. CICS includes several error handling facilities, including:

*   ABEND
*   Return codes in commands
*   DUMP
*   TRACE
*   Sending messages to system consoles where operators can respond to the problems

These are described in more detail in "Handling Errors" in Chapter 5.

Security

Security is a complex subject that requires careful planning before it is implemented; as such, it is not dealt with thoroughly here. As we have already mentioned, many people, with many different roles, interact with business applications and the security, auditability, and accuracy of the application depends on these roles being kept separate and identifiable. Therefore it is natural that security of business applications should be role-based.

Once each user's role has been understood, security can be implemented on the following basis:

Authentication
> Where the user's identities are verified, typically using a user ID and password approach

Authorization
> Where an attempted action by a user is checked to see whether it is permitted

CICS works in co-operation with OS/390 security managers (for example, Resource Access Control Facility (RACF), Access Control Facility (CA-ACF2), or TopSecret) to implement this role-based security, with CICS calling the security manager as required to provide the authentication and authorization checks. CICS can request up to three types of authorization check: transaction security, resource security, and command security.

Transaction security

This is the normal sort of security applied to business applications. All CICS applications, whether started by a user at a terminal or a program connecting to CICS, run under a transaction. Consequently, using transaction security to check the authorization of an authenticated user to initiate the transaction is usually sufficient to protect the resources accessed by the transaction.

Resource security and command security

In some situations, for example where applications require varying levels of access to different users within the same transaction, a more granular approach can be required. In these cases resource security and command security may be applied, as required, to restrict access to specific resources. For example, a transaction that prints any file might use resource-level security to prevent users printing files they are not authorized to see.

Alternatively, command-level security could be used; for example, a transaction that allows the user to select CICS commands to issue could use CICS command security to prevent a user from issuing commands that set the status of a file.

CICS security is applied only to resources owned by CICS. Although a resource security check could be made against a CICS file, this would have no relevance to the underlying security on, for example, its base implementation by a VSAM data set.

CICS resource security and CICS command security are not needed for normal business applications; indeed using them in the wrong situations can give a false sense of security. They do not protect resources from what programmers might do accidentally or deliberately. For example, use of resource security would not prevent the programmer of the payroll update transaction inserting code into the transaction which when executed by others gives the programmer unauthorized pay increases. To guard against this sort of threat, it is necessary to use anonymous peer code reviews.

Other Services for the Application Designer

CICS uses operating system services on behalf of components. However, it doesn't merely duplicate the services but adds value by providing additional services for running transactions. These services include:

- Communication with devices and subsystems.
- Recoverable access to shared databases and files, in conjunction with the various database products and data access methods that are available.

- Communication with other CICS systems and database systems, both in the same computer and in connected computer systems.

The programming facilities CICS provides are:

A choice of programming language
> You can write your application programs in IBM Assembler, COBOL, PL/I, C, C++, REXX, or Java languages.

An application programming interface
> You need know a little about how CICS works. You request services by issuing CICS commands consistent with the programming language you are using. For example, in COBOL, the EXEC CICS command, or in Java, the JCICS classes.

An execution diagnostic facility (EDF)
> This is used for displaying and changing parameters in command-level application programs, that is, those that use the EXEC CICS command interface interactively.

A remote edit, compile, and debug capability
> This is used in conjunction with the VisualAge compilers for OS/390.

Developing the Components of a Business Application

Having looked at the key elements of a business application, and how CICS addresses these elements, it's time to consider the process for developing the components of a business application. The stages of the process are:

- Design
- Programming
- Test and debug
- Deployment

Design

It's important to ensure that there is agreement on what each component is required to do. Make sure you document the design of your component thoroughly, and share it with people who are designing other components. Document your component's interface, if it has one that other components use. Include assumptions about performance and capacity.

If your component has a user interface, test it out on paper first by drawing all of the proposed screens, and asking some of the intended users to check your design by attempting to "use" the screens. Put yourself in the position of the computer, in order to check what happens when it makes a functional request.

Finding problems at the design stage is essential; it is much cheaper and quicker to fix them earlier rather than later.

For each component in our sample application, you will find that there is a chapter describing the design. In these chapters we consider the factors influencing the design of the component, which lead to the decisions made by the component designer.

Programming

Read the design document! The main job of the programmer is to implement the design, as documented. At the same time, the programmer should follow:

- Good practice for the language in which the component will be written.
- Good practice for the environment in which the component will be running.
- Local conventions with regard to file naming, and so on.

For each component in our sample application, we show how to convert the design into a working program.

Test and Debug

Testing is an integral part of any software development, and must be as carefully prepared and implemented as the development of the product itself. There are many different methods for testing and several standards have been developed. It is outside the scope of this book to describe testing standards in detail; however, here are a few useful guidelines:

- Test each component in isolation.
- Test the application as a whole, that is, from end-to-end. This book covers:
  - Visual Basic to COBOL
  - MQSeries to COBOL
  - Web to Java to COBOL
  - IBM 3270 green screen using CICS BMS (Basic Mapping Support) to COBOL
- Load/Stress the application:
  - Concurrent users
  - Running in a system with a high workload

Your testing will inevitably uncover errors in the component's logic or programming. These then need to be removed, a process known as debugging. Chapter 16, *Debugging in CICS* describes some of the debug tools available in CICS, and shows some sample debug screens.

Deployment

Once each component has been designed, programmed, tested, and debugged, it must be deployed correctly. At the same time, the configuration files for the various runtime products must be updated to recognize the components.

Appendix A describes the deployment of our sample application.

What's Next...

Enough about the background; the next chapter introduces the sample application that will be developed throughout the remainder of the book.

In this chapter:
- *The Business Case*
- *The Design of the Sample Application*
- *What's Next...*

3

Introducing the Sample Application

Chapters 1 and 2 described the essentials of a business application, and the advantages of using CICS in business applications. The remainder of this book is concerned with the design and the programming needed to build a CICS application along the lines of those described in the previous chapters. Before getting into the details, let's look at the business case and the reason why our fictitious company, KanDoIT, might want to develop a CICS application.

The Business Case

The KanDoIT company is a successful business with an IT department that includes a CICS development team and a web design group. It has thousands of customers. The customer accounts file holds the customer's name, address, telephone number, charge limit, current balance, account activity, payment history, and so on. It uses a short, unique account number that is allocated manually (this wouldn't happen in the real world but it's included here for simplicity) when a new account is opened.

The existing application creates, reads, updates, and deletes customer accounts, and it needs to be expanded to meet the expected future demand. It runs on an IBM S/390 mainframe computer that is also used for other, unrelated applications. The application was developed many years ago, and is used by staff in the accounts department and in the customer services department. The staff run, the application using 3270 terminals. The company has a web site that is used primarily as a means of advertising the company's business.

There are several business factors influencing KanDoIT's decision to develop a new business application:

- The customer services department has a high turnover of clerical staff and the manager would therefore like to spend less time on training new clerks to use the existing system. They would like their applications to present data using a graphical user interface (GUI). As well as being easier to use and learn, it would include its own online help information. The staff in the accounts department want to retain their existing terminals, familiar transactions and data presentations.

- A strategic decision has been taken to enhance the web site so that customers can access and query their own accounts.

- Head office auditors want to be able to conduct random checks on customer accounts.

A typical company may have many more requirements and demands than this. But for the moment let's consider in more detail the IT requirements for the application.

The IT Requirements

The IT requirements for the new application are:

- To replace the existing application with a new one better able to respond to business requirements.

- To create a GUI using Visual Basic or a similar product.

- To provide customers with direct access to their own account from the Internet using a web server and a Java program running in CICS.

- To support more users in the Head Office.

- To reuse the existing customer account database.

The Cross-Functional Team

So what is the process for addressing the IT requirements? KanDoIt formally starts their project by holding a "kick-off" meeting and inviting all departments affected to provide one representative to be a member of the cross-functional team. This is to ensure that all departments are familiar with the new proposal and that their concerns are aired at the meeting.

At KanDoIT's kick-off meeting, the following departments are represented. In real life, it might not be necessary to have quite such a broad cross-section of groups; nevertheless, it's always good policy to ensure that everyone involved in the project has the chance to provide input at the earliest possible stage. This can help to avoid extensive redesign later on.

Application architect
   This person directs the overall design of the application, but needs more information before submitting a proposed architecture.

Security

This group is responsible for anticipating and preventing methods of defrauding the company, and ensuring data protection for customers, especially when the system is connected to the Internet.

Audit

The Audit group is responsible for the integrity of the customer account record database. They are concerned with the diagnosis and correction of data corruption, and logging of user activity.

Visual Basic development

This group is concerned with requirements and design of the new interface for the customer services department.

Accounts department

This group would like to keep their familiar 3270 terminals and transactions.

Customer services

This group would like to replace the user interface for the customer services department with a new, user-friendly one.

Head office

This group wants the availability of data during specific business hours, and they want that data to be accessible with rapid response to achieve, for example, higher employee productivity and customer responsiveness.

Web design

This group wants to enhance the web site to develop it for e-business and e-commerce.

IT development planning

This group is concerned with project management, how much it will cost, how many people will be required, and how long it will take.

IT technical planning

This group is concerned with capacity planning, whether the customer account record database is likely to grow as a result of the enhancements, if more MIPS (million instructions per second) are required.

CICS development

This group is concerned with CICS aspects, and whether or not they can support the new features—the nature of the firewall, the operating system, and so on.

At the end of the meeting the application architect has the information required to make a first pass at defining the overall architecture. This will be reviewed and agreed by the cross-functional team before proceeding to detailed design and development. The next chapter looks in detail at the proposed design.

The Design of the Sample Application

Let us now look at the proposed architecture for the sample application. The key requirements for the KanDoIT company's new system are:

- Reuse the existing accounts file for a new application to keep track of customer accounts.

- Provide online access to the application for the accounts department, the customer services department, head office, and for customers themselves using the Internet.

- Use presentation logic and business logic components running on CICS, customer service department PCs, a web server, and so on. Server components will run on CICS to ensure that the technical requirements (see "Technical Requirements" in Chapter 1) are met.

The Initial Architecture

Let us now look in more detail at what each set of end users requires:

The customer services department requires:

- Online access to the customer accounts database using a new, user-friendly interface written in Visual Basic and running on Windows NT workstations that can be used alongside the existing call management system.

- The ability to search for records by name and to select the appropriate record easily if the search results in multiple matches.

The accounts department requires:

- An account inquiry function.

- The ability to add, delete, and change some fields unrelated to billing.

- The ability to access records by account number. The account number is always available when they are processing work or answering questions.

The head office requires:

- The ability to send an MQSeries message to obtain the full record of a customer, for audit purposes.

Customers require:

- The ability to query their own account information.

- Confidence that their account information is secure from other users.

It is clear that all users want to share the same data, and that they want a high-performance, reliable business logic component with a set of access services to the data. This leads to the initial architecture shown in Figure 3-1. They now need to refine the lines in the diagram above to give direction to each of the development groups.

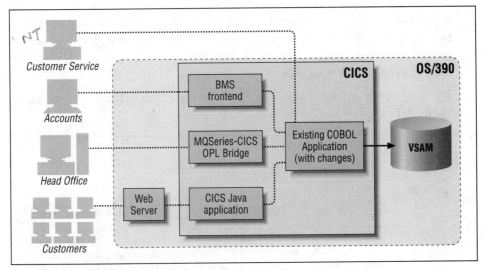

Figure 3-1. The initial architecture

Customer service

The customer services department uses Windows NT workstations, and the developers of the customer services interface are using Visual Basic. So they plan to develop a component in Visual Basic that uses the External Call Interface provided by CICS (see "Designing the Visual Basic Component" in Chapter 12) to access the COBOL business logic. The programming is simplified using the VisualAge Interspace product.

Accounts

Members of the accounts department want to continue using 3270 emulation for the repetitive tasks they perform. For this they decide to continue to use their current system, that is, a presentation logic component running in CICS using CICS 3270 presentation services.

Head office

Head office wants to access the account files using MQSeries messaging. So the application architect decided to configure MQSeries and the MQSeries-CICS DPL bridge on their system to enable this. The sample in this book shows an application written in Java that can be used to test the messaging capability. It has been kept relatively simple for the purposes of clarity. For a head office in the real world it would have to be a little more extensive.

Customers

The KanDoIT company chooses an approach that uses as many industry-standard components as possible. It includes a standard web browser connecting using HTTP to a web server and the WebSphere Web Application Server running Java servlets and Java server pages, connecting to CICS using the internet inter-orb protocol (IIOP). This is the approach that we have used in this book. However the burning issue that would have to be addressed and is beyond the scope of this book is security. One plan would have been to include a second database, unrelated to the account database, which would be used to validate customer access.

The end result of the planning stage looks like the architecture shown in Figure 3-2.

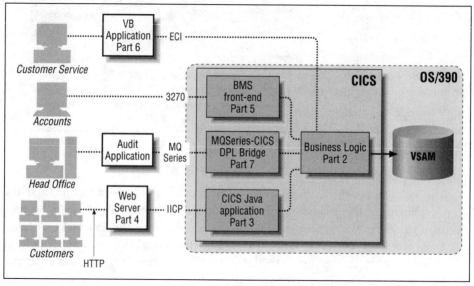

Figure 3-2. The overall architecture

What's Next...

The remainder of this book describes the steps involved in designing and developing the six components of our sample application:

- Business logic—as a COBOL program
- A CICS Java component including CORBA
- Web component including a CORBA client
- 3270 presentation
- Graphical User Interface (GUI) using Visual Basic
- Messaging using MQSeries

II

The COBOL Business Logic Component

Part I introduced the key concepts of components, transactions, and error handling for business applications, together with the KanDoIt company's new business application. This Part looks at the design and programming of the COBOL business logic component for KanDoIT's business application. It includes the following chapters:

- Chapter 4, *Designing the Business Logic*, describes the stages that you need to think about when designing the business logic which allows you to create, read, update and delete records from a keyed file.

- Chapter 5, *Programming the COBOL Business Logic*, introduces a range of CICS commands which are used in the COBOL business logic program.

4

Designing the Business Logic

The specification outline for the COBOL business logic component for the sample application is a simple one—to provide a program to perform create, read, update, delete, and browse operations on the customer account file.

The design phase for the component specifies in detail:

- The interfaces to the component

- Any errors the component may encounter and report

- Usage constraints, such as the need to call the read operation before calling the update operation

It is important to note before starting to design and develop the component that the simple and incomplete specification above could be implemented in many ways, altering the balance of responsibilities and affecting the ease of development and debugging of the total application. In the real world, the final specification only evolves after several meetings involving the architect and the component developers, and a number of redesigns. As they work through the sample to get it right first time, consultation with the users of the application is critical to ensure the correct design decisions. During the design stage, you should include the following steps:

- Determine what the COBOL component should do

- Incorporate CICS design guidelines

- Determine data handling

- Design the individual functions
- Map the functions to CICS programs
- Check business logic programs

Understanding What COBOL Components Need to Do

The first step is to ensure that you understand what your architect has said that the component must do. It is also essential to talk to the actual users of the application to find out how they do their work and how they view the functions you intend to provide.

You need to check for information or functions that nobody requested but that nevertheless may be required when real work is attempted. Inevitably the users make the same discoveries after you've completed your programming effort, and you'll be left to make changes later when it may prove difficult, rather than now when it is easy. It is very important to repeat this validation step as the design process moves along from a broad outline toward a more and more detailed specifications.

As a result of these deliberations, you decide that your COBOL component will provide interfaces to do the following:

- Return the contents of a customer account record, given an account number.
- Add a new customer account record, given an account number and customer data.
- Modify an existing account record, given an account number and modified data.
- Delete an account record, given an account number.
- Access customer account records by name; that is, given a last name or part of it, return a list of matching names with corresponding account numbers and addresses.

The component must be able to accept these requests from other components running inside or outside CICS.

A fundamental principle of the design is that users must always read a record before modifying or deleting it.

Once you understand the purpose of the component, you need to consider other aspects of the design. These include the structure of the data, environmental restrictions, and the estimated workload.

Looking at the Data Structure

Naturally, the detailed design of your business logic is going to be influenced by the established form of the existing customer data. The account file is very much at the center of this application. Its records are shown in Table 4-1.

Table 4-1. Account File Records

Field	Length	Occurs	Total	Type
Account number (Key)	5	1	5	Read/Write
Surname (Last name)	18	1	18	Read/Write
First name	12	1	12	Read/Write
Middle initial	1	1	1	Read/Write
Title (Dr., Mr. and so on)	4	1	4	Read/Write
Telephone number	10	1	10	Read/Write
Address line	24	3	72	Read/Write
Other charge name	32	4	128	Read/Write
Cards issued	1	1	1	Read/Write
Date issued	6	1	6	Read/Write
Reason issued	1	1	1	Read/Write
Card code	1	1	1	Read/Write
Approver (initials)	3	1	3	Read/Write
Special codes	1	3	3	Read/Write
Account status	2	1	2	Read-only
Charge limit	8	1	8	Read-only
Payment history:	(36)	3	108	Future Use
Balance	8			Future Use
Bill date	6			Future Use
Bill amount	8			Future Use
Date paid	6			Future Use
Amount paid	8			Future Use

The fields marked as Read/Write are the ones that are to be maintained by your online program. Those marked Read-only are updated by an existing billing and payment application.

Assessing Restrictions

As well as the users' requirements, certain other requirements are imposed by the environment in which the COBOL component runs. The component must:

- Maintain the integrity of the account file using CICS functions. This means that it must be protected from inconsistent or lost data, whether resulting from a

failure in the application or CICS or the operating system. It must also be protected from total loss, such as a device error or other catastrophe.

- Accept requests from a variety of places.

- Run the program in your CICS region.

- Use the existing account file, a VSAM key-sequenced data set containing about
  50,000 fixed length records of 383 characters each, including the 5-digit
  account number key.

Using an existing file and its predefined format illustrates one of the dilemmas
with which designers are faced. The file as defined has a numeric key of length
five so has a maximum of 99,999 records. In order to allow for future expansion,
the key should be defined as alphanumeric and with just one letter in the key can
grow to 359,964 records. Obviously the simple numeric checks that are in the code
would have to be modified to fit whatever scheme is adopted.

Secondly, the use of a fixed length record is not the best choice for the future.
This application does not use an explicit postcode or Zip Code, but if it had, the
change in length would have a major impact where the designer would have to
squeeze the elongated fields in, whereas if the record was defined as variable in
length with spare space on the end, the change would be no more than a simple
addition.

Estimating the Workload

Now is the time to find out how often the system is expected to cope with the
transactions of each type, what sort of response times are expected, what times of
the day the application has to be available, and so on. This allows you to design
programs that are efficient for the bulk of the work, and it helps you to determine
system and operational requirements.

For the sample application, you can assume that your inquiries produced the following information:

- There will be about 100 additions, 500 modifications, 50 deletions, and 2,000
  inquiries (by account number) per day in the accounting department.

- The people in accounting are unable to estimate the number of inquiries that
  they would make by name, but they like the idea, and therefore may be
  expected to make some use of this facility.

- The update and add activity is broken into separate functions, such as name
  and address changes, credit limit adjustments, and setting up a new account.
  Because these discrete activities are performed by different personnel, they
  could be attempted simultaneously for an individual customer. Another remote
  possibility is that the same account number could be erroneously assigned to

two different new accounts. In order to ensure that conflicting work is not performed at the same time, the system needs to prevent more than one person operating on the same account at the same time. (This is a new requirement, not in the original specification.)

- Customer services makes nearly 10,000 inquiries per day against account records, ninety percent of them by name. For most of these, the only items used from the complete account record are the name and address (to verify that it is the right record), and the credit status and limit. A management decision has been taken that payment history will be deferred to release 2.

- Head office will only want to query the file, and do this on an occasional basis.

- The requests from external users (customers) come in using another component that restricts access to inquiry on their account number only. The volume of these requests is unknown, but it is anticipated that this could become popular with customers, so scalability of the application is essential.

 In assessing estimates of transaction frequency, you need to account for a fact of life: if you make it much easier to do something, such as an inquiry, users will almost certainly do it more often than they used to! Indeed, the eventual transaction rates experienced with online systems are almost always higher than can be predicted from the current workload—often a reliable indication of their success.

Summary

Having identified the purpose of the component, and other aspects of the design, you can now go on to design the processing programs that you'll need. So, let's continue now with some application design considerations. This implies that some element of scalability needs to be considered at the design stage.

Incorporating CICS Design Guidelines

To convert what you have learned about the requirements for your business logic component into a detailed design, you need to be familiar with some general design principles for server components.

There are three important things you learned from your estimation of the workload:

- You need to design a highly scalable solution. By definition this means that you use the same resources in a number of different environments—thus improving your efficiency.

- You need to prevent multiple users updating the same account record at the same time.

- You need to design a clean approach to error handling.

Using Resources Efficiently

The resources you have to use efficiently are:

- Shared resources:
    — Processor storage
    — Processor time
    — Transmission capacity to auxiliary storage space
    — Communication bandwidth

- Single-user resources, which can be used by only one user at a time, such as file records being updated, scratchpad areas, and so on

Let's examine these individually and develop some guidelines for designing and programming CICS applications from them. Remember, there's bound to be conflict from time to time when trying to conserve one resource at the cost of another. The appropriate compromises vary from one program to the next.

Shared resources

You can use different techniques for locking (allowing single use of) specific types of resources. These are described in the following paragraphs:

Processor storage

In an online system, storage needs constantly change. Most exist only for the duration of a transaction, and so, in assessing storage needs you have to consider not only how much is used, but for how long. The trade-off between space and time requires the following storage consumers to be considered:

- The internal CICS data areas associated with any transaction being processed. You should therefore minimize the duration of the transaction.

- The program or programs being executed to accomplish the transaction. Don't worry about the size of programs, because they are shared by all transactions and there is only one copy in the system at a time. It is much more important to structure the code well for ease of maintenance.

- Keep the size of working storage areas as small as possible; for example, WORKING STORAGE in COBOL or large stack arrays in Java.

Processor time

In general, you need to conserve processor time. Calls for CICS or operating system services take much longer, relatively speaking, than straight application code. Avoiding unnecessary commands reduces processor time much more than fine tuning your code.

It is undesirable to do long calculations in an online program, because you may be sharing the process with thousands of other users. If such calculations are necessary, you need to use an application design approach that is beyond the scope of this book.

Auxiliary storage

Disk space and transmission capacity is optimized in an online system by minimizing input/output by, for example, creating additional indexes instead of performing sequential searches.

It is undesirable to do complex database queries in an online program. If such queries are needed, special design approaches are needed; these are beyond the scope of this book.

Communication bandwidth

There are two main principles governing community bandwidth:

Capacity

Send only the necessary data.

Latency

Send in a single message as much as is likely to be needed.

Single-user resources

Resources that can only be used sequentially by one user at a time are something that we do not want multiple transactions accessing concurrently. A file record destined for update is a perfect example of this type of resource. CICS provides a user-locking mechanism (called *EXEC CICS ENQUEUE/DEQUEUE*) for transactions to prevent concurrent use and CICS uses the mechanism internally to obtain a lock prior to using the resource and free it automatically at the end of the task or at a user syncpoint. While one transaction *owns* the lock, other transactions that wish to use this resource have to wait. Therefore, minimize the duration of transactions that require exclusive use of resources because everyone else who wants to update that resource is held in a queue until the lock is released.

CICS applications do not typically need to obtain locks explicitly, because CICS file and database operations use locks automatically to implement the Isolation property of ACID transactions. CICS locks can be held only for the duration of a single task. If a lock needs to be held for longer than this, other approaches are needed. This is discussed in more detail in the next section.

Maintaining File Integrity: Using Locking

When a user works on an account, she will bring the account details onto the screen, work with the information, optionally save changes to the database and cease working with the customer account.

There is a potential problem if two users try to do this on the same account at the same time. Both users could be making changes based on the same *old* copy of the record. Changes made by the first user to complete his work go into the file, but then changes from the second user will overwrite the first user's updates. You must ensure that, when one user starts to work with a customer account record, subsequent users are prevented from doing so. As discussed in "Transactions" in Chapter 2, *Designing Business Applications*, ACID transactions should not wait for user input. Thus, you can't use the Isolation property of ACID transactions to prevent multiple users working on the same account.

Our solution is to introduce an application-level locking scheme that locks out other users between the initial display of the account details on the screen and ceasing to work with the customer record. Note that you can still exploit the capabilities of ACID transactions during the step that saves the changes.

Use of an application locking scheme is better than using ACID transactions from the perspective of users, too. If you used a long-running ACID transaction to protect against double updating, the second user would be locked out waiting for the first user to complete his work. With an application lock, you can tell the second user to try again later, and you can even pass information as to who owns the lock so that the second user (who may have the actual customer waiting on the telephone) can discuss the problem with the first. Let's look at one way this locking mechanism could work.

Suppose that as soon as a user asked to update an account number, you make a note in a scratchpad area. (CICS provides scratchpad facilities for keeping track of things between transactions.) You can leave the number there until the update is entirely completed and then erase it. In our example, this means that if you write a scratchpad record in a subsequent transaction, it erases the earlier one. Before starting any update request, you can check to see if the account number is in use. If it is, you can tell the user this and ask him or her to resubmit the request later. Furthermore, you can let the user display the record even if it is in use.

This isn't quite all, however. Because CICS ensures that transactions are either executed completely or not at all, you have to make sure that all your protected resources get updated in what CICS regards as a single transaction to ensure the consistency of your data. In the conversational case, (see Table 10-1) the program performs all the steps in one transaction. On the other hand locks are held over two terminal output/input operations so the scalability of the system might be adversely affected by a user going to lunch in the middle of a transaction. In the pseudo-conversational case (see Table 4-2), the files are all updated in the third transaction (this is the preferred solution), but the scratchpad is updated in two different transactions (not so good). The real benefit of this design is that no locks are held while waiting for user's terminal input, so step 2 has disappeared between 1 and 3 and step 6 between 5 and 7.

Table 4-2. Example of Pseudo-Conversational Transactions

Transaction	Steps	Operations
First	1	Display menu screen
Second	3	Receive menu screen (which is presumed to contain a correct modify request)
	4	Invoke the business logic component to read the required record
	5	Display the record in formatted form
Third	7	Receive the changes
	8	Update the account file accordingly
	9	Re-display the menu screen

If the second transaction is completed successfully, but something happens to the third, the scratchpad record is written but not erased. Our data files would be consistent, which is the main concern, but you'd be unable to update the record involved until you could somehow reset the scratchpad.

You can get around this by designing a slightly more sophisticated scratchpad mechanism, for instance, by putting a limit on the time for which a transaction can *own* an account number. Then an error in the third transaction or thoughtless behavior by a user (going to lunch in the middle of a modification) will not cause an account record to become unusable for more than a short period of time. But all this involves extra coding and complications—is it worth it?

Absolutely. You can program your own mechanism for avoiding concurrent updates. Double updating is one of those problems you can tackle in a variety of ways. We chose a scratchpad. A drawback of a scratchpad, however, is that all future (and, as yet, unknown) transactions that update the account file have to refer to this scratchpad. However you can control this by the design you have chosen to separate the presentation logic from the business logic. Since all updating automatically manages the locking, this should be less of a problem than it may appear at first.

Handling Errors

As developers of a reusable component, you *must* handle errors well. Hence, your component does some or all of the following actions for each error, which correspond to the following table:

1. Ensures that the system continues without damage by cleaning up:

   — ACID transactions

   — Conversations

   — Memory

   — Locks

2. Ensures that the end user, or the calling program or component, knows what's happened by means of an on-screen message or return code, or occasionally an abnormal end (abend).

3. Ensures that CICS administrators know what's going on.

4. Ensures that you, the developer, can find out why the error happened by writing debugging information to a log file or providing a dump.

Categories of errors in a CICS transaction

The errors that can occur in a CICS transaction can be divided into five categories. For each category, you need to consider which of the error-handling actions are required.

Conditions that aren't normal from the CICS point of view but are anticipated in the program	
For example, when you try to read a record and get a "not found" response. Errors in this category should be handled by explicit logic in the program. None of the error-handling described above are needed.	*Actions needed:* 2. (If a record is not found the user should be told.)
Conditions caused by user errors and input data errors	
An error of this kind in the sample application would occur if a user tried to add an account number that already existed. Errors in this category should also be handled by explicit logic in your program. Ideally, no errors of this type should be allowed to stop the program, or do anything else to upset the user.	*Actions needed:* 2.

Conditions caused by omissions or errors in the application code	
These may result in the immediate failure of the transaction (abend) or simply in a condition that you believed "could not happen" according to your program logic. In the sample application, an attempt to add two identical records to the account file would represent this kind of error. You wouldn't expect it, because you've already tested in the frontend transaction that no record with the same key is in the file. One of the main goals of the debugging process should be to get rid of this type of error.	*Actions needed:* 1, 2, 3, 4.

Errors caused by mismatches between applications and CICS resource definitions, generation parameters and Job Control Language (JCL)	
An example is when CICS responds "no such file exists" to your read or write request. When you are first debugging an application, these problems are almost invariably your fault. Perhaps the definition of the file was not installed into the CICS system you are using to test or you spelled a name differently in the program than that used in the definition.	*Actions needed:* 1, 2, 3.
These conditions sometimes occur after the system has been put into production use as well. In this stage, they are usually the result of changes to a CICS resource definition, or a failure to install a resource definition, or JCL, more often than not related to some other application.	
This category needs the same treatment as errors in a program that you are debugging. Once the program is in actual use, however, something more is needed when one of these conditions arises. You must give users an intelligible message that they or their supervisors can relay to the operations staff, to help in identifying and correcting the problem. For example, if an administrator has disabled a file for some reason and forgotten to re-enable it, you want a message to the operations staff that says that the problem is caused by a disabled file (and which file, of course). Moreover, you should program for these eventualities from the start, as this part of the program will need debugging just as well as the rest.	

Errors related to hardware or other system conditions beyond the control of an application program	
The classic example of this is an "I/O error" while accessing a file. As far as the application programs are concerned, this category needs the same treatment as the one above. Systems or operations personnel still have to analyze the problem and fix it. The only differences are that they probably didn't cause it directly, and it may take much more effort to put right.	*Actions needed:* 1, 2, 3.

Handling Data

Having decided what you want to do, you can now determine what data is required to do it, and how to organize that data.

The Account File

In the sample application, you know that you need access to all the fields that make up records in the existing account file, because this is the data that you intend to maintain and display. You need direct access to these records by account number for several of the required operations (create, read, and so on). Happily, this file exists in a form directly usable by CICS (a VSAM key-sequenced data set (KSDS), with the exact key that you need).

This isn't pure luck or coincidence. The account number is the natural key for this file, and a VSAM key-sequenced data set is a good choice for a mixture of sequential and direct processing, such as probably occurs now in the batch programs that already use this file. Table 4-3 shows the record format for this file.

Table 4-3. Account File Record Formats

Field	Length	Occurs	Total
Account number (Key)	5	1	5
Surname (Last name)	18	1	18
First Nname	12	1	12
Middle initial	1	1	1
Title (Dr., Mr., and so on)	4	1	4
Telephone number	10	1	10
Address line	24	3	72
Other charge name	32	4	128
Cards issued	1	1	1
Date issued	6	1	6
Reason issued	1	1	1
Card code	1	1	1
Approver (initials)	3	1	3
Special codes	1	3	3
Account status	2	1	2
Charge limit	8	1	8
Payment history:	(36)	3	108
Balance	8		
Bill date	6		
Bill amount	8		
Date paid	6		
Amount paid	8		

The Name File

You'll be accessing the account file records by account number, but you also need to access them by a second key—the customer's last name. There are many ways of achieving an alternative path into a file. For example, VSAM provides a facility called an *alternate index*, which can be used in CICS.

CICS supports other data formats including SQL with the IBM DB2 relational database product, and hierarchical data access with the IBM IMS/DB DL/I product. These systems provide powerful cross-indexing facilities, and they have many other features that reduce the coding required in user applications. They support complex data structures, provide increased function and simplify the maintenance of file integrity. If you have data that you need to access by more than just a few different key fields, or if you have data that does not arrange itself into neat units like the account records in this application, you should use a database system. CICS also supports various non-IBM databases as well.

For this component you'll use a simple technique, frequently used and quite appropriate to an application of this size. You'll build *an alternate index on the customer's last name*. This requires a one-time setup, and it means that every update to the base index (account number) is also accessible by both account number and last name (surname) without any extra intervention by your application.

The Locking File

One of the requests made when discussing the Accounts Department's needs was that no conflicting work should be allowed at the same time. As considered in "Maintaining File Integrity: Using Locking" earlier in this chapter, you decided to use a "scratchpad" to implement the requirement of "locking" an account. The question then is how to implement this scratchpad. You have various alternatives, for example, temporary storage, but the easiest is to use a file. Table 4-4 shows the record format for this file.

Table 4-4. Scratchpad File Record Format

Field	Length	Format
Account number (Key)	5	Character
Owner:	12	Character
User	8	Character
Terminal	4	Character
Date	4	Packed decimal
Time	4	Packed decimal

Since the lock needs to be maintained by account, the account number is the field used. The logical *owner* of the account lock is a combination of the user field and the CICS terminal identifier since neither on its own can be guaranteed to be unique. First, CICS allows the same user to be active at multiple terminals. Second, the terminal identifier may not be relevant if entry to the system is using the CICS Client technology or Distributed Program Link (DPL). With CICS web enablement, the terminal identifier may be randomly generated.

As already discussed, the lock should have a limited lifetime. The current date and time are included when it is created. This can be tested later to see if a user has exceeded the time allowed for a lock to prevent an account from becoming unavailable.

The main drawback to this use of a file is the apparent contradiction of the resource usage guideline regarding performing unnecessary I/O operations. In fact, this can be overcome because CICS has a facility called a data table that allows the programmer to think they are accessing this use of the locking file, but in fact the data is kept in memory and no actual input/output operation takes place—the best of both worlds, simplicity and efficiency.

Recovery Requirements

As discussed already, CICS prevents loss of integrity associated with partly completed transactions. However, you must protect the account file from disasters such as a catastrophic device failure.

In some environments, you can keep an extra copy of an important file, or keep enough information to recreate it (such as backup versions and the input needed to bring it up to date). In a business application environment, this isn't so easily done. You cannot copy the file after every update. Nor can you afford to lose all the updates since the last time you copied the file. These updates were entered at terminals by many different users, who may not remember what stage they had reached when you last secured the file, who may not have ready access to the input documents any longer, and who will certainly be very cross if they have to re-key a large number of transactions!

CICS provides facilities to address this concern. If you have a file that must be protected, you ask CICS to journal the updates. CICS then keeps a copy of every change made to the file. It logs these changes on an appropriate journal. If you lose a file, you go back to the most recent copy of it and then run a restore program that applies the changes recorded on all the journals created since that copy was made.

In your sample application, the account file is clearly a file that must be protected in this way. By way of contrast, the locking file is implemented as a data table where no I/O takes place, so changes to it are not written to a journal because no actual hardening of the data ever takes place. (In other words, no physical I/O takes place to move the data from volatile to non-volatile storage for this logical file.)

The only way this data would be *destroyed* is by the failure of the entire system, which would require a restart of all of the activity anyway; in this case, you would want to reconstruct the data as far as possible.

Designing the Individual Functions

The accounts department performs additions, modifications, deletions, and inquiries by account number. Head office only needs to view and add new accounts. Customer requests will be restricted to inquiry by their account number only. These are the classic Create, Read, Update, and Delete (CRUD) functions of an application. Because the lock handling is specific to the CRUD activities, you decide to include this function in the program as well.

However, customer service performs ninety percent of its inquiries by name. This quite distinct feature does not fall into any of the normal CRUD activities. As a result you have decided to split the business logic into two distinct areas, the CRUD activities and the browse activities. However, underlying each process are the three key functions of the common error handling, creating a lock and freeing a lock:

Common error handling
> Because error handling can be invoked from a variety (and possibly increasing number) of frontend presentation programs, the first thing the backend business logic programs must do is to ensure that the data passed seems reasonable. If it is not, the backend program needs to generate an error message to be returned to the frontend caller. Other errors that are encountered need to be handled.

Creating a lock
> We have discussed the need for locks and it is not surprising that this forms an important part of our code; this is required in order to ensure only one person can update the same account at a time. A check needs to be done to ensure that no other user currently *owns* the account record.

Freeing a lock
> Because a lock must be obtained before any actual action is taken against an account, a function needs to exist to free it in case the user decides not to proceed with the original intention. A check needs to be done to ensure that the lock deletion is successful.

Figure 4-1 shows a summary of the key steps that are implemented in the business logic program. This is called *NACT02* and you will find the complete code on the CD-ROM that accompanies this book.

Creating, Reading, Updating, and Deleting Account Records

The program (*NACT02*) adds a record to the file based on the data passed to it. It uses the three functions, handling errors, creating locks, and freeing locks, that we have just described. This procedure is common for the four functions of this part of our application (creating, reading, updating and deleting). However it must check that a lock is *owned* by the user requesting the add; this implies that a lock must be created. Likewise, at the end of the transaction the lock must be freed.

The process, therefore, consists of checking to see if a lock exists (maybe the record is in use by someone else). If not, it creates a lock, adds your record, confirms that it has been added sucessfully, and either returns an error message to the caller, or if it is successful, frees the lock and returns to caller.

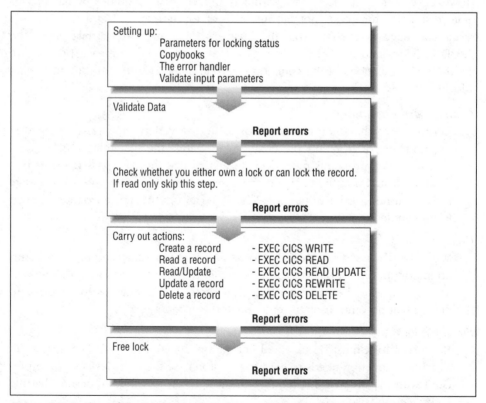

Figure 4-1. Outline of the Create, Read, Update and Delete program (NACT02)

Reading a record

This is slightly different from the process of creation, updating, and deletion in that there are actually two types of read required:

- An inquiry only function
- A read anticipating some sort of file update (thus requiring a lock)

If a lock was required, checking needs to be done to ensure that no other user currently "owns" the account. If all is well, then you attempt to read the record from the file.

Browsing Records

This logic attempts to find all matches on the accounts file for the criteria specified. The initial search uses the name file, but the application must perform more specific filtering (based on first name). The four phases of this program, which is called *NACT05*, are similar to those of the CRUD program as shown in Figure 4-1. As with CRUD, the initial phase sets up the basic function of error handling as well as validation of the correct form of user input. Copybooks are used in all the sample programs to define interfaces so that everyone has the same layout.

The browse program (*NACT05*) scans the database for records matching the input value supplied by the end user. The position within the file to start scanning is passed using an *EXEC CICS STARTBR* command. If there are no matches, the program should return an appropriate message back to the user. Browsing itself does not involve any locks, but, of course, when using last names for a search there is always the possibility of duplicates. In step 3 of Figure 4-2 the command *EXEC CICS READNEXT* is invoked to continue the browse until the key last name does not match the input and the remainder of the program returns the results and displays them.

It is good practice to use an *EXEC CICS ENDBR* command to free any pointers to the file when you have finished scanning for matches. CICS will clean this up, if this is not done, at task termination.

Error Processing

This is one of the most complex areas of the system since it needs to handle a wide variety of scenarios. In order to allow for the future expansion of the system to include other functions, this should be designed to tolerate some scenarios that cannot happen with the original specification but which might occur in the future.

These scenarios include the ability for the program to be entered in a variety of ways, either under application or CICS control. The program needs to distinguish

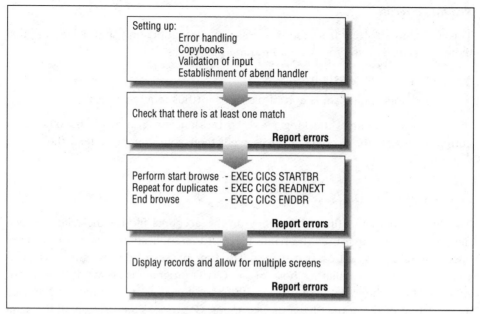

Figure 4-2. Outline of the Browse a Record program(NACT05)

between these different possibilities. Much of the logic is specific to the CICS environment and is discussed later. However, in general, the error handler needs to:

- Record information about the problem.

- Back out any changes made in the current Unit Of Work (UOW)—see the glossary for a definition.

- Send messages to the user, to a log, and possibly to the systems administrator responsible for CICS.

- Terminate the task or return to the application program requesting these services.

Figure 4-3 is a high-level overview of the error handling program. We'll discuss this in more details in the next chapter when we talk about actually programming the constituent pieces.

Mapping the Functions to CICS Programs

You've now reached the point where you can start to arrange the processing of your component into CICS programs. There is no requirement that you use exactly one program for this—a component can consist of many programs. There is no requirement that you use one program per function—the parameters and returned

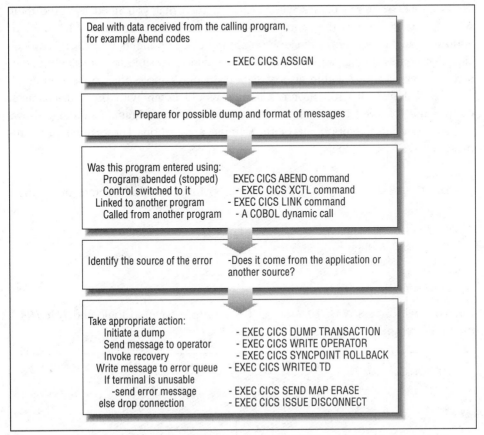

Figure 4-3. Outline of the Error Handling Program (NACT04)

values of a CICS program are in a data area called the COMMAREA and not controlled or checked by CICS. Hence you could put completely unrelated functions having entirely different parameters and returned values into the same program, providing there was at least one part of the COMMAREA that could be reliably used to determine which function the caller wanted.

You can observe that the functions that operate on a single record have many similarities. Since each of these functions requires the same sort of initial parameter verification and locking requirements it seems sensible to combine them into a single program.

On the other hand, the name search function is quite distinct in its requirements. Because there are no updates, it requires no locking logic and has a rather different set of input and output areas, so it is reasonable that this function be placed in a different program. Finally, the error handling is to be common so it should be a separate program as well. If it were not separate, the same code would need to be included in all of the other programs that would introduce a potential maintenance problem.

The scope of resource names within CICS is such that you need to agree them with the designers of other components running within the same CICS region/ address space. However, because the mapping of components to a CICS is a decision that comes during deployment, it is in practice sensible to coordinate names across all applications within an installation. In our sample, the application architect decided that all CICS program names would begin with the four-character code *NACT* followed by a different number for each program. Figure 4-4 shows the outline of the components of the sample application. These three programs make up the business logic:

NACT02

> The Create, Read, Update, Delete (CRUD) functions that operate on a single record.

NACT04

> The error handling program.

NACT05

> The name browse function.

Later we will discuss *NACT01*—the 3270 screen presentation logic and *NACT03*— the print presentation logic.

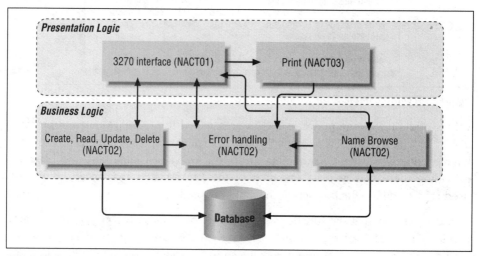

Figure 4-4. Summary of the components of the Sample Application

Looking at the Business Logic Programs

You've now defined three programs, (the business logic (*NACT02*), error handling (*NACT04*), and browsing records (*NACT05*)), that implement your component. In this section, we'll review briefly what each program does. This material repeats much that we have discussed previously but it is arranged somewhat differently. Feel free to move on to the next chapter if you are already comfortable with the program structure that we've defined.

The Create, Read, Update, and Delete Backend Progam (NACT02)

This program is *LINK*ed to by whatever frontend requires its services. It executes as a stateless task, reacting in isolation to each request without reference to what might have been requested previously by the user—that is the job of the frontend program.

When called, the program validates and analyzes the request. Once accepted, the request is acted upon according to the action demanded. Thus, locks are checked, added, or deleted as appropriate and the account file is accessed as it should be.

A key detail in the implementation of this program is that the EXEC CICS commands used should conform to the DPL subset as defined in the *CICS Application Programming Guide*. If this is done, any component can be used unchanged by the various frontend invocations.

The program uses the standard error handling approach designed for the application, and uses CICS facilities to identify program *NACT04* as the one to be invoked in the event of an abend occurring, as well as using it to process any unexpected errors that may arise.

The ABEND/Error Handler Program (NACT04)

This program implements the standard error handling actions designed for the application. It is designed in such a way as to be able to allow it to be entered in a variety of ways for maximum flexibility. It can:

- Have control transferred to it under application control (*EXEC CICS XCTL*)
- Be called using CICS services (*EXEC CICS LINK*)
- Be called using COBOL services (Dynamic CALL)
- Be entered as a result of CICS abnormal end processing (*EXEC CICS ABEND*)

As the program needs to distinguish between these different possibilities, it obtains information from CICS about its environment. Depending on how the program was entered, it obtains information about the problem from data passed to it or directly from CICS. It builds messages appropriate to the type of error. Then it initiates a transaction dump, backs out any changes made to recoverable resources (for example, the account file), and outputs the messages to the locations appropriate to its environment. It then finishes its processing in a manner that ensures the task is eventually (if not immediately) terminated.

The Name Browse Backend Program (NACT05)

This program is *LINK*ed to by whatever frontend requires its services. It executes as a stateless task, reacting in isolation to each request without reference to what might have been requested previously by the user—that is the job of the presentation logic.

When called, the program validates and analyzes the request. Once accepted, the request is acted upon according to the action demanded. Thus, records are returned to the caller based on the criteria supplied by the end-user by reading the account/name file.

Summary

Essentially these programs implement the processing described earlier in "Common error handling" and "Browsing Records." There are some important points to note about the implementation of this logic. The name browse program can return up to 80 name matches. This may be too many, but it does mean that the total length of the COMMAREA returned is less than the maximum 32,500 bytes. With this limit, this implies:

- There is a maximum number of matches that can be returned in one call.

- The program must not only implement a browse function but also a continue function to overcome that upper limit of matches that can be returned in one call.

The program implements the standard error handling approach designed for the application.

5

Programming the COBOL Business Logic

You are now ready to write the COBOL code of the sample application. This chapter describes:

- Writing CICS programs in COBOL

- Dealing with file handling in CICS programs

- Saving data using a scratchpad facility

- Moving control from one program to another in the application

- The queuing facilities of temporary storage and transient data

- Handing errors in you programs

Writing CICS Programs in COBOL

The source programs are listed on the CD-ROM that is packaged with this book. They include a step-by-step description of what the code does. This chapter is about programming the business logic component, other services including Basic Mapping Support (BMS), the CICS supplied services for formatting a green screen, are described in "Programming the 3270 Presentation Logic Component" in Chapter 11.

Invoking CICS Services

When you need a CICS system service—for example, when reading a record from a file—you just include a CICS command in your code. CICS commands look like:

```
EXEC CICS function
      [option (argument)][option ...]... [terminator]
```

The options for this command are:

Terminator

> The *terminator* is language dependent. For COBOL, the reserved word is either *END-EXEC* or a period (full stop). The full stop option should be avoided since it ends a COBOL sentence. In PL/I, C, and REXX it is the semicolon.

> This way of obtaining a CICS service is identical for PL/I, C, System/ 390 Assembler, and REXX. However a different approach is used for C++ and Java—for more information see Chapter 7.

Function

> The *function* is the thing you want to do. For example, reading a file is *READ*, writing to a terminal is *SEND*. It must be the first value after *EXEC CICS*.

Option

> An *option* or parameter is some specification that's associated with the function. The word *option* is slightly misleading since some of the options are mandatory. Options are expressed as keywords, some need an argument in parentheses after the keyword. The syntax is free format after the function; that is, the parameters (options) may appear in any sequence and layout in the code as shown in the following example:

```
EXEC CICS READ FILE(filename) RIDFLD(data-area)              * Resources
               [INTO(data-area)   SET(ptr-ref)] LENGTH(data-area)   * Storage
               KEYLENGTH(data-value) [GENERIC]              * Keys
               SYSID(systemname) [RBA   RRN   DEBKEY   DEBREC]   * Options
               CONSISTENT   REPEATABLE                      * Options
               UNCOMITTED   UPDATE [TOKEN(data-area)]       * Options
               [EQUAL   GTEQ]                               * Options
               NOSUSPEND                                    * Conditions
       END-EXEC                                             * Terminator
```

For example, the options for the *READ* command include *FILE, RIDFLD, UPDATE*. *FILE* tells CICS which file you want to read, and is always followed by a value indicating or pointing to the filename. *RIDFLD* (record identification field), that is the key that tells CICS which record within the file to address, and likewise needs a value. The values are called arguments and must appear after the keyword within parentheses (brackets). *UPDATE*, on the other hand, simply means that you intend to modify the record and update it (thereby invoking the CICS transactional protection we discussed earlier) and has no argument associated with it.

So, to read into a piece of working storage named *ACCTREC*, with intent to update, a record from a file known to CICS as *ACCTFIL*, using a key that we've stored in working storage at *ACCTC*, the command could be coded like this:

```
MOVE 'ACCTFIL' TO LF-ACCTFIL
EXEC CICS READ FILE(LF-ACCTFIL)          * Resource
          RIDFLD(ACCTC)                  * Key
          INTO (ACCTREC)                 * Storage
          UPDATE                         * Option
END-EXEC
```

When you specify a value, you can either use a character literal (enclosed in quotes), as we did for *FILE* above, or you can point to the name of a storage area that contains the value you want, as we did for RIDFLD above. In other words, we might have written:

```
EXEC CICS READ FILE(LF-ACCTFIL) UPDATE
          INTO (ACCTREC) RIDFLD(ACCTC)
END-EXEC
```

instead of our earlier command. If you use a literal, follow the usual language rules; for example, for COBOL put it in quotes unless it's a number.

Data can be moved by CICS from and into your program storage by using the FROM and INTO options (also known as move mode) or you can access the data using a pointer together with the SET parameter (also known as locate mode).

You may be curious about what the compiler does with what is a rather English-like statement. The answer? The compiler doesn't see that statement. Processing a CICS program for execution starts with a translation step. The CICS translator converts your EXEC CICS commands into native language statements; for example, for COBOL in the form of a *CALL* statement. You then compile the expanded source and link edit this in the normal way. By the way, in COBOL the generated statements never contain periods (full stops), unless you include one explicitly after the END-EXEC. This means you can use CICS commands within any COBOL construct such as IF or EVALUATE statements (by leaving the period out of the command), or you can end a sentence with the command (by including the period).

Differences from Standard COBOL Programs

The biggest difference between standard COBOL programs and CICS COBOL programs is that you don't define your files in a CICS program. Instead, they are defined using FILE definitions that are stored in a CICS table, the File Control Table (FCT), which is covered in "Handling Files" later in this chapter. Other differences are:

- You cannot use the entries in the ENVIRONMENT DIVISION and the DATA DIVISION that are normally associated with files. In particular, the entire FILE SECTION is omitted from the DATA DIVISION. Put the record formats that usually appear there in either the WORKING-STORAGE or LINKAGE sections. (WORKING-STORAGE is recommended because most COBOL programmers prefer it that way.)

- You should not use the COBOL file processing verbs (such as READ, WRITE, OPEN, and CLOSE). Requests for operating system services are all made through CICS, so CICS takes care of opening and closing files for everyone using the system.

- You should not use the COBOL console I/O verbs: ACCEPT and DISPLAY, because they interact with the operating system without CICS getting control.

Some statements and compiler functions produce code that is incompatible with the CICS environment. You must not use the STOP 'literal' form of that COBOL verb, because it stops not only yourself but everyone else who uses your CICS address space. In general, you cannot use language features and compiler options that need operating system services during execution. COBOL examples include ACCEPT, OPEN, and READ. There are similar restrictions in the other supported languages.

Because CICS is managing the shared environment:

- Certain COBOL compiler options (for example, DYNAM, NOLIB, NORENT and NORES), should not be used. Use your installation's standard setup.

- You must take care with some functions (for example, SORT) which, if used, will stop the shared system being shared. There is a full list of the functions to be avoided in the *CICS Application Programming Guide*.

CICS COBOL programs should be usually short-running if data is shared. A batch COBOL program might process all records of a file; on the other hand, a typical CICS COBOL program processes just a few requests.

These restrictions also apply to other supported languages, including PL/I, C, C++, System/390 Assembler, REXX, and Java for the same reason.

Handling Files

CICS allows you to access file data in a variety of ways. In an online system, most file accesses are random, because the transactions to be processed aren't batched and sorted into any kind of order. Therefore CICS supports the keyed access method provided by VSAM. It also allows you to access data using a variety of database managers.

This book covers only VSAM Key-Sequenced Data Sets (KSDS) that are accessed by supplying a key. Other VSAM data set format types—Entry-Sequenced Data Sets (ESDS) and Relative-Record Data Sets (RRDS) are described in more detail in the *CICS Application Programming Guide*. CICS also supports sequential access to keyed files in several forms; one of these, browsing, is covered in the next section.

The most important information kept for each file is the symbolic filename (normally the MVS DDNAME) or the data set name. When a CICS program makes a file request, it always uses a symbolic filename. CICS looks up this name in the FCT, and from the information there it makes the appropriate request of the operating system. This technique keeps CICS programs independent of the specific resources on which they are operating.

In the examples that follow, we'll use the symbolic filename *ACCTFIL* for the account file and *ACCTNAM* for the name file which is actually a path to the same data set via an alternate index on the last name (surname).

READ Commands

There are three *READ* commands:

READ
> Reads a record from a file.

READNEXT
> Reads the next record during a browse of a file.

READPREV
> Reads the previous record during a browse of a file.

The sample application uses the first two: *READ* and *READNEXT* as seen in "Browsing a File," later in this chapter.

The command to read a single record from a file is:

```
EXEC CICS READ FILE(filename)
          INTO(data-area) LENGTH(data-area)
          RIDFLD(data-area)
       options
END-EXEC
```

The options for this command are:

FILE(filename)
> Specifies the name of the file that you want to access. It is required in all *READ* commands. The entry in the CICS File Control Table (FCT) is used to find out the characteristics of the data set and whether it is on a local or remote system. Filenames can be up to eight characters long and, like any parameter value, should be enclosed in quotes if they are literals.

INTO(data-area)

Specifies the name of the data area into which the record retrieved from the data set is to be written. When *INTO* is specified, *LENGTH* must be specified or must be capable of being deduced from the *INTO* option. *INTO* is used in the sample application associated with this book.

LENGTH(data-area)

Specifies the maximum number of characters where the record is to be put. The *LENGTH* parameter is required for access to variable record length files. After the *READ* command is completed, CICS replaces the maximum value you specified with the true length of the record. For this reason, you must specify *LENGTH* as the name of a data area rather than a literal. For the same reason, you must re-initialize this data area if you use it for *LENGTH* more than once in the program. An overlong record raises an error condition. For the uses of the *READ* command we're covering in this book, the *LENGTH* option is not required because it is a fixed length file and can always be deduced from the *INTO* parameter.

RIDFLD(data-area)

Specifies the record identification field. The contents can be a key, a relative byte address (RBA for an ESDS), or relative record number (RRN for RRDS). This parameter is also required.

Immediately upon completion of the command, the *RIDFLD* data area is available for reuse by the application program, even if *UPDATE* was specified.

Other options (partial list)

Any of the following options which apply to this command can be used. Note that multiples of these may be used. Except where noted, you can use them in any combination.

UPDATE

Means that you intend to update the record in the current transaction. Specifying *UPDATE* gives your transaction exclusive control of the requested record (possibly over a whole group of records known as a control interval if you are not using VSAM's Record Level Sharing (RLS) facility). Consequently, you should use it only when you actually need it; that is, when you are ready to modify and rewrite a record.

NOHANDLE

Means that you are going to handle all exceptional conditions that CICS may raise when processing your request. Modern usage is to use RESP and RESP2 instead.

RESP(data-area)

Means that you are going to handle all exceptional conditions that CICS may raise when processing your request. This is an alternative to the older *NOHANDLE* option and requires a separate data area into which CICS places the value indicating success or otherwise in addition to the standard EIBRESP field in the EIB CICS that is always used. The EIB is explained in more detail in "The EXEC Interface Block (EIB)" in Chapter 11.

RESP2(data-area)

Returns a value that may further qualify the RESP response; the data-area value mirrors the EIBRESP2 value in the EIB.

Using the READ Command in the Sample Application

In program *NACT02*, we need to find out whether the requested record is there. The command we use is shown in Example 5-1.

Example 5-1. The EXEC CICS READ Command in the Sample Application

```
    EXEC CICS READ FILE(WS-LITS-FILES-ACCOUNT)
                INTO(NACTREC-DATA)
                RIDFLD(ACCTDO IN NACTREC-DATA)
                RESP(CA-CRUD-RESP) RESP2(CA-CRUD-REAS)
    END-EXEC
    IF CA-CRUD-RESP NOT DFHRESP(NORMAL)
*  We may have a problem and the RESP2 field may contain more information
    END-IF
```

The major return code will be placed in *CS-CRUD-RESP* and a qualifier may be supplied in *CA-CRUD-REAS*.

In this command, the record is placed in the data area named *NACTREC-DATA* so it should be a data structure corresponding to the account file record. You could define this structure directly in the program, but you'll also need it in several other programs. So instead you should put the record definition into a library in *NACCTREC* and copy it into the *NACCRUD* copybook, which is then copied into the *NACT02* program.

In *NACCCRUD:*

```
    10  NACTREC-DATA.
        COPY NACCTREC.
```

In *NACT02:*

```
    01  DFHCOMMAREA
        COPY NACCCRUD.
```

Here *ACCTDO IN NACTREC-DATA* is where the account number was passed by
the frontend that called the program. *NACTREC-DATA* is the location where the
data is to be passed back to the frontend program.

In any application, it is a good idea to keep your record layouts in a library and
copy them into the programs that need them. Even in the simplest of applications,
the same record is usually used by several programs. This procedure prevents multiple programs from using different definitions of the same thing.

This argument applies equally well to any structure used in common by multiple
programs. Map structures are a prime example, as are parameter lists and communication areas, which we'll discuss later. Apart from its value in the initial programming stage of an application, this technique greatly reduces the effort and hazards
associated with any change to a record or map format. You can make the changes
in just one place (your library) and then simply recompile all the affected programs. Example 5-1 also introduces the method of testing the major CICS return
code. The CICS translator replaces the DFHRESP(condition) with the numeric
return code so programmers are able to write intelligible code.

Example 5-2 shows the COBOL record definition we need of the account file in
the sample application. Its fields are described beginning at the 20 level in order
to allow it to be used within other structures.

Example 5-2. Record Definition for the Account File

```
20  ACCTDO       PIC X(5).    //  Account number
20  SNAMEDO      PIC X(18).   //  Last/surname
20  FNAMEDO      PIC X(12).   //  First name
20  MIDO         PIC X.       //  Middle initial
20  TTLDO        PIC X(4).    //  Title e.g., Mr./Mrs.
20  TELDO        PIC X(10).   //  Telephone number
20  ADDR1DO      PIC X(24).   //  Address line 1
20  ADDR2DO      PIC X(24).   //  Address line 2
20  ADDR3DO      PIC X(24).   //  Address line 3
20  AUTH1DO      PIC X(32).   //  Additional Authorized Card  User 1
20  AUTH2DO      PIC X(32).   //  Additional Authorized Card  User 2
20  AUTH3DO      PIC X(32).   //  Additional Authorized Card  User 3
20  AUTH4DO      PIC X(32).   //  Additional Authorized Card  User 4
20  CARDSDO      PIC X.       //  Number of cards issued to Customer
20  IMODO        PIC X(2).    //  Month card issued
20  IDAYDO       PIC X(2).    //  Day card issued
20  IYRDO        PIC X(2).    //  Year card issued
20  RSNDO        PIC X.       //  Reason code for card issued
20  CCODEDO      PIC X.       //  Card status coded e.g. G for Gold
20  APPRDO       PIC X(3).    //  Code of card issue approvers
20  SCODE1DO     PIC X.       //  Additional privilege code 1
20  SCODE2DO     PIC X.       //  Additional privilege code 2
20  SCODE3DO     PIC X.       //  Additional privilege code 3
20  STATDO       PIC X(2).    //  Account status
20  LIMITDO      PIC X(8).    //  Customer Account Credit Limit
```

Example 5-2. Record Definition for the Account File (continued)

```
20   PAY-HIST OCCURS 3.                // Pay History first of last three
        25   BAL          PIC X(8).    // Account Balance
        25   BMO          PIC 9(2).    // Month
        25   BDAY         PIC 9(2).    // Day
        25   BYR          PIC 9(2).    // Year
        25   BAMT         PIC X(8).    // Amount of balance
        25   PMO          PIC 9(2).    // Payment month
        25   PDAY         PIC 9(2).    // Payment day
        25   PYR          PIC 9(2).    // Payment year
        25   PAMT         PIC X(8).    // Payment mmount
```

The record format is already fixed and used by batch programs. Our online CICS sample program must use the same record definition.

Browsing a File

When you search by name using *NACT05,* you need to be able to point to a particular record in the file, based on end-user input which maybe anywhere in the file. Then you can start reading the file sequentially from that point on. The need for this combination of random and sequential file access—called browsing—arises frequently in online applications. Consequently, CICS provides a special set of EXEC CICS browse commands to make this job easier, namely: *STARTBR, READNEXT, READPREV,* and *ENDBR.*

Before looking at these commands, a few words about the performance implications of browsing. Transactions that produce lots of output screens can monopolize system resources. A file browse is often guilty of this. Having a long browse can put a severe load on the system, delaying other transactions and increasing overall response time.

The CICS default design model assumes the end user initiates a transaction that accesses a few data records, processes the information, and returns the results to that user. This process may involve numerous I/O waits that allow CICS to schedule and run other tasks. However, CICS is not an interrupt-driven multitasking system—tasks that involve small amounts of I/O relative to processing are able to monopolize the system regardless of priority.

Starting the browse operation

The *STARTBR* (start browse) command gets the process started. It tells CICS where in the file you want to start browsing. The format is:

```
EXEC CICS STARTBR FILE(filename)
                  RIDFLD(data-area)
                  options
END-EXEC
```

The *FILE* and *RIDFLD* parameters are described in the *READ* command. The options allowed are *EQUAL* and *GTEQ*; you cannot use them both. They are defined as follows:

EQUAL

Specifies that the search is satisfied only by a record having the same key (complete or generic) as that specified in the *RIDFLD* option.

GTEQ

Specifies that, if the search for a record having the same key (complete or generic) as that specified in the *RIDFLD* option is unsuccessful, the first record having a greater (higher in the collating sequence) key satisfies the search.

Reading the next record

Starting a browse does not make the first eligible record available to your program; it merely tells CICS where you want to start when you begin issuing read commands. To get the first record, and for each one in sequence after that, you use the *READNEXT* command:

```
EXEC CICS READNEXT FILE(filename)
                   INTO(data-area) LENGTH(data-area)
                   RIDFLD(data-area)
END-EXEC
```

The *FILE, INTO* and *LENGTH* parameters are defined in the same way as they are in the *READ* command. You need the *FILE* parameter because CICS allows you to browse several files at once, and the *FILE* parameter tells which one to read.

You cannot execute a *READNEXT* command for a file unless you've first executed a successful *STARTBR* command for that file.

The RIDFLD parameter is used in a somewhat different way. On the READ and STARTBR commands, RIDFLD carries information from the program to CICS; on READNEXT, the flow is primarily in the other direction: RIDFLD points to a data area into which CICS will "feed back" the key of the record it just read. Make sure that RID-FLD points to an area large enough to contain the full key; otherwise any adjacent fields in storage will be overwritten. Don't change it, either, because you'll interrupt the sequential flow of the browse operation. Note that this area must be the same one used in the STARTBR command.

There *is* a way to do what is called "skip sequential" processing in VSAM by altering the contents of this key area between *READNEXT* commands. Although we won't be covering this here, we mention it only to explain why you should not inadvertently change the contents of the data-area in *RIDFLD* while browsing the file.

Finishing the browse operation

When you've finished reading a file sequentially, terminate the browse with the *ENDBR* command:

```
EXEC CICS ENDBR FILE(filename)
END-EXEC
```

Here *FILE* functions as it did in the *READNEXT* command; it tells CICS which browse is being terminated, and obviously must name a file for which a successful *STARTBR* has been issued earlier.

Using the browse commands in the sample application

The first thing you have to do is construct a key that starts the browse in the right place. The key of the name file consists of the last name (surname). The idea is to build a key that consists of the characters the user keyed in as the last name (surname). Then you can use the *GTEQ* option on our *STARTBR* command to get the first qualifying record. For example:

```
05  WS-LIMIT-NAMES.
    10  WS-BROWSE-SNAME        PIC X(18) VALUE SPACES.
    10  WS-MAX-SNAME           PIC X(18) VALUE SPACES.
    10  WS-MIN-FNAME           PIC X(12) VALUE SPACES.
    10  WS-MAX-FNAME           PIC X(12) VALUE SPACES.
```

You can then set up the parameters for the search limits. This data comes from the area passed to the *NACT05* program which performs this name search. You also need to know where to stop the browse.

Certainly this stops when you overflow the capacity of the data passing area, but you may run out of eligible names before that. So you need to construct a last name value that is the highest alphabetically that could meet your match criteria. If the last name in the record exceeds this value, you know that you've read all the (possibly) eligible records. This limiting value is named *WS-MAX-SNAME*.

Finally, as you read, you need to test whether the forename matches sufficiently to return the record to the caller or not. If you define *WS-MIN-FNAME* as the smallest allowable value and *WS-MAX-FNAME* as the largest, then you need the following code to set up all of the relevant areas:

```
B-010.
    MOVE SNAMEDO IN CA-BRWS-ENTRY (1) TO WS-PASSED-SNAME
                                        WS-BROWSE-SNAME
                                        WS-MAX-SNAME
*
    INSPECT WS-MAX-SNAME REPLACING ALL SPACES BY HIGH-VALUES
*
    MOVE FNAMEDO IN CA-BRWS-ENTRY (1) TO WS-PASSED-FNAME
                                        WS-MAX-FNAME
                                        WS-MIN-FNAME
*
    INSPECT WS-MAX-FNAME REPLACING ALL SPACES BY HIGH-VALUES
    INSPECT WS-MIN-FNAME REPLACING ALL SPACES BY LOW-VALUES
```

SNAMEDO IN CA-BRWS-ENTRY(1) is where the input last name is passed to the program. Similarly *FNAMEDO IN CA-BRWS-ENTRY(1)* is where the input forename is passed to the program.

So we can now look at how the code is put together with these commands. But we need to introduce a couple of controlling values:

```
05  WS-AVAILABILITY-IND         PIC X.
    88  SOME-AVAILABLE          VALUE 'Y'.
    88  NONE-AVAILABLE          VALUE 'N'.
```

WS-AVAILABILITY-IND is used to control the reading loop. Also we need to note a part of the area passed to the program:

```
10  CA-BRWS-FOUND               PIC 9(4).
    88  CA-BRWS-NONE-FOUND      VALUE ZERO.
10  CA-BRWS-MORE                PIC 9(4).
10  CA-BRWS-MORE-X REDEFINES CA-BRWS-MORE
                                PIC X(4).
    88  CA-BRWS-NO-MORE         VALUE '0000'.
```

CA-BRWS-FOUND indicates how many matches were found for the criteria supplied. *CA-BRWS-MORE* indicates if there were more matches than the number allowed for. These are copied into *NACT05* from copybook *NACCBRWS*. Example 5-3 shows the copybook. It is also found on the CD-ROM in *Cobol Application\PC\source\copy*.

Example 5-3. Sample of the NACCBRWS Copybook

```
* The interface to the Browse program is described in a copy book
* in order to ensure consistency. The values in this area designed
* to be in character format to enable ease of translation when the
* program is invoked from a remote system which uses a different
* encoding scheme (e.g., ASCII) than the EBCDIC of the mainframe.
*
* This is the working storage version of the interface to the
* Browse program.
*
    05  WS-BRWS-COMMAREA.
*
```

Example 5-3. Sample of the NACCBRWS Copybook (continued)

```
* This is an "Eyecatcher" and integrity check field.
*
        10  WS-BRWS-VERSION            PIC XXX VALUE SPACES.
            88  WS-BRWS-CORRECT-VERSION VALUE 'V1A'.
*
* Only two functions are provided by the Browse program:
* initiation of a Browse and Continuation of a previously
* initiated browse.
*
        10  WS-BRWS-FUNCTION           PIC X VALUE SPACE.
            88  WS-BRWS-REQ-BROWSE     VALUE 'B'.
            88  WS-BRWS-REQ-CONTINUE   VALUE 'C'.
            88  WS-BRWS-VALID-REQUEST  VALUE 'B' 'C'.
*
* The response field is designed to conform to the CICS EIBRESP
* characteristics which always contains a numeric value. There
* are also architected values to indicate errors detected by the
* Browse program itself. If there was an interface error, this
* contains a special value of 'FRMT'.
*
        10  WS-BRWS-RESP               PIC 9(4) VALUE ZERO.
        10  WS-BRWS-RESP-X REDEFINES WS-BRWS-RESP
                                       PIC X(4).
            88  WS-BRWS-NO-ERROR       VALUE '0000'.
            88  WS-BRWS-BAD-FORMAT     VALUE 'FRMT'.
*
* The reason field is designed to conform to the CICS EIBRESP2
* characteristics which always contains a numeric value. There
* are also architected values to indicate errors detected by the
* Browse program itself. If there was an interface error, this
* contains 'VERE' for Version Error, 'LENE' for Length Error (if
* possible), 'REQE' for Request Error, 'LIME' for Limit Error or
* 'MORE' for More Error (only occurs for a continuation request).
*
        10  WS-BRWS-REAS               PIC 9(4) VALUE ZERO.
        10  WS-BRWS-REAS-X REDEFINES WS-BRWS-REAS
                                       PIC X(4).
            88  WS-BRWS-VERSION-ERROR  VALUE 'VERE'.
            88  WS-BRWS-LENGTH-ERROR   VALUE 'LENE'.
            88  WS-BRWS-REQUEST-ERROR  VALUE 'REQE'.
            88  WS-BRWS-LIMIT-ERROR    VALUE 'LIME'.
            88  WS-BRWS-MORE-ERROR     VALUE 'MORE'.
*
* If the response contains a numeric value, this contains the
* character representation of the EIBFN value giving rise to
* the exception condition.
*
        10  WS-BRWS-CICS-FUNCTION      PIC 9(5) VALUE ZERO.
        10  WS-BRWS-CICS-FUNCTION-X
                REDEFINES WS-BRWS-CICS-FUNCTION
                                       PIC X(5).
*
```

Example 5-3. Sample of the NACCBRWS Copybook (continued)

```
* In order to prevent excessive searches, the caller must specify
* the maximum number of matches (s)he is prepared to handle.
* Also because a COMMAREA is limited to a maximum of approximately
* 32,000 bytes, the maximum limit has been set at 80.
*
        10  WS-BRWS-LIMIT-TO-GET          PIC 9(4) VALUE ZERO.
        10  WS-BRWS-LIMIT-TO-GET-X REDEFINES WS-BRWS-LIMIT-TO-GET
                                          PIC X(4).
*
* The Browse program indicates the number of matches found.
* The range is zero to the limit.
*
        10  WS-BRWS-FOUND                 PIC 9(4) VALUE ZERO.
            88  WS-BRWS-NONE-FOUND        VALUE ZERO.
*
* After satisfying the limit, the Browse program will place
* either '0000' in here if there are no more records satisfying
* the search criteria or a number if there are more. On a
* continuation request this number must be returned to the Browse
* program since it is used to reposition the request.
*
        10  WS-BRWS-MORE                  PIC 9(4) VALUE ZERO.
        10  WS-BRWS-MORE-X REDEFINES WS-BRWS-MORE
                                          PIC X(4).
            88  WS-BRWS-NO-MORE           VALUE '0000'.
*
* The records found on file for a match. Input is in the
* surname and first name fields of the first Entry.
*
        10  WS-BRWS-MATCHES.
            15  WS-BRWS-ENTRY             OCCURS 80.
*
* The description of the account record is placed in a copy book.
*
            COPY NACWTREC.
```

The code shown in Example 5-4 initializes the browse of the file using the *STARTBR* command and sets the availability indicator based on the possibility of a match.

Example 5-4. Sample Showing the Start of the Browse Procedure

```
  C-START-BROWSE SECTION.
*
*
* This routine initializes the browse of the file via the
* STARTBR command and sets the availability indicator based
* on the possibility of a match.
*
      SET CA-BRWS-NONE-FOUND TO TRUE
*
      EXEC CICS STARTBR FILE(WS-LITS-FILES-NAME)
```

Example 5-4. Sample Showing the Start of the Browse Procedure (continued)

```
                    RIDFLD(WS-BROWSE-SNAME)
                    RESP(RESPONSE) RESP2(REASON-CODE)
        END-EXEC
*
        EVALUATE RESPONSE
            WHEN DFHRESP(NORMAL)
                SET SOME-AVAILABLE  TO TRUE
            WHEN DFHRESP(NOTFND)
                SET NONE-AVAILABLE  TO TRUE
                SET CA-BRWS-NO-MORE TO TRUE
*
* If any other condition other than success or NOTFND
* occurs, then a serious problem has occurred, so the
* error handler is invoked.
*
            WHEN OTHER
                PERFORM Z-ERROR-HANDLER
        END-EVALUATE
*
  END-C-START-BROWSE.
      EXIT.
```

The code shown in Example 5-5 attempts to read a record from the file and sets
the availability indicator based on its success.

Example 5-5. Sample Showing a Read of a Record

```
  Y-READ-ONE SECTION.
*
* This code attempts to read a record from the file and
* sets the availability indicator based on its success.
*
* This section is performed from the following sections -
*       D-FILL-IN-MATCHES
*       E-CONTINUE-BROWSE
*
  Y-010.
      EXEC CICS READNEXT FILE(WS-LITS-FILES-NAME)
                      INTO(AN-ACCTREC)
                      RIDFLD(WS-BROWSE-SNAME)
                      RESP(RESPONSE) RESP2(REASON-CODE)
      END-EXEC
    EVALUATE RESPONSE
*
* If either condition occurs, it means a record was read.
*
        WHEN DFHRESP(NORMAL)
        WHEN DFHRESP(DUPKEY)
*
* But it may not match the full criteria.
*
                IF  SNAMEDO IN AN-ACCTREC > WS-MAX-SNAME
                    SET NONE-AVAILABLE TO TRUE
                ELSE
```

Example 5-5. Sample Showing a Read of a Record (continued)

```
                    SET SOME-AVAILABLE TO TRUE
                    ADD 1 TO WS-RECORDS-READ
            END-IF
*
* If we have exhausted the file, then there
* are obviously no more matches.
*
            WHEN DFHRESP(ENDFILE)
                SET NONE-AVAILABLE TO TRUE
*
* If any other condition occurs, then a serious problem
* has occurred, so the error handler is invoked.
*
            WHEN OTHER
                PERFORM Z-ERROR-HANDLER
        END-EVALUATE
*
 END-Y-READ-ONE.
    EXIT.
    EJECT.
```

The code shown in Example 5-6 terminates the browsing operations against the file.

Example 5-6. Terminating Browsing Operations

```
F-TERMINATE-BROWSE SECTION.
*
* This code terminates the browsing operation against the file.
*
F-010.
    EXEC CICS ENDBR FILE(WS-LITS-FILES-NAME)
            RESP(RESPONSE) RESP2(REASON-CODE)
    END-EXEC
```

Write Commands

There are three file output commands:

REWRITE
    Modifies a record that is already on a file.

WRITE
    Adds a new record.

DELETE
    Deletes an existing record from a file.

Rewriting a file record

The *REWRITE* command updates the record you've just read. You can use it only after you've performed a "read for update" by executing a *READ* command for the same record with *UPDATE* specified. *REWRITE* looks like this:

```
EXEC CICS REWRITE FILE(filename)
                  FROM(data-area)
                  RESP(data-area) RESP2(data-area)
END-EXEC
```

The options for this cḩommand are:

FILE(filename)

>The same meaning as in the *READ* command: it is the CICS name of the file you are updating. This parameter is required.

FROM(data-area)

>The name of the data area that contains the updated version of the record to be written to the file. This parameter is required.

LENGTH(data-value)

>The length of the (updated) version of the record. You must specify length, as in a *READ* command for variable length records, but for fixed length records as in this book, the *LENGTH* option is not required.

Adding (writing) a file record

The *WRITE* command adds a new record to the file. The parameters for *WRITE* are almost the same as for *REWRITE*, except that you have to identify the record with the *RIDFLD* option. (You do not do this with the *REWRITE* command because the record was identified by the previous *READ UPDATE* operation on the same data set.) The format of the *WRITE* command is:

```
EXEC CICS WRITE FILE(filename)
                FROM(data-area) LENGTH(data-value)
                RIDFLD(data-value)
                RESP(data-area) RESP2(data-area)
END-EXEC
```

The key option for this command is:

RIDFLD(data-area)

>The data area containing the key of the record to be written. If the key is located at the front of the record, its argument will be the same as the *FROM* argument.

Deleting a file record

The *DELETE* command deletes a record from the file, and looks like this:

```
EXEC CICS DELETE FILE(filename)
                 RIDFLD(data-area)
                 RESP(data-area) RESP2(data-area)
END-EXEC
```

The parameters are defined in the same way as for the *WRITE* and *REWRITE* commands. You can delete a record directly, without reading it for update first. When you do this you must specify the key of the record to be deleted by using *RIDFLD*. Alternatively, you can decide to delete a record after you've read it for update. In this case, you must omit *RIDFLD*.

Using the write commands in the example application

Program *NACT02* uses all three of the file output commands. For add requests, it issues the command:

```
EXEC CICS WRITE FILE(WS-LITS-FILES-ACCOUNT)
                FROM(NACTREC-DATA)
                RIDFLD(ACCTDO IN NACTREC-DATA)
                RESP(CA-CRUD-RESP) RESP2(CA-CRUD-REAS)
END-EXEC
```

ACCTDO IN NACTREC-DATA is where the frontend program passed the data of the record to be added.

For a modification, the program first reads the record in question, with *UPDATE* specified:

```
EXEC CICS READ FILE(WS-LITS-FILES-ACCOUNT) UPDATE
               INTO(OLD-ACCTREC)
               RIDFLD(ACCTDO IN NACTREC-DATA)
               RESP(CA-CRUD-RESP) RESP2(CA-CRUD-REAS)
END-EXEC
```

Then it merges this old data with the new version of the record, again at *ACCTDO IN NACTREC-DATA*. Finally, it replaces the old record with the new one, in the command:

```
EXEC CICS REWRITE  FILE(WS-LITS-FILES-ACCOUNT)
                   FROM(NACTREC-DATA)
                   RESP(CA-CRUD-RESP) RESP2(CA-CRUD-REAS)
END-EXEC
```

For a deletion, the program issues the command without reading it for update. Therefore the key (*RIDFLD*) is required in the *DELETE* command, which is:

```
EXEC CICS DELETE  FILE(WS-LITS-FILES-ACCOUNT)
                  RIDFLD(ACCTDO IN NACTREC-DATA)
                  RESP(CS-CRUD-RESP) RESP2(CS-CRUD-REAS)
END-EXEC
```

If you have created a lock with a *READ UPDATE* command and then decide that you don't need it, you use an *EXEC CICS UNLOCK FILE(fileName) RIDFLD(key)* command to release it.

Errors on file commands

A wide variety of conditions can arise when using file commands. Here are some of the conditions passed to your program in the *RESP* field that can arise when you use the file commands that have just been described. A mapping between the response value and the following name can be found in the *NACT04* program:

DISABLED

Occurs if a file is disabled. A file may be disabled because:

— It was initially defined as disabled and has not been enabled since.

— It has been disabled by an *EXEC CICS SET* command or by the CEMT* transaction.

DUPKEY

Means that if a VSAM record is retrieved by way of an alternate index with the *NONUNIQUEKEY* attribute; another alternate index record with the same key follows. It does not occur as a result of a *READNEXT* command that reads the last of the records having the non-unique key.

DUPREC

Means that there is already a record in the file with the same key as the one that you are trying to add with a *WRITE* command. This condition may result from a user error or may be expected by the program. In either of these cases, there should be specific code to handle the situation. This condition is handled in the *NACT02* program when dealing with the locking file, since this could mean another user has already locked the account.

It can also fall into the *should-not-occur* category. In this case no special code is required beyond logging information that may help find the problem, cleaning up if necessary, and identifying the problem to the user.

ENDFILE

Means that you've attempted to read sequentially beyond the end of the file in a browse (using the *READNEXT* command). This is a condition that you should program for in any browse operation. In the example application, for instance, a search on "Zuckerman" or a similar name might cause *ENDFILE*, and you code for it explicitly as shown in Example 5-4 in the C-START-BROWSE SECTION in the browse program, *NACT05*.

---

* CEMT is a CICS-supplied transaction that enables administrators to query and alter the state of CICS resources.

FILENOTFOUND

Means that the symbolic filename in a file command cannot be found in the File Control Table. This is often a coding error; look for a difference in spelling between the command and the FCT entry. If it happens after the program is put into actual use ("in production"), look for an accidental change to the definition for that file. The file may be on another system or it hasn't been created; there are any number of possibilities that could cause this response.

ILLOGIC

Is a catch-all class for errors detected by VSAM that don't fall into one of the other categories that CICS recognizes. The RESP2 value will tell you the specific error.

INVREQ

Means that CICS regards your command as an invalid request for one of the following reasons:

— You requested a type of operation (write, update, browse, and so on) that wasn't included in the "service requests" of the definition for the file in question.

— You tried to *REWRITE* a record without first reading it for update.

— You issued a *DELETE* command without specifying a key (*RIDFLD*), and without first reading the target record for update.

— You issued a *DELETE* command specifying a key (*RIDFLD*) for a VSAM file when a read for update command is outstanding.

— After one read for update, you issued another read for update for another record in the same file without disposing of the first record (by a *REWRITE, UNLOCK,* or *DELETE* command).

— You issued a *READNEXT, READPREV* or an *ENDBR* command without first doing a *STARTBR* on the same file.

Almost all of these INVREQ situations result from program logic errors and should disappear during the course of debugging. The first one, however, can also result from an inadvertent change to the allowed *service requests* in the FCT entry for the file.

IOERR

Means that the operating system is unable to read or write the file, presumably because of physical damage. This can happen at any time, and there is usually nothing to do in the program except to abend the transaction and inform the user of the problem.

ISCINVREQ

Means that the remote system indicates a failure which does not correspond to a known condition.

LENGERR

Is usually caused by a coding error and could result from one of the following reasons:

— The length you specified on a *WRITE* or *REWRITE* operation was greater than the maximum record size for the file. (See the description of the *LENGTH* option in the *CICS Application Programming Reference*.)

— You indicated a wrong length on a *READ, READNEXT, WRITE* or *REWRITE* command to a file containing fixed-length records.

NOSPACE

Means that there's no space in the file to fit the record you've just tried to put there with a *WRITE* or *REWRITE* command. This doesn't mean that there's no space at all in the data set; it simply means that the record with the particular key you specified will not fit until the file is extended or reorganized. Like IOERR, this may occur at any time, and should be handled accordingly.

NOTAUTH

Means that a resource or command security check has failed.

NOTFND

Means that there is no record in the file with the key specified in the *RIDFLD*, parameter on a *READ, READNEXT, READPREV, STARTBR,* or *DELETE* command. *NOTFND* may result from a user error, may be expected by the program, or may indicate an error in the program logic:

```
IF NOT WS-CRUD-BAD-LOCK
    EVALUATE WS-CRUD-RESP
        WHEN DFHRESP(NORMAL)
          CONTINUE
        WHEN DFHRESP(NOTFND)
           IF NOT CA-SENT-MENU
              PERFORM TA-BAD-CRUD-RESPONSE  (Handle abend)
           END-IF
        WHEN OTHER
           PERFORM TA-BAD-CRUD-RESPONSE
    END-EVALUATE
    END-IF
```

When adding:

```
    EVALUATE TRUE
**
* when this account already exists, the user must be informed
*
```

```
WHEN WS-CRUD-NO-ERROR
        SET MSG-DUPLICATE TO TRUE
        MOVE-1   TO ACCTML
        MOVE DFHBMBRY TO ACCTMA
        SET WS-BB-ERROR-PRESENT TO TRUE
        .
        .
        .
END-EVALUATE
```

In program *NACT01*, when you check to see if the requested
account record is on file, you expect *NOTFND* if the request is to
add a record. The actual work was done in *NACT02*. However, it
shows a user error (in the account number) if it happens on any
other type of request. For both these cases, you need to provide
recovery code.

NOTOPEN

Occurs if:

— The requested file is *CLOSED* and *UNENABLED*. The *CLOSED,
UNENABLED* state is reached after a close request has been received
against an *OPEN ENABLED* file and the file is no longer in use.

— The requested file is still open and in use by other requests, but a close
request against the file has been received. Existing users are allowed to
complete.

— This condition can occur only during the execution of the following commands: *READ, WRITE, DELETE,* or *STARTBR.* Other commands cannot raise
this condition because they are part of an active request.

— This condition does not occur if the request is made to either a *CLOSED,
ENABLED* file or a *CLOSED, DISABLED* file. In the first case, the file is
opened as part of executing the request. In the second case, the
DISABLED condition is raised.

As you have probably gathered from this description, *NOTOPEN* usually
results from an operations problem, and you may want to notify the operations staff of the problem, or send a message to the user to do so.

SYSIDERR

Means that the SYSID option specifies either a name of a CICS system that is
not defined in the intersystem table or a system to which the link is closed.

There are ways within CICS of updating multiple records within a single transaction. They are not covered in this book, but details can be found in the *CICS Application Programming Guide.*

Other File Services

Before leaving the topic of file commands, we'll list some of the other facilities that are available. You can find guidance information on using file control in the *CICS Application Programming Guide,* and a full list of commands, options, and exceptional conditions in the *CICS Application Programming Reference.* Both of these books are part of the CICS library and are found on the CD-ROM.

Saving Data: Using a Scratchpad Facility

Sequential file facilities are provided because of the need to save data from the execution of one transaction, passing it on to another that occurs later. There are two instances of this requirement in the sample application:

- The first resulted from the decision to use *pseudo-conversational transactions;* this arises from the need to save data from one interaction with the terminal user to the next, even though no task exists for that terminal for most of the intervening time. For this you need something to save state, for example, a scratchpad facility.

- The second requirement came from the need to log the changes to the account file. Here you require some sort of queuing facility: a way to add items to a list (one in each update transaction) and read them later (in the log-print transaction).

There are several different scratchpad areas in CICS that you can use to transfer and save data, within or between transactions. See "Queuing Facilities: Temporary Storage and Transient Data," later in this chapter. The *CICS Application Programming Reference* gives you a complete list of the commands you can use to get access to these areas:

Communication Area or COMMAREA

This is an area used for passing data between both programs within a transaction and transactions at a given terminal. It's described later in connection with the program control commands in "Controlling Programs," later in this chapter. The COMMAREA is the recommended scratchpad area.

The COMMAREA offers an alternative solution to the double updating problem. For example, it would be perfectly feasible for the *NACT01* program to pass the contents of the account file record over to the *NACT02* program in the COMMAREA. The *NACT02* program could then re-retrieve the account record for update and compare it with the version passed in COMMAREA. Any difference would show that some other task had changed the account record.

Although this solution may be easier to code, it isn't as good from the user's point of view. You see, with this scheme, you don't find out about any conflict over the record until you're ready to update it. Unfortunately, that means you then have to tell one user that his or her update cannot be made, but you can't tell them until they've keyed in all the changed data.

Common Work Area (known as the CWA)

Any transaction can access the CWA, and since there's only one CWA for each CICS address space, the whole system, the format and use of this area must be agreed upon by all transactions in all applications that use it. *Avoid* this method; the affinities created cause major problems if groups of transactions have to be split up sometime in the future.

Transaction Work Area (TWA)

The TWA exists only for the duration of a transaction. Consequently, you can use it to pass data among programs executed in the same transaction (like COMMAREA), but not between transactions (unlike COMMAREA). The TWA isn't commonly used now (and probably *shouldn't be*) as a scratchpad area in modern CICS programs.

Affinities

An *affinity* is created when a resource that contains state data of a pseudo-conversation is tied to one instance of a CICS. If the KanDoIT company takes over other companies, they will want to run multiple machines with many CICS regions/ address spaces and if the state of one credit card is on one machine and the data on another, the application will not scale up because the transaction may (will) have an affinity to the first machine. The first place that this normally occurs is in the use of a resource that is tied to one CICS region, for example, a CWA. Secondly, it is using temporary storage with a key that uses a resource name that is unique to that CICS, for example, a termid. This is a highly complex subject; see the *CICS Application Programming Guide* for more information.

Controlling Programs

A transaction (task) may use several programs in the course of completing its work.

Associating Programs and Transactions

The *installed program definition* contains one entry for every program used by any application in the CICS system. Each entry holds, among other things, three particularly important pieces of information:

- The language in which the program is written, which CICS needs to know in order to set up its linkages and control blocks properly

- How many tasks are using the program at the moment

- Where the program is (in main storage and/or on disk)

The *installed transaction definition* has an entry for every transaction identifier in the system (using "transaction" in the CICS sense of the word). The important information kept about each transaction is the transaction identifier and the name of the first program to be executed on behalf of the transaction.

You can see how these two sets of definitions work in concert:

- The user types in a transaction identifier at the terminal (or the previous transaction may have determined it).

- CICS looks up this identifier in the list of installed transaction definitions.

- This tells CICS which program to invoke first.

- CICS looks up this program in the list of installed program definitions, finds out where it is, and loads it if it isn't already in main storage.

- CICS builds the control blocks necessary for this transaction, using information from the definition of the transaction, program, and principle facility. For programs in command-level COBOL, like ours, this includes making a private copy of working storage to make it re-entrant for this particular execution of the program.

- CICS passes control to the program, which begins running using the environment that has been set up. This program may pass control to any other program in the list of installed program definitions or may autoinstall a program on its first reference, if necessary, in the course of completing the transaction.

Commands for Passing Program Control

There are two CICS commands for passing control from one program to another. One is the *LINK* command, which is similar to a CALL statement in COBOL. The other is the *XCTL* (transfer control) command, which has no COBOL counterpart. When one program links to another, the first program in working storage and remains in main storage. When the second (linked-to) program finishes and gives up (*RETURN*s) control, the first program resumes at the instruction after the *LINK.*

The linked-to program is considered to be operating at one logical level lower than the program that does the linking.

In contrast, when one program transfers control (*XCTL*) to another, the first program is considered terminated, and the second program operates at the same level as the first. When the second program finishes, control is returned not to the first program, but to whatever program last invoked it.

Some people like to think of CICS itself as the highest program level in this process, with the first program in the transaction as the next level down, and so on. If you look at it from this point of view, CICS links to the program named in the list of installed transaction definitions when it initiates the transaction (see Figure 5-1). When the transaction is complete, this program (or another one operating at the same level) returns control to the next higher level, which happens to be CICS itself.

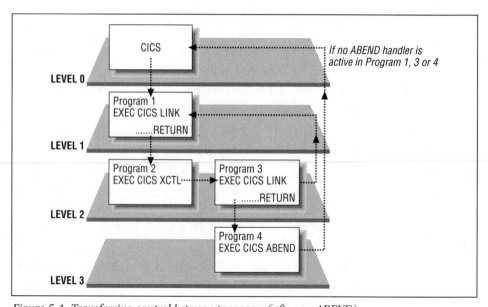

Figure 5-1. Transferring control between programs (after an ABEND)

The LINK Command

The *LINK* command is used to link to another program expecting return. The syntax of the *LINK* command looks like this:

```
EXEC CICS LINK PROGRAM(name)
               COMMAREA(data-area) LENGTH(data-value)
               RESP(data-area) RESP2(data-area)
END-EXEC
```

PROGRAM(name)

Specifies the identifier (1–8 characters) of the program to which control is to be passed unconditionally. The linked-to program can execute either in the same region/address space as its caller (default) or may execute remotely if a remote SYSID is specified. This type of link is known as a distributed program link (DPL).

COMMAREA(data-area)

Specifies a communication area that is to be made available to the invoked program. In this option the data area is passed, and you must give it the name DFHCOMMAREA in the receiving program. (See the section about passing data to other programs in the *CICS Application Programming Guide.*)

LENGTH(data-value)

Specifies the length in bytes of the COMMAREA (communication area) and must not exceed 32,500 bytes. This need not be specified as the length can be inferred from the COMMAREA argument.

The XCTL Command

The *XCTL* command is used to transfer control from one program to another:

```
EXEC CICS XCTL PROGRAM(name)
               COMMAREA(data-area) LENGTH(data-value)
               RESP(data-area) RESP2(data-area)
END-EXEC
```

The parameters are the same as for the *LINK* command.

The RETURN Command

The *RETURN* command returns control to the previous program within a transaction. The syntax is simply:

```
EXEC CICS RETURN
END-EXEC
```

When the program at the highest level for the transaction returns control to CICS, however, there are two additional options that you can specify:

- You can say what transaction is to be executed when the next input comes from the same terminal. (This is how you get into pseudo-conversational mode.)

- You can specify data that's to be passed on to that next transaction.

In this case the *RETURN* command is slightly longer:

```
EXEC CICS RETURN TRANSID(nextid)
               COMMAREA(data-area) LENGTH(data-value)
END-EXEC
```

TRANSID(nextid)

Specifies the transaction identifier (1–4 characters) to be used with the next input message entered from the terminal with which the task that issued the *RETURN* command has been associated. The specified name must have been defined as a transaction to CICS.

COMMAREA(data-area)

Specifies a communication area that is to be made available to the next program that receives control. In a COBOL receiving program, you must give this data area the name DFHCOMMAREA. (See the *CICS Application Programming Guide* for more information about the CICS COMMAREA.) Because the data area is freed before the next program starts, a copy of the data area is created and a pointer to the copy is passed.

LENGTH(data-value)

Specifies the length in bytes of the COMMAREA. The maximum as before is 32,500 bytes but, as always, the shorter the better. This need not be specified as the length can be inferred from the COMMAREA argument.

The COBOL CALL Statement

As well as passing control to other programs by means of *LINK* and *XCTL* commands, a CICS COBOL program can invoke another program with a COBOL *CALL* statement. Although there's somewhat less system overhead (in other words, a shorter path length) with this method, there are some considerations that may count against it. For example:

- A called program remains in its last-used state after it returns control, so a second call finds the program in this state. *LINK* and *XCTL* commands, on the other hand, always find the *new* program in its initial state.

- With static calls, you must link-edit the calling and called programs together and present them to CICS as a single unit, with one name. This has two consequences:

  — It may result in a module that is quite large.

  — It prevents two programs that call the same program from sharing a copy of the called program.

- With dynamic calls, *CALL* data-area have the advantage over *LINK* in terms of shorter length as long as the program is called more than twice.

- Programs that are called are different than *LINK*ed programs:

  — They use the conventional *GOBACK* statement to return to their caller rather than *EXEC CICS RETURN*.

  — No CICS trace entries are created on the *GOBACK*; problem analysis is more difficult.

Subroutines

Now, the answer to that problem we met earlier—whether and how to break up a large routine. For single-task efficiency, generally inline code is best, *PERFORM* next, straight CALL third, *XCTL* next, and *LINK* last. However, any of the first three choices may make for a long load module, and that can impact future understanding as to how the whole thing works when it comes to fixing bugs in later years.

Always use *XCTL* if it will do, of course, rather than *LINK*. In the *NACT01* program there is one use of *XCTL*. That's just a program logic issue; you either need control back or you don't. In the example, as you'll see, we've broken our own rule and used a *LINK* (rather than an *XCTL*) to the error handling program. However, we do have an excuse ready. See "Handling Errors," earlier in this chapter.

The probability of the code being re-used is another issue. If you have a long complex routine for calculating withholding tax for veterans in a payroll system, but you use it only if salary or dependents change and you have hardly any veterans, then by all means put it in a separate routine and *LINK* to it.

Examples of Passing Control and Data Between Programs and Transactions

The previous sections provide the background about passing data from one transaction to another; you may be wondering how the receiving program accesses this data. When the sample application meets an error from which it cannot recover, it transfers control to the general-purpose error program, *NACT04*. We pass three items of information to the *NACT04* program:

- The name of the program that passed control (and where the error was detected)
- The function that failed
- The return code from the command that failed

The copybooks used to pass this information to the error handling program by the other modules in the COBOL application are shown in Example 5-7.

Example 5-7. Sample of the NACCCERRH Copybook

```
*
* This is the working storage version of the interface to the
* Error Handler program.
*
    05  WS-ERRH-ERROR-COMMAREA.
*
* This is an "Eyecatcher" and integrity check field.
*
```

Example 5-7. Sample of the NACCCERRH Copybook (continued)

```
        10  WS-ERRH-VERSION              PIC XXX VALUE SPACES.
            88  WS-ERRH-CORRECT-VERSION VALUE 'V1A'.
        10  FILLER                       PIC X   VALUE SPACES.
*
* The error field is designed to conform to the CICS EIBRESP
* characteristics which always contains a numeric value. There
* are also architected values to indicate errors detected by the
* various programs in the applications suite.
*
        10  WS-ERRH-ERROR                PIC 9(4) VALUE ZERO.
        10  WS-ERRH-ERROR-X REDEFINES WS-ERRH-ERROR
                                         PIC X(4).
*
* The reason field is designed to conform to the CICS EIBRESP2
* characteristics which always contains a numeric value. There
* are also architected values to indicate errors detected by the
* various programs in the applications suite.
*
        10  WS-ERRH-REASON               PIC 9(4) VALUE ZERO.
        10  WS-ERRH-REASON-X REDEFINES WS-ERRH-REASON
                                         PIC X(4).
*
* If the response contains a numeric value, this contains the
* character representation of the EIBFN value giving rise to
* the exception condition.
*
        10  WS-ERRH-CICS-FUNCTION        PIC 9(5) VALUE ZERO.
        10  WS-ERRH-CICS-FUNCTION-X
                REDEFINES WS-ERRH-CICS-FUNCTION
                                         PIC X(5).
*
* Since the Error Handler can be LINKed or XCTLed to as well as
* being entered via CICS ABEND handling, this field allows the
* program trapping the error to identify itself.
*
        10  WS-ERRH-PROGRAM              PIC X(8) VALUE SPACES.
*
* This is set by the Error Handler to indicate the number of
* messages it generated from the error information. This is
* intended to allow a program which has LINKed to the Error
* Handler to use the information in a manner it deems suitable.
*
        10  WS-ERRH-NUMBER               PIC 9(4) VALUE ZERO.
*
* The array of messages generated.
*
        10  WS-ERRH-MESSAGES.
            15  WS-ERRH-MESSAGE          PIC X(120) OCCURS 3.
```

The data is passed to the *NACT04* program using the *XCTL* command:

```
    EXEC CICS XCTL PROGRAM(ABEND-PROGRAM)
               COMMAREA(WS-ERRH-ERROR-COMMAREA)
               RESP(RESPONSE) RESP2(REASON-CODE)
    END-EXEC
```

Communicating Between Transactions in the Sample Application

The *LINK* command is used to connect the *NACT01* program to the *CRUD* *(NACT02)* program and also to the *BRWS (NACT05)* program:

```
EXEC CICS LINK PROGRAM(CRUD-PROGRAM)
               COMMAREA(WS-CRUD-COMMAREA)
               RESP(RESPONSE) RESP2(REASON-CODE)
END-EXEC
```

Accessing the COMMAREA in the called program

In the *NACT02* code you will see how this is done. To the *NACT02* program, CICS makes it look like you are receiving one parameter:

```
LINKAGE SECTION
01 DFHCOMMAREA
    COPY NACCCRUD
```

Examples of EXEC CICS RETURN use

There are several different types of return to CICS. The simplest occurs in program *NACT02*, after the user has indicated a wish to exit from the application. No next *TRANSID* (transaction identifier) is set, and no data is passed forward to the next transaction. The return command is just:

```
EXEC CICS RETURN
END-EXEC
```

In program *NACT01*, in contrast, we need to indicate that the next transaction to be executed from the same terminal is the same as the current one whose transaction ID is stored in *EIBTRNID* of the EIB, so the *RETURN* command is written:

```
EXEC CICS RETURN TRANSID(EIBTRNID)
               COMMAREA(DFHCOMMAREA)
END-EXEC
```

Errors on the Program Control Commands

CICS recognizes these exceptional conditions on program control commands:

INVREQ

This means that one of two things happened:

— You specified COMMAREA or *LENGTH* on a *RETURN* command in a program that was not at the highest level (that is, a RETURN that would not terminate the transaction by returning control to CICS),

— You specified the *TRANSID* option on a *RETURN* from a task that had no terminal associated with it. In either form, *INVREQ* usually means a programming error.

LENGERR

This means that the length of the data, specified using the *RETURN* command with the length option, is outside the valid range of 1 to 32,500.

NOTAUTH

This means that a resource or command security check has failed. There is a complete list of reasons for such failures in the section on *NOTAUTH* in the *CICS Application Programming Reference.*

PGMIDERR

This means that the program to which control was passed, on a *LINK* or an *XCTL* command, cannot be found in the list of installed program definitions, isn't in the library, or has been disabled. It corresponds to *FILENOTFOUND* on a file command, and has similar causes. If it occurs during the testing phase, look for a spelling mismatch; if it occurs once the system has been put into actual use (*in production*), have your systems people check the list of installed program definitions.

Abending a Transaction

In addition to the normal return sequences, there is another command that is used in abnormal circumstances. This is the *ABEND* command. It returns control to CICS directly, as shown in Figure 5-1, if no *ABEND* handlers are active in any of the previous programs.

Use the *ABEND* command when a situation arises that the program cannot handle. This may be a condition beyond the control of the program (such as an input/output error on a file) or it may simply be a combination of circumstances that *should not occur* if the program logic is correct. In either case, *ABEND* is the right command to terminate the transaction. The format is:

```
EXEC CICS ABEND ABCODE(name)
END-EXEC
```

The option for this command is:

ABCODE(name)

Simply a four-character code identifying the particular *ABEND* command. It does two jobs: it tells CICS that you want a dump of your transaction, and it identifies the dump. Enclose it in quotes if it is a literal.

In addition, if no *ABEND* handlers are active and the program is at the highest level (Level 1 as described in Figure 5-1) control will be returned to CICS. The *ABEND* command has another very important property: it causes CICS to undo (back out) all of the changes made by this unit of work to recoverable resources.

Do not start the name of an **ABEND** code with the letter A, because it is reserved for CICS itself.

In our example application, we use this command at the end of program *NACT04*, where we send control when we've encountered a situation that prevents us from continuing the requested transaction. The code is:

```
EXEC CICS ABEND ABCODE(WS-LITS-SPECIAL)
END-EXEC
```

Suppose, for example, that program *NACT02* successfully adds a new record to the account file, but meets a *NOSPACE* condition when trying to add the corresponding new record to the index file. The resulting *ABEND* command issued in program *NACT04*:

- Produces a dump of all the main storage areas related to the transaction. A dump isn't always needed.

- Removes the new record or any changes from the account file, so that the two files are still synchronized with each other, even after the failure.

- Returns control to the *ABEND* handler further up the stack, if none to CICS.

Other Program Control Commands

There are two other program control commands that we'll mention here, but not cover in detail.

The *LOAD* command brings a program (any phase (VSE) or load module (MVS) in the list of installed program definitions or in the DFHRPL concatenation) into main storage but doesn't give it control. This is useful for tables of the type that are assembled and stored in a program library, but doesn't contain executable code.

The *RELEASE* command tells CICS that you've finished using such a program.

Queuing Facilities: Temporary Storage and Transient Data

CICS provides two queuing facilities: *temporary storage* and *transient data*. The following paragraphs tell you how to use temporary storage, both for queuing and as a scratchpad. There is a brief description of transient data in the following section, outlining the differences between the two facilities, and suggests when you might use one or the other.

Temporary Storage

Temporary storage is a set of sequential files, implemented using a VSAM data set on a disk, an area of main storage, or a coupling facility.

The CICS temporary storage facilities allow a task to create a queue of items, stored under a name (16 characters long in CICS TS for OS/390 Version 1.3 and 8 characters in all previous releases) selected by the user program. Each queue, which you can think of as a minature sequential file, exists until some task deletes it. The task that deletes it isn't usually the same task that created it, although it could be. The queue can contain up to 32,767 items and any number of different tasks can add to it, read it from any point within it, or change the contents of any items in it.

When there is just one item in a queue, we think of this facility as a scratchpad; when there is more than one, we think of it as a queuing facility. The items can be of almost any length up to 32,767 bytes, and they can be of different lengths within the same queue. If you are using the queue as a temporary sequential file, you can think of each item in it as a record.

The simplest use of temporary storage is:

```
EXEC CICS READQ TS QUEUE(name)
        INTO(data-area)
        RESP(response) RESP2(reason)
```

There are options to allow you to start where you like, read the next, and find out how many items there are in the queue.

Transient Data

There is another facility in CICS, called transient data, which comes in two flavors—*intrapartition* and *extrapartition:*

Intrapartition transient data

Intrapartition transient data is similar to temporary storage. Both temporary storage and transient data allow you to write and read queues of data items, which are often essentially small sequential files and each queue requires a resource definition called the *Destination Control Table* (DCT) entry. Like temporary storage queues, intrapartition transient data queues are implemented as a single VSAM data set managed by CICS. However, temporary storage items can be reread whereas with transient data a read is a destructive read. Also, temporary storage items can be read in any order, whereas with transient data they are read in the order that they are written. Table 5-1 illustrates the differences between temporary storage and transient data.

Extrapartition transient data

Extrapartition transient data is the means by which CICS supports standard sequential access method (SAM) files. The commands used for extrapartition queues are the same as for intrapartition queues, and each queue also requires a DCT entry. In this case, however, a read or write operation is actually a read or write to a sequential file, and each queue is a file. You can either read or write an extrapartition queue, but not both.

Table 5-1. Differences Between Temporary Storage and Transient Data

	Temporary Storage	Transient Data
Queue name	1–16 characters (CICS TS 1.3) 1–8 characters (Earlier releases)	1–4 characters
Queue name definition	Dynamic or pre-defined	Pre-defined
Cursor position	From ITEM value	From top
Read mode	Ordinary	Destructive

The EXEC CICS WRITEQ TD Command

The *WRITEQ TD* command writes transient data to a predefined symbolic destination. The syntax is as follows:

```
EXEC CICS WRITEQ TD QUEUE(name)
                FROM(data-area)
                RESP(data-area) RESP2(data-area)
END-EXEC
```

The options for this command are:

QUEUE(name)

Specifies the symbolic name (1–4 alphanumeric characters) of the queue to be written to. The named queue must have been defined to CICS.

FROM(data-area)

Specifies the data that is to be written to the transient data queue.

The EXEC CICS WRITEQ TD command as used in the NACT04 program

By default we produce messages that are sent to transient data. We also want to display these at the terminal if we have one. In the *NACT04* program, transient data is used to send error information to the CICS-supplied extrapartition transient data queue, CSSL. The code is as follows:

```
MOVE 2 TO WS-ERRH-NUMBER
EXEC CICS WRITEQ TD QUEUE(LO-ERROR-QUEUE)
                FROM(MA-STD-INFO)
                RESP(MA-RESP) RESP2(MA-REASON)
END-EXEC
```

Handling Errors

The *NACT04* program is a general-purpose error routine. It isn't invoked directly by any transaction, but instead receives control from programs *NACT01, NACT02,* and *NACT03* when they meet a condition from which they cannot recover.

The program sends a screen to the terminal user (see Figure 5-2) with a text description of the problem and a request to report it. The text is based on the CICS command that failed and the particular error that occurred on it. The name of the transaction and the program (and, if applicable, the file) involved are also shown. The command, error type, and program name are passed to the *NACT04* program from the program that transferred control to it; other items come from the CICS EXEC Interface Block (EIB). The EIB is a CICS control block associated with a task, containing information accessible to the application program. We'll look at it in more detail in "The EXEC Interface Block (EIB)" in Chapter 11.

After writing the screen, the program abends, so that any updates to recoverable resources performed in the half-completed transaction get *backed out*.

You'll see the *NACT04* program in action in the Execution Diagnostic Facility (EDF) session described in Chapter 16, *Debugging in CICS*.

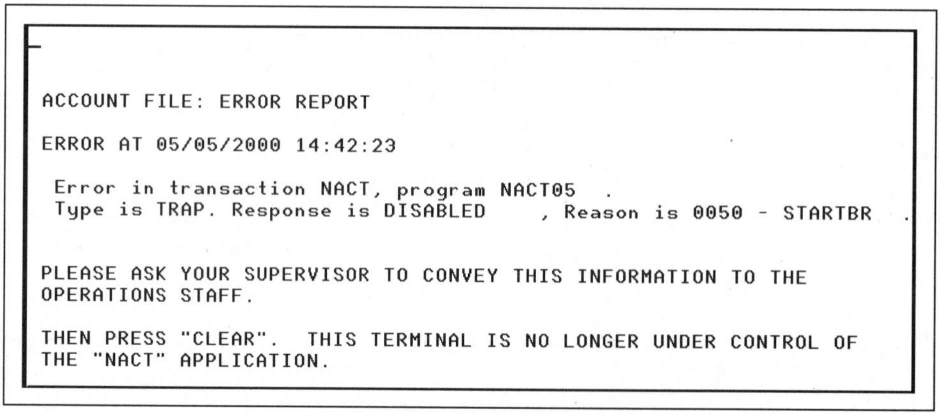

```
ACCOUNT FILE: ERROR REPORT

ERROR AT 05/05/2000 14:42:23

  Error in transaction NACT, program NACT05  .
  Type is TRAP. Response is DISABLED     , Reason is 0050 - STARTBR  .


PLEASE ASK YOUR SUPERVISOR TO CONVEY THIS INFORMATION TO THE
OPERATIONS STAFF.

THEN PRESS "CLEAR".  THIS TERMINAL IS NO LONGER UNDER CONTROL OF
THE "NACT" APPLICATION.
```

Figure 5-2. An example of a transaction error screen

As you saw in Figure 4-3, the *NACT04* program begins by issuing an *EXEC CICS ASSIGN* command. This command obtains information from CICS about the environment and the problem. This helps you diagnose a problem and determine whether the *NACT04* program was entered using an *EXEC CICS ABEND* command or whether the application program passed control to it using an *EXEC CICS XCTL* command or called it using an *EXEC CICS LINK* command. Alternatively, it could have been called by a COBOL dynamic CALL, although this is not used in the sample application program.

The EXEC CICS ASSIGN Command

The *CICS ASSIGN* command requests values from outside the application program's local environment. The syntax is as follows:

```
EXEC CICS ASSIGN ABCODE(data-area)
                 ABPROGRAM(data-area)
                 ASRAINTRPT(data-area)
                 ASRAKEY(cvda)
                 ASRAPSW(data-area)
                 ASRAREGS(data-area)
                 ASRASPC(cvda)
                 ASRASTG(cvda)
                 FCI(data-area)
                 INVOKINGPROG(data-area)
                 NETNAME(data-area)
                 PROGRAM(data-area)
                 RETURNPROG(data-area)
                 STARTCODE(data-area)
                 TERMCODE(data-area)
                 RESP(data-area) RESP2(data-area)
     END-EXEC
```

The options in this command are:

ABCODE(data-area)

Returns a four-character abend code. (Abend codes are documented in the *CICS Messages and Codes* manual that is on the CD-ROM). If an abend has not occurred, the variable is set to blanks.

ABPROGRAM(data-area)

Returns an eight-character name of the failing program for the latest abend. If the abend originally occurred in a DPL server program running in a remote system, *ABPROGRAM* returns the DPL server program name.

This field is set to binary zeros if it is not possible to determine the failing program at the time of the abend.

ASRAINTRPT(data-area)

Returns an eight-character program status word (PSW) containing interrupt information at the point when the latest abend with a code of ASRA, ASRB, ASRD, or AICA occurred.

The field contains binary zeros if no ASRA, ASRB, ASRD, or AICA abend occurred during the execution of the issuing transaction, or if the abend originally occurred in a remote DPL server program.

ASRAKEY(cvda)

Returns the execution key at the time of the last ASRA, ASRB, AICA, or AEYD, abend, if any. CVDA values are:

CICSEXECKEY

Returned if the task was executing in CICS-key at the time of the last ASRA, ASRB, AICA, or AEYD abend.

 All programs execute in CICS key if CICS subsystem storage protection is not active.

USEREXECKEY

Returned if the task was executing in user-key at the time of the last ASRA, ASRB, AICA, or AEYD abend.

NONCICS

Returned if the execution key at the time of the last abend was not one of the CICS keys; that is, not key 8 or key 9.

NOTAPPLIC

Returned if there has not been an ASRA, ASRB, AICA, or AEYD abend.

ASRAPSW(data-area)

Returns an eight-character program status word (PSW) at the point when the latest abend with a code of ASRA, ASRB, ASRD, or AICA occurred.

The field contains binary zeros if no ASRA, ASRB, ASRD, or AICA abend occurred during the execution of the issuing transaction, or if the abend originally occurred in a remote DPL server program.

ASRAREGS(data-area)

Returns the contents of general registers 0–15 at the point when the latest ASRA, ASRB, ASRD, or AICA abend occurred.

The contents of the registers are returned in the data area (64 bytes long) in the order 0, 1..., 14, 15.

ASRASPC(cvda)

Returns the type of space in control at the time of the last ASRA, ASRB, AICA, or AEYD abend, if any. The CVDA values on the ASRASPC option are:

SUBSPACE

Returned if the task was executing in either its own subspace or the common subspace at the time of the latest ASRA, ASRB, AICA, or AEYD abend.

BASESPACE

Returned if the task was executing in the base space at the time of the last ASRA, ASRB, AICA, or AEYD abend.

All tasks execute in base space if transaction isolation is not active.

NOTAPPLIC

Returned if there has not been an ASRA, ASRB, AICA, or AEYD abend.

ASRASTG(cvda)

Returns the type of storage being addressed at the time of the last ASRA or AEYD abend, if any. The CVDA values are:

CICS

Returned if the storage being addressed is CICS-key storage. This can be in one of the CICS dynamic storage areas (CDA or ECDA).

USER

Returned if the storage being addressed is user-key storage in one of the user dynamic storage areas (UDSA or EUDSA).

READONLY

Returned if the storage being addressed is read-only storage in one of the read-only dynamic storage areas (RDSA or ERDSA) when CICS is running with the PROTECT option on the RENTPGM system initialization parameter.

NOTAPPLIC

Returned if:

— There is no ASRA or AEYD abend found for this task.

— The affected storage in an abend is not managed by CICS.

— The ASRA abend is not caused by an 0C4 abend.

— An ASRB or AICA abend has occurred since the last ASRA or AEYD abend.

FCI(data-area)

Returns a one-byte facility control indicator. This indicates the type of facility associated with the transaction; for example, X'01' indicates a terminal or logical unit. A value is always returned.

INVOKINGPROG(data-area)

Returns the eight-character name of the application program that used the LINK or XCTL command to link or transfer control to the current program. If you issue the *ASSIGN INVOKINGPROG* command:

— In a remote program that was invoked by a distributed program link (DPL) command, CICS returns the name of the program that issued the DPL command.

— In an application program at the highest level, CICS returns eight blanks.

— In a user-replaceable program, a Bridge Exit program or a program list table program, CICS returns eight blanks.

— From a global user exit, task-related exit, or application program linked to from such an exit, CICS returns the name of the most recent invoking program that was not a global user exit (GLUE) or task-related user exit (TRUE).

NETNAME(data-area)

Returns the eight-character name of the logical unit in the VTAM network. If the task is not initiated from a terminal, *INVREQ* occurs. If the principal facility is not a local terminal, CICS returns the netname of the remote terminal. If this command was issued by a user transaction that was started by a bridged-to transaction, the value returned is the termid of the Bridge Facility.

Program(data-area)

Returns an eight-character name of the currently running program.

RETURNPROG(data-area)

Returns the eight-character name of the program to which control is to be returned when the current program has finished executing. The values returned depend on how the current program was given control, as follows:

— If the current program was invoked by a *LINK* command, including a distributed program link, *RETURNPROG* returns the same name as *INVOKINGPROG*.

— If the current program was invoked by an *XCTL* command, *RETURNPROG* returns the name of the application program in the chain that last issued a *LINK* command.

If the program that invoked the current program with an *XCTL* command is at the highest level, CICS returns eight blanks.

— If the *ASSIGN RETURNPROG* command is issued in the program at the top level, CICS returns eight blanks.

— If the *ASSIGN RETURNPROG* command is issued in a user-replaceable module, or a program list table program, CICS returns eight blanks.

— If the *ASSIGN RETURNPROG* is issued in a global user exit, task-related exit, or application program linked to from such an exit, CICS returns the name of the program that control is returned to when all intermediate global user exit and task-related user exit programs have completed.

STARTCODE(data-area)

Returns a two-byte indicator showing how the transaction issuing the request was started. It can have the following values:

Code	Transaction Start By
D	A distributed program link (DPL) request that did not specify the *SYNCONRETURN* option. The task cannot issue I/O requests against its principal facility, nor can it issue any syncpoint requests.
DS	A distributed program link (DPL) request, as in code D, that did specify the *SYNCONRETURN* option. The task cannot issue I/O requests against its principal facility, but can issue syncpoint requests.
QD	Transient data trigger level.
S	*START* command without data.
SD	*START* command with data.
SZ	*FEPI START* command.
TD	Terminal input or permanent transid.
U	User attached task.

TERMCODE(data-area)

Returns a two-byte code giving the type and model number of the terminal associated with the task. The first byte is a code identifying the terminal type, derived from the terminal resource definition. This is the *DEVICE* attribute (described in the *CICS Resource Definition Guide*). The second byte is a single-character model number as specified in the *TERMMODEL* attribute.

The EXEC CICS ASSIGN command as used in the NACT04 program

First we obtain various information from CICS about the environment and the problem. We use this to determine what actions to take and whether the program was entered using CICS *ABEND* handling or whether an application program transferred control to it using a CICS *XCTL* command or called it using a CICS *LINK* or COBOL Dynamic *CALL*. The syntax is as follows:

```
EXEC CICS ASSIGN ABCODE(AA-ABCODE)
                 ABPROGRAM(AA-ABPROGRAM)
                 ASRAINTRPT(AA-ASRAINTRPT)
                 ASRAKEY(AA-ASRAKEY)
                 ASRAPSW(AA-ASRAPSW)
                 ASRAREGS(AA-ASRAREGS)
                 ASRASPC(AA-ASRASPC)
                 ASRASTG(AA-ASRASTG)
                 FCI(AA-FCI)
                 INVOKINGPROG(AA-INVOKINGPROG)
                 NETNAME(AA-NETNAME)
                 PROGRAM(AA-PROGRAM)
                 RETURNPROG(AA-RETURNPROG)
```

```
                    STARTCODE(AA-STARTCODE)
                    TERMCODE(AA-TERMCODE)
                    RESP(AA-RESP)
      END-EXEC
```

The EXEC CICS INQUIRE PROGRAM Command

Having determined how the error handling program received control (through the *LINK* or *XCTL* command), the *EXEC CICS INQUIRE PROGRAM* is used in two ways: one to confirm that this was the program where the error occurred, and secondly, if it is not, then to browse the other programs to see if it can find the culprit.

The syntax of the *EXEC CICS INQUIRE PROGRAM* is as follows:

```
EXEC CICS INQUIRE PROGRAM(name)
                  LOADPOINT(ptr-ref) ENTRYPOINT(ptr-ref)
                  LENGTH(data-area)
      END-EXEC
```

Description

The *INQUIRE PROGRAM* command returns information about a particular program, map set, or partition set installed in your CICS system. All of these resources are load modules and, therefore, CICS uses the same *INQUIRE* command for all three. To avoid confusion, we use the word module to refer to the object of your inquiry, except in some cases where the option applies only to executable programs.

CICS determines the information you request from both the resource definition and, where applicable, the load module. Information from the module takes precedence over that in the definition if there is a conflict. However, CICS inspects a module only if it is already loaded and is the copy currently available for use. CICS does not do a load for an *INQUIRE PROGRAM* command, nor attempt to auto-install a resource for which it has no definition.

ENTRYPOINT(ptr-ref)

Returns the entry point address of the module, if it is loaded. The top bit of the address is set on if the addressing mode is 31 and off if it is 24. If the module has not been loaded, or is a remote program, or is a Java Virtual Machine (JVM) program, a null pointer (X'FF000000') is returned.

LENGTH(data-area)

Returns a full-word binary field giving the length of the module in bytes. A value of 0 is returned if the module has not been loaded in the current CICS session. A value of −1 is returned if it is a remote program, or a JVM program.

LOADPOINT(ptr-ref)

> returns the load address of the module. If it is not currently loaded, or if the program is running under a JVM, a null pointer (X'FF000000') is returned.

Browsing

You can also browse through the definitions of these three attributes of resources in your system by using the browse options (*START, AT, NEXT,* and *END*) on *INQUIRE PROGRAM* commands. In browse mode, the definitions are returned in alphabetical order, and you can specify a starting point with the *AT* option if you wish.

This command has introduced an argument value of *cvda*, which stands for a CICS-value data area. It is implemented in a similarly to DFHRESP, so to test the value returned in the *ASRAKEY* argument, you would code:

```
IF AA-ASRAKEY = DFHVALUE(USEREXECKEY)
```

The EXEC CICS INQUIRE PROGRAM as used in the NACT04 program

NACT04 uses the *INQUIRE PROGRAM* command as follows:

```
EXEC CICS INQUIRE PROGRAM(AA-ABPROGRAM)
               ENTRYPOINT(WF-ENTRY-POINT) LOADPOINT(WF-LOAD-POINT)
               LENGTH(WF-LENGTH)
               RESP(WF-RES)
END-EXEC
```

And for browsing:

```
EXEC CICS INQUIRE PROGRAM START
               RESP(WF-RES)
END-EXEC
PERFORM UNTIL (MA-ABPROGRAM NOT = '*UNKNOWN')
       OR    (WF-RESP = DFHRESP(END))
    EXEC CICS INQUIRE PROGRAM(AA-ABPROGRAM) NEXT
               ENTRYPOINT(WF-ENTRY-POINT) LOADPOINT(WF-LOAD-POINT)
               LENGTH(WF-LENGTH)
               RESP(WF-RES)
    END-EXEC
      ADD WF-LENGTH TO    WF-LOAD-POINT
               GIVING WF-END-POINT
      IF  AA-ASRAPSW-NSI < WF-END-POINT
      AND AA-ASRAPSW-NSI > WF-LOAD-POINT
          MOVE AA-ABPROGRAM   TO MA-ABPROGRAM
      END-IF
END-PERFORM
EXEC CICS INQUIRE PROGRAM END
               RESP(WF-RES)
END-EXEC
```

The EXEC CICS DUMP TRANSACTION Command

The *DUMP TRANSACTION* command dumps all, a series, or any single main storage area related to a task, any or all of the CICS resource definitions (DCT, FCT,
SIT, or TCT), or all of these together.

 If you issue a *DUMP TRANSACTION* for a *DUMPCODE* that is defined
in the transaction dump table with *SYSDUMP*, you also get a system
dump.

If there is no entry in the system dump table for the specified *DUMPCODE*, a temporary entry is made. This entry is lost on the next CICS start. The system dump
table is described in the *CICS Problem Determination Guide*. The syntax for this
command is:

```
EXEC CICS DUMP TRANSACTION DUMPCODE(name)
          RESP(data-area)
END-EXEC
```

The option in this command is:

DUMPCODE(name)

Specifies a name (1–4 characters) that identifies the dump. If the name contains any leading or imbedded blanks, the dump is produced but *INVREQ* is
raised. No entry is added to the system dump table.

If you omit all the options except *DUMPCODE*, you get the same dump as if
you specified *TASK*, but without the DL/I control blocks.

EXEC CICS DUMP TRANSACTION as used in NACT04

We take a dump but with a code based on the type of error we have encountered. This way we ensure we do not conflict with any CICS dump codes. Note
that if these are not wanted, they can be suppressed by operational procedures:

```
EXEC CICS DUMP TRANSACTION DUMPCODE(DUMP-CODE)
          RESP(AA-RESP)
END-EXEC
```

The EXEC CICS SYNCPOINT ROLLBACK Command

The *SYNCPOINT ROLLBACK* command backs out any updates to protected
resources and returns them to a state they were in before this transaction began.
The syntax is as follows:

```
EXEC CICS SYNCPOINT ROLLBACK
END-EXEC
```

ROLLBACK specifies that all changes to recoverable resources made by the task since its last syncpoint are to be backed out. This option can be used to tidy up protected resources in a *HANDLE ABEND* routine, or to revoke database changes after the application program finds irrecoverable errors in its input data.

A failure occurring during the backout phase (phase 2) of syncpoint processing does not return an error condition and the transaction is not abnormally terminated. Subsequent units of work in the transaction are allowed to continue normally. See *CICS Recovery and Restart Guide* for further information.

The EXEC CICS SYNCPOINT ROLLBACK command as used in the NACT04 program

In order to reset all CICS recoverable resources because the transaction has not finished we backout the current UOW by performing the following command:

```
EXEC CICS SYNCPOINT ROLLBACK
END-EXEC
```

The EXEC CICS WRITE OPERATOR Command

The *WRITE OPERATOR* command enables an application to write a message to one or more system consoles and, if necessary, wait for a reply. The command can specify route codes. This is of particular use to application packages that need to issue their own system operator messages.

As a result of a change in the way CICS handles messages sent to the console, text lengths of greater than 113 characters are split into two lines:

```
EXEC CICS WRITE OPERATOR
        TEXT(data-value)
END-EXEC
```

If *ACTION* (or one of the equivalent CVDA values below) is specified, the message is retained until the console operator explicitly deletes it or CICS terminates.

The option for this command is:

TEXT(data-value)

A data value containing the text to be sent. In COBOL programs use a data-area that contains the text to be sent to the operator, rather than a data-value.

The EXEC CICS WRITE OPERATOR command as used in the NACT04 program

By writing these messages out to the sytem operator, we enable automated operations policies to be implemented and this will depend on the way your CICS systems are set up for running transactions. The syntax for this command is:

```
EXEC CICS WRITE OPERATOR
          TEXT(MA-STD-INFO)
END-EXEC
```

In the code there is another *WRITE OPERATOR* that sends a second message held in data variable *MA-XTR-INFO.*

Other Commands

In addition to the previous commands, the error handling program also uses a number of other commands including those which enable you to add a date and time stamp in a variety of formats to the messages. They are *EXEC CICS ASKTIME* and *EXEC CICS FORMATTIME.* Finally, the command *EXEC CICS ISSUE DISCONNECT* is used when you need to drop the session of the end user's terminal. For the details of these commands, look in the *CICS Application Programming Reference.*

What's Next...

The last two chapters have given us a clear idea of what is involved in setting up the business logic of a simple CICS application. Most of the remainder of this book looks at the various forms of the presentation logic you can use to access your data.

III

The CICS Java Component

One of the KanDoIT company's aims is to give its customers the ability to easily check their accounts using the Web without requiring any special client application software. The solution will connect to the existing business logic component, retrieve account data, and return a dynamically generated web page.

The business logic to retrieve customer account records is already in place—it's the set of *NACTnn* COBOL programs we developed elsewhere in the book. Because we have designed it in the way we have, we will be able to reuse it for the Web.

How do we go about creating such a web application and benefit from the power of CICS on the mainframe? CICS TS for OS/390 Version 1.3 now supports the Java programming language and the Internet Inter-ORB Protocol (IIOP), which is part of the Common Object Request Broker Architecture (CORBA). These technologies are ideal for this type of application. Java allows development of applications that can run on any platform with a Java Virtual Machine (JVM). CORBA lets Java objects communicate with other objects across the Internet. This is exactly what we want to achieve: to expose our existing business logic to the outside world for any remote client that knows how to invoke its methods (subject to security constraints).

In this part we describe how to *wrapper* the existing COBOL CICS application using CICS Java classes, how to encapsulate the customer account as a CORBA object and how to configure CICS to route requests for information to this object and return data to remote clients.

Development of the user interface, the web server components that will request information from the CICS Java object, and how account data can be returned to the user is left for Part IV, *The Web Component.* This part contains Chapter 6, *Designing the CICS Java Component* and Chapter 7, *Programming the CICS Java Component.*

6

Designing the CICS Java Component

The KanDoIT company already has a strong web presence where customers can read sales and marketing information, company details, and contact KanDoIT departments and individuals directly. However, just like many companies, this information is general, seldom updated and likely to be old printed literature represented in HTML. To maintain customer business it's time to take a step towards dynamically generated information that is directly relevant to individual customers—into the world of e-business.

The existing CICS application that handles business logic (as described in Part II) is to be re-used. It can now be easily connected to the Web using two new features of CICS TS for OS/390 Version 1.3—Java classes for CICS and Internet Inter-Orb Protocol (IIOP) support. How these technologies will form part of the overall solution is illustrated in Figure 6-3. In this setup, the CICS Java component acts as an account data server which communicates using IIOP with a client application which runs on a web server. The details of the client-side part of the component implemented on the web server are discussed in Part IV, *The Web Component.*

This chapter describes the background and design of the CICS Java component that will allow KanDoIT to integrate data generated by existing CICS applications directly into web pages. Chapter 7, *Programming the CICS Java Component* describes the detailed steps to build and implement a working application. The CD-ROM that accompanies this book includes all the code that is developed in this chapter and Chapter 7.

The topics described in this chapter are: *Common object request broker architecture*

- The background to Java and CORBA in a CICS environment

- Understanding what the CICS Java component needs to do

- Describing a customer account object with Interface Definition Language (IDL)

- Designing the CICS Java component

- Implementing the CICS Java component

Background to Java and CORBA in a CICS Environment

The benefits of object-oriented development are well known: faster development cycles, reduced maintenance, higher quality, reusability, portability, and lower cost, achieved through encapsulation and inheritance. The Java programming language offers these benefits and at the same time draws on the better features of older object-oriented languages such as Smalltalk and C++. Java removes many of the complexities and pitfalls of these earlier languages and provides a clean, safe, portable, reliable and efficient object-based development platform. Objects communicate by passing messages and this paradigm matches the needs of distributed, client-server systems. Java technology is well suited to these heterogeneous environments.

CICS TS for OS/390 Version 1.3 supports the Internet Inter-ORB Protocol (IIOP) used by distributed objects for communication. This protocol is part of the Common Object Request Broker Architecture (CORBA) 2.0 specification. Let's look at how Java and IIOP fit into the CICS picture.

Java in a CICS Environment

You can write CICS application programs in Java with CICS TS Version 1.3 that provides a library of Java classes to access important CICS services. These classes allow you to read files, write to transient data, start transactions, link to other programs, enqueue resources, and access many other resources in CICS.

The Java class library for CICS, known as JCICS, is supplied in the Java archive file *dfjcics.jar*. By default, this is located in the HFS directory *$CICS_HOME/classes* during CICS installation.

CICS resources, such as programs or temporary storage queues, are represented by instances of the appropriate Java class. Resources are defined to CICS in the usual way, for example using *CEDA*. See the *CICS Resource Definition Guide* for information about defining CICS resources.

Use the CEDA transaction to define resources to your CICS system while the system is running. With CEDA, you can update both the CICS system definition (CSD) file and the running CICS system.

The CICS translator (as used by other CICS supported languages) is not required for Java. You can develop Java programs on a workstation, or in the OS/390 Unix System Services shell on OS/390, using an editor of your choice, or in a visual composition environment such as VisualAge for Java, and then compile them.

The CICS approach to running Java programs allows you to link to and from CICS programs written in Java. Thus you can capitalize on the advantages of Java in new applications and migrate to Java by converting one program at a time. Data is passed in COMMAREAs, which are byte arrays of up to 32,500 bytes long.

With the link interface, you can take advantage of Java in CICS and even work in a cross-language environment. For example, the invoking program can be a Java program that was started through an IIOP request, and the invoked program can be a COBOL program containing the actual business logic. This setup is the basis for our sample application.

In summary, CICS TS for OS/390 Version 1.3 support for Java:

- Allows CICS application development in Java.

- Allows CICS Java programs to interoperate with CICS programs written in any other CICS supported language.

- Allows CICS Java programs to access CICS services.

- Provides a Java version of the CICS API known as the JCICS class library.

- Supports Java development tools such as IBM VisualAge for Java.

Introduction to CORBA

Because of mergers, acquisitions, and the fast rate of change in the IT industry, companies often have to manage and evolve diverse systems, on different hardware, different operating systems, and in different programming languages. Enabling these applications to communicate over networks is a necessity. The growth of the Web exacerbates the problem, especially for providing individual access to current business data, sometimes known as legacy data, from web browsers.

The traditional client/server approach typically uses server-dependent implementations of a client, meaning that maintenance of the server application or indeed the hardware it runs on often requires changes to individual clients. Deployment and management of these *fat clients* is both time and resource consuming.

How can companies utilize component-based, object-oriented applications, and at the same time build on their existing business functions and data? Is there a programming language that is portable, robust and object oriented that can run on all the different available hardware platforms and operating systems? Is there a transport mechanism that allows inter-object communication across the global network?

The answer is yes to both. Java provides an object implementation independent of platform and operating system, and there are many publications written about this. A good starting point would be the Sun Java web site at *http://java.sun.com*. Java applications will run anywhere there is a Java Virtual Machine implementation. Common Object Request Broker Architecture (CORBA) is the answer to providing a complete, standard, distributed object infrastructure.

CORBA is based on the OMG Object Model which defines common object semantics to have the same external visible characteristics between objects. To communicate with each other, CORBA-compliant objects implement a language-independent interface, the Interface Definition Language (IDL).

The object's methods and attributes are defined in IDL and then mapped to a specific programming language. In the case of Java, an IDL-to-Java compiler converts the IDL description into a set of Java classes, known as the *stub* or *skeleton*.

When a CORBA-compliant object wants to invoke a method located in another object, it calls the stub. The stub then uses the local Object Request Broker (ORB), a CORBA component that locates the requested service on the network, to send the request, and to receive the response. The object does not need to know anything about the ORB or the actual location of the server. All CORBA clients and servers communicate through ORBs.

The ORB is the only portion of CORBA that must be present to build a CORBA-compliant application. Many ORBs ship without some or any of the CORBA services or facilities, and you must create or purchase these services yourself. However, without the ORB, a CORBA application cannot function.

The most visible function of a CORBA ORB is to respond to requests from your application or from another ORB. During the life cycle of a CORBA application, the ORB may be asked to do many different things, including:

- Looking up and instantiating objects on remote machines.
- Marshalling parameters from one programming language (such as Java) to another (such as C++).
- Invoking methods on a remote object, using the static method invocation described by a downloaded stub.
- Invoking methods on a remote object, using dynamic method invocation.
- Automatically starting objects that are not currently running.

On the server side, the stub is called a skeleton. It plays the symmetric role to the (client) stub: it gathers the request's parameters and sends back the response. The skeleton is also generated by the IDL-to-Java compiler. Figure 6-1 shows an object invoking a remote method through an ORB proxy and IIOP.

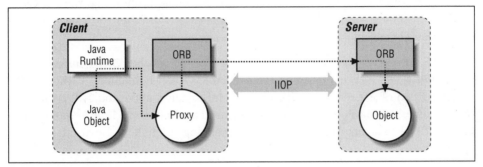

Figure 6-1. Java object invoking a remote method

To summarize these concepts, CORBA objects can:

- Be located anywhere on a network.

- Interoperate with other CORBA objects on other platforms.

- Be written in any programming language to which there is a mapping from OMG IDL. Mappings currently specified include Java, C++, C, Smalltalk, COBOL, and Ada.

Using CORBA, you can design a distributed system where various components (for example, user interface, business logic, and database access) are packaged in separate programs running on different machines. Each component communicates with the other only through its published interface and can therefore be maintained separately.

Detailed information about CORBA can be found at the OMG web site at *http:// www.omg.org/corba*. The Web also has many CORBA articles and tutorials.

CICS IIOP Support

IIOP is the standard network protocol that CORBA uses for inter-object communication across networks. With CICS support for inbound IIOP (CICS always acts as the server), you can take a true object oriented (OO) approach to interfacing with CICS Java programs.

CICS TS for OS/390 Version 1.3 provides a subset of CORBA services suitable for distributed objects that have evolved from existing CICS applications. The CICS-provided solution has strong advantages over the full-function ORB solution in that CICS manages many services such as security, transaction services, and other characteristics such as state management and data storing mechanisms. This means existing investment in CICS can be reused and migration to distributed object programming can be done incrementally at low risk. There are performance benefits too, in that processor and memory resource utilization on the server is better than that in a full-function ORB solution. The server-side application that runs in CICS, has access to most CICS facilities, can communicate with other CICS systems, and can access all available and existing data sources.

The CICS ORB does not use a naming service like many other ORBs. Instead, a client locates a server object using an Interoperable Object Reference (IOR). The IOR is a stringified object reference that contains information about the TCP/IP address of the server machine and the port being used for incoming IIOP requests. The CICS ORB classes provide a utility for generating an IOR to be used in client applications.

CICS CORBA IIOP applications are defined as interfaces and operations in IDL and implemented in Java. Components of such applications are:

The IDL
> Before you can write a CORBA client or server application, you must create an OMG IDL file that contains the definitions of the interfaces the server implementation will support. The IDL file describes the data types, operations, and objects that a client can use to make a request and that a server must provide for an implementation of a given object.

A server program that implements the interfaces defined in the IDL
> You process IDL definitions with a suitable IDL-to-Java compiler. You must use a compiler provided by the server environment (CICS) to generate the server-side skeletons and helper classes.

A client program that makes calls to the server based on the IDL definition
> You must use a compiler provided by the client environment to generate the client-side stub (sometimes called the proxy) and helper classes. The proxies and skeletons provide the object-specific information needed for an ORB to distribute a method invocation.

CICS definitions for execution of the server program
> To generate the server-side skeleton and server classes you must use the IDL compiler provided by CICS in *dfjcidl.jar*.

Figure 6-2 illustrates the application development process for a CICS CORBA IIOP application.

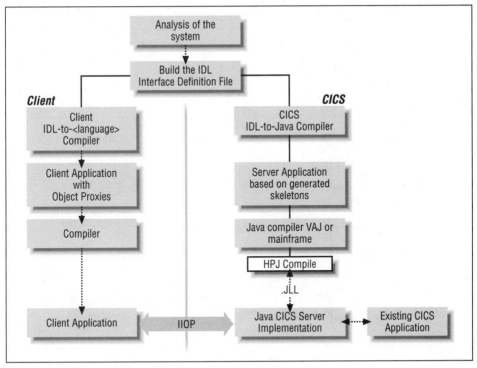

Figure 6-2. CICS CORBA IIOP application development process

 If you are running both client and server IDL compilers on the same workstation, ensure that the CLASSPATH locates the correct compiler in each case, and that the output is written to separate directories.

The client can be a CORBA 2.0 compliant client written in any language. If the client is developed in Java, it can run as an applet or Java application and connect through IIOP to the CICS ORB server application program.

Understanding What This Component Needs to Do

The key steps that we need to develop for our sample application are to:

- Implement a server object that represents a customer account, as defined in IDL. This account object must provide methods to allow clients to request account data by account number.

- Wrapper the COBOL (*NACT02*) program as a Java program. The JCICS classes are used to link to the COBOL program, request account data.

- Set the account fields, returned by the COBOL program, in the account object and return to the client.

The overall solution is illustrated in Figure 6-3.

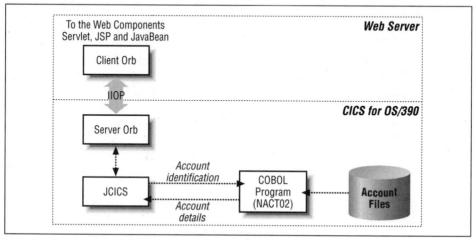

Figure 6-3. Overview of the CORBA server/client relationship using IIOP

Describing a Customer Account Object with IDL

The IDL defines a contract between the client and server, specifying what objects are available on the server and the operations a client can invoke against those objects. The IDL file you create contains the definitions of the interfaces the server implementation will support. It describes the data types, operations and objects that a client can use to make a request and that a server must provide for the implementation of a given object.

For the KanDoIT sample application, we need to describe an object that represents a customer account, including all the fields we want to make available to the customer such as account number, last name, telephone number, etc. We also need to provide a method by which a client application can request information for a given account number. The IDL file for such an account object looks like Example 6-1.

Example 6-1. Sample IDL File

```
module accountObject {

    struct AccountData {
        string respcode;
```

Example 6-1. Sample IDL File (continued)

```
            string reascode;
            string cicsfunc;
            string acctid;
            string lastname;
            string firstname;
            string midinit;
            string title;
            string telnum;
            string addr1;
            string addr2;
            string addr3;
            string auth1;
            string auth2;
            string auth3;
            string auth4;
            string cards;
            string issuemonth;
            string issueday;
            string issueyear;
            string reason;
            string code;
            string approver;
            string scode1;
            string scode2;
            string scode3;
            string status;
            string limit;
        };
      interface AccountInterface {
            //getter methods
            accountObject::AccountData getAccount(in string acctno);
        };
};
```

The account data structure, called AccountData, is a convenient way of keeping all the account fields together in one logical piece. It also allows the client to retrieve an entire account structure in one request rather than having getter methods for each and every field which is less efficient.

The interface is called AccountInterface and this must be implemented by the server application we write. The server application must also provide a method called getAccount, which is how the client application will make its request on the customer account. The syntax for getAccount is:

```
    AccountData getAccount(in string acctno)
```

This says that this method takes (specified by 'in') a string of characters containing an account number as input, and returns a data structure in the format of AccountData.

You then process the IDL file with an IDL-to-Java compiler. You must use a compiler provided by the server environment (in this case *dfjcidl.jar*) to generate server-side skeleton and helper classes.

For the client side, you must use an IDL-to-Java compiler suitable for that environment to generate client-side stub (also known as proxy) and helper classes. The proxies and skeletons provide the object-specific information needed for an ORB to distribute a method invocation across the network.

The client can be a CORBA 2.0–compliant client written in any language. If the client is developed in Java, it can run as an applet or Java application and connect through IIOP to the CICS ORB server application program. In the case of the Kan-DoIT application, the client will be written in Java and integrated with a servlet running on a web server.

Details of how to write and compile the IDL are provided in Chapter 7.

Design of the CICS Java Component

With the skeleton and helper classes generated by the IDL-to-Java compiler process, we now need to write a Java class that will specifically implement the getAccount method we defined in the IDL. With the JCICS Java class library, our CORBA server implementation can perform a program link to (or wrapper) the existing *NACT02* program that is written in COBOL and request customer account details. The program is encapsulated by the Java implementation class we write and there is no need to make any changes to the COBOL application. For providing access to legacy CICS applications, the JCICS library is very powerful.

The program link passes parameters using the COMMAREA. The implementation class we write must prepare a COMMAREA suitable for the *NACT02* program to include type of request (read), the customer account number, and provide return fields for response, reason and error codes, and of course the account details themselves.

After an IIOP request invokes the *getAccount* method, the customer account details for the given account number must be returned in the *AccountData* format.

For our sample application, we split these tasks into three methods:

getAccount()
> Puts request parameters into a string and invokes the *callCRUD()* method. Returned account data is then extracted and set in the *AccountData* format.

callCRUD()
> Invokes *buildCA()* to prepare the COMMAREA, then performs a program link to the *NACT02* program.

buildCA( )
    Converts a COMMAREA string into a byte array.

Specific information on developing the Java class and its methods is described in Chapter 7.

Implementing CICS Java Components

The next step is to compile the implementation class together with the various skeleton and helper classes. You will require CORBA classes from *dfjcorb.jar* and the CICS API Java classes found in *dfjcics.jar* to be in your CLASSPATH. The Java bytecode output of this process may be interpreted by a JVM running in CICS or transferred (if necessary) to OS/390 Unix System Services and further compiled by the High Performance Java (HPJ) compiler included in the Enterprise Toolkit for OS/390 (ET/390) component of VisualAge for Java, Enterprise Edition 2.0 (and higher). The ET/390 binder produces program objects as OS/390 Java executable files (*.jll* or *.exe*) in OS/390 partitioned data set extended (PDSE) libraries, which can be loaded and executed by CICS.

CICS loads the program from the PDSE on first invocation and executes it in an LE run unit, similarly to a C++ program, using runtime support in the CICS region provided by the Java runtime component of ET/390.

You can use the VisualAge for Java Integrated Development Environment (IDE) to develop Java applications to run in the OS/390 Unix or CICS TS Version 1.3 for OS/390 environments. To let you control the ET/390 actions that you want to perform, every object (project, package, class) has its own set of ET/390 properties. The panels in ET/390 properties allow you to set the bytecode binder options, Language Environment runtime options, OS/390 environment variables, and Java command options so that the following ET/390 actions can be successfully performed at the host:

- Export and bind Java bytecode into an OS/390 Java executable or DLL
- Run the OS/390 Java executable (optionally with tracing) in the OS/390 shell
- Run Java bytecode in the OS/390 JVM
- Debug the OS/390 Java executable as it runs in the OS/390 shell
- Debug the Java bytecode as it runs in the OS/390 JVM

The following CICS resource definitions are required so that the program objects respond to external IIOP requests:

TCPIPSERVICES
    Specifies which port is used for IIOP requests.

REQUESTMODEL

Associates inbound requests with a TRANSID.

TRANSID

Defines execution characteristics for this IIOP request.

The sample definitions are supplied in Appendix A, *Configuring Your CICS for OS/390 Environment.*

What's Next...

Let's look now at the detailed steps to build a complete CORBA application developed entirely and run from the VisualAge for Java environment. This is described in more detail in Chapter 7.

7

Programming the CICS Java Component

In this chapter you will be using VisualAge for Java Enterprise Edition to develop the CICS Java component together with the Enterprise Toolkit/390 (ET/390) that comes with it. The procedure is based on VisualAge for Java Version 2. The panels and screens in Version 3 are different.

Before you can complete the procedure in this chapter you need to install the COBOL application and have all the definitions outlined in Appendix A set up.

The IIOP client/server programming model starts with interface definitions. Here are the steps for developing a CORBA application:

- Write a definition for each object using IDL.

- Compile the IDL code using an IDL-to-Java compiler to produce server skeleton code and client stub code.

- Create and add the Java implementation classes.

- Build the server application (Export and bind to a CICS region).

- Build the client application.

Tools

The main tool detailed in this chapter is VisualAge for Java for Windows NT, Enterprise Edition, which is an end-to-end Java application development tool that lets you develop Java code on the workstation and deploy it on OS/390. It provides a comprehensive Integrated Development Environment (IDE) that supports browsing, editing, compiling, testing, debugging, and deployment. The Enterprise Toolkit for OS/390 (ET/390), a feature of VisualAge for Java Enterprise Edition, provides OS/390 support. It provides a SmartGuide to export class files to the OS/390 Hierarchical File System (HFS) for native compilation and debugging. Native code built on PDSEs is a dynamic link library (DLL) that, while not portable, is suited for high-performance server programs.

Setting Up Your Development Environment

This section shows how to prepare your Windows NT environment before you start developing your CORBA application using VisualAge for Java. The CICS ORB classes and the JCICS APIs are shipped with VisualAge for Java 3.0 Enterprise Edition as additional features. If you are working with Version 2.0, you need to copy the required packages from the CD-ROM that accompanies this book, set up the CICS IDL environment, and configure the ET/390 environment, as explained here:

Downloading the required packages from CICS Transaction Server

To develop a JCICS IIOP application on the workstation, you need, at a minimum, the CICS ORB and IDL compiler. If your application uses JCICS classes, you need the JCICS package as well. CICS TS for OS/390 Version 1.3 provides these packages and utilities in the HFS directory called *$CICS_HOME/classes* during CICS installation. FTP them to your workstation in binary format. They are also on the CD-ROM that accompanies this book in the directory that is called *\cicsadp\CORBA Server\CICS classes*. The three jar files supplied with CICS are:

dfjcics.jar

The JCICS API classes, required for compilation of Java server programs that uses JCICS to access CICS services.

dfjcorb.jar

The CICS ORB classes, required to build the IIOP server application. This also contains the GenericFactory utility that is used to help build your client program.

dfjcidl.jar

The CICS IDL compiler to be used in building the IIOP server application.

After transferring the required packages to the workstation, import them into the VisualAge for Java IDE so their references can be resolved when you develop your application using the package classes.

Importing the JCICS classes

To import the JCICS classes, use the following steps:

1. Go to the menu bar and select *File* and then *Import.* The Import Smart-Guide dialog is displayed.

2. Choose *Jar File* and select *Next.*

3. In the *Import from a jar/zip file* SmartGuide dialog, click *Browse* and navigate to the directory containing the *dfjcics.jar* file. This is on the CD-ROM in the directory called *\cicsadp\CORBA Server\CICS classes.*

4. Select the file, *dfjcics.jar,* and click *Open* to return to the *Import from a jar/zip file* SmartGuide dialog.

5. Ensure that the checkboxes for class and resource are checked.

6. In the *Project* field, type in a name to identify the JCICS project, such as JCICS Classes and click *Finish.*

   A question box appears stating that the JCICS Classes project does not exist and asking if you want to create it. Click *Yes* and wait until it finishes importing.

   The JCICS classes contain bean classes, so you are prompted to create a bean category for the bean classes. Select *New Category* and type a name for the new category, such as JCICS. Ensure that all beans under *Available beans* are selected and that the new category JCICS is selected, click *Add to Category.*

7. Finally, click *OK.*

Figure 7-1 shows the results of this procedure, including the JCICS beans:

Importing the CICS ORB classes and the CICS IDL compiler

After importing the JCICS classes, use the same procedure to import the CICS ORB classes into the IDE. These are in the file called *dfjcorb.jar.* Unlike the JCICS classes, the CICS ORB does not contain any bean classes in the package, so you won't be asked to create a bean category.

Now repeat the process to import the CICS IDL compiler; this is found in the file called *dfjcidl.jar.*

VisualAge for Java Enterprise Edition Version 3.0 includes the CICS ORB and JCICS classes. To ensure that you are using these classes, you need to add them as a feature. Select *File → Quickstart → Feature → Add Feature* and click *OK.* From the list select *JCICS Application Programming Library 3.0,* then *OK.* If you are using Version 2.0, add these features to the IDE as shown in this section.

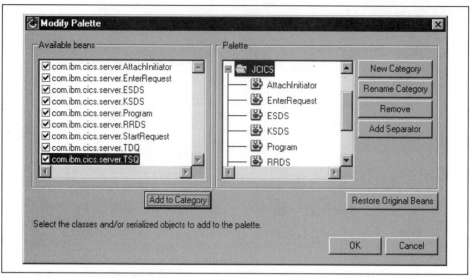

Figure 7-1. VisualAge for Java: Modify Palette panel

Preparing the IDL development environment

The IDL development environment is an additional feature of VisualAge for Java. It provides an environment to create IDL objects and generate server skeletons and client stubs by invoking the IDL-to-Java compiler. To add the IDL development environment into the IDE:

1. From the Workbench, go to the menu bar and select *File* and click *Quick Start*. The Quick Start SmartGuide dialog is displayed. Alternatively press the F2 key.

2. Ensure that *Features* is highlighted in the left column, then select *Add Feature* and click *OK*. The Selection Required SmartGuide dialog is displayed.

3. Navigate the list and highlight *IDL Development Environment 2.0*, then click *OK*.

The IDL development environment is added to the IDE and is ready for use.

Mounting a network drive

In order to export and bind the Java code so that it works in your CICS region, you need to have HFS mounted as one of the drives in your development environment; you need to install an NFS client. Hummingbird's NFS Maestro Solo is a client-based program that allows Windows NT and Windows 95/98 users to access file and print resources of other network attached machines, or any other system that supports NFS. To do this:

1. Start *NFS Maestro Solo—NFS Network Access*. Select *Start → Programs → NFS Maestro → NFS Network Access*.

2. Enter your *Network Path*, for example, *winmvs26\/hfs/u/horswil,binary*, a *Drive* letter, *Username* and *Password*. On the remainder of the screen change *Read Size* to 4096 and the *Write Size* to 8192, and finally select *Preserve Case*. Figure 7-2 shows you the settings that we used.

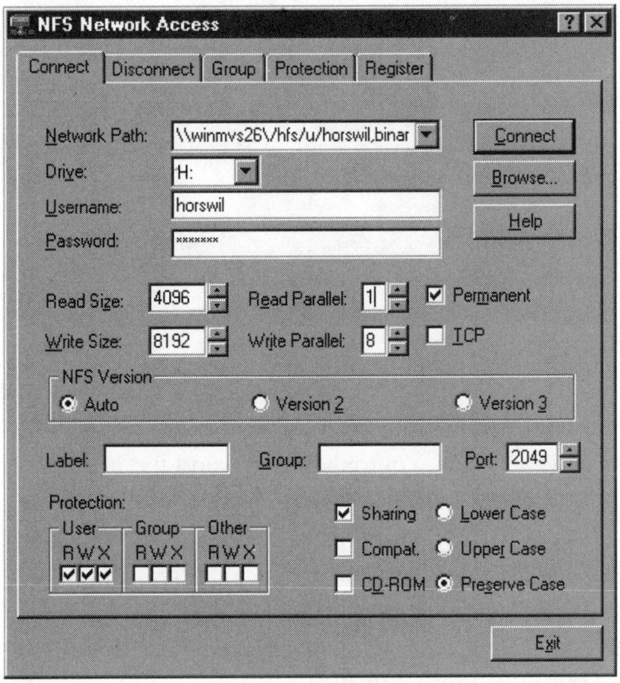

Figure 7-2. NFS Maestro Solo: NFS Network Access dialog

Configuring your ET/390 host environment

When you use ET/390 to bind and run your OS/390 Java applications, you have to provide the OS/390 host session information to VisualAge for Java. A sample ET/390 Java Install Data file can be found in your ET/390 install tree on OS/390. It describes your working environment and where the ET/390 bytecode binder is installed. You can modify it to fit your working environment. When you add the host session, ET/390 downloads a copy of the ET/390 Java Install Data file to the workstation and saves a copy for your ET/390 development work. The information in the Data file is used by ET/390 to locate the host where it exports the class files and binds the application. To add an ET/390 host session:

1. Go to the menu bar of the Workbench page and select *Workspace* → *Tools* → *ET/390* → *Host sessions* → *Add*. Figure 7-3 shows the panel.

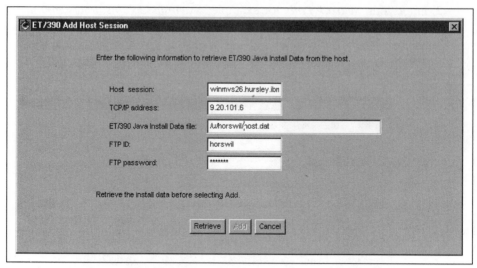

Figure 7-3. VisualAge for Java: ET/390 Add Host session panel

2. Enter the information appropriate to your host system and user ID, select *Retrieve* and then *Add*. You only need to add the host session once before you first use ET/390. The file names are case sensitive.

3. We have provided a sample file on the CD-ROM called \cicsadp\CORBA Server\host.dat. You will have to edit this file to point to your own system. Example 7-1 shows a sample file definition that works for our environment. You have now done all the preparation work and you can start writing your IIOP application.

Example 7-1. Sample of host.dat file

```
@@HPJHostName: Host machine address
@@HPJHome: /u/hpj/extract.spe23/hpj.dev
@@HPJBinderExecutablesPDSE: HPJ.R14.TOBEY.JAV2R0M0.SPE23
@@HPJBinderMessagesPDSE: HPJ.R14.TOBEY
@@HPJLERuntimeBind: PP.ADLE370.OS39025.SCEELKED:PP.ADLE370.OS39025.SCEELKEX:PP.
ADLE370.OS39025.SCEEOBJ:PP.ADLE370.OS39025.SCEECPP
@@HPJLERuntimeRun: PP.ADLE370.OS39025.SCEERUN
@@HPJRuntime: HPJ.BUILD.JAV2R0M0.SPE23.LOAD
@@HPJDebugger: HPJ.DEBUG.VISUAL.SEQAMOD
@@HPJProfiler:
@@HPJJavaHome: /usr/lpp/java114/J1.1
@@HPJPICLHome:
@@HPJCICSRegion: regionName
@@HPJCICSEXCI: CTS130.GA3.CICS.SDFHEXCI
```

Creating and Compiling the IDL Definition

This procedure describes how to write the IDL definition and operations that generate the necessary classes for a customer account object.

If you haven't done this already, create a *KanDoIT Server* project in your VisualAge for Java Workbench. From the main menu bar, select *File* and *Quickstart* (or press F2), highlight *Basic* and *Create project*, and click *OK*. Enter the project name in the *Create a new project named:* field and click *Finish*.

To make life easier for you, we'll describe the import process and use the files that we have supplied on the CD-ROM. The procedure below imports the *accountObject.idl* file which is part of the sample application. To import an existing IDL into the project:

1. From the Workbench, double-click on your project name; this will show the project's screen. Select the IDLs tab (it's on the right hand side). Go to the menu bar and select *IDLs* and *Import*. The *Import SmartGuide* appears; see Figure 7-4.

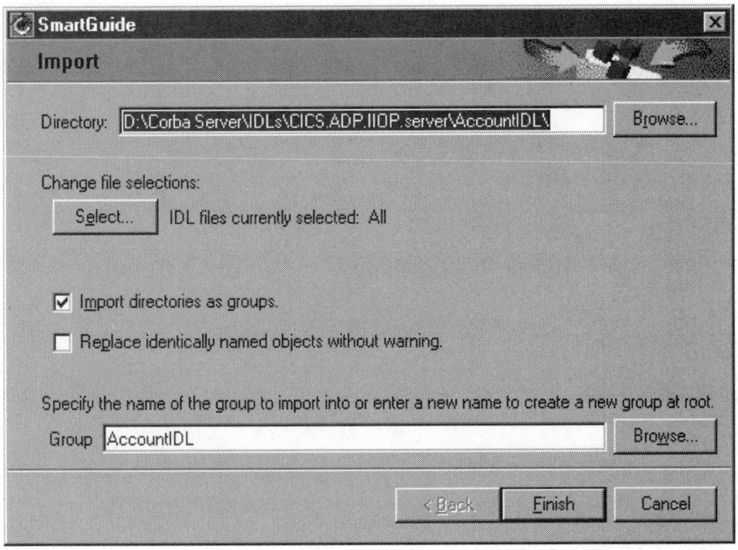

Figure 7-4. VisualAge for Java: Importing an IDL file

2. In the *Directory* field, enter the directory (*CORBA Server**IDLs**CICS.ADP. IIOP.Server**AccountIDL*) where the IDL file is located. Ensure that *Import directories as groups* checkbox is selected.

3. In the *Group* field, enter an IDL group name, for example, AccountIDL, to
identify this group of objects and click *Finish*. The IDL file is imported into the
KanDoIT Server project. The IDL defines the interface to the accountObject
object and its methods (operations). This is done by the following two lines of
code which is at the end of the IDL definition:

```
interface AccountInterface
        accountObject::AccountData getAccount(in string acctno);
```

Example 7-2 shows the complete IDL definition.

Example 7-2. The IDL Definition

```
module accountObject {
        string respcode;
        string reascode;
        string cicsfunc;
        string acctid;
        string lastname;
        string firstname;
        string midinit;
        string title;
        string telnum;
        string addr1;
        string addr2;
        string addr3;
        string auth1;
        string auth2;
        string auth3;
        string auth4;
        string cards;
        string issuemonth;
        string issueday;
        string issueyear;
        string reason;
        string code;
        string approver;
        string scode1;
        string scode2;
        string scode3;
        string status;
        string limit;
    };
    interface AccountInterface {
        //getter methods
        accountObject::AccountData getAccount(in string acctno);
    };
```

Once the IDL definition has been imported, invoke the CICS IDL-to-Java compiler
to compile it in the form of both stub and skeleton code. The VisualAge for Java

IDL development environment lets you specify compiler options before you invoke the compiler:

1. In the IDLs pane, select the *AccountIDL* group and right-click, select *Change Compile Options....* The *Change IDL-to-Java Compile Options* dialog screen appears, as shown in Figure 7-5.

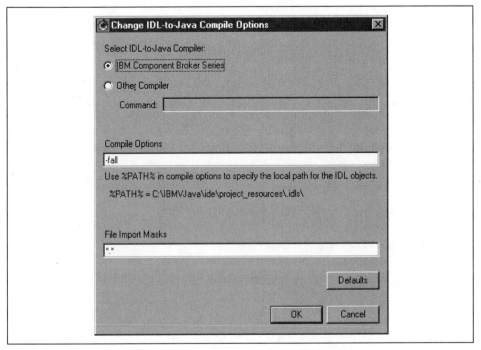

Figure 7-5. VisualAge for Java: Change IDL-to-Java Compile options

2. Ensure that the radio button *IBM Component Broker Series* is selected. The ORB that ships with CICS TS for OS/390 1.3 is part of the IBM Component Broker Series.

3. In the *Compile Options* field, type *-fall* to instruct the compiler to omit all bindings and click *OK*. This returns you to the IDL pane.

4. Having set the options for compiling, you are now ready to generate the code. Select the *AccountIDL* group and right-click, then select *Generate Java* and *All Objects.*

If no errors occur, one or more Java classes and interfaces are generated for the IDL objects contained in *AccountIDL* group. The Java classes and interface are displayed in the *Types* pane.

An X icon will appear beside any IDL object in error. Error messages are displayed in the *Log* window. The status bar at the bottom of the window also indicates errors.

Now all the server skeletons and helper classes are generated, you can move on to write the server implementation class. At this point you should return to the main Workbench window and select your project (in our case, the *KanDoIT Server* project).

Writing the Server Implementation Class

You create the server application by extending the base implementation class, *_AccountInterfaceImplBase*, which is generated by the IDL compiler as seen in Example 7-3. The class name of the server implementation must be *_AccountInterfaceImpl*.

Example 7-3. Code from the _AccountInterfaceImplBase Class

```
/**
accountObject/_AccountInterfaceImplBase.java
* Generated by the IBM IDL-to-Java compiler, version 1.0
* from accountObject.idl
* 25 February 2000 18:22:35 o'clock GMT-05:00
*/

public abstract class _AccountInterfaceImplBase extends com.ibm.CORBA.portable.
ObjectImpl implements accountObject.AccountInterface, com.ibm.CORBA.portable.Skeleton
{
   private static com.ibm.CORBA.portable.OperationDescriptor __dispatchTable[][] = new
com.ibm.CORBA.portable.OperationDescriptor[1][0];

   static {
__dispatchTable[0] = accountObject._AccountInterfaceStub._get_operations ();
   }

   // Type-specific CORBA::Object operations
   private static String[] __ids = {
"IDL:accountObject/AccountInterface:1.0"  };
}
```

In the Workbench you will see that there are a number of classes and one interface created in the *accountObject* package. You can see the list in Figure 7-6. The interface was created as a result of the interface defined in the IDL called AccountInterface. The interface contains one method called *getAccount* method. We will be implementing the *getAccount* method in our *implementation* class and that is expecting to receive an account number and return the *AccountData* structure.

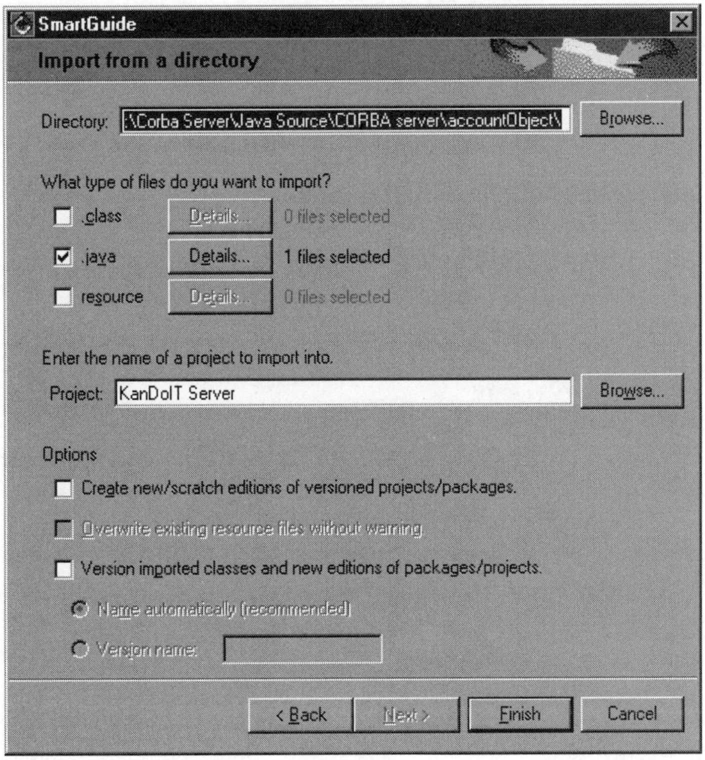

Figure 7-6. VisualAge for Java: Workbench showing the classes of the accountObject package

Example 7-4. Class Declaration

```
import com.ibm.cics.server.*;
import java.io.*;
/**
 * This type was created in VisualAge.
 */
public class _AccountInterfaceImpl extends _AccountInterfaceImplBase {
    CommAreaHolder crudCA;
    Program cobolProg;
}
```

An Implementation class for the sample application is supplied on the CD-ROM. Import the file called *_AccountInterfaceImpl.java* into your project as follows:

1. Highlight the *KanDoIT Server* project, right-click and select *Import*.

2. Select the *Directory* radio button to indicate the file that is to be imported from a directory and click *Next*. The *Import from a directory* SmartGuide dialog appears as seen in Figure 7-7.

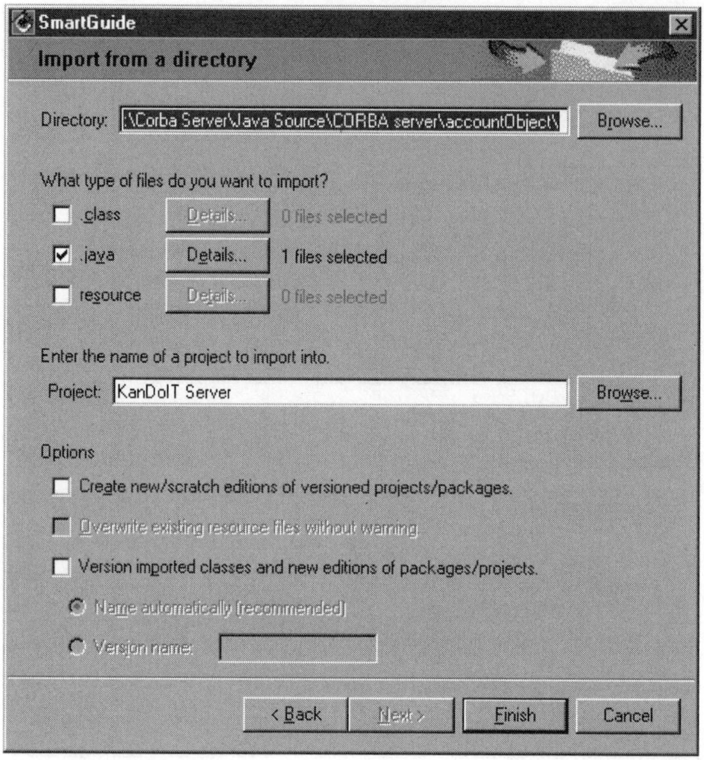

Figure 7-7. VisualAge for Java: Import from a directory

3. In the *Directory* field, browse to find the directory on the CD-ROM where the file is located, for example, *cicsadp\CORBA Server\Java Source\CORBA Server\accountObject*.

4. Ensure that only the *.java* file type checkbox is selected, select *Details* next to .java and ensure that the *_AccountInterfaceImpl.java* file is the only file that is checked. Now select *OK* and then *Finish*.

The *.java* file will be compiled into bytecode and the package is created under the *KanDoIT* Server project. This adds a further class to the *accountObject* class and extends the *_AccountInterfaceImplBase* class that was generated from the IDL definition. You can view the source code for the class and see the methods it contains. Examples 7-4 through 7-7 show the resulting code. Figure 7-8 shows the resulting structure.

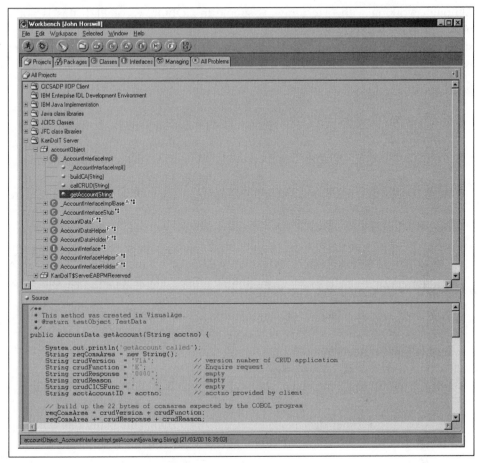

Figure 7-8. VisualAge for Java: Workbench

Examining the Methods in the _accountInterfaceImpl Class

There are three methods in the *_accountInterfaceImpl* class:

getAccount( )

Builds a request string and invokes the *callCRUD( )* method to retrieve account data; it then sets each field in the account object.

callCRUD( )

Links to another CICS program, in this case, the *NACT02* program.

buildCA( )

Builds a COMMAREA and converts it to a byte array.

Although working with byte arrays is simple in COBOL, C, or PL/I, this is not a normal way of working with data in Java. In this sample application we've used string manipulation to keep the sample simple and clear. A better way to work with this data is to use the IBM Java Record Framework.

getAccount( )

This is the method specified in the IDL definition of *accountObject* that will be invoked by CORBA clients. The declaration for the method shows that the method will take an account number (as a string) and return an *AccountData* structure. Several variables are then declared and initialized with values in the order that the *NACT02* program expects them. We only want to request data from the *NACT* application, so *crudFunction* is set to E to specify an enquire request. *crudResponse*, *crudReason*, and *crudCICSFunc* are set to zero or blank values to ensure false errors are not detected when the *NACT02* program returns with customer account information. These string variables are concatenated to form the 22 bytes that will make up the request COMMAREA accepted by the *NACT02* program, into a string variable called reqCommArea. This is passed to another method in *_AccountInterfaceImpl* class called *callCRUD*, which will convert *reqCommArea* into a byte array and link to the *NACT02* program, and finally return the customer account record into a variable *returnedCommArea*.

At this point *returnedCommArea* is just a string of characters. A new variable result is declared of type *AccountData*, to hold the customer data in the format the client expects, and as defined in the IDL. The next block of code then extracts the customer data fields from *returnedCommArea* using the matching field in result, which is then returned to the requesting client application.

Example 7-5. getAccount( ) Method

```
public AccountData getAccount(String acctno) {
    String reqCommArea = new String();
    String crudVersion  = "V1A";        // version number of CRUD application
    String crudFunction = "E";          // Enquire request
    String crudResponse = "0000";       // empty
    String crudReason   = "    ";       // empty
    String crudCICSFunc = "      ";     // empty
    String acctAccountID = acctno;      // acctno provided by client
    // build up the 22 bytes of commarea expected by the COBOL program
    reqCommArea = crudVersion + crudFunction;
    reqCommArea += crudResponse + crudReason;
    reqCommArea += crudCICSFunc + acctAccountID;
    // pass the request data to the COBOL CRUD program and receive account into
    // returnedCommArea
    String returnedCommArea=callCRUD(reqCommArea);
    // create objects to hold returned account data
    AccountData result = new AccountData();
    try {
```

Example 7-5. getAccount( ) Method (continued)

```
// extract the returned data and set each field in account object
        result.respcode = returnedCommArea.substring(4,8);
        result.reascode = returnedCommArea.substring(8,12);
        result.cicsfunc = returnedCommArea.substring(12,17);
        result.acctid = returnedCommArea.substring(17,22);
        result.lastname = returnedCommArea.substring(22,40);
        result.firstname = returnedCommArea.substring(40,52);
        result.midinit = returnedCommArea.substring(52,53);
        result.title = returnedCommArea.substring(53,57);
        result.telnum = returnedCommArea.substring(57,67);
        result.addr1 = returnedCommArea.substring(67,91);
        result.addr2 = returnedCommArea.substring(91,115);
        result.addr3 = returnedCommArea.substring(115,139);
        result.auth1 = returnedCommArea.substring(139,171);
        result.auth2 = returnedCommArea.substring(171,203);
        result.auth3 = returnedCommArea.substring(203,235);
        result.auth4 = returnedCommArea.substring(235,267);
        result.cards = returnedCommArea.substring(267,268);
        result.issuemonth = returnedCommArea.substring(268,270);
        result.issueday = returnedCommArea.substring(270,272);
        result.issueyear = returnedCommArea.substring(272,274);
        result.reason = returnedCommArea.substring(274,275);
        result.code = returnedCommArea.substring(275,276);
        result.approver = returnedCommArea.substring(276,279);
        result.scode1 = returnedCommArea.substring(279,280);
        result.scode2 = returnedCommArea.substring(280,281);
        result.scode3 = returnedCommArea.substring(281,282);
        result.status = returnedCommArea.substring(282,284);
        result.limit = returnedCommArea.substring(284,292);
    }   catch (Exception e) {
  System.err.println("Exception occurred trying to build response: " + e.toString());
    }
    // return the account object to the client
    return result;
}
```

callCRUD( )

This method links to another CICS program, in this case the *NACT02* program. This method is invoked by the *getAccount* method which provides a string variable containing the 22 bytes to be passed to the *NACT02* program. The first step is to instantiate a new program object, *cobolProg*, which is one of the classes in the JCICS class library. The program object represents the *NACT02* program to be linked to, and the name is specified using the *setName( )* method.

Next, a new instance of a *CommAreaHolder* object, *crudCA*, is created to contain the COMMAREA data. Before linking to *NACT02*, the request data must be converted to byte array format. This is done by invoking the *buildCA( )* method and providing the request data *requestCA* as a parameter. The *buildCA( )* method returns the byte array and we store it into the value property of *crudCA*.

The next line performs the link to *NACT02*, passing the request COMMAREA in *crudCA.value*. The requestCA.length parameter specifies the length of the COMMAREA being passed—in this case 22 bytes. The link populates *crudCA. value* with the response from the *NACT02* program, which will be the entire customer account record. The method then converts the returned COMMAREA to a string and returns to the *getAccount( )* method.

Example 7-6. callCRUD( ) Method: Links to NACT02

```
public String callCRUD(String requestCA)  {
  try  {
      cobolProg=new Program();
      cobolProg.setName("NACT02");           // the CRUD COBOL CICS program
      crudCA=new CommAreaHolder();
      crudCA.value=buildCA(requestCA);       // requestCA is the string of COMMAREA passed
                                             // to linked program
      cobolProg.link(crudCA.value, requestCA.length()); // cah.value is type converted
                                             // to byte array
    }       catch (Exception e)  {
      System.err.println("Problem with program link to NACT02");
      System.err.println("> " + e.toString());
    }
      return new String(crudCA.value);
}
```

buildCA( )

This method converts a request string to a byte array. This method takes the request string passed by the *callCRUD( )* method and converts it to byte-array format, required by the progam link. The request string, passed in the variable value, is appended to a string of spaces long enough to contain the COMMAREA that will be returned by the *NACT02* program. This string is written to the *ByteArrayOutputStream baos* using the *OutputStreamWriter osw*. The method converts the *ByteArrayOutputStream* to byte-array format using the *toByteArray( )* method and returns to *callCRUD( )*.

Example 7-7. buildCA( ) Method: Converts a Request String into a Byte Array

```
public byte[] buildCA(String value)    {
    ByteArrayOutputStream baos = new ByteArrayOutputStream();
    try  {
        DataOutputStream dos = new DataOutputStream(baos);
        OutputStreamWriter osw = new OutputStreamWriter(dos);
        // add a character string big enough to hold returned COMMAREA
        // This is a long string of spaces the same length as the returned COMMAREA
        // Note This line has been shortened in this example to fit the page
        // Your data will be truncated.  You should use the code from the CD-ROM
        osw.write(value + "                                                        ");
```

Example 7-7. buildCA( ) Method: Converts a Request String into a Byte Array (continued)

```
        osw.flush();
        dos.flush();
           }    catch (Exception e) {
    System.err.println("Unable to build commarea");
    System.err.println(">" + e.toString());
    }
    return baos.toByteArray();
}
```

Exporting and Binding the Server Application to the CICS Region

At this point you have extended the base classes generated from the IDL and provided an implementation class to build a request COMMAREA, converted it to byte array format, performed the link to the COBOL program, retrieved account data, and returned it to the calling program. The *accountObject* package now needs to be deployed in a CICS region. ET/390 uses FTP to export class files on OS/390. You should have already mounted a drive on your machine using an NFS client, which points to your host.

Check that your CICS region has the correct parameters defined. See "Configuring the CICS Java Component" in Appendix A for the details about setting up the sample definitions on OS/390.

In the VisualAge for Java Workbench:

1. Highlight the *KanDoIT Server* project, right-click and select *Tools → ET/390 → Properties*. The ET/390 property panel will appear, which allows you to define the *Export and Bind Session* properties. These settings affect the entire project, but can be overridden at the package level. Fill out the panel as follows:

   Host session
      Host session you added to VisualAge for Java in the preparation step.

   Bind CLASSPATH
      Classpath on the host you use to bind your application. To bind the sample application, ensure that ORB (*dfjcorb.jar*) and JCICS (*dfjcics.jar*) are in the classpath; for example, */usr/lpp/java114/J1.1.1/lib/classes.zip:/usr/lpp/cicsts/satinc07/classes/dfjcorb.jar:/usr/lpp/cicsts/satinc07/classes/dfjcidl.jar*.

   Directory for objects and lists
      HFS directory where you want to save the object and list files on the host.

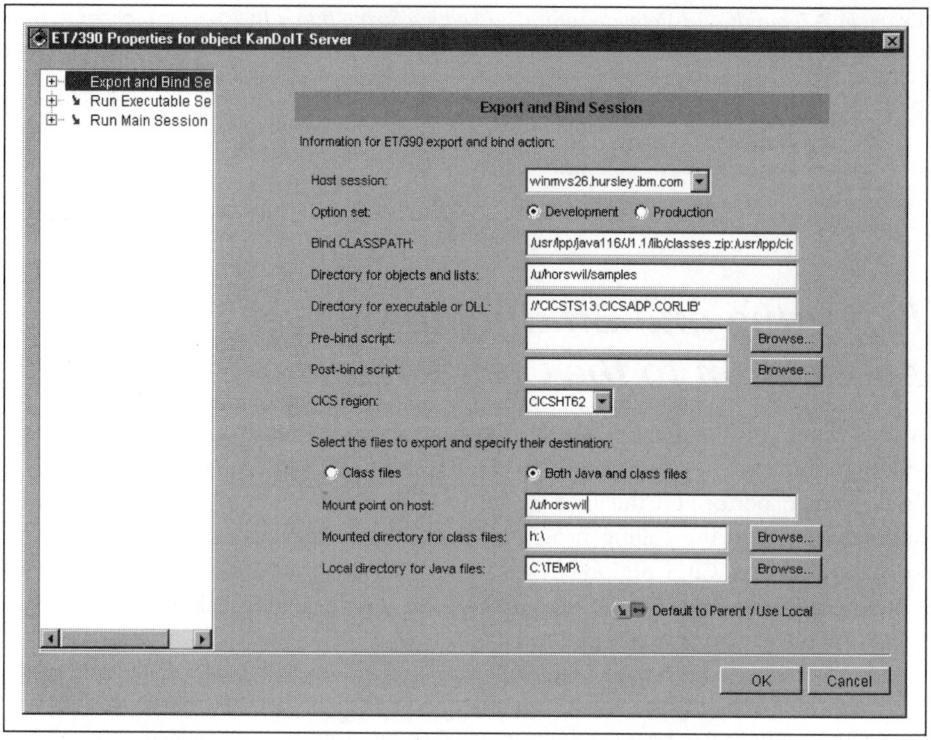

Figure 7-9. VisualAge for Java: ET/390 properties for exporting and binding

Directory for executable or DLL

> PDSE name where you want to save the DLL. Specify the PDSE *//'CICSTS13.CICSADP.CORLIB'* to save the DLL.

CICS region

> The *applid* of the CICS region where your DLL is loaded.

2. Expand the *Export and Bind Session* and select *Bind Options*. Ensure that the *Rebuild all, CICS application,* and *Refresh CICS program* checkboxes are all selected and the *Build a Java DLL* radio button is selected, see Figure 7-10. *Rebuild all* instructs the compiler to compile all the classes in the package. Finally, select *OK*.

3. We now have to define the properties that are specific to this package. Some of the ET/390 properties will have been inherited from the project. To do this, expand the *KanDoIT Server* project and select the *accountObject* package. Right-click and select *Tools → ET/390 → Properties.* Expand the *Export and Bind Session* and select *Bind Options.* Enter a PDSE member name, for example, *ZSRV02,* to identify the package you are building, see Figure 7-11 and click *OK.*

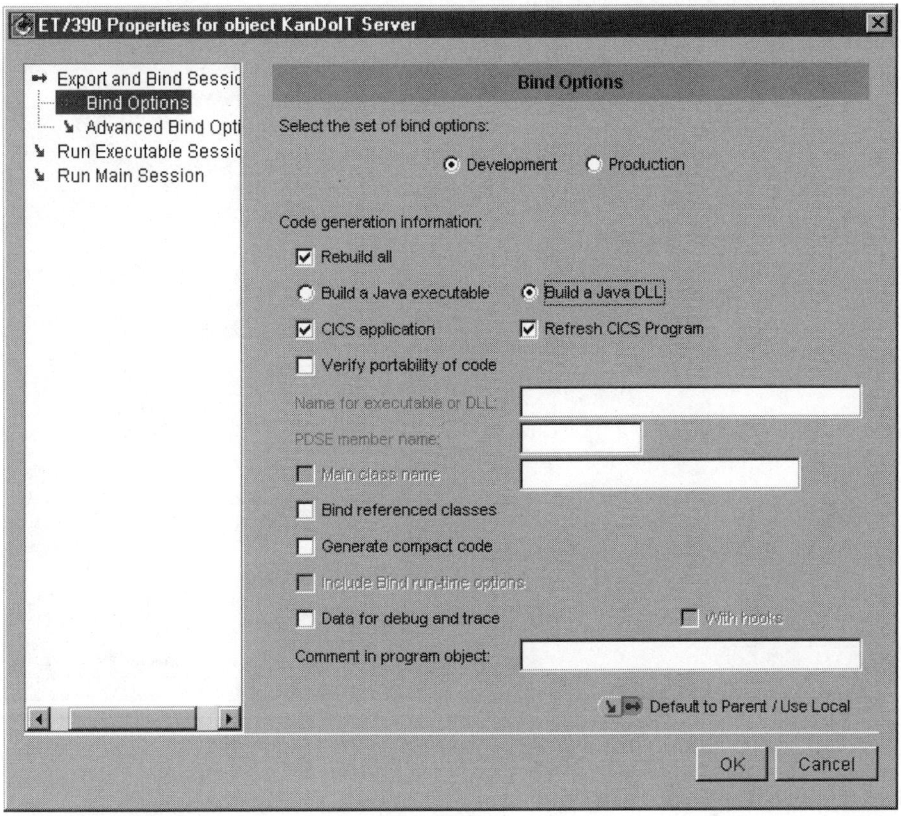

Figure 7-10. VisualAge for Java: ET/390 Properties for object KanDoIT Server

4. You are now ready to export the package to OS/390. Select the *accountObject* package, right-click and choose *Tools → ET/390 → Export and bind.* If the OS/390 Logon Data dialog appears, enter your host user ID and password and select *Save.* While this is happening a progress bar appears.

Any output from the bind is written to the VisualAge for Java log window. If the export and bind fails, access your host system and you will see a bin file in */tmp.* Copy this to the subdirectory where you are saving your classes and run it with the Unix Services Shell on OS/390 to determine what is wrong.

Creating the CORBA Client

So far we have created the IDL definition, written the server-side application and exported that application to an OS/390 server. Now we need to write a CORBA client to test the CORBA server code that we have just created.

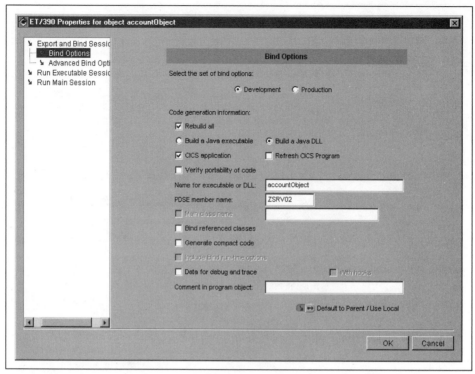

Figure 7-11. VisualAge for Java: ET/390 Properties for object accountObject

Normally there are two steps:

1. Compile the IDL to create client stub classes.

2. Generate an IOR file. This uses the input of hostname, port number and output directory.

 In VisualAge for Java, the compilation of IDL in our *KanDoIT Server* project has already created helper classes and stub files so we will re-use them in the client implementation.

Creating the Client Program

To create the client program, return to VisualAge for Java Workbench and create a new project called, for example, CICSADP IIOP Client:

1. Select the *Add New or Existing Project to Workbench* button on the toolbar and the screen shown in Figure 7-12 appears. Enter the name of your project and select *Finish*. The project is added to your VisualAge for Java Workbench.

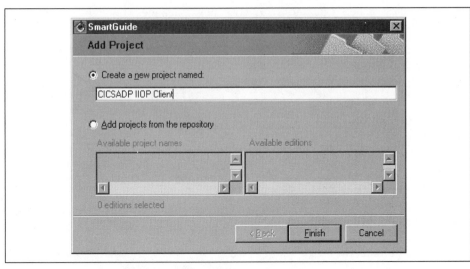

Figure 7-12. VisualAge for Java: Add Project

2. Add a package called *testIIOPClient* to the project. Highlight the name of your project, right-click and select *Add* followed by *Package*. Enter *testiiopclient* (lowercase) in the *Create a new package named:* field; see Figure 7-13. Select *Finish* (not *Next*).

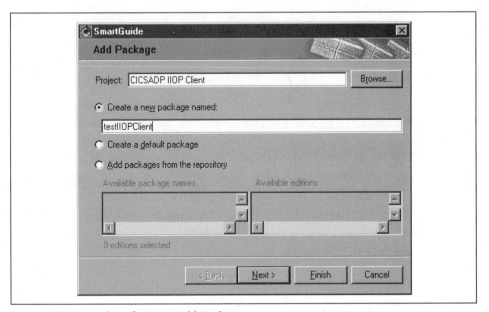

Figure 7-13. VisualAge for Java: Add Package

3. Add a class called *ClientStub* to your new package. Highlight the name of your package, right-click and select *Add* following by *Class*. Figure 7-14 shows you the panel. Enter *ClientStub* in the *Class name* field and click *Next*.

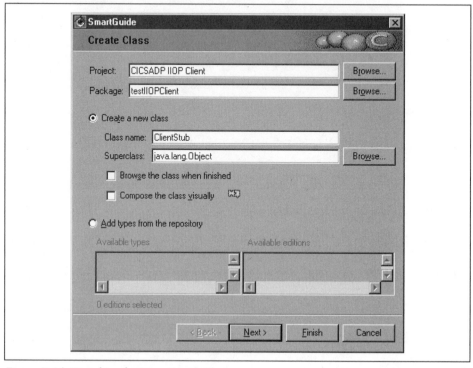

Figure 7-14. VisualAge for Java: Create Class

4. Select the *Add Package...* button. Add the packages that you need to import as shown in Figure 7-15. The packages are *accountObject, java.io, .org .omg CORBA, org .omg .CosLifeCycle, org .omg .CosNaming*. Ensure that the *Public, Methods* and *Copy constructors* checkboxes are selected, then click *Finish*.

5. Add a method called *getFactoryIOR*, specifying that it returns a String (to contain the IOR). To do this highlight the *clientStub* class, right-click and select *Add* following by *Method*. Figure 7-16 shows the Create Method panel. Select the Types button and choose String and then add *getFactoryIOR( )* in the input field. Click *Next*.

6. Specify that the method throws an *IOException*. To do this select the *Add* button and choose *IOException* from the list. Click the *Add* button and then *Close*, see Figure 7-17.

7. Add user code to the *getFactoryIOR( )* method so that it reads a *genfac.ior* file from the local file system. You may wish to change the location of the *genfac.ior* file in the following example so that it is correct for your system. Cut and paste the relevant section from Example 7-8 or *cicsadp\Corba*

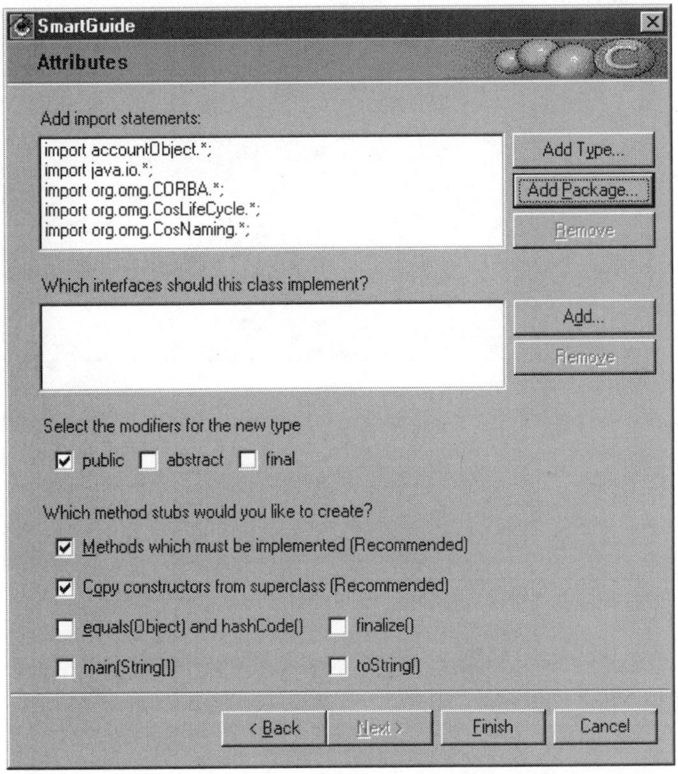

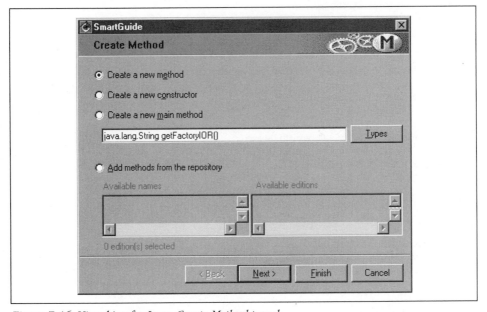

Figure 7-15. VisualAge for Java: Defining Class attributes

Figure 7-16. VisualAge for Java: Create Method panel

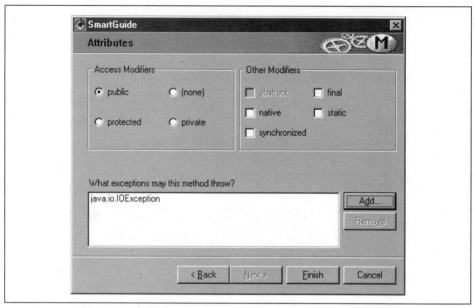

Figure 7-17. VisualAge for Java: attributes

Server\Java Source\CORBA client\testIIOPClient\ClientStub.java into your *getFactoryIOR()* method.

Example 7-8. Sample to Show getFactoryIOR() Method

```
/**
 * This method was created in VisualAge.
 * @return java.lang.String
 * @exception java.io.IOException The exception description.
 */
public String getFactoryIOR() throws IOException {
    String line;
    final String filename = "C://IORFiles/genfac.ior";
    FileInputStream in = null;
    InputStreamReader isr = null;
    BufferedReader br = null;
    try {
        in = new FileInputStream(filename);
        isr = new InputStreamReader(in);
        br = new BufferedReader(isr);
    }   catch(IOException e) {
        System.out.println("Client: Error opening file " + filename);
        throw e;
    } try {
        line = br.readLine();
    }   catch(IOException e)  {
        System.out.println("Client: Error reading file " + filename);
        throw e;
     }
    return line;
}
```

8. Now modify the *ClientStub* constructor so that it returns a string and add user code to create a reference to the remote object. Cut and paste the code from Example 7-9 or from *cicsadp\Corba Server\Java Source\CORBA client\testI-IOPClient\ClientStub.java* into your *ClientStub* constructor:

Example 7-9. Modifying the ClientStub Constructor

```
/**
 * ClientStub constructor comment.
 */
public ClientStub(String acctID) {
    String factoryIOR;
    AccountInterface ai = null;
    try {
        // create and initialize the ORB
        System.out.println("Client: creating and initializing the ORB");
        ORB orb = ORB.init();

        // create the generic factory
        System.out.println("Client: creating the generic factory");
        factoryIOR = getFactoryIOR();
        org.omg.CORBA.Object genFacRef = orb.string_to_object(factoryIOR);
        System.out.println("Client: narrowing the generic factory");
        GenericFactory fact = GenericFactoryHelper.narrow(genFacRef);

        // use generic factory to make accountObject object
        System.out.println("Client: using generic factory to make testObject
object");
        NameComponent nc = new NameComponent("accountObject::AccountInterface",
"object interface");
        NameComponent key[] = {nc};
        NVP mycriteria[] = {};

        System.out.println("about to create object reference");
        org.omg.CORBA.Object objRef = fact.create_object(key, mycriteria);
        System.out.println("about to narrow");
        ai = AccountInterfaceHelper.narrow(objRef);
       getDetails(ai, acctID);
    }

     // Catch NoFactory
    catch (org.omg.CosLifeCycle.NoFactory nf)  {
    System.out.println("Client: NoFactory thrown by create_object for accountObject:
:AccountInterface");
    System.out.println("                     - check server program with alias
accountObject.jll is available on the CICS server");
    }

    // Catch any unexpected exceptions
    catch (Exception e)  {
    System.out.println("Client: Unexpected exception : " + e);
    e.printStackTrace(System.out);
    }
}
```

9. You will notice a number of red X's appearing, don't worry, when we complete the code they should all resolve themselves. Now you need to add another method called *getDetails* that takes *accountObject.AccountInterface* and *String* as its parameters. The *accountObject.AccountInterface* is the reference to the remote object and the *String* is the account ID we want to retrieve data for. To do this highlight the *ClientStub* class, right-click and select *Add* and *Method*. The user code is shown in Example 7-10.

Example 7-10. The getDetails Method

```
/**
 * This method was created in VisualAge.
 * @param ai accountObject.AccountInterface
 */
public void getDetails(accountObject.AccountInterface ai, String acctID) {
        // Invoke the getAccount method
        System.out.println("Client: invoking getAccount method on accountObject
object");
        AccountData acctData = ai.getAccount(acctID);
        if (acctData.respcode.equals("0000") && acctData.reascode.equals("0000"))  {
            System.out.println("Account ID: " + acctData.acctid);
            System.out.println("First name: " + acctData.firstname);
            System.out.println("Last name: " + acctData.lastname);
            System.out.println("Mid init: " + acctData.midinit);
            System.out.println("Title: " + acctData.title);
            System.out.println("Tel Number: " + acctData.telnum);
            System.out.println("Address 1: " + acctData.addr1);
            System.out.println("Address 2: " + acctData.addr2);
            System.out.println("Address 3: " + acctData.addr3);
            System.out.println("Auth 1: " + acctData.auth1);
            System.out.println("Auth 2: " + acctData.auth2);
            System.out.println("Auth 3: " + acctData.auth3);
            System.out.println("Auth 4: " + acctData.auth4);
            System.out.println("Cards: " + acctData.cards);
            System.out.println("Issue Date: " + acctData.issueday + "/" +
                            acctData.issuemonth + "/" + acctData.issueyear);
            System.out.println("Reason: " + acctData.reason);
            System.out.println("Code: " + acctData.code);
            System.out.println("Approver: " + acctData.approver);
            System.out.println("Scode 1: " + acctData.scode1);
            System.out.println("Scode 2: " + acctData.scode2);
            System.out.println("Scode 3: " + acctData.scode3);
            System.out.println("Status: " + acctData.status);
            System.out.println("Limit: " + acctData.limit);
        } else {                                       // non-zero return code
            System.out.println("An error occurred: ");
            System.out.println("Response Code: " + acctData.respcode);
            System.out.println("Reason Code: " + acctData.reascode);
            System.out.println("Account ID: " + acctData.acctid);
            System.out.println("CICS Function: " + acctData.cicsfunc);
        }
}
```

For diagnosing problems and so we can see the response from the server, we send all the returned fields to the console using System.out. As we'll see later, this forms the basis for the code we'll export to the web server which will be called by a servlet.

Create genfac.ior File

The *GenFacIOR* utility supplied on the CD-ROM in *Corba Server\GenFac utility*\ *mygenfac* is used to generate the *genfac.ior* file. Use the following guidelines for compiling:

1. Import the Java package into VisualAge for Java. Use the *File* and *Import* options.

2. Expand *mygenfac* package and the *DoIt* class to edit the main method. Change the host name, port number, and the directory where the resulting file is to be stored.

3. Now compile the package.

4. Alternatively, you can use the JDK from the command line to create the *genfac.ior* file. Check that you have *dfjcorb.jar* in your classpath. At a command prompt (DOS shell), enter:

```
java com.ibm.cics.server.ts.iiop.GenFacIOR -host hname -port pnum -d C:\IORFiles
```

where *hname* is the appropriate hostname and *pnum* is the appropriate port-number.

Creating the RunClient Class

Still in the *testIIOPClient* package, we need to add another class called *RunClient*. This has a *main( )* method so we can run and test the client-server interactions within the VisualAge environment. To do this:

1. Highlight the *testIIOPClient* package and select the *Create Class* button on the toolbar. Enter RunClient in the *Class name* field as shown in Figure 7-18.

2. Click *Next* and on the SmartGuide Attributes dialog box, check the *main(String [ ])* option, see Figure 7-19 and select *Finish*.

3. In the main method of the RunClient class, add user code to instantiate a new ClientStub object, passing an account number as its input parameter. The code is shown in Example 7-11.

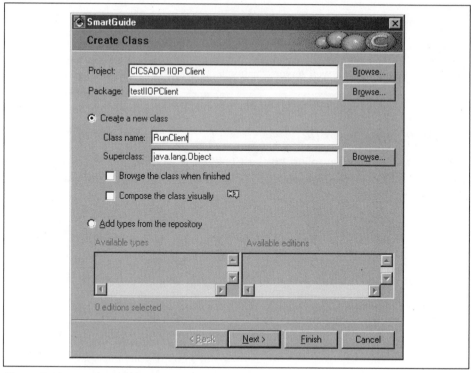

Figure 7-18. VisualAge for Java: Create Class

Example 7-11. The RunClient Class

```
/**
 * Starts the application.
 * @param args an array of command-line arguments
 */
public static void main(java.lang.String[] args) {
        new ClientStub("10000");              // 5-digit account number used for testing
}
```

4. Right-click the *RunClient* class and from the popup menu that appears. Choose *Run* and then *Check Class Path...*; see Figure 7-19 for details. Click the *Compute Now* button; this adds the necessary Class Path for the runtime code. This is used for testing only.

5. The computed class path appears in the project path text area; see Figure 7-20. Now click *OK*.

Testing the Client

To test the client, select the *RunClient* class and click the *running man* button on the toolbar. The console panel should appear with output from the *ClientStub* class. See Figure 7-21 for a sample output.

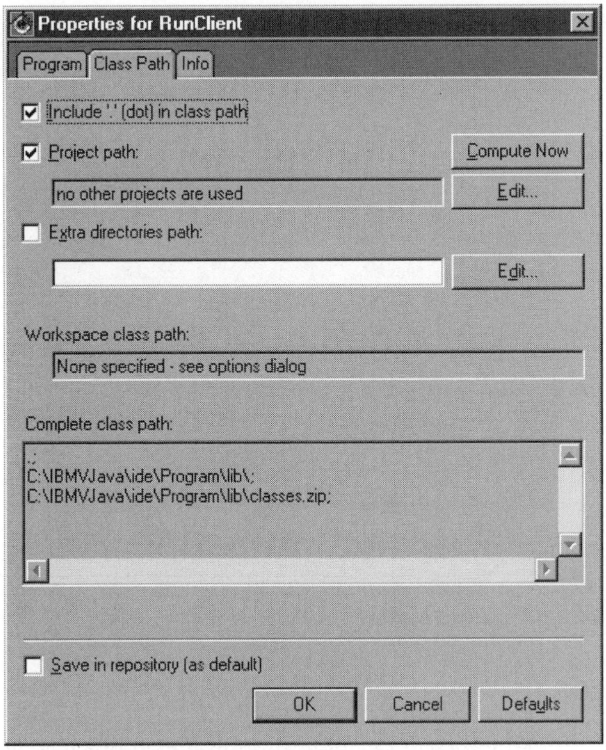

Figure 7-19. VisualAge for Java: Class Path for RunClient

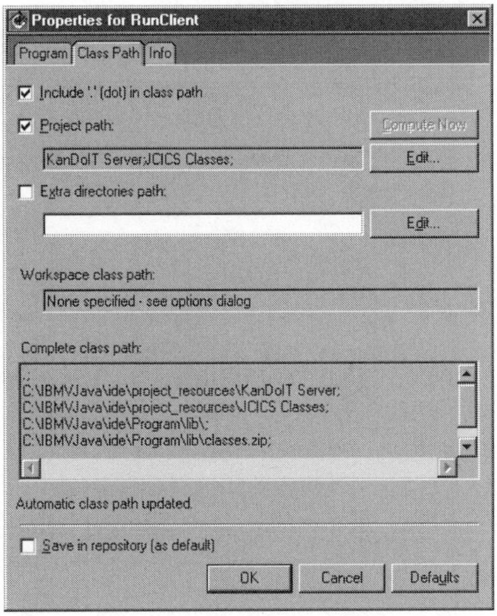

Figure 7-20. VisualAge for Java: Properties for RunClient

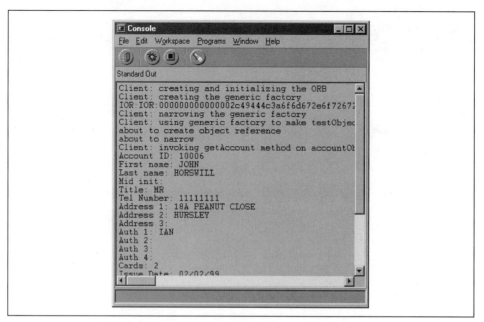

Figure 7-21. VisualAge for Java: The Console Panel

What's Next...

So now we have a working CORBA application in which our test client, running in the VisualAge for Java IDE is invoking methods on the accountObject object running in the CICS region. To build a complete web application, we now need to incorporate our CORBA client into a web server environment. This allows Kan-DoIT customers to retrieve their account data from the Web using their browsers. This is described in detail in Part IV.

IV

The Web Component

In the space of just a few short years, the World Wide Web has changed from being a repository of static information, inhabited only by computer enthusiasts with considerable technical expertise, to a huge and vibrant marketplace in which both small and large corporations do much of their business. It is also a place to which virtually everyone has easy, low-cost access.

Most information on the Web is presented using HyperText Markup Language (HTML). Today a greater proportion of web pages are generated dynamically, delivering data to customers quickly and which is directly relevant to their request. Customer information is still managed to a large extent by backend servers which handle data processing.

CICS provides several means by which legacy applications (such as those that pay your salary) can be re-used and accessed from remote clients, including web browsers. CICS TS for OS/390 Version 1.3 supports CORBA (as described in Part III, *The CICS Java Component*) and CORBA clients can be implemented at web servers (and even directly in web browsers) that allow CICS applications to be run from the Web.

For our sample application, we describe the development of a browser frontend and how a CORBA client can be implemented on a web server. This Part contains the following chapters:

- Chapter 8, *Designing the Web Component*
- Chapter 9, *Programming the Web Component*

In addition to the usual software requirements, this part also makes extensive use of the following products:

- Web browser: for example, Netscape Communicator 4.5 or MicroSoft Internet Explorer 5.0.

- Web Server with appropriate servlet support: for example, IBM HTTP Server Version 1.3.3 with IBM WebSphere Application Server Version 2.0.

The next three products are those that are used in this book but you can use any equivalent software:

- Servlet/JSP/JavaBean development: IBM WebSphere Studio Release 1.0.

- Servlet/JSP/JavaBean source editing: NetObjects ScriptBuilder Version 3.0.

- Web site building tool: NetObjects Fusion Version 4.0.

8

Designing the Web Component

As we described in Part I, the KanDoIT company wants to provide an enhanced service for its customers. The aim is to provide new pages in the KanDoIT web site that allow clients to check their accounts online, using a browser. The web pages presented to customers must comply with existing corporate style guidelines and be easy to maintain without any need to change application code. The solution will connect to the existing business logic component, access customer data and return a dynamically generated web page without the user ever knowing that CICS is performing the data processing behind the scenes.

This Part builds on Part III, *The CICS Java Component*, and essentially covers the implemention of a CORBA client in a web server environment. The sample application presented here to meet these requirements is quite simple in its design and it does not address the complex issues of security.

For the web component we describe how to create the HTML pages by which customers can make requests, how to write a Java servlet to handle requests and retrieve data from CICS using CORBA, and how to create dynamically generated web pages using Java Server Pages (JSP) and JavaBeans. The design is typical for a web application, in that it follows the three-tier model, or perhaps more accurately, the n-tier model.

In this model, the user interface, the business logic, and the backend data management processes are separated by platform. Figure 8-1 shows the overall design.

The Java component, which *wrappers* the COBOL program on CICS, is described in Chapter 7, *Programming the CICS Java Component*.

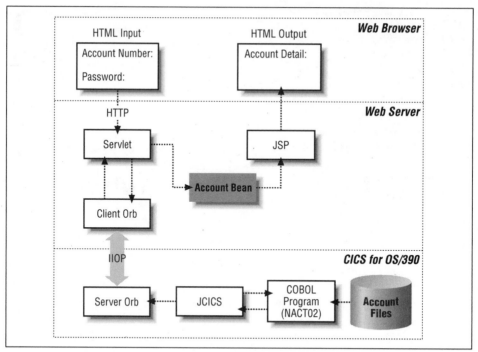

Figure 8-1. Overall design for the web component

Understanding What the Component Needs To Do

For the KanDoIT users, customers with web access, the web component needs to provide:

- An input form into which customers can enter their account number and password

- An output screen to display the customer's account details

This is the presentation layer for the component; the customer submits the input form and views the account details on their web browser. The design of the presentation layer is described in more detail in the next section, "Designing the Web Interface."

Between the user submitting a request with their input parameters, and receiving output (of their account details) in their browser, there must be some processing to generate a response. The input parameters must be checked for validity, and then passed on to the CICS application to retrieve the appropriate customer data from its database. Then, using that data, a new web page is generated and returned to the user.

A web server (a server connected to the Internet, dedicated to serving web pages) is typically used to deliver static web pages in response to users requesting HTML documents via HTTP from their web browsers. However, the web server could also return the output of a program, which in this case we want to be the data returned by the CICS application. In our example, the web server provides the following services:

- Listens for an HTTP request for account details, issued by the user's web browser.

- Invokes a program to connect to and request data from the CICS application.

- Formats the data returned from the CICS application into HTML.

- Returns the HTML document to the user's web browser.

The design of the data processing logic is described in more detail in "Designing the Web Server Components" later in this chapter.

Designing the Web Interface

The design of the user interface that KanDoIT's customers will use to access their account data should adhere to the existing corporate web style guidelines. Three new web pages are required to support the new customer account application:

View Account
> To allow users to enter their account number.

Account Details
> To display returned account details.

Error
> To display error messages should things go wrong.

The View Account page (see Figure 8-2) design might be sketched out like this:

The standard navigation links for KanDoIT's web site appear to the left. Two form fields marked *Account ID* and *Password* allow the user to enter required input parameters. The *Request* button is used to send the request to the web server and the *Clear* button can be used to reset the form fields.

The KanDoIT web designers decide that the *Account Details* page should show the same information as the original COBOL application running in CICS (see Part V). The fields to display might be formatted as shown in Figure 8-3.

Again, the KanDoIT navigation links are placed to the left, and the remaining data fields organized into logical groups, such as customer details, authorized cardholders, and card details.

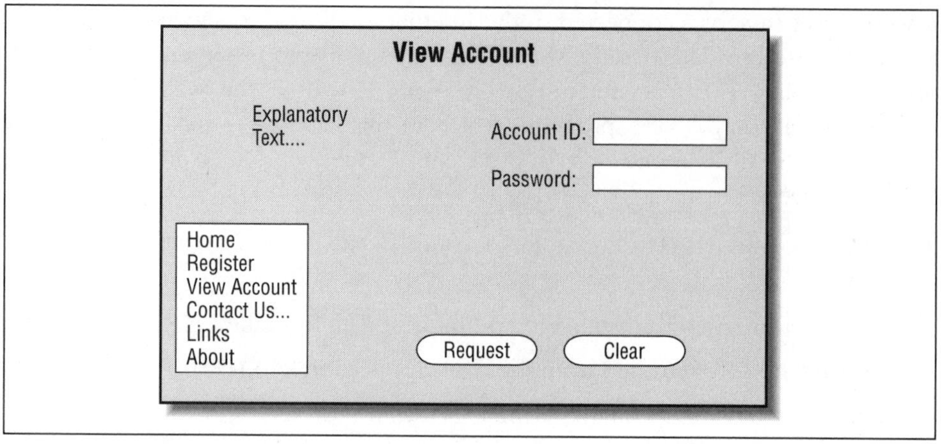

Figure 8-2. Design for the View Account page

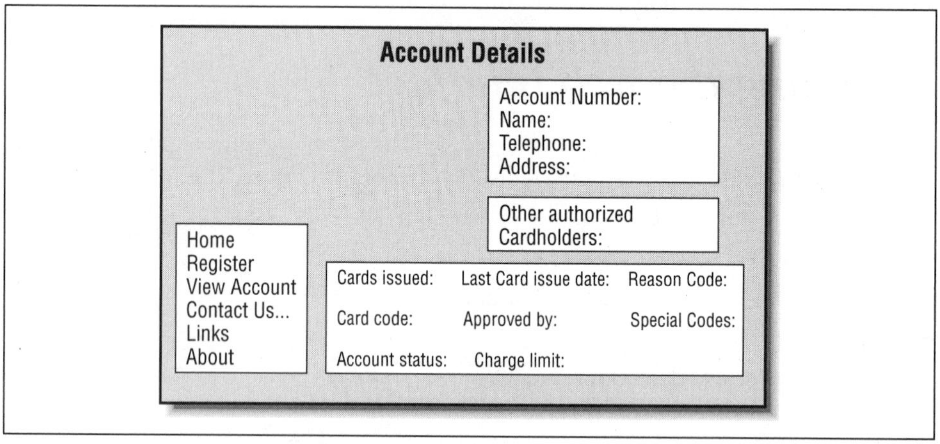

Figure 8-3. Design for the Account Details page

The *error* page uses the same basic structure. See Figure 8-4 for details.

How we go about converting these page designs into actual web browser compatible pages is described in detail in Chapter 9, *Programming the Web Component.*

Designing the Web Server Components

The web server's job is to listen for requests for account details, validate input parameters, connect to CICS, pass on the request to the CICS application, format the returned data into HTML and return a web page to the user's browser. All of these tasks can be handled by a special type of program running in the web server environment called a servlet.

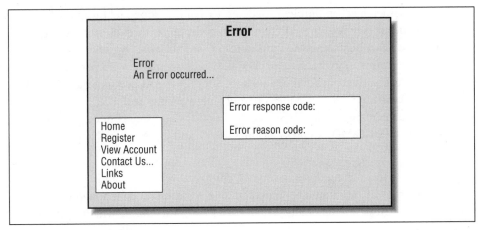

Figure 8-4. Design for the Error page

In Chapter 9, we can divide the specific tasks further among three distinct components:

- A Java servlet to process the request and connect to CICS

- A JavaBean to temporarily hold information about the customer

- Java Server Pages (JSP) to automatically format the returned data into HTML

Let's look at these web server components in more detail.

The Java Servlet

The Common Gateway Interface (CGI) was one of the first practical techniques for creating dynamic content. With CGI, a web server can forward HTTP requests to an external program. The output of this program is then returned to the client browser. CGI is more-or-less platform-independent and is very popular. However, CGI has many drawbacks that affect web application performance and it is particularly resource-intensive. There are several proprietary solutions that work only on certain web servers, such as server extension APIs, Active Server Pages, and server-side JavaScript. These are by no means perfect solutions, as they can be difficult to develop, increase the risk of crashing the web server, or they work in very specific environments.

A *servlet* is a Java program (class) that runs on a web server. It can be loaded dynamically to expand the function of a server. Servlets are commonly used in web servers to replace CGI scripts. A servlet is similar to a proprietary server extension, except it runs inside a Java Virtual Machine (JVM) on the server, so it is safe and portable.

Unlike CGI, which uses multiple processes to handle separate programs and/or separate requests, servlets are all handled by separate threads within the web server process. This means servlets are efficient and scalable. Another advantage is portability: Java runs anywhere there is a JVM and all major web servers support servlets. Because servlets are written in Java, they give you access to all the benefits that the Java language provides, namely networking and URL access, multithreading, image manipulation, data compression, database connectivity, remote method invocation (RMI), CORBA connectivity, and object serialization, among others.

Servlets inherit the strong type safety of the Java language and, because Java doesn't use pointers, servlets are generally safe from memory management problems. Servlets handle errors safely using exception processing, which won't crash the server.

Servlet code is clean, object-oriented, modular, and quite simple. Servlets can take advantage of a huge library of third-party Java classes and JavaBean components, including new Enterprise JavaBeans.

For the purposes of our example web application, the servlet we will develop performs the following functions:

1. Checks that the account number and password parameters entered by the user are in a valid format.

2. Instantiates a JavaBean to store the parameters and the details that are received from CICS.

3. Invokes a method on a remote Java Account object running in CICS, using IIOP.

4. Returns the appropriate Java Server Page (JSP) to the browser.

The servlet is automatically invoked whenever a request for this specific servlet is received from a web browser. The request is initiated when a customer submits the View Account page by clicking on the *Request* button.

The JavaBean

A JavaBean, often referred to simply as a bean, is a reusable Java component built using Sun's JavaBeans technology. In our sample application, our JavaBean is called *AccountBean*. The purpose of *AccountBean* is to store the details of the customer account returned from the call to the Account object in CICS. So, for example, it contains first name, last name, telephone number, account balance, and so on. This information is then used by the JSP to build the HTML that is returned to the user's web browser.

The Java Server Pages (JSP files)

Java Server Pages (JSP files) technology is a convenient way to generate dynamic page content. JSP files allow the application server to dynamically add content to your HTML pages before they are sent to a requesting browser. The dynamic content can come from any available databases and file systems to provide web visitors with timely and accurate data.

The JSP files created by the WebSphere Studio wizards contain the following HTML tags and JSP tags defined by the JSP specification. This allows us to retrieve data directly from JavaBeans:

A JSP <BEAN> tag
> To access a JavaBean when the page is processed

JSP <INSERT> tags
> To embed variables in the page

HTML tags
> To format the variable data

JSP <REPEAT> tags
> To repeat a block of HTML tagging that contains <INSERT> tags and the HTML formatting tags

When the Application Server processes the JSP file, it:

* Instantiates the JavaBean

* Puts the resulting data into the output page (replacing the special tags)

* Returns it as an HTML file

You can customize the JSP file, adding your own text and images using Java-Script, HTML, or JSP tagging. These tags and script are included in the HTML file created by the application server and returned to the requesting browser.

For our sample, we make use of the account details stored in our AccountBean JavaBean. As an example, if we want to include the account number property in the HTML output we would include a tag similar to this in the account details JSP file:

```
<INSERT BEAN="KanDoItServlet" PROPERTY="accountnum"></INSERT>
```

For more information, see "Creating the Java Server Page File" in Chapter 9.

Why Design It This Way?

There are many ways the web component could have been designed. So why have we done it this way? There are several compelling reasons:

- By using a servlet rather than an applet, we are ensuring that any customer with web access can use the component, regardless of what web browser they are using.

- Servlets produce better performance than CGI programs performing a similar function.

- Because the servlet and JSPs run on the web server we can upgrade or even completely change function and presentation of data without any dependency on user's client software.

- Using CORBA (see below) we can communicate directly with our account object running in the CICS server over a TCP/IP network.

- CORBA is both cross-platform and cross-language—we've implemented our CORBA client in Java so we can invoke it directly within our servlet.

- The servlet could have included code to perform HTML conversion, but it would then be doing two jobs: processing and presentation. If you later wished to change the way in which data was presented in the web browser, you would have to change the servlet and recompile it. By using JSP to generate the HTML, and inserting placeholders for any dynamic data, the presentation logic is kept apart from the processing logic and it is easier to maintain and update.

Designing the CORBA Client Implementation

In Part III we introduced CORBA and described how to define and implement a Java object in the CICS environment that can be invoked by a remote client.

Normally, the developer of the CORBA client code would start work from the same IDL description of the server object as the developer of the CORBA server implementation and generate client stub classes. Since we already developed a test client in Part III, we will integrate it into the web server component part of our sample application.

The CORBA client can be instantiated by the servlet to invoke the remote methods on our account object (in CICS). The CORBA client performs the following tasks:

- Instantiates and initializes the client ORB

- Locates the server using a stringified object reference (see "Programming the Web Component" in Chapter 9)

- Obtains a reference to the remote object

- Invokes the getAccount method on the remote object
- Stores the returned account details (and error codes) in the corresponding AccountBean fields

What's Next...

Now that you have some idea what we are trying to achieve, Let's look at the actual programming that is involved in Chapter 9.

9

Programming the Web Component

This chapter introduces a number of recent web technologies and describes how to build a website, build and deploy servlets, create Java Server Pages (JSP), and create and build a JavaBean. In addition, this chapter shows you how to incorporate the CORBA client that you developed in Part III.

Tools

This section describes the configuration of those tools so that you can follow through the sample application more easily. You need to have access to the following: a web server, this book uses WebSphere Application Server (WAS) to provide servlet support, WebSphere Studio for the development of your servlets, and NetObjects Fusion or other web page servers to develop your web pages.

Install and Configure a Web Server

When you have successfully installed your web server (for example, IBM HTTP Server), you can create an alias to point your web server at the directory where you have your HTML files. To do this:

1. Edit the *httpd.conf* file found in the *\Program Files\IBM HTTP Server\conf* directory and add a directive for a user directory to contain your web pages:

   ```
   UserDir "C:/userpages"
   ```

   UserDir may already be defined for your web server.

2. Set up an alias for */cicsadp*. This will redirect requests for *http://servername/cicsadp/* to the *index.html* file in the folder */userpages/cicsadp/index.html*:

   ```
   Alias /cicsadp/ "C:/userpages/cicsadp/"
   ```

3. Use Windows Explorer to create a *cicsadp* folder under */userpages*.

Using WebSphere Studio

To use WebSphere Studio, you need to set up a project and configure a publishing server so that when you have completed your development work you can transfer the files to a directory on the web server. When WebSphere Studio is successfully installed, create an empty project called KanDoIT; we'll populate with files from the CD-ROM later. The following instructions guide you through setting up a project:

1. Start WebSphere Studio, and create a new project called KanDoIT. To do this select *File* and *New project*, as shown in Figure 9-1. In the New project dialog box, enter details about the project then click *OK*.

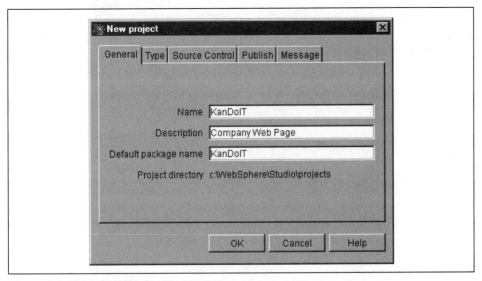

Figure 9-1. WebSphere Studio: New project

2. Select the KanDoIT project. Go to the Toolbar and select *Options* and *Publishing Servers...* Either edit the local definition or add a new publishing server setup. Figure 9-2 shows the screen.

3. Select *Edit* and enter the pathname for your HTML files and classes, for example:

```
html destination:C:\userpages\cicsadp
classes destination:'C:\WebSphere\AppServer\web\classes'
```

Select the *Browse* button and find the directory where you plan to publish your HTML and class files; see Figure 9-3. Then click *OK* twice.

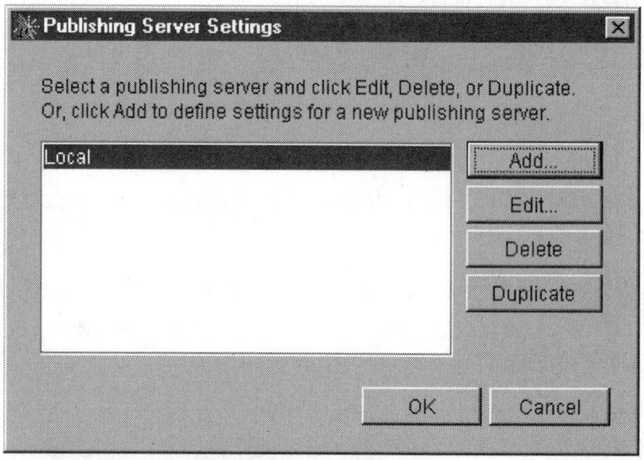

Figure 9-2. WebSphere Studio: Publishing Server Settings

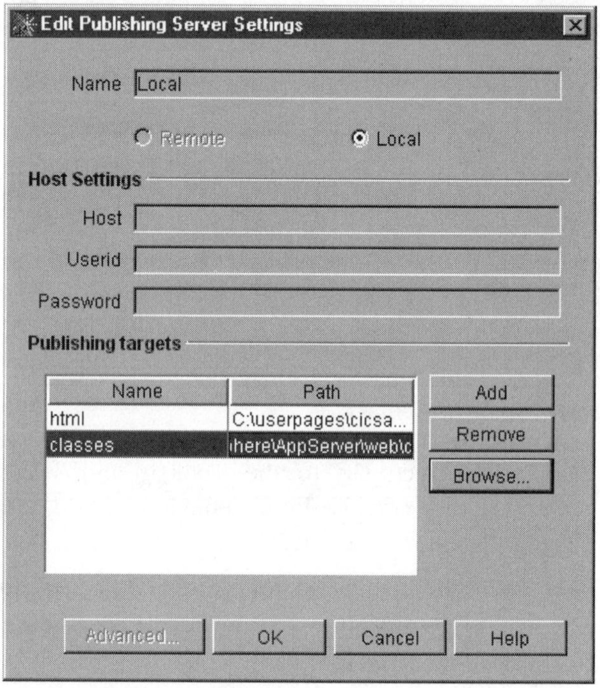

Figure 9-3. WebSphere Studio: Edit Publishing Server Settings

Servlet Configuration

WebSphere Application Server Version 2.0 provides your web server with support for servlets. Before you can use it with our sample application, you need to add the name of your servlet and create an alias that can be used in the form of the input page later. This will identify the servlet that it should invoke when it is submitted. To add your servlet's name and create an alias, follow these guidelines:

1. When WebSphere Application Server is successfully installed and sample web pages are deployed, open your web browser and enter the URL *http:// servername:9527* to bring up the Websphere Application Server administration screen. Alternatively use the *Start* menu → *Programs* → *IBM WebSphere* → *Application Server V2.0* → *Administration* and you'll see the panel as shown in Figure 9-4.

Figure 9-4. WebSphere Application Server: Administration login panel

2. Log in as administrator (admin and your password) and select *Setup* followed by *Java Engine*. This allows you to check that the CLASSPATH environment variable is correctly configured for your system. In this example, we're using JDK 1.1.8, which is supplied on the CD-ROM in the folder: *\Web Component\ JDK1.1.8.*

Building the Web Site

Although it is quite possible to create web pages by starting with an empty file and writing your own HTML, there are numerous products which make it much easier to create and maintain web pages by generating HTML. You can then customize the HTML, to refine the design or adhere to your own corporate style. Such products include NetObjects Fusion, Microsoft FrontPage, Macromedia's Dream-Weaver, or Borland's JBuilder.

The web designers at the KanDoIT company decide to use the NetObjects Fusion product to generate their new web interface. NetObjects Fusion enables you to create web sites quickly and efficiently in a WYSIWYG environment. There are page layout systems that allow you to draw the various components you want for your site and arrange them on a page. The tool then generates all the HTML.

Their first objective is to create a view account request form that reflects the design described in "Designing the Web Interface" in Chapter 8. We have called the HTML file that is generated by NetObjects Fusion for the *view account* form, *view-acct.html.* We are not only designing the look of the form but also we are setting the properties of the form (see Figure 9-5), so that when the user clicks the *Request* button, the KanDoIT servlet is invoked. The form settings properties dialog box allows you to set these.

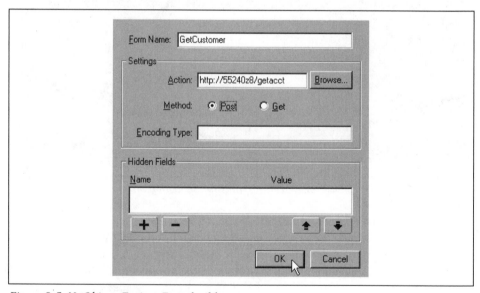

Figure 9-5. NetObjects Fusion: Form builder

In the HTML of *view-acct.html,* the definition of the form begins as follows:

```
<FORM METHOD=POST ACTION="/getacct">
```

In this line the action is */getacct*. That is the alias we defined through the Web-Sphere Application Server administration tool earlier in this chapter. In our example, */getacct* is mapped to the *KanDoIt.KanDoItServlet*. The POST method is used to ensure that we don't reveal the parameters we used to call the servlet (which would happen if we used a get). Figure 9-6 shows the finished form.

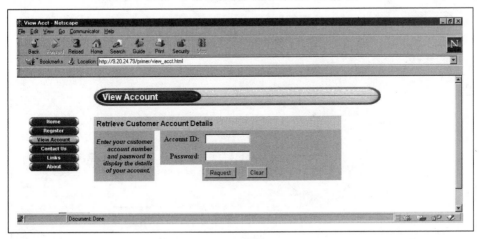

Figure 9-6. The View Account form

The Account Details output screen that is returned to the customer after they have entered a valid account number and password is also generated using NetObjects Fusion. Figure 9-7 shows the Account Details page. When you are creating this form it is important to remember that what you are creating is the basis of the Java Server Page (JSP) file that we want to call from the servlet. We have designed the *details.html* file so that it satisfied corporate standards but then we hardcoded the data fields, so that we know what to replace with dynamically generated data, that is, the hardcoded items are used as placeholders. After we have edited the file to replace the placeholders with the bean reference field, we will rename this file from *details.html* to *details.jsp*:

```
<INSERT BEAN="KanDoITServlet" PROPERTY="acctStatus"></INSERT>
```

The remainder of this chapter describes the creation of the programs that are involved in the process, from the moment a customer enters their account ID and password, until the moment the account details appear on the screen.

Programming the Web Server Components

As described in "Designing the Web Server Components" in Chapter 8, there are three web server components in the overall design of the web application:

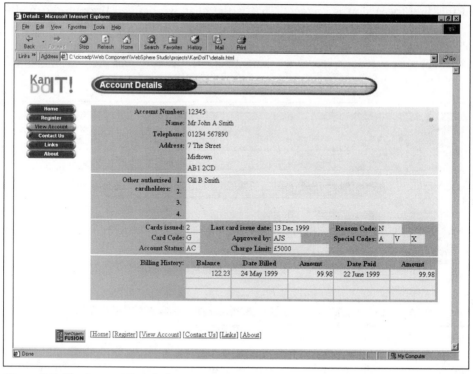

Figure 9-7. The Account Details form

- A Java servlet, which we're naming *KanDoItServlet*. (See "Creating KanDoIt-Servlet")

- A JavaBean, which we're naming *AccountBean*. (See "Creating AccountBean")

- A Java Server Pages (JSP) file, which we'll name *details.jsp*. (See "Creating the Java Server Page File")

A final stage is incorporating the CORBA client into the *KanDoItServlet* (See "Incorporating the CORBA Client").

We decided to use IBM's WebSphere Studio product to create these components as it was a product that drew together the development and the deployment of servlets, JavaBeans, and JSP pages. WebSphere Studio is a visual layout tool for creating and maintaining dynamic web pages using JSPs, full HTML, and JavaScript. It uses wizards to help you generate database-driven pages.

It would be possible to use other tools, such as VisualAge for Java, or generate the code manually, using your favorite editor. In this chapter, we walk you through the process of creating the code using WebSphere Studio, as well as looking at the code itself.

The overall design of the web component, as shown in Figure 8-1, shows how the web server components fit together. The best sequence for creating these components is:

- *AccountBean*

- *KanDoItServlet*

- *details.jsp* and *error.jsp* file

The reason for this is that the servlet wizard requires a bean, and the changes to the JSP file require knowing the field names in the bean. However, before creating any of the components, the first stage, using WebSphere Studio, is to create a project to contain the components.

Creating a WebSphere Studio Project

WebSphere Studio is the main development tool that we will be using in this chapter. If you followed the configuration of WebSphere Studio, you will have already created a new project called KanDoIT. If you didn't, then you need to create one now:

1. Start WebSphere Studio, and create a new project called *KanDoIT*. To do this, go to the toolbar, select *File → New Project*. In the New project dialog box, enter details about the project then click *OK*; see Figure 9-8 for an example of the screen.

2. A new project is created with an empty classes folder. This chapter describes in detail the steps that you need to follow to build up your own project.

   Alternatively, you can copy the directory and its contents from \ *Web Component\Websphere Studio\projects\KanDoIT* to the \ *WebSphere\studio\ projects* directory. This was created when you set up the *KanDoIT* project.

3. If you loaded the files into the *KanDoIt* project, you have to refresh the project before they become visible. Highlight the *KanDoIT* project, right click, and select *Refresh*.

Now we can get down to the business of understanding the working parts of the web component.

  The rest of this chapter describes how to develop this project from the beginning so all you need at this point is an empty KanDoIT project. So if you don't have the CD-ROM, it doesn't matter.

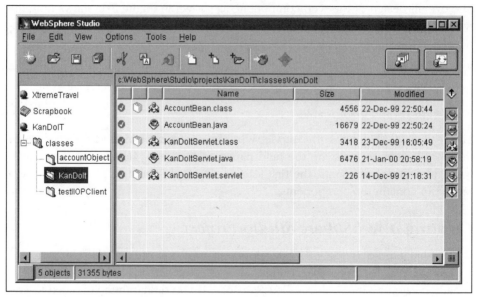

Figure 9-8. WebSphere Studio initial window

Creating AccountBean

The process of creating *AccountBean* using WebSphere Studio means that you need to know the names of all of the properties that you want to store in the bean. These properties are the names of the fields that we have used in other parts of this book—in both Part V and Part VI. To create *AccountBean* using Web-Sphere Studio:

1. Highlight your KanDoIT project root folder and click on the Studio Wizard icon 🔳 (top righthand corner), as shown in Figure 9-8.

2. In the dialog box that appears (see Figure 9-9), select *JavaBean*, and click *Next*.

3. Specify the name of your JavaBean (in the case of the sample application, *AccountBean*), then click *Next* to enter Properties; see Figure 9-10.

4. Add the names of all of the properties that you want to store in the JavaBean. Here, we want to match the names of the account detail fields in the customer VSAM file. See Example 9-1 for the list of property names you should enter for the sample. Figure 9-11 shows the Properties panel for the JavaBean Wizard.

5. Click *Next* to move to the *Imports page* tab, leave these settings as they are. Click *Next* and then *Finish* to complete the wizard. A message appears saying that the code is being compiled.

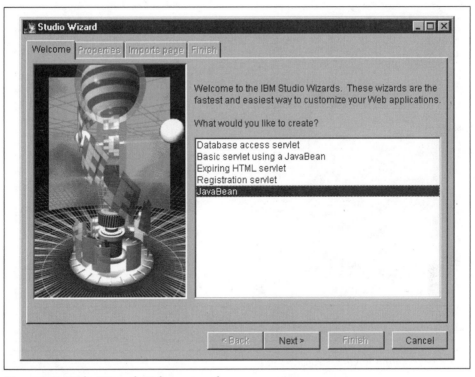

Figure 9-9. Studio Wizard: Welcome panel

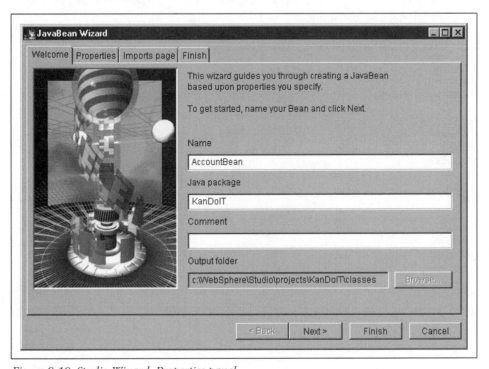

Figure 9-10. Studio Wizard: Properties panel

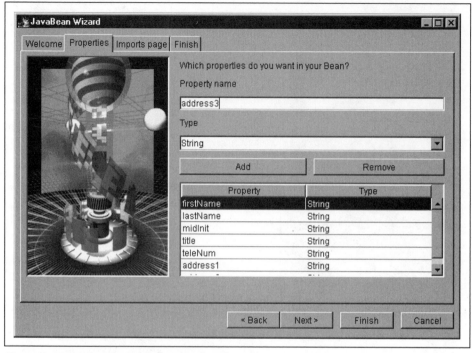

Figure 9-11. Studio Wizard: Properties panel

6. Select the KanDoIt project, right-click and select *Refresh* to see the results of your efforts. The usual fastpath of F5 is available as well.

Example 9-1. Property Names for the AccountBean

```
FirstName
LastName
MidInit
Title
TeleNum
Address1
Address2
Address3
Auth1
Auth2
Auth3
Auth4
NumIssues
IssueDay
IssueMonth
IssueYear
IssueReason
CardCode
ApproverCode
SpecialCode1
```

Example 9-1. Property Names for the AccountBean (continued)

```
SpecialCode2
SpecialCode3
AcctStatus
CreditLimit
```

The classes folder is now populated with a *KanDoIT* folder that contains the following files:

- *AccountBean.java* (the source code)

- *AccountBean.class* (the compiled code)

See Figure 9-12 for the details.

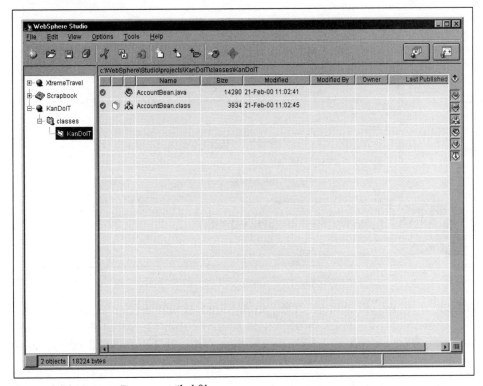

Figure 9-12. AccountBean compiled files

 The icon next to *AccountBean.class* shows that this file is set to be published. This means that it is ready to be copied to the correct location on the target web server.

Looking at the coding in AccountBean

If you want to view or edit the source Java code for *AccountBean*, double-click on the *AccountBean.java* file. This invokes your editor, in our case NetObjects Script-Builder Version 3.0, as shown in Figure 9-13. You can see the code that has been generated by the WebSphere Studio wizard.

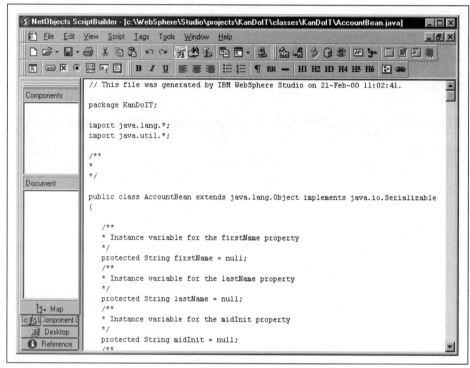

```
// This file was generated by IBM WebSphere Studio on 21-Feb-00 11:02:41.

package KanDoIT;

import java.lang.*;
import java.util.*;

/**
 *
 */

public class AccountBean extends java.lang.Object implements java.io.Serializable
{

    /**
     * Instance variable for the firstName property
     */
    protected String firstName = null;
    /**
     * Instance variable for the lastName property
     */
    protected String lastName = null;
    /**
     * Instance variable for the midInit property
     */
    protected String midInit = null;
    /**
```

Figure 9-13. Editing the Java source code

What follows are declarations of the string variables you defined in the *Properties* tab. These match the fields in the VSAM customer data file. All of these variables are defined as protected, which means they can only be modified by methods defined within the *AccountBean* class, as shown in Example 9-2.

Example 9-2. AccountBean Code: String Variables for Account Number and Password

```
/**
 * Instance variable for the accountNum property
 */
    protected String accountNum = null;

/**
 * Instance variable for the password property
 */
    protected String password = null;
```

These string variables are used to hold the account's variable fields—account number and password, as shown in Example 9-3. These are the same account number and password that the customer enters in the *View Account* form on the web browser.

Example 9-3. AccountBean Code: String Variable for the Last Name and First Name

```
/**
* Instance variable for the lastName property
*/
     protected String lastName = null;
/**
* Instance variable for the firstName property
*/
     protected String firstName = null;
```

The remaining fields will contain the customer information from the VSAM data file, for example address, telephone number, and so on.

Further down the *AccountBean* code, we find the getter and setter methods for each variable, as shown in Example 9-4. These enable other Java classes to read the value of a property or set the value of a property, without modifying the property directly.

Example 9-4. AccountBean Code: Getter and Setter Methods

```
/* Get method for the accountNum property
* @return the value of the property
*/
public String getAccountNum()    {
       return accountNum;
       }
/* Set method for the accountNum property
*
* @param value the new value for the proprety
*/
public void setAccountNum(String value)    {
       this.accountNum = value;
       }
```

Creating KanDoItServlet

The KanDoItServlet servlet has three main tasks:

- Instantiates the *AccountBean* and sets parameters (account number and password) in it.

- Invokes a method on the account object installed in CICS, using IIOP.

- Calls the JSP file that extracts data from *AccountBean* to generate the output HTML.

The process for creating *KanDoItServlet* using WebSphere Studio is described here:

1. Select the KanDoIT root folder to highlight it, then click the *Studio Wizard* button on the toolbar—as you did in Figure 9-8.

2. In the wizard dialog box that appears (Figure 9-14), select *Basic servlet using a JavaBean*, click *Next*. Specify the name of your servlet (in this case, *KanDoItServlet*) and click *Next*.

3. Select *KanDoIT.AccountBean* from the pull-down list, and check the *Store this Bean in the user's session* option, click *Next* to move to the *Input page* tab.

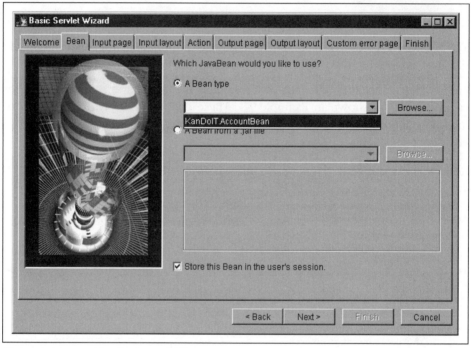

Figure 9-14. Basic Servlet Wizard: The Bean

4. In the Input page (Figure 9-15), the fields you specified in `AccountBean` appear in the window. Select *No, thank you* in response to the question *Do you want an input page?*, click *Next* to move to the *Action* page; see Figure 9-14.

5. On the *Action* page, select *No, thank you*, click *Next* to move to the *Output* page.

6. On the *Output* page tab (Figure 9-16), click *Yes, please* and check all of the properties you want to display. In the sample application, this is everything except *password, errorReason, errorResponse,* and *class*. This indicates that we

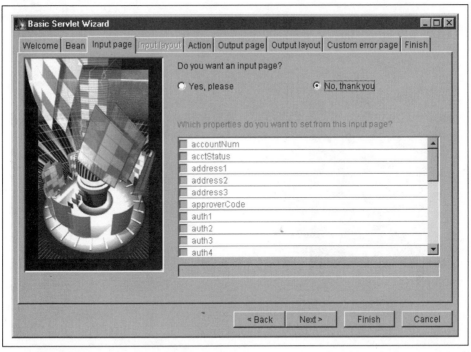

Figure 9-15. Basic Servlet Wizard: The Input page

want to generate a sample JSP page which will come in useful when we convert our HTML files to JSP files. Click *Next* to move to the *Output Layout* page; see Figure 9-16.

7. In the *Output layout* page (Figure 9-17), you can arrange the fields so that they are displayed in the order you want by selecting the fields and using the arrow keys.

8. Finally, click *Next* to move to the Custom error page tab. Select *No, thank you*, click *Next* to move to the *Finish* tab, then click *Finish* to complete the wizard.

Now when you look at the KanDoIT folder (Figure 9-18), you will find three new files:

- *KanDoItServlet.java* (the source code for the servlet)

- *KanDoItServlet.class* (the compiled code for the servlet)

- *KanDoITServlet.servlet* (an XML configuration file for the servlet).

The 🗍 icon next to *KanDoItServlet.class* and *KanDoItServlet.servlet* shows that these files are set to be published. If you click on the *KanDoIT* project folder, you'll see that there is also one new file in the root folder.

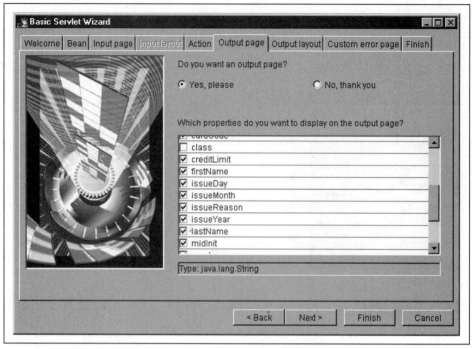

Figure 9-16. Basic Servlet Wizard: The Output page

WebSphere Studio has automatically created a skeleton JSP file, and named it *KanDoItServletOutputPage.jsp*. This is in the KanDoIT root folder; see Figure 9-19.

Creating the Java Server Page File

The *KanDoItServletOutputPage.jsp* file is generated by WebSphere Studio. It contains the code that displays the contents of the specified fields in **AccountBean**, but without any HTML formatting. What we want to do now is to take the HTML file that was generated in the HTML editor, for example, NetObjects Fusion, and convert it into a JSP file that references dynamically generated data:

1. Double-click on *KanDoItServletOutputPage.jsp* in the KanDoIT root folder. This opens the NetObjects ScriptBuilder and allows you to edit the file.

2. Locate the *details.html* file in the KanDoIt root directory. If it isn't in your project folder, use *File, Add File* and browse to find the file on the CD-ROM.

3. Edit the *details.html* file in NetObjects ScriptBuilder, use *windows → tile* option so that you can see both the *details.html* and *KanDoItServletOutputPage.jsp* source files, as shown in Figure 9-20.

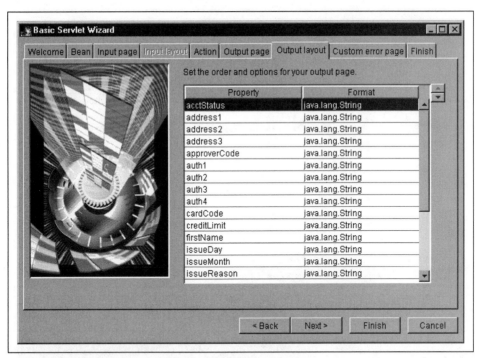

Figure 9-17. Basic Servlet Wizard: The Output layout page

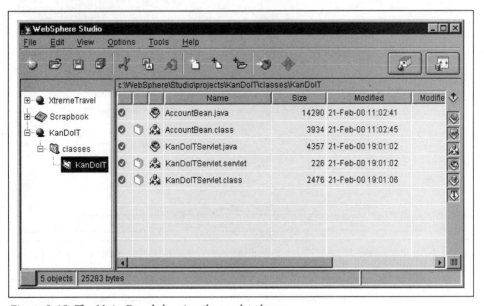

Figure 9-18. The Main Panel showing the servlet classes

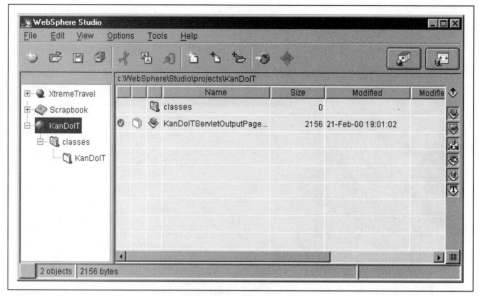

Figure 9-19. WebSphere Studio: The main window showing the JSP file

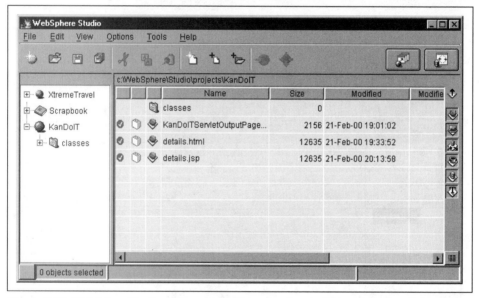

Figure 9-20. WebSphere Studio: The main window showing the JSP and the details.html files

4. Locate the hard-coded field values in *details.html*. In Figure 9-21 this is, for example, *12345* and replace them with the corresponding tags from the sample JSP file; see Figure 9-22). For example:

```
<INSERT BEAN="KanDoITServlet" PROPERTY="accountNum"></INSERT>
```

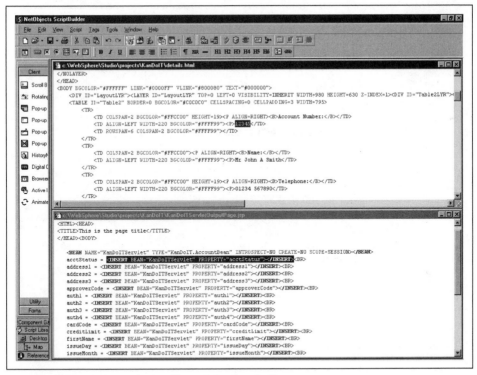

Figure 9-21. Comparing the JSP file and the details file

5. After making the required changes, save the modified *details.html* file as *details.jsp*. Close ScriptBuilder and return to WebSphere Studio and refresh the project display (F5). The *details.jsp* file will now appear in the list of project files in the *KanDoIt* root directory.

Examining the details of the Java Server Page

The early part of the file is standard HTML, as generated by your web editor. The changes begin after the <BODY... tag, as shown in Example 9-5.

In Example 9-5, the first highlighted line in the code fragment shows the <BEAN ... tag, in which a reference to the JavaBean is created. This is used by the <INSERT BEAN... tags that follow. Rather confusingly, WebSphere Studio uses as its reference ID the name of the Java servlet, in this case *KanDoItServlet*. If you wish, you can change this name to avoid potential confusion.

Later in the code fragment, you'll see an <INSERT BEAN... tag, which inserts the *accountNum* value that has been stored in *AccountBean*. The value is displayed next to the text string *Account Number*, as defined two lines earlier. The same change has to be made for all the other fields.

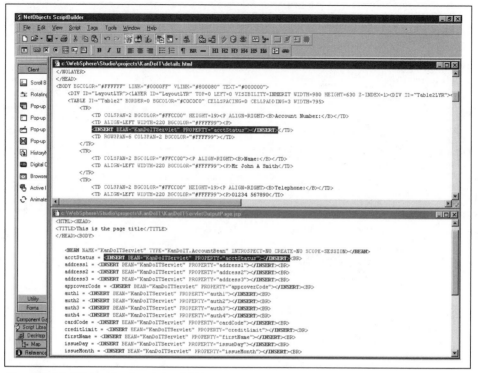

Figure 9-22. Editing the details.html file

Example 9-5. Code of the details.jsp file

```
<BODY BGCOLOR="#FFFFFF" LINK="#0000FF" VLINK="#800080" TEXT="#000000">
<BEAN NAME="KanDoITServlet" TYPE="KanDoIT.AccountBean" INTROSPECT=NO CREATE=NO
SCOPE=SESSION></BEAN>
    <DIV ID="LayoutLYR"><LAYER ID="LayoutLYR" TOP=0 LEFT=0 VISIBILITY=INHERIT
WIDTH=980 HEIGHT=630 Z-INDEX=1><DIV ID="Table2LYR"><LAYER ID="Table2LYR"
VISIBILITY=INHERIT TOP=90 LEFT=177 WIDTH=795 HEIGHT=470 Z-INDEX=1>
    <TABLE ID="Table2" BORDER=0 BGCOLOR="#C0C0C0" CELLSPACING=0 CELLPADDING=3
WIDTH=795>
        <TR>
            <TD COLSPAN=2 BGCOLOR="#FFCC00" HEIGHT=19><P ALIGN=RIGHT><B>Account
Number:</B></TD>
            <TD ALIGN=LEFT WIDTH=220 BGCOLOR="#FFFF99"><P>
            <INSERT BEAN="KanDoITServlet" PROPERTY="accountNum"></INSERT></TD>
            <TD ROWSPAN=6 COLSPAN=2 BGCOLOR="#FFFF99"></TD>
```

We now have a JavaBean named *AccountBean*, a JSP file that will generate output HTML with data picked up directly from *AccountBean*, and a Java servlet. The final stage is to modify the servlet that was generated by WebSphere Studio, so that it does the following:

- Performs basic validation on the account number and password entered by the customer.

- Calls CICS using IIOP.

- Depending on the result from CICS, calls the appropriate JSP output file to display either the account details or the error message page.

Before we go further we need to create an equivalent *error.jsp* file using the same method we have described earlier.

Creating the Error JSP File

There are three steps needed to set up the error JSP file. They are:

- Create an *error.html* file

- Edit the *error.html* so that it includes the reason and response BEAN tags

- Save the resulting *error.jsp* file

The process is very similar to the one described for the creation of the *details.jsp* file (see "Creating the Java Server Page File," earlier in this chapter).

If a customer does fail to enter a password, the panel as shown in Figure 9-23 is displayed.

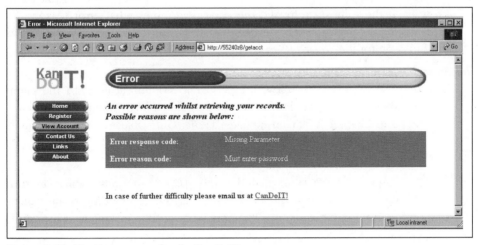

Figure 9-23. The Error screen for the KanDoIT company

Incorporating the CORBA Client

To incorporate the CORBA client you have to modify two files:

- *KanDoItServlet.java*

- *ClientStub.java*

Modifying KanDoItServlet.java

There are two methods that you need to include in the sample: deciding which JSP page to return to the user, and instantiating the ClientStub class so that we can get data from CICS using IIOP:

Deciding which JSP page to return

The servlet determines which JSP file to output whether it should be the *details.jsp* or the *error.jsp*. Initially we have to add a variable to hold the name of the JSP file that we want to display. The code to do this is:

```
String pageToDisplay;
```

Later in the code you will see that it returns the *error.jsp* file if either the account number is incorrect or the password has not been entered. The code for this is:

```
String inAcctNum = getParameter(request, "custacno", true, true, true, null);
String inPassword = getParameter(request, "password", true, true, true, null);
    pageToDisplay = "/~CICS_Primer/error.jsp";
```

Depending on the response code from CICS, we can set the *pageToDisplay* variable to either *details.jsp* or *error.jsp*. If the account number and the password are valid entries, then *pageToDisplay* returns the *details.jsp*. This causes the JSP file to be compiled and replace all the BEAN tags with the appropriate values from the *AccountBean*. The *Account Details* page is sent to the client browser. If the values are invalid the code determines what error reason and error response to return with the *error.jsp* file to the user. Example 9-6 shows the full code for the *KanDoItServlet* servlet.

Instantiating the ClientStub object

The purpose of this is to allow the servlet to communicate with the client ORB. At the beginning of the file, we import the *testIIOPClient* class that we developed in Chapter 7. This instantiates a *ClientStub* object so we can request data from CICS using IIOP. The code to do this is:

```
import testIIOPClient.*;
```

This package (*testIIOPClient*) includes the *ClientStub* class, which in turn imports the necessary *AccountObject helper* classes. After doing some validation on the input parameters (see Example 9-6) we then instantiate *ClientStub*:

```
new ClientStub(inAcctNum, KanDoItServlet);
```

After you have completed the modifications you need to recompile *KandoItServlet. java*. Example 9-6 shows the code is the *Kandoitservlet.java* file. The lines that you need to edit are highlighted.

Example 9-6. Code from the Kandoitservlet.java File

```
// This file was generated by IBM WebSphere Studio Release 1.0 on 14-Dec-99 16:18:31.
package KanDoIt;
import testIIOPClient.*;
/**
*
*/
public class KanDoItServlet extends com.ibm.servlet.PageListServlet implements java.
io.Serializable    {
* Process incoming requests for information
*
* @param request Object that encapsulates the request to the servlet
* @param response Object that encapsulates the response from the servlet
*/
public void performTask(javax.servlet.http.HttpServletRequest request,
                        javax.servlet.http.HttpServletResponse response)        {
    String pageToDisplay;
    try   {
            javax.servlet.http.HttpSession session = request.getSession(true);
            // Instantiate the bean and store it in the request so it can be accessed
            //  by the called page
            KanDoIt.AccountBean KanDoItServlet = null;
            KanDoItServlet = (KanDoIt.AccountBean)
            java.beans.Beans.instantiate (getClass().getClassLoader(),
                    "KanDoIt.AccountBean");
            // Store the bean in the session so it can be accessed by other servlets as
            //  the user navigates the site
            session.putValue("KanDoItServlet", KanDoItServlet);
        // get input parameters from HTTP request
        String inAcctNum = getParameter(request, "custacno", true, true, true, null);
        String inPassword = getParameter(request, "password", true, true, true, null);
        pageToDisplay = "/~CICS_Primer/error.jsp";
        // check we have both input parameters - if not issue error
        if ( inAcctNum.equals("") || inPassword.equals("") ) {
            KanDoItServlet.setErrorResponse("Missing Parameter");
            if ( inAcctNum.equals("") ) {
              KanDoItServlet.setErrorReason("Must enter account code");
            } else {
              KanDoItServlet.setErrorReason("Must enter user password");
            else if ( inAcctNum.length() != 5 || inPassword.length() > 8 ) {
        KanDoItServlet.setErrorResponse("Length error");
                if ( inAcctNum.length() != 5 ) {
                KanDoItServlet.setErrorReason("Account code must be 5 characters");
                } else {
                    KanDoItServlet.setErrorReason("Password is 1-8 characters");
                    }
                } else {
                // Initialize the bean accountNum property from the parameters
                KanDoItServlet.setAccountNum(inAcctNum);
                // Initialize the bean password property from the parameters
                KanDoItServlet.setPassword(inPassword);
                // Pass acccount bean reference to Client stub and retrieve
                // accountdata directly into the account bean
```

Example 9-6. Code from the Kandoitservlet.java File (continued)

```
                new ClientStub(inAcctNum, KanDoItServlet);
                // if no error from CICS, set URL of JSP to display with account
                // details
                if (KanDoItServlet.getErrorReason().equals("0000") && KanDoItServlet.
getErrorResponse().equals("0000")) {
                        pageToDisplay = "/~CICS_Primer/details.jsp";
                } else {
                    if (KanDoItServlet.getErrorResponse().equals("0013") &&
                        KanDoItServlet.getErrorReason().equals("0080")) {
                        KanDoItServlet.setErrorResponse("Not found");
                        KanDoItServlet.setErrorReason("Account " + inAcctNum + "
                                                     does not exist");

                    }
                }
            }
            // Use callPage to invoke the JSP file and pass the current request object
            ((com.sun.server.http.HttpServiceResponse)
                                response).callPage( pageToDisplay, request);
        } catch (Exception theException)  {
            handleError(request, response, theException);
        }
    }
/*****************************************************************************
 * Returns the requested parameter
 *
 * @param request Object that encapsulates the request to the servlet
 * @param parameterName The name of the parameter value to return
 * @param checkRequestParameters when true, the request parameters are searched
 * @param checkInitParameters when true, the servlet init parameters are searched
 * @param isParameterRequired when true, an exception is thrown when the parameter
cannot be found
 * @param defaultValue The default value to return when the parameter is not found
 * @return The parameter value
 * @exception java.lang.Exception Thrown when the parameter is not found
 */
public java.lang.String getParameter(javax.servlet.http.HttpServletRequest request,
java.lang.String parameterName, boolean checkRequestParameters, boolean
checkInitParameters, boolean isParameterRequired, java.lang.String defaultValue)
throws  java.lang.Exception {
    java.lang.String[] parameterValues = null;
    java.lang.String paramValue = null;
    // Get the parameter from the request object if necessary.
    if (checkRequestParameters)  {
        parameterValues = request.getParameterValues(parameterName);
        if (parameterValues != null)
            paramValue = parameterValues[0];
    }
    // Get the parameter from the servlet init parameters if
    // it was not in the request parameter.
      if ( (checkInitParameters) && (paramValue == null) )
          paramValue = getServletConfig().getInitParameter(parameterName);
    // Throw an exception if the parameter was not found and it was required.
```

Example 9-6. Code from the Kandoitservlet.java File (continued)

```
            // The exception will be caught by error processing and can be
            // displayed in the error page.
            if ( (isParameterRequired) && (paramValue == null) )
                throw new Exception(parameterName + " parameter was not specified.");
            // Set the return to the default value if the parameter was not found
            if (paramValue == null)
                paramValue = defaultValue;
            return paramValue;
    }
    /*************************************************************************
    * Process incoming HTTP GET requests
    *
    * @param request Object that encapsulates the request to the servlet
    * @param response Object that encapsulates the response from the servlet
    */
    public void doGet(javax.servlet.http.HttpServletRequest request, javax.servlet.http.
    HttpServletResponse response)  {
        performTask(request, response);
        }
    /*************************************************************************
    * Process incoming HTTP POST requests
    *
    * @param request Object that encapsulates the request to the servlet
    * @param response Object that encapsulates the response from the servlet
    */
    public void doPost(javax.servlet.http.HttpServletRequest request, javax.servlet.http.
    HttpServletResponse response) {
        performTask(request, response);
        }
}
```

Modifying ClientStub.java

There are a number of small changes that you need to make to the *ClientStub.java*
file. They are:

- Change the constructor so that it includes a reference to the *AccountBean*:

  ```
  public ClientStub(String acctID, KanDoIt.AccountBean KanDoItServlet)
  ```

- Invoke the **getDetails** method including that *AccountBean* reference:

  ```
  getDetails(ai, acctID, KanDoItServlet);
  ```

- Add these line to set the error response and reason fields in the *AccountBean*:

  ```
  KanDoItServlet.setErrorReason(acctData.reascode);
  KanDoItServlet.setErrorResponse(acctData.respcode);
  ```

- Change all the System.out.println lines to set the corresponding fields in the
  AccountBean with the values returned from the IIOP request:

  ```
  KanDoItServlet.setFirstName(acctData.firstname);
  KanDoItServlet.setLastName(acctData.lastname);
  ```

The *AccountBean* class source code is generated by the bean wizard in Web-Sphere Studio. It contains all the fields we specified that we want to store from the account Object. The contents are picked up by the JSP file, *detail.jsp*.

After you have completed the modifications you need to recompile *ClientStub. java.*

Example 9-7 shows the code is the *ClientStub.java* file. The lines that you need to edit are highlighted.

Example 9-7. Code from ClientStub.java

```
package testIIOPClient;
import accountObject.*;
import java.io.*;
import org.omg.CORBA.*;
import org.omg.CosLifeCycle.*;
import org.omg.CosNaming.*;
/**
 * This type was created in VisualAge.
 */
public class ClientStub {
/**
 * ClientStub constructor comment.
 */
public ClientStub(String acctID, KanDoIt.AccountBean KanDoItServlet) {
String factoryIOR;
AccountInterface ai = null;
try {
    // create and initialize the ORB
    System.out.println("Client: creating and initializing the ORB");
    ORB orb = ORB.init();
    // create the generic factory
    System.out.println("Client: creating the generic factory");
    factoryIOR = getFactoryIOR();
    org.omg.CORBA.Object genFacRef = orb.string_to_object(factoryIOR);
    System.out.println("Client: narrowing the generic factory");
    GenericFactory fact = GenericFactoryHelper.narrow(genFacRef);
    // use generic factory to make HelloWorld object
    System.out.println("Client: using generic factory to make accountObject object");
    NameComponent nc = new NameComponent("accountObject::AccountInterface", "object
interface");
    NameComponent key[] = {nc};
    NVP mycriteria[] = {};
    System.out.println("about to create object reference");
    org.omg.CORBA.Object objRef = fact.create_object(key, mycriteria);
    System.out.println("about to narrow");
    ai = AccountInterfaceHelper.narrow(objRef);
    getDetails(ai, acctID, KanDoItServlet);
}
// Catch NoFactory
catch (org.omg.CosLifeCycle.NoFactory nf)  {
```

Example 9-7. Code from ClientStub.java (continued)

```
    System.out.println(
    "Client: NoFactory thrown by create_object for accountObject::AccountInterface");
    System.out.println("                        - check server program with alias +
                        accountObject.jll is available on the CICS server");
}
// Catch any unexpected exceptions
catch (Exception e)  {
    System.out.println("Client: Unexpected exception : " + e);
    e.printStackTrace(System.out);
}
}
/**
 * This method was created in VisualAge.
 * @param ai accountObject.AccountInterface
 */
public void getDetails(accountObject.AccountInterface ai, String acctID, KanDoIt.
AccountBean KanDoItServlet) {
    // Invoke the getAccount method
    System.out.println("Client: invoking getAccount method on accountObject object");
    AccountData acctData = ai.getAccount(acctID);
    KanDoItServlet.setErrorReason(acctData.reascode);
    KanDoItServlet.setErrorResponse(acctData.respcode);
    if (acctData.respcode.equals("0000") && acctData.reascode.equals("0000")) {
        KanDoItServlet.setFirstName(acctData.firstname);
        KanDoItServlet.setLastName(acctData.lastname);
        KanDoItServlet.setMidInit(acctData.midinit);
        KanDoItServlet.setTitle(acctData.title);
        KanDoItServlet.setTeleNum(acctData.telnum);
        KanDoItServlet.setAddress1(acctData.addr1);
        KanDoItServlet.setAddress2(acctData.addr2);
        KanDoItServlet.setAddress3(acctData.addr3);
        KanDoItServlet.setAuth1(acctData.auth1);
        KanDoItServlet.setAuth2(acctData.auth2);
        KanDoItServlet.setAuth3(acctData.auth3);
        KanDoItServlet.setAuth4(acctData.auth4);
        KanDoItServlet.setNumIssues(acctData.cards);
        KanDoItServlet.setIssueDay(acctData.issueday);
        KanDoItServlet.setIssueMonth(acctData.issuemonth);
        KanDoItServlet.setIssueYear(acctData.issueyear);
        KanDoItServlet.setIssueReason(acctData.reason);
        KanDoItServlet.setCardCode(acctData.code);
        KanDoItServlet.setApproverCode(acctData.approver);
        KanDoItServlet.setSpecialCode1(acctData.scode1);
        KanDoItServlet.setSpecialCode2(acctData.scode2);
        KanDoItServlet.setSpecialCode3(acctData.scode3);
        KanDoItServlet.setAcctStatus(acctData.status);
        KanDoItServlet.setCreditLimit(acctData.limit);
    } else {                                // non-zero return code
        System.out.println("An error occurred: ");
        System.out.println("Response Code: " + acctData.respcode);
        System.out.println("Reason Code: " + acctData.reascode);
        System.out.println("Account ID: " + acctData.acctid);
        System.out.println("CICS Function: " + acctData.cicsfunc);
    }
```

Example 9-7. Code from ClientStub.java (continued)

```
}
/**
 * This method was created in VisualAge.
 * @return java.lang.String
 * @exception java.io.IOException The exception description.
 */
public String getFactoryIOR() throws IOException {
String line;
final String filename = "C://IORFiles/genfac.ior";
FileInputStream in = null;
InputStreamReader isr = null;
BufferedReader br = null;
try {
    in = new FileInputStream(filename);
    isr = new InputStreamReader(in);
    br = new BufferedReader(isr);
}
catch(IOException e)  {
    System.out.println("Client: Error opening file " + filename);
    throw e;
} try {
    line = br.readLine();
    System.out.println("IOR:" + line);// for diagnostics
    }
    catch(IOException e)  {
        System.out.println("Client: Error reading file " + filename);
        throw e;
    }
return line;
    }
}
```

Publishing Your Files

Now that you have completed the WebSphere Studio project, you have all the HTML, JSP, servlets, Java classes that you need together with the CORBA client Java and class files. At this point you need to publish the files on the web server:

1. Select the *KanDoIT* project, right-click and choose *Publish*. All the files that are marked for publication will be transferred to your web server. You will be prompted to select a publishing server, for example, local. This was defined at the beginning of this chapter.

2. Shut down and restart your web server to apply your changes. If you are using the latest version of WebSphere Application Server, you may not have to do this.

3. To define the servlet and its alias, select *Servlets* followed by the *Configuration* option. Later in the chapter we will be describing how to develop the servlet. Figure 9-24 shows the screen.

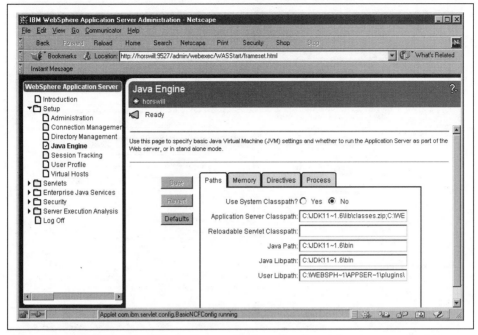

Figure 9-24. WebSphere Application Server: Checking the Classpath

4. Click the *Add* button to add a servlet and enter *KanDoIt.KanDoItServlet* for the servlet name and class name; now click *Add.* Figure 9-25 shows the screen.

5. Now you need to create an alias that you will use later to access the servlet. Select *Servlets* followed by the *Configuration* option, now click *Add* (see Figure 9-26).

6. Click the *Add* button to add an alias and enter /getacct for the alias and *KanDoIt.KanDoItServlet* for the servlet invoked, now click *Save.*

7. You are finally ready to test your work.

Testing the Sample

1. Open your web browser and enter the URL *http://servername/cicsadp/* where *cicsadp* is the name you defined in the *httpd.conf* file of your web server. This brings up the home page for the KanDoIT web site.

2. Navigate to the View Account page, click the view account button and enter an account number, for example, 10000 and password (any password since we have not covered security at all). This should return the account details page, populated with information for account number 10000.

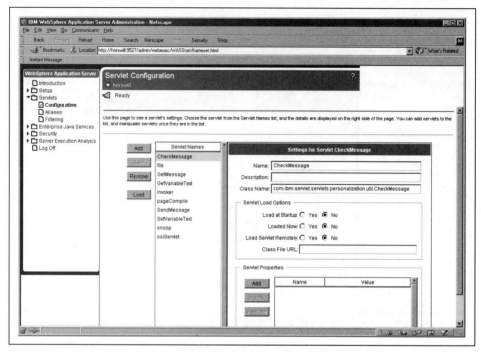

Figure 9-25. WebSphere Application Server: Servlet Configuration

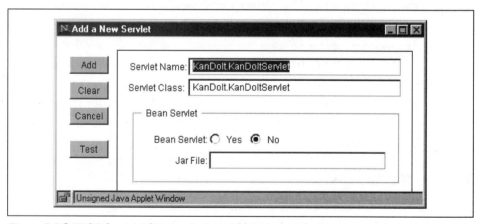

Figure 9-26. WebSphere Application Server: Add a new servlet

3. Now test the error page. Return to the home page and enter the account number but this time without a password. This should return the error page with the error reason code and the error response code as shown in Figure 9-23.

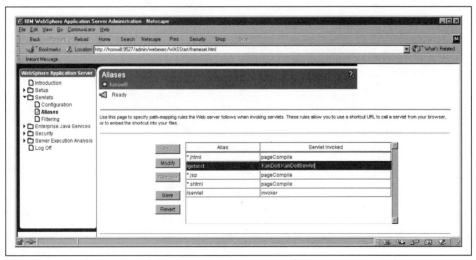

Figure 9-27. WebSphere Application Server: Aliases

What's Next...

With the code we have developed in in Parts III and IV, you should now have a working web sample. Next, we describe setting up a frontend using BMS maps for a typical greeen (3270) screen.

V

The 3270 Interface

The limitations of 3270 devices are usually compensated for by designing and building the system for high performance, with typical response times for a query usually being less that half a second. From the early 1970s, 3270 devices brought transaction processing to the end user. The design point was to produce useful data to the end user in less than a second over a network which had a bandwidth that would be considered to be abnormally narrow today. If the end users were paid by the number of transactions they finish, a terse layout is the right design and implementation for this interaction with their company system.

There are two reasons why you may have a need to understand the information in this part:

- Because you are writing a new 3270 application. Even in this case, the CICS facilities hide most of the technical details of the hardware from your program.

- Because there is an existing 3270 application that you need to invoke from your own program. You will be issuing API calls that the existing program interprets as user keystrokes. Again, there are CICS and other facilities that hide the technical details.

This Part provides detailed information about the 3270 interface for our sample CICS application and contains Chapter 10, *Designing the Presentation Logic*, and Chapter 11, *Programming the 3270 Presentation Logic Component*.

10

Designing the Presentation Logic

In the KanDoIT company, the accounts department has decided that it is very happy with its existing 3270-based applications. So here we describe the background to a 3270 user interface and the design principles behind writing the presentation logic.

This chapter describes the design of the presentation logic of the Accounts system. There are two key stages that you need to consider in your design. They are:

- Designing the user interface, including checks for valid data, and the ability for the users to correct their input. There are two sections describing what the presentation logic has to do and another describing the ways to incorporate the CICS design guidelines.

- Sending and receiving the information to your appropriate business logic component. This describes how information is sent from the screen to the business logic and also how the data is returned to the screen.

Understanding What the Presentation Logic Component Needs to Do

The basic design behind each of the frontends that we describe in this book is:

- To create a clear, easy-to-use screen so that the users can enter their data quickly and easily.

- To transfer data to the business logic.

- To receive information from the business logic to display on the screen.

The plan to achieve that for this component is to:

- Display a customer account record, given the account number.
- Add new account records.
- Modify existing account records.
- Delete account records.
- Print a list of the changes made to the account file.
- Print a single copy of a customer account record.
- Access records by name.
- Read and update the stored data using the account business logic component.

First, a little about 3270 terminals, how 3270 data streams work, and how CICS starts transactions. Then we can start thinking about how our application might look to the end user.

IBM 3270 Information Display System

The 3270 information display system is a family of display and printer terminals. Today, most people who require 3270 devices use PCs to emulate them. There were many 3270 device types and models that differed in screen sizes, printer speeds, features (like color and special symbol sets) and manner of attachment to the processor, but they all used essentially the same data format. You need to know a little about this format to understand the *Basic Mapping Support* (BMS) services that CICS provides to ease the job of communicating with these devices.

The IBM 3278 Display Station Model 2 has a display screen and a keyboard. This device is used for both input and output, and in both cases the screen (or rather a buffer that represents it) was the crucial medium of exchange between the terminal and the processor. The purpose of the keyboard is to modify the screen, in preparation for input, and to signal when that input is ready to be sent to the server.

When your application program writes to a 3278, the server sends a stream of data in the special format used by 3270 devices. Most of the data in the stream is the text that is to be displayed on the screen; the rest of it is control information that defines where the text should go on the screen, whether it can be overtyped from the keyboard later, and so on.

The printers that correspond to the 3278 can use this same data stream, so a stream built for a display device can be used equally well for a printer. More about printers later.

3270 Field Structure

The screen of the 3278 Model 2 can display up to 1920 characters, in 24 rows and 80 columns. That is, the face of the screen is logically divided into an array of positions, 24 deep and 80 wide, each capable of displaying one character, with enough space around it to separate it from the next character.

Each of these 1920 character positions is individually addressable. This means that your COBOL application program can send data to any position on the screen, without having to space it out with space characters to get it into the right location. Your program does not, however, give an address for each character you want displayed. Instead, within your program, you divide your display output into *fields*. A field on the 3278 screen is a consecutive set of character positions, all having the same display characteristics (high intensity, normal intensity, protected, not protected, and so on). Normally, you use a 3270 field in exactly the same way as a field in a file record or an output report to contain one item of data.

Planning Your 3270 Screen Layout: Using a Menu Screen

You will mainly use the presentation logic component to design the 3270 screen.

For many applications, users need to remember just one transaction identifier. When they want to do any transaction in that application (in our case, create, display, print, and so on) they enter just the one transaction identifier. In response, the screen displays a menu of things that the users can do in this application. The menu has formatted fields for the data items that are required on input and also shows help instructions in case users don't remember exactly what to do.

The chief advantage of this technique is that the user has to remember almost nothing, a big help if they were infrequent users of our sample application.

There are some other benefits as well: you can diagnose errors in the request input in the same convenient way that we described for the add screen, so that the user gets a good explanation of the problem and has to do a minimum of re-keying to correct the errors. Also, when you complete a transaction such as an add, you can combine your confirmation message with this menu screen. This way, the user knows that the previous entry was successful, and is all ready to enter the next request.

Probably the only disadvantage to this menu technique is that a user has to go through one extra screen for the first transaction of a session, and one extra step (clearing the screen in this case) to escape. The only time this is a serious matter is when users need to mix transactions from different application suites constantly.

Before proceeding much further for our sample application, we should consult the users in the accounts department, showing them the sample screens (hand-drawn if necessary) and asking them to *use* them. Now let's consider how a modify transaction will work:

1. The user keys in the four-character transaction identifier (in our case, *NACT*) to get started.

2. The menu screen is displayed in response (see Figure 10-1).

3. The user enters M (for modify) for the request type, keys in an account number, and presses Enter.

If there's a problem, the user sees the same screen with the error fields highlighted and an explanatory message at the bottom saying what's wrong.

Otherwise, the response displays the record to be modified, ready for the user to change. The user changes the fields to be modified, and then presses the Enter key to send the screen back. If there are errors in the changes, the transaction returns the input with the errors highlighted and a message, if necessary. If (when) the user gets it right, the transaction updates the file, and sends back the menu screen, with a message at the bottom saying that the modification just requested was completed successfully. The user then enters the next request, or clears the screen to quit our application.

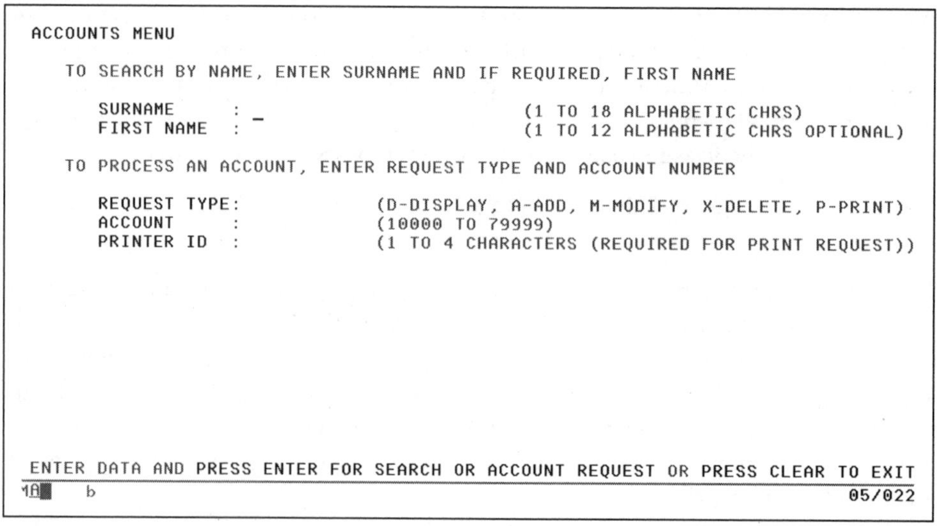

```
ACCOUNTS MENU

    TO SEARCH BY NAME, ENTER SURNAME AND IF REQUIRED, FIRST NAME

        SURNAME    : _                    (1 TO 18 ALPHABETIC CHRS)
        FIRST NAME :                      (1 TO 12 ALPHABETIC CHRS OPTIONAL)

    TO PROCESS AN ACCOUNT, ENTER REQUEST TYPE AND ACCOUNT NUMBER

        REQUEST TYPE:         (D-DISPLAY, A-ADD, M-MODIFY, X-DELETE, P-PRINT)
        ACCOUNT     :         (10000 TO 79999)
        PRINTER ID  :         (1 TO 4 CHARACTERS (REQUIRED FOR PRINT REQUEST))




    ENTER DATA AND PRESS ENTER FOR SEARCH OR ACCOUNT REQUEST OR PRESS CLEAR TO EXIT
 1A    b                                                              05/022
```

Figure 10-1. The sample menu screen

Interface Design Principles

In reaching our current idea of how your user interface will look, most of your decisions are based on what is easiest for the user. Indeed, that should be the cardinal rule. Human time has now become so much more valuable than computer time that it's worth a lot of effort and coding to make the user as productive as possible.

It isn't always obvious how to do this to the best advantage, and what is best for one user may not be best for another. This applies especially to occasional users of an application. In fact, the style of conversation between users and computers has changed significantly as people have learned more about the human factors of online systems.

Though there are no hard and fast rules, and though there can be many good designs for the user interface, here are five guidelines that we can safely propose:

1. Make screens easy to understand:

   — Keep to the rules used in forms design: try to give the screen layout an uncluttered appearance and, to the extent possible, a columnar structure, so that the reader's eye moves easily from one item to the next and doesn't have to jump long distances.

   — Put a title on the screen, so that users know where they are in the current transaction.

   — Be consistent from screen to screen. If you put the title on the top center of one screen, put it there on all the screens. If you put the messages at the bottom of one screen, put them there on all the screens.

   — If the user is reading from a form for input to a screen, make the screen look as much as possible like the form. Put the fields in the same order, and use the same placement as much as possible.

   — Likewise, if a screen is used to display information that the user is accustomed to seeing printed on a form, make the screen resemble the form as much as possible.

2. Reduce what the user must remember:

   — If there are more than a few fields to be filled in; use a formatted screen with labels and instructions.

   — Where possible, put instructions on the screen to show what the user can do next.

— Use consistent procedures, both within and across application programs. For example, if the CLEAR key is used to cancel in one transaction, use it that way in all transactions.

3. Protect users from themselves:

— If a user is about to do something that's hard to undo, such as a file deletion, get the user to confirm that it's the right action.

4. Save the user's time and patience:

Minimize the number of characters that have to be keyed.

Make the user change screens as little as possible.

Make it as easy as possible to correct errors. There are many ways to do this. In our application, for example, we do the following:

— Redisplay the user's input in the same screen in which it was entered.

— Diagnose all the errors at once.

— Highlight fields that have errors.

— If the user misses any required fields, fill with asterisks and highlight.

— Place the cursor under the start of the first field in error.

— Display an explanatory message if the error may not be obvious.

— Minimize the number of times that the users have to skip over fields.

5. Reassure users:

— Give a positive confirmation that a requested action has been done successfully.

— When you know a particular response time is likely to be longer than usual (because of the operation being performed) consider sending an intermediate display.

Incorporating CICS Design Guidelines

In addition to the screen design, we need to take into account some features that are common to transaction processing systems. The main one here is to understand the difference between conversational and pseudo-conversational transactions.

Conversational or Pseudo-conversational Transactions?

Now that we've established guidelines for design, let's return to the issue of defining the transactions that make up the sample application. Earlier we described the processing required for the various transaction types that the user sees: add, modify, display, and so on. If we were to define our CICS transactions along these functional lines, we can foresee several problems:

- There is much repetitive processing, which suggests that we should at least use common programs for some of the transactions, or combine transactions.

- Every transaction involves a wait for the user to enter data, and the update transactions contain two such waits. This means that these transactions will be running for a relatively long time, which is a violation of the guideline to keep program duration short.

- The modify and delete transactions will be holding on to a one-user-at-a-time resource during one of the waits, contradicting the guideline to minimize the duration of transactions that use such resources.

- Because CICS places no restriction on user input, CICS allows the systems programmer to place a limit on the number of concurrent transactions in each CICS address space internally to stop it becoming flooded and running out of resources. So if you have a conversational transaction open while the end-user goes to lunch, that slot within CICS is wasted and if the transaction is holding onto a lock, anybody else who wishes to access the same resource will have to wait until that user returns from lunch and completes his task.

Take, for example, the modify transaction. If programmed for a 3270 terminal as outlined earlier, the sequence of major events would be as shown in Table 10-1.

Table 10-1. Conversational Sequence of the Modify Transaction

Step	Operation
1	Display the menu screen
2	Wait for response
3	Receive menu screen (which is presumed to contain a correct modify request)
4	Invoke the business logic component to read the required record
5	Display the record in formatted form
6	Wait for the user to enter changes
7	Receive the changes
8	Update the account file accordingly
9	Re-display the menu screen

In CICS, this is called a *conversational transaction*, because the programs being executed enter into a conversation with the user. In contrast, a *non-conversational transaction* processes one input (which was read by CICS and which started the task), responds, and ends (disappears). It never pauses to read a second input from the terminal, so there is no real conversation. The important difference between the two types is transaction duration.

Conversational transactions

Because the time required for a response from a terminal user is much longer than the time required for the computer to process the input, conversational transactions last that much longer than non-conversational transactions. This means that conversational transactions use storage, maintain locks and other resources much more heavily than non-conversational ones because they retain their resources for so long. Whenever one of these resources is critical, you have a compelling reason for using non-conversational (pseudo-conversational) transactions if at all possible.

Pseudo-conversational transactions

This leads to a technique in CICS called *pseudo-conversational processing*, in which a series of non-conversational transactions gives the appearance (to the user) of a single conversational transaction. In the case we were just looking at, the pseudo-conversational structure is shown in Table 10-2.

Table 10-2. Pseudo-Conversational Transactions

Transactions	Steps	Operations
First	1	Display menu screen
Second	3	Receive menu screen (which is presumed to contain a correct modify request)
	4	Invoke the business logic component to read the required record
	5	Display the record in formatted form
Third	7	Receive the changes
	8	Update the account file accordingly
	9	Re-display the menu screen

Notice that Steps 2 and 6 of the conversational version have disappeared. No transaction exists during these waits for input; CICS takes care of reading the input when the user gets around to sending it.

A word about transactions. If we seem to be using the word in two different ways, well . . . yes, we are. We defined the word earlier in the way that the user sees a transaction: a single item of business, such as an add, a display operation, and so on. This is a correct use of the word. However, what the user sees as a transaction isn't necessarily what CICS sees.

To CICS, a transaction is a task that begins (usually on request from a terminal), exists for long enough to do the required work, and then disappears. It may last milliseconds or it may last hours. As we've just explained, you can use either one or several CICS transactions to do what the user regards as a single transaction. We're still deciding what we should define to CICS as transactions to accomplish the user transactions in our example problem. At the moment, the pseudo-conversational approach seems promising; it uses shorter programs (which are desirable in CICS as any other transaction processing system) and although there may be more of them, the programming does not look any more complicated.

The main way one transaction passes data to the next is by using the COMMAREA (for *communication area*). The same facility is available to pass data between programs within a transaction.

There are other facilities for storing data between transactions. One of these is a CICS facility known as temporary storage, which can be used as an application scratchpad.

Handling Errors

Error handling was discussed in some detail when we developed the COBOL business logic component (see "Handling Errors" in Chapter 4). The same principles apply here, especially dealing with user errors, invalid input, mismatches in resources and applications, hardware faults, omissions in the code, and so on.

Designing the Functions

This section provides detailed information about the 3270 presentation logic component of our sample application.

The first point to note is that we must always present the user with a "menu" of choices. So we'll start by displaying this menu and analyzing the request entered on it. The requests may be:

To exit the application
    In this case, we simply end the transaction.

To display, print, modify, add, or delete an account
    In this case, we invoke the appropriate business logic as described in Part II.

To search the accounts by name
    In this case, we invoke the appropriate business logic as described in Part II.

None of the above
    In this case, we send an error message to the user and repeat from the analysis step.

After invoking the appropriate business logic, we must check for errors and inform the user if one has occurred. For successful requests, we must perform the action desired for each request:

Display requests

We must present the data to the user.

Print requests

We must schedule the print activity.

Modify requests

We must lock the account, present the data to the user, accept any changes made to the data, and invoke the update business logic.

Add requests

We must get an account number, ensure it does not already exist, lock it, solicit input from the user, accept the input data, and invoke the add business logic.

Delete requests

We must lock the account, present the data to the user, solicit confirmation of the delete, and invoke the delete business logic.

Searches by name

You must invoke the browse logic and display the results.

You must allow for the user to abandon any of these functions at any time that may require freeing any locks previously obtained. Once an activity has been completed we should display a confirmation message.

11

Programming the 3270 Presentation Logic Component

There are three steps that are necessary to build up this component:

- Defining screens using Basic Mapping Support (BMS)

- Sending and receiving data (*NACT01*)

- Local printing (*NACT03*)

Part way through the chapter, we'll have a digression and introduce a little background about symbolic description maps.

First, a recap about the purpose of the component that we are going to write. This program is the first one executed when the *NACT* transaction is entered on a 3270 terminal. Apart from local printing, all of the code in the presentation logic has been placed in a single program. This is because the application is not big enough to justify multiple programs. *NACT01*, the name of our program, displays the menu screen, which prompts the user for request input, and ends when it returns control to CICS. In returning, it specifies that the same transaction (*NACT*) is to be executed when the next input is received from this terminal. *NACT01* will be invoked repeatedly to process the input from the menu. A typical piece of code that does this is:

```
X-RETURN-COM-AREA SECTION.
*
* This routine saves data and ends the task
*
* This section is performed from the following sections -
* B-GET-MENU-DATA
* DB-SEND-DETAIL-WITH MESSAGE
* DE-SEND-MENU-WITH-MESSAGE
* U-SEND-EMPTY-MENU
* W-LINK-FOR-BROWSE
```

```
*
   X-010.
      EXEC CICS RETURN TRANSID(EIBTRNID)
               COMMAREA(DFHCOMMAREA)
      END-EXEC

   END-X-RETURN-COM-AREA.
      EXIT.
```

Once input is received from the user, the program performs the necessary validation, invokes the appropriate back-end process (in this case *NACT02*), or sched-
ules a print action, depending on the user request. It displays the data required,
accepts and validates account data, and displays appropriate messages to keep the
user informed of the results of their actions.

There are some important points to note about the implementation of this logic,
which are considerations when using 3270 terminals:

- If a message is returned as the result some part of your program's logic, the
  whole screen is refreshed and the message is displayed.

- The Browse request logic must be adapted to the fact that there may be more
  matches found on file than can be displayed at one time. This actually leads to
  a change in the specification of the browse back-end (*NACT05*) program to
  limit the output and to accept a resume browse request.

- The *NACT* transaction expects the program to supply the data in a form suitable for printing, when it performs the print scheduling function.

The program implements the standard error handling approach designed for the
application. It uses CICS facilities to identify the error handling program (*NACT04*)
as the one to be invoked in the event of an abend occurring as well as using it to
process any unexpected errors that may arise.

Defining Screens with Basic Mapping Support (BMS)

At the beginning of the first program (*NACT01*), one of the first things you need to
do is to write a formatted screen to the input terminal. This requires the use of
CICS terminal input/output services and the most common tool that is used is
Basic Mapping Support (BMS). This is probably the easiest way to set up the 3270
interface. That said, let's now plunge in and try to code our sample application. If
you are new to BMS, you may find some of this a little tedious, but once you have
coded a few maps, the coding discipline becomes quite understandable.

First, some background information. CICS supports a wide variety of terminals,
from ATMs to retail store systems. In this book, however, we cover only the most
common CICS terminals—those of the IBM 3270 system. The sample in this book

is relatively simple, so there are only features that do not depend on a particular terminal access method, and we only cover formatted output. For detailed information, see the *CICS Application Programming Guide* on the CD-ROM.

What Is BMS and What Does It Do?

BMS simplifies your programming job, keeping your code largely independent of any changes in your network of terminals and of any changes in the terminal types. It's probably easiest to define what BMS does by examining the menu screen that is part of our initial program; see Figure 11-1. It all looks quite straightforward, even if there is a lot of detail.

```
ACCOUNTS MENU

    TO SEARCH BY NAME, ENTER SURNAME AND IF REQUIRED, FIRST NAME

        SURNAME    : _                   (1 TO 18 ALPHABETIC CHRS)
        FIRST NAME :                     (1 TO 12 ALPHABETIC CHRS OPTIONAL)

    TO PROCESS AN ACCOUNT, ENTER REQUEST TYPE AND ACCOUNT NUMBER

        REQUEST TYPE:                    (D-DISPLAY, A-ADD, M-MODIFY, X-DELETE, P-PRINT)
        ACCOUNT     :                    (10000 TO 79999)
        PRINTER ID  :                    (1 TO 4 CHARACTERS (REQUIRED FOR PRINT REQUEST))




    ENTER DATA AND PRESS ENTER FOR SEARCH OR ACCOUNT REQUEST OR PRESS CLEAR TO EXIT
 1A     b                                                                  05/022
```

Figure 11-1. The menu screen

You define this screen with BMS macros, which are a form of System/390 Assembler language. When you've defined the whole map, put some job control language (JCL) around it and assemble it. You assemble it twice, in fact. One of the assemblies produces the *physical map*. This gets stored in one of the execution-time libraries, just like a program, and CICS uses it when it executes a program using this particular screen. However, this physical map does not contain any executable code—the physical map is stored in a program library to enable it to be loaded and unloaded like code.

The physical map contains the information BMS needs to:

- Build the screen, with all the titles and labels in their proper places and all the proper attributes for the various fields.

- Merge the variable data from your program in the proper places on the screen when the screen is sent to the terminal.

- Extract the variable data for your program when the screen is received.

The information is in an encoded form comprehensible only to BMS; fortunately we never need to examine this ourselves.

The other assembly produces a structure which we call the *symbolic description map*. This structure defines all of the variable fields (the ones you might read or write in your program), so that you can refer to them by name. The data structure gets placed in a library along with similar copy/include structures like file record layouts, and you simply introduce it into your program in the normal way.

If your company uses a software tool to create maps, like Screen Definition Facility II (SDF II), you can go directly to "Copying the Map Structure into a Program."

Defining a Menu Map Using BMS Macros

To show you how this works, let's go ahead and define the menu map. There are three map-definition macros that you need: DFHMDF to generate a map definition for a field, DFHMDI to generate a map definition, and DFHMSD to generate a map set definition. Don't be put off by the syntax; it's really quite simple when you get used to it. We'll go from the inside out, starting with the individual fields, but be aware that the program object used by BMS is called a MAPSET, which contains one or more maps which, in turn, contain one or more fields.

The DFHMDF macro: generate a map definition for a field

For each field in a map, you need one DFHMDF macro, which looks like this:

```
fldname DFHMDF POS=(line,column),LENGTH=number,
               INITIAL='text',OCCURS=number,
               ATTRB=(attr1,attr2,....)
```

The items in this macro are:

fldname

This is the name of the field, as it is used in the program. Name every field that you intend to read or write in your program, but don't name any field that's constant, other labels, or the stopper fields that define the end of the input field in this screen. For example, see the DFHMDF macro with LENGTH=1 after the FNAMED definition in Example 11-1. The name must begin with a letter, contain only letters and numbers, and can be up to 30 characters long.

DFHMDF

The DFHMDF macro defines a field within a map defined by the DFHMDI macro. A map contains one or more fields.

POS=(line, column)

This is the position on the screen where the field should appear. (In fact, it's the position relative to the beginning of the map. For the purposes of this book, however, screen and map position are the same.) Remember that a field starts with its attribute byte, so if you code POS=(1,1), the attribute byte for that field is on line 1 in column 1 (the top left corner), and the actual data starts in column 2. For the type of maps in this book, you need this parameter for every field.

LENGTH=number

This specifies the length (1–256 bytes) of the field or group of fields. This length should be the maximum length required for application program data to be entered into the field; it should not include the one-byte attribute indicator appended to the field by CICS for use in subsequent processing. The length of each individual subfield within a group must not exceed 256 bytes.

If the *LENGTH* specification in a DFHMDF macro causes the map-defined boundary on the same line to be exceeded, the field on the output screen is continued by wrapping.

INITIAL='text'

This specifies constant or default data for an output field. *INITIAL* is used to specify data in character form; *XINIT* is used to specify data in hexadecimal form. For fields with the detectable (*DET*) attribute, initial data that begins with one of the following characters: ? > & blank that should be supplied.

GRPNAME='name'

This is the name used to generate symbolic storage defintions and to combine specific fields under one group name. For example, a group of fields such as a continuous string of characters, (04 11 2000) can be displayed on the screen as 04:11:2000 where the additional characters can be inserted from the map.

OCCURS='number'

This specifies that the indicated number of entries for the field are to be generated in a map, and that the map definition is to be generated in such a way that the fields are addressable as entries in a matrix or an array. This permits several data fields to be addressed by the same name (subscripted) without generating a unique name for each field.

OCCURS and *GRPNAME* are mutually exclusive; *OCCURS* cannot be used when fields have been defined under a group name. If this operand is omitted, a value of *OCCURS*=1 is assumed.

ATTRB=(attr1,attr2,...)

These are the attributes of the field, and there are a number of different characteristics you can specify. The first is the display intensity of the field, and your choices are:

NORM, BRT, DRK

NORM normal display intensity.

BRT specifies that a high-intensity display of the field is required. Because of the 3270 attribute character bit assignments, a field specified as *BRT* is also potentially detectable. However, for the field to be recognized as detectable by BMS, *DET* must also be specified.

DRK specifies that the field is nonprint/nondisplay. *DRK* cannot be specified if *DET* is specified.

ASKIP, PROT, UNPROT, NUM

ASKIP (autoskip) is the default and specifies that data cannot be keyed into the field and causes the cursor to skip over the field.

PROT specifies that data cannot be keyed into the field. If data is to be copied from one device to another attached to the same 3270 control unit, the first position (address 0) in the buffer of the device to be copied from must not contain an attribute byte for a protected field. Therefore, when preparing maps for 3270s, ensure that the first map of any page does not contain a protected field starting at position 0.

UNPROT specifies that data can be keyed into the field.

NUM ensures that the data entry keyboard is set to numeric shift for this field unless the operator presses the alpha-shift key, and prevents entry of nonnumeric data if the Keyboard Numeric Lock feature is installed.

FSET, IC, DET

FSET specifies that the modified data tag (*MDT*) for this field should be set when the field is sent to a terminal. Specification of *FSET* causes the 3270 to treat the field as though it has been modified. On a subsequent read from the terminal, this field is read back, whether or not it has been modified. The *MDT* remains set until the field is rewritten without *ATTRB=FSET*, or until an output mapping request causes the *MDT* to be reset.

Insert Cursor *IC* specifies that the cursor is to be placed in the first position of the field. The *IC* attribute for the last field for which it is specified in a map is the one that takes effect. If not specified for any fields in a map, the default location is zero. Specifying *IC* with *ASKIP* or *PROT* causes the cursor to be placed in an unkeyable field.

DET specifies that the field is potentially detectable. The first character of a 3270 detectable field must be one of the following: ? > & blank . If ? or >

the field is a selection field; if *&* or *blank*, the field is an attention field. A field for which *BRT* is specified is potentially detectable to the 3270, because of the 3270 attribute character bit assignments, but is not recognized as such by BMS unless *DET* is also specified.

DET and DRK are mutually exclusive

You don't need the *ATTRB* parameter. If you omit it, the field will be *ASKIP* and *NORM*, with no *FSET* and no *IC* specified. If you specify either the protection or the intensity characteristics, however, it will be clearer if you specify both, because the specification of one can change the default for the other.

The DFHMDI macro: generate BMS map definition

At the beginning of each map there is a macro, DFHMDI, which provides the control information:

```
mapname DFHMDI SIZE=(line,column),
               CTRL=(ctrl1,ctrl2,...)
```

The items in this macro are:

mapname

This is the name (1–7 characters) of the map.

DFHMDI

This is the macro identifier, also required. It shows that you're starting a new map.

SIZE=(line, column)

This parameter gives the size of the map. You need it for the type of maps we're using. BMS allows you to build a screen using several maps, and this parameter becomes important when you are doing that. In this book, however, we'll keep to the simpler situation where there's only one map per screen. In this case, there's no point in using a size other than the screen capacity.

CTRL=(ctrl1,ctrl2,...)

This defines characteristics of IBM 3270 terminals. This parameter shows the screen and keyboard control information that you want sent along with a map. Use of any of the control options in the *SEND MAP* command overrides all control options in the DFHMDI macro, which in turn overrides all control options in the DFHMSD macro.

PRINT

This must be specified if the printer is to be started; if omitted, the data is sent to the printer buffer but is not printed. This operand is ignored if the mapset is used with 3270 displays without the Printer Adapter feature.

LENGTH

This indicates the line length on the printer; length can be specified as L40, L64, L80, or HONEOM. L40, L64, and L80 force a new line after 40, 64, or 80 characters, respectively. HONEOM causes the default printer line length to be used. If this option is omitted, BMS sets the line length from the terminal definition.

FREEKB

This causes the keyboard to be unlocked after the map is written. If *FREEKB* is not specified, the keyboard remains locked; data entry from the keyboard is inhibited until this status is changed.

ALARM

This activates the 3270 audible alarm. For non-3270 VTAM terminals, it sets the alarm flag in the command section of the data stream (FMH) passed to the device.

FRSET

This specifies that the modified data tags (MDTs) of all fields currently in the 3270 buffer are to be reset to a not-modified condition (that is, field reset) before map data is written to the buffer. This allows the DFHMDF macro with the *ATTRB* operand to control the final status of any fields written or rewritten in response to a BMS command.

The DFHMSD macro: generate BMS map set definition

You can put several maps together into a map set. In fact, all maps (even a single map) must form a map set. For efficiency reasons, it's a good idea to put related maps that are generally used in the same transactions in the same map set. All the maps in a map set get assembled together, and they're loaded together at execution time as well. So far you have defined only one map but our sample uses more than one map; see "Map Definitions for the Sample Application."

When you've defined all the maps for a set, you put another macro in front of all the others to define the map set. This is the DFHMSD macro:

```
mapset DFHMSD TYPE=type,MODE=mode,LANG=COBOL,
              STORAGE=AUTO,TIOAPFX=YES,
              CTRL=(ctrl1,ctrl2,...)
```

The items in this macro are:

mapset

This is the name of the map set. You use it when you issue a CICS command to read or write one of the maps in the set; it's required. Like a field name, it must start with a letter, consist of only letters and numbers, and be no more than seven characters long.

Because this name goes into the list of installed program definitions, make sure your system programmer (or whoever maintains these lists) knows what the name is, and that neither of you changes it without telling the other. It is the load module name.

DFHMSD

This is the macro identifier, also required. It shows that you're starting a map set.

TYPE=type

This specifies the type of map to be generated using the definition. Both types of map must be generated before the mapset can be used by an application program. If aligned symbolic description maps are required, you should ensure that you specify *SYSPARM=ADSECT* and *SYSPARM=AMAP* when you assemble the symbolic and physical maps respectively:

DSECT

This specifies that a symbolic description map is to be generated. Symbolic description maps must be copied or included into the source program before it is compiled.

MAP

This specifies that a physical map is to be generated. Physical maps must be assembled or compiled, link-edited, and cataloged in the CICS program library before an application program can use them. TYPE governs whether the assembly produces the physical map or the symbolic description (DSECT).

As we pointed out in "What Is BMS and What Does It Do?", you do your assembly twice, once with *TYPE=MAP* specified and once with *TYPE=DSECT* specified. The *TYPE* parameter is required; see "Symbolic Description Maps."

MODE=mode

This shows whether the maps are used only for input, *MODE=IN;* only for output, *MODE=OUT;* or for both, *MODE=INOUT.*

LANG=COBOL

This specifies the source language of the application programs into which the symbolic description maps in the mapset are copied. This option need only be coded for *DFHMSD TYPE=DSECT.* If a mapset is to be used by more than one program, and the programs are not all written in the same source language, a separate version of the mapset must be defined for each programming language. This decides the language of the DSECT structure for copying into the application program. For the examples in this book, the language is COBOL. However, you can program in Assembler, PL/I, C, or C++ (in which case you would code an appropriate LANG= statement).

STORAGE=AUTO

The meaning of this operand depends upon the language in which application programs are written. For a COBOL program, *STORAGE=AUTO* specifies that the symbolic description maps in the mapset are to occupy separate (that is, not redefined) areas of storage. This operand is used when the symbolic description maps are copied into the working-storage section and the storage for the separate maps in the mapset is to be used concurrently. For other languages, see the *CICS Application Programming Reference.*

TIOAPFX=YES

This specifies whether BMS should include a filler in the symbolic description maps to allow for the unused TIOA prefix. The alternatives are YES or NO.

CTRL=(ctrl1,ctrl2,...)

This parameter has the same meaning as in the DFHMDI macro. Control specifications in the DFHMSD macro apply to all the maps in the set; those on the DFHMDI macro apply only to that particular map, so you can use the DFHMDI options to override those of the DFHMSD macro.

Since all the maps in the sample application are used together, we'll put them all into a single map set and call it *NACTSET.* The DFHMSD macro we need, then, is:

```
NACTSET DFHMSD TYPE=MAP,MODE=INOUT,LANG=COBOL,TIOAPFX=YES,STORAGE=AUTO
```

The only thing now missing from our map definition is the control information to show where the mapset ends. This is very simple: It's another macro, DFHMSD TYPE=FINAL, followed by the Assembler *END* statement:

```
DFHMSD TYPE=FINAL
END
```

Rules on macro formats

When you write assembler language (which is what you are doing when using these macros), you have to observe some syntax rules. Here's a simple set of format rules that works. This is by no means the only acceptable format:

- Start the mapset, map, or field name (if any) in column 1.
- Put the macro name (DFHMDF, DFHMDI, or DFHMSD) in columns 9 through 14 (*END* goes in 9 through 11).
- Start your parameters in column 16. You can put them in any order you like.
- Separate the parameters by one comma (no spaces), but do not put a comma after the last one.
- If you cannot get everything into 71 columns, stop after the comma that follows the last parameter that fits on the line, and resume in column 16 of the next line.

- The *INITIAL* parameter is an exception to the rule just stated, because the text portion may be very long. Be sure you can get the word *INITIAL*, the equal sign, the first quote mark, and at least one character of text in by column 71. If you can't, start a new line in column 16, as you would with any other parameter. Once you've started the *INITIAL* parameter, continue across as many lines as you need, using all the columns from 16 to 71. After the last character of your text, put a final quote mark.

- Where you have more than one line for a single macro (because of initial values or any other parameters), put an "X" (or any character except a space) in column 72 of all lines except the last. This continuation character is very important. It's easy to forget, but this upsets the Assembler.

- Always surround initial values by single quote marks. If you need a single quote within your text, use two successive single quotes, and the Assembler will know you want just one; similarly with a single "&" character. For example:

```
INITIAL='MRS. O''LEARY''S COW && BULL'
```

- If you want to put a comment into your map, use a separate line. Put an asterisk (*) in column 1, and use any part of columns 2 through 71 for your text. Do not go beyond column 71.

Map Definitions for the Sample Application

Now that you have all the information you need for building maps, you've done the menu map, we'll look at the next map in a lot more detail.

Defining the account detail map

Figure 11-2 shows the map in an account record screen. It's used for displaying and printing the record, and for additions, modifications, and deletions.

Example 11-1 shows the map definition for this screen; after the code there are notes on some of the macros.

Notes on the Account Detail map

The highlighted numbers (1-6) are not part of the code:

1. There is a suffix on each of the labels to tell which map the field is from; in this map the suffix is "D", for detail. This is the same in the menu (M) and is repeated in subsequent maps. Thus, the account number is ACCTM in the menu map and ACCTD in the detail map. This is simply for clarity and to avoid having to use COBOL qualifiers to distinguish between fields with the same name. You could just as easily have used a prefix instead of a suffix; neither is a BMS requirement.

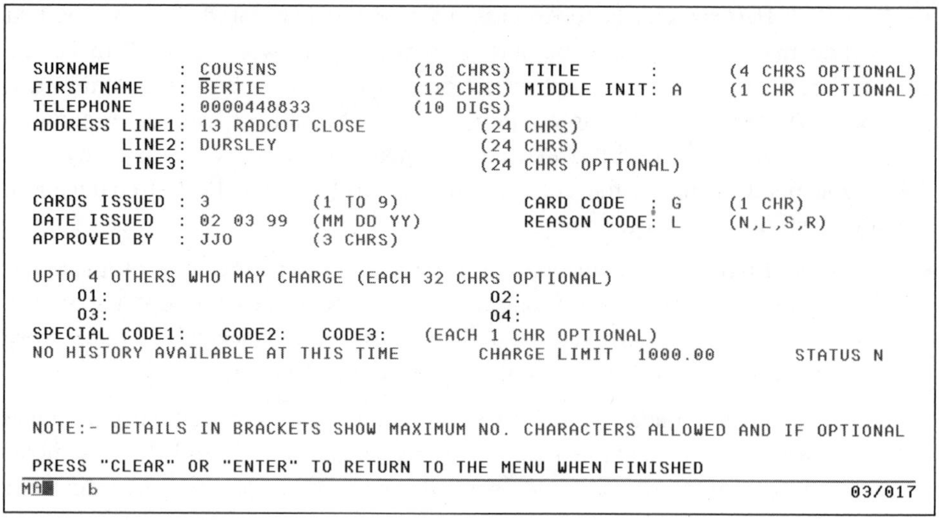

```
   SURNAME      : COUSINS          (18 CHRS) TITLE    :      (4 CHRS OPTIONAL)
   FIRST NAME   : BERTIE           (12 CHRS) MIDDLE INIT: A  (1 CHR  OPTIONAL)
   TELEPHONE    : 0000448833       (10 DIGS)
   ADDRESS LINE1: 13 RADCOT CLOSE     (24 CHRS)
           LINE2: DURSLEY             (24 CHRS)
           LINE3:                     (24 CHRS OPTIONAL)

   CARDS ISSUED : 3       (1 TO 9)      CARD CODE  : G   (1 CHR)
   DATE ISSUED  : 02 03 99  (MM DD YY)  REASON CODE: L   (N,L,S,R)
   APPROVED BY  : JJO      (3 CHRS)

   UPTO 4 OTHERS WHO MAY CHARGE (EACH 32 CHRS OPTIONAL)
      01:                          02:
      03:                          04:
   SPECIAL CODE1:   CODE2:   CODE3:   (EACH 1 CHR OPTIONAL)
   NO HISTORY AVAILABLE AT THIS TIME       CHARGE LIMIT  1000.00      STATUS N



   NOTE:- DETAILS IN BRACKETS SHOW MAXIMUM NO. CHARACTERS ALLOWED AND IF OPTIONAL

   PRESS "CLEAR" OR "ENTER" TO RETURN TO THE MENU WHEN FINISHED
 MA█    b                                                             03/017
```

Figure 11-2. The Account Detail screen

Example 11-1. The Account Detail Screen BMS Macro Definitions

```
ACCTDTL DFHMDI SIZE=(24,80),CTRL=(FREEKB,PRINT)
        DFHMDF POS=(01,01),ATTRB=(ASKIP,BRT),LENGTH=8,           X
               INITIAL='ACCOUNTS
TITLED  DFHMDF POS=(01,19),ATTRB=(ASKIP,NORM),LENGTH=10,         X    1
               INITIAL='DETAILS OF'                                   2
        DFHMDF POS=(01,30),ATTRB=(ASKIP,NORM),LENGTH=14,         X
               INITIAL='ACCOUNT NUMBER'
ACCTD   DFHMDF POS=(01,45),ATTRB=(ASKIP,BRT),LENGTH=5
        DFHMDF POS=(01,51),ATTRB=(ASKIP,NORM),LENGTH=1
        DFHMDF POS=(03,01),ATTRB=(ASKIP,BRT),LENGTH=7,INITIAL='SURNAME'
        DFHMDF POS=(03,14),ATTRB=(ASKIP,BRT),LENGTH=1,INITIAL=':'
LNAMED  DFHMDF POS=(03,16),ATTRB=(UNPROT,NORM,IC),LENGTH=18           3
        DFHMDF POS=(03,35),ATTRB=(ASKIP,NORM),LENGTH=9,          X
               INITIAL='(18 CHRS)'
        DFHMDF POS=(03,45),ATTRB=(ASKIP,BRT),LENGTH=5,INITIAL='TITLE'
        DFHMDF POS=(03,56),ATTRB=(ASKIP,BRT),LENGTH=1,INITIAL=':'
TTLD    DFHMDF POS=(03,58),ATTRB=(UNPROT,NORM),LENGTH=4
        DFHMDF POS=(03,63),ATTRB=(ASKIP,NORM),LENGTH=17,         X
               INITIAL='(4 CHRS OPTIONAL)'
        DFHMDF POS=(04,01),ATTRB=(ASKIP,BRT),LENGTH=10,          X
               INITIAL='FIRST NAME'
        DFHMDF POS=(04,14),ATTRB=(ASKIP,BRT),LENGTH=1,INITIAL=':'
FNAMED  DFHMDF POS=(04,16),ATTRB=(UNPROT,NORM),LENGTH=12
        DFHMDF POS=(04,29),ATTRB=(ASKIP,NORM),LENGTH=1
        DFHMDF POS=(04,35),ATTRB=(ASKIP,NORM),LENGTH=9,          X
               INITIAL='(12 CHRS)'
        DFHMDF POS=(04,45),ATTRB=(ASKIP,BRT),LENGTH=12,          X
               INITIAL='MIDDLE INIT:'
MID     DFHMDF POS=(04,58),ATTRB=(UNPROT,NORM),LENGTH=1
        DFHMDF POS=(04,60),ATTRB=(ASKIP,NORM),LENGTH=1
        DFHMDF POS=(04,63),ATTRB=(ASKIP,NORM),LENGTH=17,         X
```

Example 11-1. The Account Detail Screen BMS Macro Definitions (continued)

```
              INITIAL='(1 CHR  OPTIONAL)'
         DFHMDF POS=(05,01),ATTRB=(ASKIP,BRT),LENGTH=9,             X
              INITIAL='TELEPHONE'
         DFHMDF POS=(05,14),ATTRB=(ASKIP,BRT),LENGTH=1,INITIAL=':'
TELD     DFHMDF POS=(05,16),ATTRB=(NUM,NORM),LENGTH=10
         DFHMDF POS=(05,27),ATTRB=(ASKIP,NORM),LENGTH=1
         DFHMDF POS=(05,35),ATTRB=(ASKIP,NORM),LENGTH=9,            X
              INITIAL='(10 DIGS)'
         DFHMDF POS=(06,01),ATTRB=(ASKIP,BRT),LENGTH=14,            X
              INITIAL='ADDRESS LINE1:'
ADDR1D   DFHMDF POS=(06,16),ATTRB=(UNPROT,NORM),LENGTH=24
         DFHMDF POS=(06,41),ATTRB=(ASKIP,NORM),LENGTH=9,            X
              INITIAL='(24 CHRS)'
         DFHMDF POS=(07,09),ATTRB=(ASKIP,BRT),LENGTH=6,INITIAL='LINE2:'
ADDR2D   DFHMDF POS=(07,16),ATTRB=(UNPROT,NORM),LENGTH=24
         DFHMDF POS=(07,41),ATTRB=(ASKIP,NORM),LENGTH=9,            X
              INITIAL='(24 CHRS)'
         DFHMDF POS=(08,09),ATTRB=(ASKIP,BRT),LENGTH=6,INITIAL='LINE3:'
ADDR3D   DFHMDF POS=(08,16),ATTRB=(UNPROT,NORM),LENGTH=24
         DFHMDF POS=(08,41),ATTRB=(ASKIP,NORM),LENGTH=18,           X
              INITIAL='(24 CHRS OPTIONAL)'
         DFHMDF POS=(10,01),ATTRB=(ASKIP,BRT),LENGTH=14,            X
              INITIAL='CARDS ISSUED :'
CARDSD   DFHMDF POS=(10,16),ATTRB=(NUM,NORM),LENGTH=1
         DFHMDF POS=(10,18),ATTRB=(ASKIP,NORM),LENGTH=1
         DFHMDF POS=(10,26),ATTRB=(ASKIP,NORM),LENGTH=8,            X
              INITIAL='(1 TO 9)'
         DFHMDF POS=(10,45),ATTRB=(ASKIP,BRT),LENGTH=12,            X
              INITIAL='CARD CODE  :'
CCODED   DFHMDF POS=(10,58),ATTRB=(UNPROT,NORM),LENGTH=1
         DFHMDF POS=(10,60),ATTRB=(ASKIP,NORM),LENGTH=1
         DFHMDF POS=(10,63),ATTRB=(ASKIP,NORM),LENGTH=7,            X
              INITIAL='(1 CHR)'
         DFHMDF POS=(11,01),ATTRB=(ASKIP,BRT),LENGTH=14,            X
              INITIAL='DATE ISSUED  :'
IMOD     DFHMDF POS=(11,16),ATTRB=(NUM,NORM),LENGTH=2
IDAYD    DFHMDF POS=(11,19),ATTRB=(NUM,NORM),LENGTH=2
IYRD     DFHMDF POS=(11,22),ATTRB=(NUM,NORM),LENGTH=2
         DFHMDF POS=(11,25),ATTRB=(ASKIP,NORM),LENGTH=11,           X
              INITIAL=' (MM DD YY)'
         DFHMDF POS=(11,45),ATTRB=(ASKIP,BRT),LENGTH=12,            X
              INITIAL='REASON CODE:'
RSND     DFHMDF POS=(11,58),ATTRB=(UNPROT,NORM),LENGTH=1
         DFHMDF POS=(11,60),ATTRB=(ASKIP,NORM),LENGTH=1
         DFHMDF POS=(11,63),ATTRB=(ASKIP,NORM),LENGTH=9,            X
              INITIAL='(N,L,S,R)'
         DFHMDF POS=(12,01),ATTRB=(ASKIP,BRT),LENGTH=14,            X
              INITIAL='APPROVED BY  :'
APPRD    DFHMDF POS=(12,16),ATTRB=(UNPROT,NORM),LENGTH=3
         DFHMDF POS=(12,20),ATTRB=(ASKIP,NORM),LENGTH=1
         DFHMDF POS=(12,26),ATTRB=(ASKIP,NORM),LENGTH=8,
              INITIAL='(3 CHRS)'
```

4

Example 11-1. The Account Detail Screen BMS Macro Definitions (continued)

```
         DFHMDF POS=(14,01),ATTRB=(ASKIP,NORM),LENGTH=52,INITIAL='UPTO
                OTHERS WHO MAY CHARGE (EACH 32 CHRS OPTIONAL)'
         DFHMDF POS=(15,05),ATTRB=(ASKIP,BRT),LENGTH=3,INITIAL='01:'
AUTH1D   DFHMDF POS=(15,09),ATTRB=(UNPROT,NORM),LENGTH=32
         DFHMDF POS=(15,42),ATTRB=(ASKIP,BRT),LENGTH=3,INITIAL='02:'
AUTH2D   DFHMDF POS=(15,46),ATTRB=(UNPROT,NORM),LENGTH=32
         DFHMDF POS=(15,79),ATTRB=(ASKIP,NORM),LENGTH=1
         DFHMDF POS=(16,05),ATTRB=(ASKIP,BRT),LENGTH=3,INITIAL='03:'
AUTH3D   DFHMDF POS=(16,09),ATTRB=(UNPROT,NORM),LENGTH=32
         DFHMDF POS=(16,42),ATTRB=(ASKIP,BRT),LENGTH=3,INITIAL='04:'
AUTH4D   DFHMDF POS=(16,46),ATTRB=(UNPROT,NORM),LENGTH=32
         DFHMDF POS=(16,79),ATTRB=(ASKIP,NORM),LENGTH=1
         DFHMDF POS=(17,01),ATTRB=(ASKIP,BRT),LENGTH=14,
                INITIAL='SPECIAL CODE1:'
SCODE1D  DFHMDF POS=(17,16),ATTRB=(UNPROT,NORM),LENGTH=1
         DFHMDF POS=(17,18),ATTRB=(ASKIP,BRT),LENGTH=6,INITIAL='CODE2:'
SCODE2D  DFHMDF POS=(17,25),ATTRB=(UNPROT,NORM),LENGTH=1
         DFHMDF POS=(17,27),ATTRB=(ASKIP,BRT),LENGTH=6,INITIAL='CODE3:'
SCODE3D  DFHMDF POS=(17,34),ATTRB=(UNPROT,NORM),LENGTH=1
         DFHMDF POS=(17,36),ATTRB=(ASKIP,NORM),LENGTH=21,
                INITIAL='(EACH 1 CHR OPTIONAL)'
HISTTLD  DFHMDF POS=(18,01),ATTRB=(ASKIP,NORM),LENGTH=33,          X   5
                INITIAL='NO HISTORY AVAILABLE AT THIS TIME'
         DFHMDF POS=(18,35),ATTRB=(ASKIP,NORM),LENGTH=1
LIMTTLD  DFHMDF POS=(18,41),ATTRB=(ASKIP,NORM),LENGTH=12,          X
                INITIAL='CHARGE LIMIT'
LIMITD   DFHMDF POS=(18,54),ATTRB=(ASKIP,NORM),LENGTH=8
         DFHMDF POS=(18,63),ATTRB=(ASKIP,NORM),LENGTH=1
STATTLD  DFHMDF POS=(18,69),ATTRB=(ASKIP,NORM),LENGTH=6,           X
                INITIAL='STATUS'
STATD    DFHMDF POS=(18,76),ATTRB=(ASKIP,NORM),LENGTH=2
         DFHMDF POS=(18,79),ATTRB=(ASKIP,NORM),LENGTH=1
VFYTLD   DFHMDF POS=(20,01),ATTRB=(ASKIP,BRT),LENGTH=26
VFYD     DFHMDF POS=(20,28),ATTRB=(ASKIP,NORM),LENGTH=1                 6
         DFHMDF POS=(20,30),ATTRB=(ASKIP,NORM),LENGTH=1
         DFHMDF POS=(22,01),ATTRB=(ASKIP,NORM),LENGTH=78,          X
                INITIAL='NOTE:- DETAILS IN BRACKETS SHOW MAXIMUM NO. CHAX
                RACTERS ALLOWED AND IF OPTIONAL'
MSGD     DFHMDF POS=(24,01),ATTRB=(ASKIP,BRT),LENGTH=60
         DFHMDF POS=(24,62),ATTRB=(ASKIP,NORM),LENGTH=1
```

2. In this field, this value applies to the most common situation: display record details. This initial value is not a constant, as it is in the fields without labels, but a default. The field is set to a different value by the program for adds, modifies, and other uses of the screen. Notice that it has a label, so that the program has access to it.

3. This is normally the first field into which the user is to enter data, and therefore is a good place to put the cursor. This is a default specification; the program can and often overrides it.

4. You don't need a stopper field for an input field if another input field follows immediately.

5. These title fields should appear on all the displays except the skeleton screen for adding new records. It's easiest to put them in the map, therefore, and simply remove for an add operation. All you have to do is to set the attribute byte to *nondisplay* in that one case. To enable the program to access the attribute bytes, you need to add labels on the fields.

6. This field is used only for deletions, so the default value for the attribute byte will be autoskip (ASKIP). That way the user won't even be aware of the field when using the map for other transactions. For deletions, the program changes the attribute byte to be unprotected.

Defining the error map

When CICS abends our transaction, it is stopped in its tracks; detected errors are also processed by the same logic (*NACT04*). This screen (shown in Figure 11-3) is used to display error information if the transaction abended and was run at a 3270 terminal.

```
ACCOUNT FILE: ERROR REPORT

ERROR AT 25/04/2000 16:02:46

 Error in transaction NACT, program NACT05  .
 Type is TRAP. Response is DISABLED    , Reason is 0050 - STARTBR


PLEASE ASK YOUR SUPERVISOR TO CONVEY THIS INFORMATION TO THE
OPERATIONS STAFF.

THEN PRESS "CLEAR".  THIS TERMINAL IS NO LONGER UNDER CONTROL OF
THE "NACT" APPLICATION.
```

Figure 11-3. The Error screen

The Mapset

If we put together the three maps that we've now defined (the menu map, detail map, and error map), the results are shown in Example 11-2.

Example 11-2. Example of the DFHMSD Macro

```
ACCTSET DFHMSD TYPE=MAP,MODE=INOUT,LANG=COBOL,
               STORAGE=AUTO,TIOAPFX=YES
    *       MENU MAP.
ACCTMNU DFHMDI SIZE=(24,80),CTRL=(PRINT,FREEKB)
        DFHMDF ... (all macros for the menu map)
    *
    *       DETAIL MAP.
ACCTDTL DFHMDI SIZE=(24,80),CTRL=(PRINT,FREEKB)
        DFHMDF ... (all macros for the detail map)
    *
```

Example 11-2. Example of the DFHMSD Macro (continued)

```
*     ERROR MAP.
ACCTERR DFHMDI SIZE=(24,80),CTRL=FREEKB
        DFHMDF ... (all macros for the error map)
        DFHMSD TYPE=FINAL
        END
```

Symbolic Description Maps

Assembling the macros with *TYPE=MAP* specified in the DFHMSD macro produces the physical map that CICS uses at execution time. After you've done this assembly, you do it all over again, this time specifying *TYPE=DSECT*. This second assembly produces the *symbolic description map*, a structure that you copy or include into your program. It's stored in the copybook or include library specified in the JCL, and its name in that library is the map set name specified in the DFHMSD macro.

This structure is a set of data definitions for all the display fields on the screen, plus information about those fields. It allows your program to refer to these display data fields by name and to manipulate the way in which they are displayed, without worrying about their size or position on the screen.

Copying the Map Structure into a Program

To copy the structures for the maps in a mapset into a program in COBOL, you write a *COPY* statement like this:

```
COPY mapset (name).
```

For other languages you use the appropriate include syntax, for example use the import statement in Java or the include statement in C or C++.

Here, *mapset (name)* is the name of the mapset. This *COPY* statement usually appears in WORKING-STORAGE, although later you may find reasons to put it in the LINKAGE SECTION. We'll cover only the WORKING-STORAGE situation. To get the symbolic descriptions for our maps in a program, write:

```
COPY NACTSET.
```

Example 11-3 shows you the first few lines of what is copied into your program as a result of this *COPY* statement. The part shown is generated by the first map in the set, the menu map. It's followed by similar structures for the other maps. They are very long and very similar in form. They're all on the accompanying CD-ROM; see "Configuring Your CICS for OS/390 Environment" in Appendix A for details.

Example 11-3. Actual Structure That Is Copied into Your Program (Part Shown Only)

```
01  ACCTMNUI.
    02  FILLER PIC X(12).
    02  SNAMEML    COMP PIC  S9(4).
    02  SNAMEMF    PICTURE X.
    02  FILLER REDEFINES SNAMEMF.
       03 SNAMEMA    PICTURE X.
    02  SNAMEMI  PIC X(12).
    02  FNAMEML    COMP PIC  S9(4).
    02  FNAMEMF    PICTURE X.
    02  FILLER REDEFINES FNAMEMF.
       03 FNAMEMA    PICTURE X.
```

In Example 11-2, you defined the map set to be used for both input and output (by coding *MODE=INOUT* in the DFHMSD macro); the resulting structure has two parts. The first part corresponds to the input screen, and is always labeled (at the 01 level) with the map name, suffixed by the letter I (for *input*). The second part corresponds to the output screen, and is labeled with the map name followed by the letter O. The output map always redefines the input map. If you'd specified *MODE=IN*, only the input part would have been generated, and similarly, *MODE=OUT* would have produced only the output part. Notice that for each of these map fields, five data subfields are generated.

Notes on DSECTs

Here are some things to keep in mind about *DSECTs*:

- Because of the way the input and output parts of the map structure overlay each other, the -I and the -O subfields for a given map field always redefine each other. That is, SNAMEMI and SNAMEMO occupy the same storage that FNAMEMI and FNAMEMO do, and so on. This turns out to be convenient in coding.

- The flag and attribute subfields occupy the same space (REQMF overlays REQMA, ACCTMF overlays ACCTMA, and so on). You don't have to worry about removing these flags when you're sending output. Because the four input flag values (X'82', X'80', X'02' and X'00') don't represent acceptable output attribute byte values, BMS can distinguish on output between a leftover flag and a new attribute.

- When you send a map, you don't have to put anything in the length field. BMS knows how long the field is from the information in the physical map. The only time you use the length field for an output field is to set the cursor position; this will be explained shortly.

Sending a Map to a Terminal

Now that you've defined your maps, you can think about writing them to a terminal. The terminal to which you write, of course, is the one that sent the input and thereby invoked the transaction. This is the only terminal to which a transaction can write directly.

The SEND MAP Command

The *EXEC CICS SEND MAP* command writes formatted data to a terminal. It looks like this:

```
EXEC CICS SEND MAP(name) MAPSET(name)
        options
            ...
END-EXEC
```

The items in this macro are:

MAP (name)

> This specifies the name of the map you want to send. It is limited to 1–7 characters and it's required. Put it in quotes if it's a literal.

MAPSET (name)

> This specifies the unsuffixed name (1–7 characters) of the mapset that you want to send. The mapset must reside in the CICS program library. The mapset can be defined either by using RDO or by the autoinstall program when the mapset is first used. If this option is not specified, the name given in the *MAP* option is assumed to be that of the mapset.

> The number of maps per mapset is limited to a maximum of 9998. Put the name in quotes if it's a literal.

options

> There are a number of options that you can specify; they affect what's sent and how it is sent. Except where noted, you can use any combination of them. The possibilities are:

> *ALARM*

>> This means the same thing in the *SEND* command as it does in the DFHMSD and DFHMDI macros for the map: it causes the audible alarm to be sounded. The alarm sounds if you specify *ALARM* in either the map definition or the *SEND* command.

> *CURSOR(data-value)*

>> This can be used in two ways to position the cursor. If you specify a value after *CURSOR*, it's the relative position on the screen where the cursor is

to be put. Use a single number, such as *CURSOR*(81) for line 2, column 2 (counting starts at zero and goes across the lines, which on an IBM 3270-system display Model 2 are 80 characters wide). Why column 2? Because the attribute byte goes in column 1, and we want the cursor to appear under the first character of data.

Alternatively, you can specify *CURSOR* without a value, and use the length subfields in the output map to show which field is to get the cursor; see "Positioning the Cursor." In general, we recommend you to position the cursor in this second manner, rather than the first, so that changes in the map layout don't lead to changes in the program. Both kinds of *CURSOR* specification override the cursor placement specified in the map.

DATAONLY

This is the logical opposite of *MAPONLY*. You use it to modify the variable data in a display that's already been created. Only the data from your program is sent to the screen. The constants in the map aren't sent; so you can use this option only after you've sent the same map without using the *DATAONLY* option. We'll see an example when we send the results of a name search to the terminal in program *NACT01*.

ERASE

This causes the entire screen to be erased before what you're sending is shown.

ERASEUP (erase all unprotected fields)

This in contrast to *ERASE*, causes just the unprotected fields on the screen (those with either the *UNPROT* or *NUM* attribute) to be erased before your output is placed on the screen. It's most often used in preparing to read new data from a map that's already on the screen. Don't use it at the same time as *ERASE*; *ERASE* makes *ERASEAUP* meaningless.

FRSET (flag reset)

This turns off the modified data tag in the attribute bytes for all the fields on the screen before what you're sending is placed there. Once set on, whether by the user or the program, a modified data tag stays on until turned off explicitly, even over several transmissions of the screen. It can be turned off by the program sending a new attribute byte, an *FRSET* option, or an *ERASE*, or an *ERASEAUP*, or by the user pressing the CLEAR key. Like *ERASEAUP*, the *FRSET* option is most often used in preparing to read new data from a map already on the screen. It can also reduce the amount of data resent on an error cycle, as we'll explain in coding our example.

FREEKB

> This means the same thing as it does in the map definition: the keyboard is unlocked if you specify *FREEKB* in either the map or the *SEND* command.

MAPONLY

> This specifies that only default data from the map is to be written. In our example application, this option is used when we send the menu map the first time, because there is no information to put into it.

PRINT

> This allows the output of a *SEND* command to be printed on a printer, just as it does in the map definition. It is in force if specified in either the map or the command.

FORMFEED

> This causes the printer to restore the paper to the top of the next page before the output is printed. This specification has no effect on maps sent to a display, to printers without the features which allow sensing the top of the form, or to printers for which the *formfeed* feature is not specified in the CICS Terminal Control Table.

Using SEND MAP in the sample application

The first time a map is sent to a terminal occurs in program *NACT01*, the menu screen is displayed. The command we need is:

```
EXEC CICS SEND MAP('ACCTMNU') MAPSET(WS-LITS-MAPSET)
          CURSOR(EIBCPOSN) MAPONLY FRSET FREEKB
          RESP(RESPONSE) RESP2(REASON-CODE)
END-EXEC
```

The option *MAPONLY* states that only the constants within your map are to be sent, so initializing the screen. *NACT01* uses the *DATAONLY* option when the screen has the constants displayed and only the data fields are to be sent. If either of these options is not set then both the constants and the data are sent. CICS would expect the data to be used for filling in the map to be in a structure whose name is the name (as specified in the *MAP* option) suffixed with the letter O. So, when we issue the command:

```
EXEC CICS SEND MAP('ACCTDTL') MAPSET(WS-LITS-MAPSET)
          ERASE FREEKB CURSOR
          RESP(RESPONSE) RESP2(REASON-CODE)
END-EXEC
```

CICS expects the data for the map to be in a structure within the program (of exactly the sort generated by the map structure generation) named *ACCTDTLO*. This structure is usually in your WORKING-STORAGE section, but it might be in a LINKAGE area instead.

There's an option on the *SEND MAP* command that lets you specify a data structure other than the one assumed by CICS. We won't cover it here, but you can find guidance on using it in the *CICS Application Programming Guide.*

Let's look at the more common situation in which we're merging program data into the map. In program *NACT01,* we're supposed to build a detail display map for one record and send it to the screen. Since the contents of the screen vary somewhat with the type of request, and we're using the same screen for all types, this entails the following:

- Putting the appropriate title on the map (add, modify, or whatever it happens to be).

- Moving the data from the file record to the symbolic map (except for adds).

- Adjusting the attribute bytes. The input fields must be protected in a display or delete operation; the *verify* field must be unprotected for deletes, and the titles at the bottom of the screen must be made nondisplay for adds.

- Putting the appropriate user instructions (about what to do next) into the message area.

- Putting the cursor in the right place.

Examples 11-4 through 11-7 show how the necessary code might look for the display of a record.

Example 11-4. Building the Acount Detail Display Map (Part 1)

```
PERFORM BBAB-MOVE-TO-DETAIL-MAP
MOVE -1 TO SNAMEDL
MOVE 'PRESS "CLEAR" OR "ENTER" TO RETURN TO THE MENU WHEN FINISHED'
 TO  MSGDO
PERFORM BBAC-PROTECT-DETAILS
SET CA-DISPLAYING TO TRUE
```

The need to move the details read from the file to the map area occurs in several places, so it has been placed in a common routine (*BBAB-MOVE-TO-DETAIL-MAP*). In order to ensure that the cursor is placed at the beginning of the surname field, its Length field is set to the special value of −1. (More about this later.) An explanatory/operational message is also placed in the map for transmission to the user. Finally the details on display are not modifiable, so we need to protect them by setting their attributes to autoskip (ASKIP). This requirement also occurs in several places so it has been placed in a common routine (*BBAC-PROTECT-DETAILS*).

Example 11-5. Building the Account Detail Display Map (Part 2)

```
BBAB-MOVE-TO-DETAIL-MAP SECTION.
*
* This routine populates the detail map from the data obtained.
*
BBAB-010.
    MOVE ACCTDO    IN NACTREC-DATA TO ACCTDO    IN ACCTDTLO
    MOVE SNAMEDO   IN NACTREC-DATA TO SNAMEDO   IN ACCTDTLO
    MOVE FNAMEDO   IN NACTREC-DATA TO FNAMEDO   IN ACCTDTLO
    MOVE MIDO      IN NACTREC-DATA TO MIDO      IN ACCTDTLO
    MOVE TTLDO     IN NACTREC-DATA TO TTLDO     IN ACCTDTLO
    MOVE TELDO     IN NACTREC-DATA TO TELDO     IN ACCTDTLO
    MOVE ADDR1DO   IN NACTREC-DATA TO ADDR1DO   IN ACCTDTLO
    MOVE ADDR2DO   IN NACTREC-DATA TO ADDR2DO   IN ACCTDTLO
    MOVE ADDR3DO   IN NACTREC-DATA TO ADDR3DO   IN ACCTDTLO
    MOVE AUTH1DO   IN NACTREC-DATA TO AUTH1DO   IN ACCTDTLO
    MOVE AUTH2DO   IN NACTREC-DATA TO AUTH2DO   IN ACCTDTLO
    MOVE AUTH3DO   IN NACTREC-DATA TO AUTH3DO   IN ACCTDTLO
    MOVE AUTH4DO   IN NACTREC-DATA TO AUTH4DO   IN ACCTDTLO
    MOVE CARDSDO   IN NACTREC-DATA TO CARDSDO   IN ACCTDTLO
    MOVE IMODO     IN NACTREC-DATA TO IMODO     IN ACCTDTLO
    MOVE IDAYDO    IN NACTREC-DATA TO IDAYDO    IN ACCTDTLO
    MOVE IYRDO     IN NACTREC-DATA TO IYRDO     IN ACCTDTLO
    MOVE RSNDO     IN NACTREC-DATA TO RSNDO     IN ACCTDTLO
    MOVE CCODEDO   IN NACTREC-DATA TO CCODEDO   IN ACCTDTLO
    MOVE APPRDO    IN NACTREC-DATA TO APPRDO    IN ACCTDTLO
    MOVE SCODE1DO  IN NACTREC-DATA TO SCODE1DO  IN ACCTDTLO
    MOVE SCODE2DO  IN NACTREC-DATA TO SCODE2DO  IN ACCTDTLO
    MOVE SCODE3DO  IN NACTREC-DATA TO SCODE3DO  IN ACCTDTLO
    MOVE STATDO    IN NACTREC-DATA TO STATDO    IN ACCTDTLO
    MOVE LIMITDO   IN NACTREC-DATA TO LIMITDO   IN ACCTDTLO
*
END-BBAB-MOVE-TO-DETAIL-MAP.
    EXIT.
```

Each field is moved individually to the map area. This looks a bit tedious when coding, but is something which must be done. With a good block editor, this can be done in just a few minutes.

Example 11-6. Building the Account Detail Display Map (Part 3)

```
BBAC-PROTECT-DETAILS SECTION.
*
* This routine protects the detail data fields from modification.
*
BBAC-010.
    MOVE DFHBMASK TO SNAMEDA
                     FNAMEDA
                     MIDA
                     TTLDA
                     TELDA
                     ADDR1DA
                     ADDR2DA
```

Example 11-6. Building the Account Detail Display Map (Part 3) (continued)

```
                          ADDR3DA
                          AUTH1DA
                          AUTH2DA
                          AUTH3DA
                          AUTH4DA
                          CARDSDA
                          IMODA
                          IDAYDA
                          IYRDA
                          RSNDA
                          CCODEDA
                          APPRDA
                          SCODE1DA
                          SCODE2DA
                          SCODE3DA
*
  END-BBAC-PROTECT-DETAILS.
      EXIT.
```

All of the data fields on the screen need to be protected from modification, so the same attribute (DFHBMASK, AUTOSKIP) is set for all of them.

Example 11-7. Building the Account Detail Display Map (Part 4)

```
      EXEC CICS SEND MAP('ACCTDTL') MAPSET(WS-LITS-MAPSET)
                  ERASE FREEKB CURSOR
                  RESP(RESPONSE) RESP2(REASON-CODE)
      END-EXEC
```

Finally, the *SEND MAP* command instructs BMS to create and send a data stream to the device by identifying which *MAP* to use (*ACCTDTL*) in which *MAPSET*. Note this latter option references a data name which is included in source code which is copied into the program. The reason for this is to allow flexibility in naming of the objects referenced by the application. The *ERASE* option is included to ensure residual data on the screen is removed. The *FREEKB* option ensures that the user is able to continue work without needing to reset the device. The *CURSOR* option is explained in the following section. The *RESP* option is used in order to allow the program to deal with an abnormal return in a standard way.

Positioning the Cursor

We said earlier how vital it is to put the cursor where the user wants to start entering data on the screen. One small piece of source code from you can save hundreds of users a couple of seconds each and every time they use your application.

In the first *SEND MAP*, we relied on the cursor position specified in the map definition. This puts the cursor under the first data position of the surname field, which is where we want it. In subsequent uses, however, we don't necessarily want the cursor where the map definition puts it. Where we're using the detail map, we want to use the map default (the *LNAMED* field) for adds and modifies. For display operations, it doesn't matter much, there are no fields into which the user may key. For deletes, however, the cursor should be under the verify (*VFY*) field. In the case of user input errors, we want the cursor under the first field where the user entered incorrect information.

As we said, there are two ways to override the position specified by the IC specification in the map definition:

- You can specify a screen position, relative to line 1, column 1 (that is, position 0) in the *CURSOR* option on the *SEND MAP* command. (This can be used to ensure that the cursor remains in the same position that the user left it by using the *EIBCPOSN* field as the argument. This field is described along with the others in the special CICS control area called the EXEC Interface Block (EIB) later.)

- You can show that you want the cursor placed under a particular field by setting the associated length subfield to minus one (−1) and specifying *CURSOR* without a value in your *SEND MAP* command. This causes BMS to place the cursor under the first data position of the field with this length value. If several fields are flagged by this special length subfield value, the cursor is placed under the first one (as opposed to the last one with *ATTRB=IC*).

The second procedure is called *symbolic cursor positioning*, and is a very handy method of positioning the cursor for, say, correcting errors. As the program checks the input, it sets the length subfield to −1 for every field found to be in error. Then, when the map is redisplayed for corrections, BMS automatically puts the cursor under the first field that the user has to correct.

To place the cursor under the verify field on a delete, therefore, all we have to do is:

```
MOVE -1 TO VFYDL
```

and specify *CURSOR* in our *SEND MAP* command.

Sending Control Information Without Data

In addition to the EXEC CICS *SEND MAP* command, there is another terminal output command called *SEND CONTROL*. It allows you to send control information to the terminal without sending any data. That is, you can free/unlock the keyboard, erase all the unprotected fields, and so on, without sending a map.

The *SEND CONTROL* command looks like this:

```
EXEC CICS SEND CONTROL
        options

           ...
        RESP(RESPONSE) RESP2(REASON-CODE)
END-EXEC
```

The options you can use are the same as on a *SEND MAP* command: *ERASE, ERASEUP, FRSET, ALARM, FREEKB, CURSOR, PRINT,* and *FORMFEED*.

There's an example of this command in program *NACT01*. The terminal user has just cleared the screen (of the menu map) to indicate that they want to exit from the control of the online account application. The program is supposed to free/unlock the keyboard before returning control to CICS.

Normally, you would do this when writing a message to the terminal. But since we're not doing that at this point, we must free/unlock the keyboard by an explicit command, instead. Within the sample application the command is:

```
BA-SEND-CONTROL SECTION.
*
* End the pseudo-conversational series of tasks.
* Free the user's keyboard and end without saving
* any data.
*
BA-010.
    EXEC CICS SEND CONTROL
            FREEKB ERASE
            RESP(RESPONSE) RESP2(REASON-CODE)
    END-EXEC
```

We've added the *ERASE* option to the previous command, so that the user would be ready to start a new transaction. This isn't strictly necessary if the user has just cleared the screen, but no harm is done to include it.

Receiving Input from a Terminal

There are two ways to receive input from a terminal, either from the *RECEIVE MAP* command or from input from the keyboard.

The RECEIVE MAP command

When you want to receive input from a terminal, you use the *RECEIVE MAP* command, which looks like this:

```
EXEC CICS RECEIVE MAP(MAPNAME) MAPSET(MAPSETNAME)
                RESP(RESPONSE) RESP2(REASON-CODE)
END-EXEC.
```

The *MAP* and *MAPSET* parameters have exactly the same meaning as for the *SEND MAP* command. *MAP* is required and so is *MAPSET*, unless it is the same as the map name. Again, it does no harm to include it for documentation purposes.

The form of the *RECEIVE MAP* command below does not specify where the input data is to be placed. This causes CICS to bring the data into a structure whose name is the map name suffixed with the letter I, which is assumed to be in either your WORKING-STORAGE or LINKAGE area.

For example, program *NACT01* requires that we receive the filled-in account detail map. The command to do this is:

```
*
  DA-RECEIVE-DETAIL SECTION.
*
* This routine get the detail input from the user.
*
  DA-010.
      MOVE LOW-VALUES TO ACCTDTLI
*
      EXEC CICS RECEIVE MAP('ACCTDTL') MAPSET(WS-LITS-MAPSET)
                    RESP(RESPONSE) RESP2(REASON-CODE)
      END-EXEC
```

It brings the input data into a data area named ACCTDTLI, which is expected to have exactly the format produced by the map generation structure ACCTDTL.

As soon as the map is read in, we have access to all the data subfields associated with the map fields. For example, we can test whether the user made any entry in the request field of:

```
      IF REQML = 0
```

Or we could discover if the user erased the field:

```
      IF REQMF = DFHBMEOF ...
```

Or we could examine the input in that field:

```
      IF REQMI = 'A'
```

This last case is discouraged. Generally we need to retain the data the user has input in a separate area that we will keep across the pseudo-conversational series of transactions used to perform the business function. We will therefore need to *merge* the current user input with whatever had been entered (if relevant) in any previous CICS task relevant to this business operation. Thus any validation or logic determination will be performed from this special area rather than the input directly. One of the main reasons for this relates to the fact that the Input and Output map areas are really descriptions of the same storage as mentioned earlier.

Although it generally does not affect your program logic, you should be aware that the first time in a transaction that you use the *RECEIVE MAP* command, it has a slightly different effect from subsequent times. Since it is input from the terminal that causes a transaction to get started in the first place, CICS has always read the first input by the time the transaction starts to execute. Therefore, on this first *RECEIVE MAP* command, CICS simply arranges the input it already has into the format dictated by your map, and puts the results in a place accessible to your program.

On subsequent *RECEIVE MAP* commands *in the same task*, CICS actually waits for and reads input from the terminal. These subsequent *RECEIVE MAPs* are what make a task conversational. By contrast, a pseudo-conversational task executes at most one *RECEIVE MAP* command. This is the technique we use in the sample application.

Finding Out What Key the Operator Pressed

There is another technique you may wish to use for processing input from a terminal. The 3270 input stream contains an indication of which attention key caused the input to be transmitted (Enter, Clear, or one of the PA or PF keys).

You can use the EXEC Interface Block Attention Identifier (EIBAID) field to change the flow of control in your program based on which of these attention keys was used.

The EXEC Interface Block (EIB)

Before we explain how to find out what key was used to send the input, we need to introduce one CICS control block. This is the EXEC Interface Block (EIB), and it is the only one that you need to know anything about for the type of applications described in this book.

You can write programs without using even this one, but it contains information that is very useful and is sometimes really essential.

There is one EIB for each task, and it exists for the duration of the task. Every program that executes as part of the task has access to the same EIB. You can address the fields in it directly in your COBOL program without any preliminaries. You should only read these fields, however, not try to modify them. All of the EIB fields are discussed in detail in the *CICS Application Programming Reference*, but the ones that are of general use follow.

EIBAID

> Contains the attention identifier (AID) associated with the last terminal control (for example, which keyboard key was last pressed) or basic mapping support (BMS) input operation from a display device such as the 3270. It is coded as shown in later "AID byte definitions."

EIBCALEN

> Contains the length of the communication area that has been passed to the application program from the last program, using the COMMAREA and LENGTH options. If no communication area is passed, this field contains zeros.

EIBCPOSN

> Contains the position of the cursor (the cursor address) at the time of the last input command for 3270-like devices only. This position is expressed as a single number relative to position zero on the screen (row 1, column 1), in the same way that you specify the *CURSOR* parameter on a *SEND MAP* command. This field was mentioned earlier (in the section "Positioning the Cursor") when indicating that there is a technique for retaining the current position of the cursor on the screen.

EIBDATE

> Contains the date the task is started; this field is updated by the *ASKTIME* command. The date is in packed decimal form (0CYYDDD+) where C shows the century with values 0 for the 1900s and 1 for the 2000s. For example, the dates 31 December 1999 and 1 January 2000 have *EIBDATE* values of 0099365 and 0100001, respectively.

EIBDS

> Contains the symbolic identifier of the last data set (file) referred to in a file control request (command), for example, read a record, write a record.

EIBFN

> Contains a code that identifies the last CICS command issued by the task in "PIC X(2)" format. The first byte of this two-byte field indicates the type of command. File commands have a code of X'06', BMS commands are X'18', and so on. The second byte tells which particular command: X'0602' means *READ*, X'0604' means *WRITE*, and so on. A list of the codes for the API appears in the *CICS Application Programming Reference*; a list of the codes for the SPI appears in the *CICS System Programming Reference*. These books are included on the CD-ROM that comes with this book.

EIBRESP

> Contains a number corresponding to the *RESP* condition that has been raised. There is a complete list of symbolic names for these numbers in the *CICS Application Programming Reference*.

EIBRESP2

> Contains more detailed information that may help explain why the RESP condition has been raised. This field contains meaningful values for specific commands.

 The values in the *EIBRESP* and *EIBRESP2* fields of the EIB can also be interrogated using the *RESP* and *RESP2* values on an EXEC CICS command; see Example 11-9.

EIBRSRCE

> Contains the symbolic identifier (name) of the resource being accessed by the latest executed command. For file commands, this value is the *FILE* parameter, so that *EIBRSRCE* has the same value as *EIBDS* after such a command. For BMS commands it is the name of the terminal (the four-character name of the input terminal, or *EIBTRMID* in the context of this book).

EIBTASKN

> Contains the task number assigned to the task by CICS. This number appears in trace table entries generated while the task is in control. CICS assigns a sequential number to each task it executes, and this number is used to identify entries for the task in the Trace Table (if you want to know more about trace and dump refer to the *CICS Problem Determination Guide*).

EIBTIME

> Contains the time at which the current task started, also in "PIC S9(7) COMP-3" form, with one leading zero: "0HHMMSS+". Note that for simpler date processing, we recommend the use of the *ASKTIME* and *FORMATTIME* commands.

EIBTRMID

> Contains the name of the terminal (terminal or logical unit) associated with the task.

EIBTRNID

> Contains the symbolic transaction identifier of the task.

AID byte definitions

Getting back to the attention identifier, we can also tell what key was used to send the input by looking at the *EIBAID* field, as noted above.

When a transaction is started, *EIBAID* is set according to the key used to send the input that caused the transaction to get started. It retains this value through the first *RECEIVE* command, which only formats the input already read, until after a subsequent *RECEIVE*, at which time it is set to the value used to send that input from the terminal.

EIBAID is one byte long and holds the actual attention identifier value used in the 3270 input stream. As it is hard to remember these values and hard to understand code containing them, it is a good idea to use symbolic rather than absolute values when testing *EIBAID*. CICS provides you with a precoded set which you simply copy into your COBOL program by writing:

```
COPY DFHAID.
```

in your *WORKING-STORAGE SECTION*. For other languages the data structure gets placed in a library along with similar copy or include statements to add it into your program in the normal way. Example 11-8 shows some of the definitions this brings into your program.

Example 11-8. The Standard Attention Identifier Values

```
01  DFHAID.
        02  DFHNULL      PIC X VALUE IS ' '.
        02  DFHENTER     PIC X VALUE IS ''''.
        02  DFHCLEAR     PIC X VALUE IS '_'.
        02  DFHCLRP      PIC X VALUE IS ' '.
        02  DFHPEN       PIC X VALUE IS '='.
        02  DFHOPID      PIC X VALUE IS 'W'.
        02  DFHMSRE      PIC X VALUE IS 'X'.
        02  DFHSTRF      PIC X VALUE IS ' '.
        02  DFHTRIG      PIC X VALUE IS '"'.
        02  DFHPA1       PIC X VALUE IS '%'.
        02  DFHPA2       PIC X VALUE IS '>'.
        02  DFHPA3       PIC X VALUE IS ','.
        02  DFHPF1       PIC X VALUE IS '1'.
        02  DFHPF2       PIC X VALUE IS '2'.
             . . .
             . . .
        02  DFHPF23      PIC X VALUE IS '.'.
        02  DFHPF24      PIC X VALUE IS '<'.
```

DFHENTER is the Enter key, DFHPA1 is Program Attention (PA) Key 1, DFHPF1 is Program Function (PF) Key 1, and so on. As in the case of the DFHBMSCA macro, any values above that appear to be spaces are not; they correspond to bit patterns for which there is no printable character.

Errors on BMS Commands

As we cover each group of commands in this book, we'll discuss what can go wrong. We'll classify errors according to the categories and suggest how you might want to handle them in your coding.

There is really only one type of error that we can expect to occur in the subset of BMS commands and map options that we've covered here. This is known as *MAPFAIL*. There are other types of failure and they are listed in the *CICS Application Programming Reference*.

MAPFAIL errors

MAPFAIL occurs on a *RECEIVE MAP* command when there are no fields at all on the screen for BMS to map for you. This happens if you issue a *RECEIVE MAP* after the user has pressed a Clear or a Program Attention key. These are known as "short-read" keys because the only data that flows from the termial is the keycode, no data from the terminal is passed. It can also occur even if the user does not use a short-read key. If, for example, you send a screen to be filled in (without any fields in which the map or the program turns on the modified-data tag), and the user presses the Enter key or one of the program function keys without keying any data into the screen, you'll get *MAPFAIL*.

The reason for the failure is essentially the same in both cases. With the short read, the terminal does not send any screen data; hence no fields. In the other case, there are no fields to send; no modified-data tags have been turned on.

MAPFAIL is almost invariably a user error (and, hence, an expected program condition). It may occur on almost any *RECEIVE MAP*, and therefore you should handle it explicitly in the program. For instance, Example 11-9 shows the code that the example application contains to deal with a *MAPFAIL* that occurs when the menu map is received.

Example 11-9. Code to Handle MAPFAIL

```
 BB-MENU-DATA-ENTERED SECTION.
*
* Obtain the input (if any) from the user.
*
 BB-010.
     MOVE LOW-VALUES TO ACCTMNUI
*
     EXEC CICS RECEIVE MAP('ACCTMNU') MAPSET(WS-LITS-MAPSET)
             RESP(RESPONSE) RESP2(REASON-CODE)
     END-EXEC
*
     IF  (RESPONSE NOT = DFHRESP(NORMAL) )
     AND (RESPONSE NOT = DFHRESP(MAPFAIL))
         PERFORM Y-UNEXPECTED-ERROR
     END-IF
```

This code is designed to make the occurrence of *MAPFAIL* somewhat transparent to the program. It is important to realize the difference in what BMS does when there *is* and there *is not* data to map. If BMS finds data to map, it clears the target map area to nulls (LOW-VALUES) before setting up the appropriate Length, Flag and Input fields. If BMS finds no data to map, it immediately raises the *MAPFAIL* condition and leaves the target map area exactly as it was.

In order to ensure the basic logic of the program can proceed regardless of the input, it primes the target map area with LOW-VALUES (nulls) before requesting BMS services. We then detect that the response from BMS is acceptable by the test of the EIBRESP value. Note that the key causing the initiation of the transaction was tested before we reached this part of the program, so we know it isn't the *CLEAR* key.

Starting Another Task, and Other Time Services

CICS allows one transaction (task) to start another one, as we noted in our discussion about printed output. The usual reason for doing this is the one that arose in our example: the originating task needs access to some facility it does not own, usually a terminal other than the input terminal. In our case, we needed a printer to print the log of account file changes. There are sometimes other reasons as well. You might want a task to be executed at a particular time, or you might want it to run at a different priority from the original task, for instance.

Starting Another Task

The command to start another task is:

```
EXEC CICS START TRANSID(name) TERMID(termid)
                FROM(data-area)  LENGTH(data-value)
                options
END-EXEC
```

The options for this command are:

TRANSID(name)

Specifies the identifier (1–4 characters) of the transaction that is to be started. This parameter is required. If the identifier is a literal, enclose it in quotes.

TERMID(name)

Specifies the symbolic identifier (1–4 alphanumeric characters) of the principal facility associated with a transaction to be started as a result of a *START* command. When this parameter is omitted the started task runs without a principal facility.

FROM(data-area)

Specifies the name of the data area that contains data to be passed to the transaction being started. This parameter is optional.

LENGTH(data-value)

Specifies the length of the data to be passed for the new task.

options (can be either INTERVAL or TIME)

 INTERVAL(hhmmss)

  Specifies the expiration time as an interval of time that is to elapse from the time at which the *START* command is issued. The mm and ss are each in the range 0–59. The time specified is added to the current clock time by CICS when the command is executed to calculate the expiration time.

TIME(hhmmss)

> Specifies the time when a new task should be started. When using the C language, you are recommended to use the *AFTER/AT HOURS, MINUTES,* and *SECONDS* options, as C does not provide a packed decimal data type. You may use *TIME,* but if the value specified is not an integer constant, the application is responsible for ensuring that the value passed to CICS is in packed decimal format.

> If you don't specify either *INTERVAL* or *TIME,* CICS assumes that you would like INTERVAL(0), which means right away.

Retrieving data passed to the START command

If data is passed in the *START* command, the transaction that gets started uses the EXEC CICS *RETRIEVE* command to get access to this data. The syntax of the *RETRIEVE* command looks like this:

```
EXEC CICS RETRIEVE
          INTO(data-area)LENGTH(length)
END-EXEC
```

Notice the difference between this *RETRIEVE* command and the *RECEIVE* command described in "The RECEIVE MAP command." Both commands may be used to get the initial input to a transaction, but they aren't interchangeable: *RECEIVE* must be used in transactions that are initiated by input from a terminal, and *RETRIEVE* must be used in transactions that were started by another transaction. The options for this command are:

INTO(data-area)

> Specifies the user data area into which retrieved data is to be written.

LENGTH(data-value)

> Specifies the length of the data area the retrieved data is written into.

Using the START and RETRIEVE commands in the sample application

In our sample application, program *NACT01* uses the *START* command when a user asks for a record to be printed:

```
EXEC CICS START TRANSID(PRINT-TRANSID) TERMID(CA-PRINTER)
          FROM(ACCTDTLO)
          RESP(RESPONSE) RESP2(REASON-CODE)
ENDEXEC
```

This *START* command tells CICS to start transaction *PRINT-TRANSID* as soon as possible after the printer whose name is in data area CA-PRINTER is available to be its terminal.

Program *NACT03*, running on behalf of this transaction, in turn issues the following *RETRIEVE* command to retrieve the data passed from program *NACT01*:

```
EXEC CICS RETRIEVE
          INTO(ACCTDTLI)
          RESP(RESPONSE)  RESP2(REASON-CODE)
END-EXEC
```

ACCTDTLO and *ACCTDTLI* refer to the symbolic map structure, located in WORK-ING-STORAGE in both programs. The map, of course, contains the data read by transaction *NACT*. This data is to be printed by transaction *NACP*.

Errors on the START and RETRIEVE commands

A number of different problems may arise in connection with the *START* and *RETRIEVE* commands that we've described. Possible errors are:

INVTSREQ

> Means that the CICS system support for temporary storage, which is required for *START* commands that specify the *FROM* option, was not present when a *RETRIEVE* command was issued. This error is an example of the system/application mismatch (category 4) described in "Handling Errors" in Chapter 4.

IOERR

> Means an input/output error on the temporary storage data set where the data to be passed is stored on a *RETRIEVE* or *START* command.

LENGERR

> Occurs when the length of the data retrieved by a *RETRIEVE* command exceeds the value specified in the *LENGTH* parameter for the command. *LENGERR* usually means an error in the program logic.

NOTFND

> Means that the requested data could not be found in temporary storage on a *RETRIEVE* command. If a task issuing a *RETRIEVE* command was not started by a *START* command, or if it was started by a *START* command with no *FROM* parameter (in other words, no data), this condition will occur. Again, it usually means a programming error.

TERMIDERR

> Occurs when the terminal specified in the *TERMID* parameter in a *START* command cannot be found in the Terminal Control Table. During the test phase it usually indicates a problem in the program logic; on a production system, it usually means that something has happened to the terminal.

TRANSIDERR

> Means that the transaction identifier specified in a *START* command cannot be found in the list of installed transaction definitions. Like *TERMIDERR*, it usually means a programming error during the development of an application, or table damage if it occurs on a production system.

Local Printing (NACT03): Requests for Printing

This program is invoked asynchronously in order to print on a CICS-attached printer. It prints the data passed to it in the same form as it appears on a display screen as generated by *NACT01*.

Essentially this program implements the local print processing. There are some important points to note about the implementation of this logic:

- The input data is expected to be in a form already suitable for printing.

- The *Return to caller* implies ending the CICS task.

The program implements the standard error handling approach designed for the application. It uses CICS facilities to identify program *NACT04* as the one to be invoked in the event of an abend occurring as well as using it to process any unexpected errors that may arise.

NACT03 does several jobs, all related to printed output (as opposed to display output). When it is invoked by transaction *NACP*, it completes the request for printed output of a record in the account file.

NACP should not be confused with network abend control program DFHNACP. In this book it is used to refer to the print transaction.

Transaction *NACT* processed the initial stages of the print request, checking the input, reading the record to be printed, and building the detailed screen from the information in the file record. It then requested that transaction *NACP* be started with the required printer as its terminal. The processing in *NACP* is outlined here:

1. Retrieve the screen image prepared and saved for this purpose in program *NACT01*:

```
EXEC CICS RETRIEVE
        INTO(ACCTDTLO)
        RESP(RESPONSE) RESP2(REASON-CODE)
END-EXEC
```

2. Send this screen to the terminal, in this case the printer, named by the user in the print request.

```
EXEC CICS SEND MAP('ACCTDTL') MAPSET(WS-LITS-MAPSET)
        PRINT ERASE
        RESP(RESPONSE) RESP2(REASON-CODE)
END-EXEC
```

3. Transfer control to the error handling program in one of the following two ways:

```
EXEC CICS XCTL PROGRAM(ABEND-PROGRAM)
            COMMAREA(WS-ERRH-ERROR-COMMAREA)
            RESP(RESPONSE) RESP2(REASON-CODE)
END-EXEC
```

    or:

```
EXEC CICS ABEND ABCODE(WS-LITS-ABEND-ERROR-ABEND)
END-EXEC
```

4 Return control to CICS. Don't set any next transid because there's no need to do so for terminals that never send unsolicited input. Also, we don't know what transaction should be executed next at this printer.

```
EXEC CICS RETURN
END-EXEC
```

What's Next...

That's all about the 3270 interface. Chapter 12, *Designing the Visual Basic Component* describes how to create a similar interface, but this time designing the screen using Visual Basic and then linking that to the business logic by a CICS client.

12

Designing the Visual Basic Component

In Part I of the book, we looked at the various departments in the KanDoIT company, and their requirements for the new business application. Now let's look in a little more detail at the customer services department.

The customer services department is, as its name implies, driven by KanDoIT's customers. Typically, much of its work is following up customer account enquiries, most of which are received over the telephone. Sometimes customers will know their account number; often they won't. Finding the correct information quickly is always going to be a critical need.

The purpose of the Visual Basic component is to provide the customer services department with an easy-to-use graphical user interface (GUI), for their work with customer account records. Of course it's important that representatives of the customer services department work closely with the Visual Basic programmers to ensure that the design of the GUI really meets the department's requirements.

Understanding What the Component Needs to Do

In Chapter 4, *Designing the Business Logic*, we decided which services that the COBOL business logic component would provide within the sample application.

It would:

- Return the contents of a customer account record, given an account number.

- Add a new customer account record, given an account number and customer data.

- Modify an existing account record, given an account number and modified data.

- Delete an account record, given an account number.

- Access customer account records by name; that is, given a name or part of a name, return a list of matching names with corresponding account numbers and addresses.

The Visual Basic GUI supplies the interfaces to the services provided by the COBOL component. The first four services are supplied by the program *NACT02* (the business logic); the last is supplied by *NACT05* (the browse component).

Security is handled by means of a Log In panel when the Visual Basic component is started. The user must supply a valid user ID and password where this is required by the CICS server.

Most Visual Basic applications would typically include:

- A print option to print a displayed form.

- Online help facilities to guide the user through the application. These should include details of how to contact the helpdesk.

- Data validation, for checking data in the application.

We will build these options into our application.

Designing the Graphical User Interface

To the user (in this case, staff in the customer services department), the user interface is the application; first impressions are critical in determining whether or not the application will be a success. Therefore it is vital that its design is carefully thought out. The user interface designer needs to consider such things as whether to use a single document interface (SDI) or multiple document interface (MDI), how many forms will be required, the level of help needed by the user, and so on. The *Programmer's Guide* provided with Visual Basic documents the different options available in detail.

There may also be company standards that you have to follow. For example there may be rules relating to the naming of windows, so that your helpdesk is able to identify a user's problem more easily.

The design used for the GUI in this application is simply an example of what can be done. It is not meant to be a definitive guide, and it could no doubt benefit from further modifications. Design should be an ongoing, iterative process based on the needs, observations, and new demands of users.

Three forms are required for the KanDoIT application: a Log In panel, a Main Menu, and an Accounts Details form. Since only one form needs to be displayed at a time, the Visual Basic GUI makes use of an SDI design.

Where there are a limited set of options that the user can choose from it is useful to use either a *list box* (also known as a *Selection menu*) or *combo box* (also known as *textarea menu*) to make these available to the user. A list box provides the user with a series of options from which to select. A combo box allows the user to either type in a value or select from a list.

So having decided that you need three panels, what do you need to include in each panel and what design considerations should you take into account?

Designing the Log In panel

The Log In panel (see Figure 12-1) appears when the application is first started. The User Name and Password required are those defined to the CICS Server for security purposes for the particular user. In our case simple Visual Basic routines have been used to convert the input to uppercase.

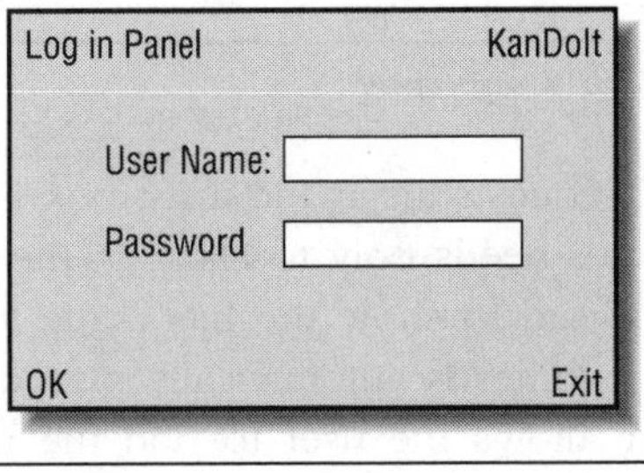

| Log in Panel | KanDoIt |

User Name: [   ]

Password [   ]

OK   Exit

Figure 12-1. Design of the Log In panel

Information typed in the Log In panel is passed to CICS, where the user is authenticated.

Designing the Main Menu

Once the user has logged in, Figure 12-2 appears on the screen. It comprises two main parts:

Search by Name

Makes use of the Browse application, *NACT05*. On a screen, most users read from left to right and top to bottom, so the input fields for User Name (rurname) and Password have been placed in the top left-hand corner as this is the point at which their eyes will look first.

Account Request

Makes use of the CRUD application (*NACT02*) and requires the Account Number.

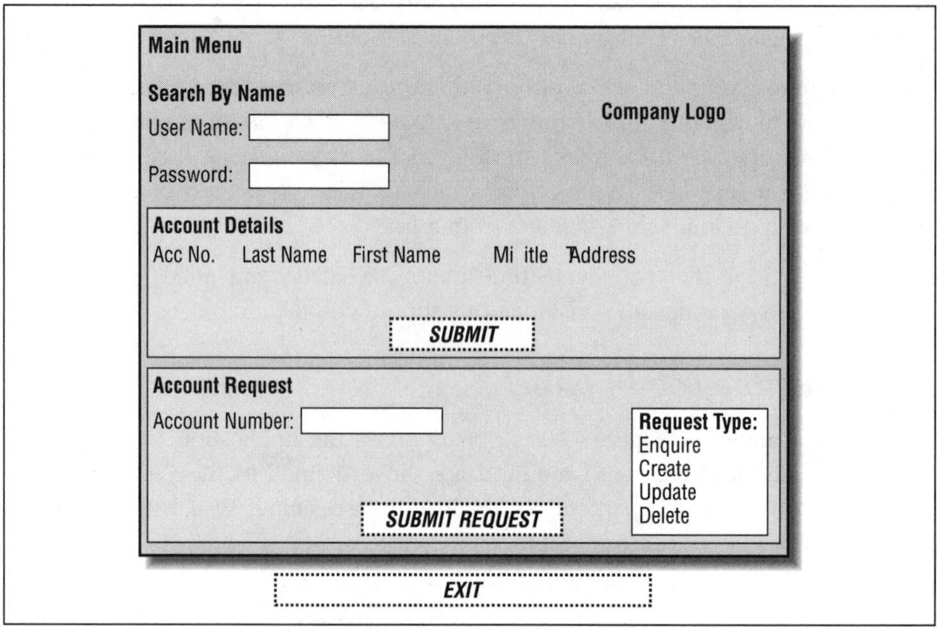

Figure 12-2. Design of the Main Menu panel

To ensure that only valid requests are made a list box is used to show the available request types. The user needs only to click on the required entry shown in the list. A list box is also used to show the hits made for a search. The account number of the selected customer is automatically placed in the Account Number field. A vertical scroll bar allows the user to find the required entry where the length of the list exceeds the display space.

In addition to list boxes, other GUI components used in the Main Menu include:

Tab Indexes

These are used for the various data input fields and ensure that the cursor is positioned correctly. Initially the cursor is placed in the first field we would normally expect the user to complete. Pressing the Tab key then takes the user through the various data input fields on the menu page in the order we would expect them to be completed.

Shortcuts or Fast Paths

These have been set up for the command buttons and menu bar choices. A shortcut is set up by prefacing one of the letters in the caption with the ampersand symbol (&). For example, &Submit Search appears on the corresponding command button as <u>S</u>ubmit Search, and can be activated by the shortcut <*Alt*> S.

Experienced users may choose to use the tabs and shortcuts provided rather than using the mouse pointer (assuming a mouse is available), to select fields and click on the command buttons.

In many cases a user would search for a particular customer name, and then do an account request based on an entry from the list displayed. Selecting an entry from the resulting list box causes the selected account number to be entered in the Account Number box for the Account Request part of the form.

The Account Details form is based on the input form on which details are supplied to the operator. Because the details required for the various request options are generally the same, it makes sense to use the same basic form with minor alterations to tailor it for the individual options.

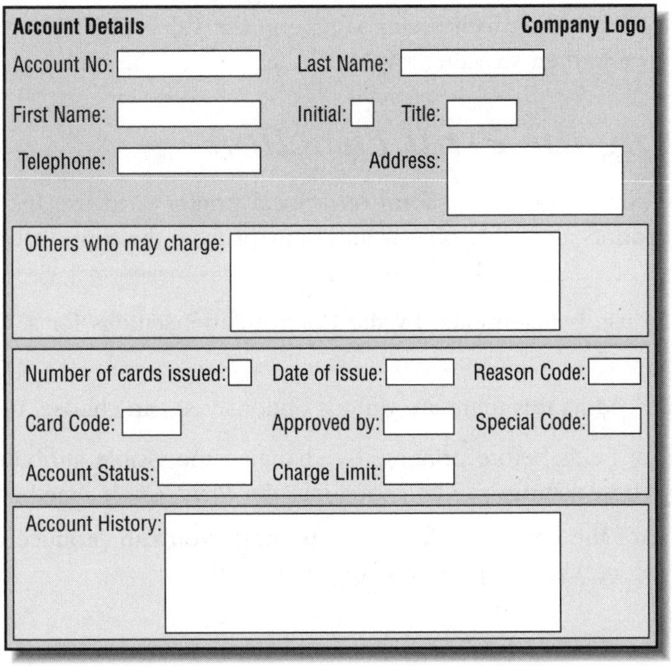

Figure 12-3. Design of the Account Details form

Two command buttons for particular request types have been added to the Account Details form: *Confirm Delete* and *Create Account.* Depending on the request made, these are displayed or hidden as appropriate. The window shown in Figure 12-3 is an enquiry screen, so the command button doesn't appear. Similarly, when creating a new account the user has no requirement for the history section at the bottom of the form, so this is hidden.

As with the Main Menu, the Tab Index property of the various input objects has been set to provide the user with a logical progression through the data entry fields on the form.

A combo box has been used for the Reason Code to allow users to either type in the appropriate letter directly, or display a list of the available codes from which they can select. The Reason Code is a one-character code used to identify the reason for a charge card being issued. Valid codes are:

- *N* for New
- *L* for Lost
- *S* for Stolen
- *R* for Replacement

An experienced user may well prefer to type in the value directly rather than displaying the list and then selecting a value.

Designing the Print Function

The simplest way of printing a form on a local printer is to use the `PrintForm` method. This prints all visible objects and bitmaps from the form that the user has opened.

The printer to use is determined by the Control Panel settings for a Windows NT workstation.

When you are coding this there are various options you can choose, including:

- Removal of fields before printing, by changing the visible attribute from True to False. These settings can be coded into the *Print_Click()* method.
- Changing of the color attributes. For example, you can produce a black and white printout where color tones are not desired.

Designing the Online Help

The purpose of the online help is to provide information at the point when the user needs it. There are various types of help information that are available using Visual Basic:

Tooltip text
> Information is displayed to the user when the mouse pointer passes over a given GUI object such as an input field or command button. This provides a simple contextual help aid.

WhatsThisHelp facility
> This can be invoked by the user in different ways, but like tooltip text, it is always context-sensitive. One of the most common techniques is to set up a WhatsThisHelp button on the title bar. The user then clicks the button, drags the WhatsThisHelp icon to a control, then clicks again to see the associated help. WhatsThisHelp can be used where a more detailed explanation than that which would normally be given in a tool tip is required.

Help options
> The menu bar for Visual Basic applications normally includes a Help option. The sub-menu from this normally includes an About item giving details of the release of the Visual Basic application and any copyright information. This model has been implemented in our application.

> Additional help items give the user more details about each of the main options called from the Main Menu, namely Search by Name and Account Request. As the Account Request item is more complex than the Search by Name item the help has been further broken down to include not only a brief description of the application but further details on each of the request types that can be used as separate items.

> A similar setup is used on the Account Details form. Help relative to the chosen action, such as create account or delete account, will appear in the option list depending on the choice made on the menu form. Only those topics relevant to the chosen action are made available when the menu is displayed.

Helpdesk
> Instructions need to be provided telling the user how to contact the helpdesk.

Designing the Data Validation

To reduce the overhead in CICS client to server calls, it is best to validate the data being sent within the Visual Basic application itself. This means that our component should never receive server-based application error messages. So we need to add data validation routines to the Visual Basic application.

It is important to have a clear understanding of what checks are performed in the existing BMS map-based application and, where appropriate, mirror these in the new Visual Basic application. Here are some of the things we need to consider:

- Which fields need to contain just numeric values?

- Are supplied numeric values within the value range for that field?

- Which fields must contain only alphabetic characters?

- Is the length of supplied field valid?

- Do date fields contain a properly formatted date value (for example, dd/mm/yyyy format) acceptable to the CICS application? Also, is the date valid (for example, not 31 February 2000)?

- Which fields can be assumed to contain default values when left empty?

- Have all required fields been completed?

- Which fields need to be converted to uppercase for key matching in the CICS application?

Designing Access to and Control of the CICS Application

To communicate with our CICS business logic application on the OS/390 server, the Visual Basic component uses the CICS External Call Interface (ECI) API. This is explained later in "Understanding the CICS External Call Interface (ECI)." The ECI enables a non-CICS client application to call a CICS program synchronously or asynchronously, as a subroutine. The client program communicates with the server CICS program, using a data area called a COMMAREA. Check back with "Saving Data: Using a Scratchpad Facility" in Chapter 5 if you have forgotten what a COMMAREA means in CICS.

In making use of the CICS ECI, we have chosen to implement two different access methods, so that you can compare and contrast the approaches:

- The first of these uses the native CICS API. This requires the Visual Basic application programmer to have a reasonable understanding of what CICS requires in terms of the COMMAREA field definitions used by the CICS applications, as well as the ability to set up various buffers that are needed in the sending and receiving of the data. The bulk of the code for this method is contained in the Visual Basic module *comsubs.bas*.

- The second method makes use of the VisualAge Interspace product. This product enables the Visual Basic application programmer to make use of CICS applications easily, without the need to understand exactly what CICS is doing. Within Interspace, the programmer can create the module that is required to communicate with a given CICS application, and then include it in any Visual Basic application that needs to use that CICS application.

- Both of these methods are discussed in greater detail later in this chapter. Whichever of these two methods is used, the underlying form of communication is the same; this is illustrated in Figure 12-4.

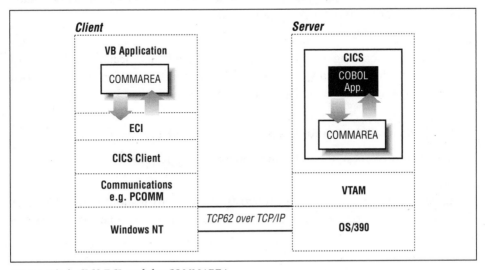

Figure 12-4. CICS ECI and the COMMAREA

The COMMAREA is passed to the CICS server on the call, and the CICS program typically populates it with data accessed from files or databases. The data is then returned to the client for manipulation or display.

In line with good coding practice, the two programs in the business logic component (*NACT02* and *NACT05*) that are used for our example only make use of field definitions of data type CHAR for the COMMAREA. This greatly simplifies the conversion of data flowing between the Windows NT workstation and the OS/390 server.

The use of the CICS ECI requires us to think about the number of communication flows that need to be transmitted between the CICS client and the CICS server.

Taking the *NACT02* application as an example, we are provided with a choice of the following commands. In each case, the actual value entered in the COMMAREA is the initial letter:

Enquiry (Read without Lock)
Create
Delete

Update
Read with Lock
Lock
Free

For a simple Enquiry, only one communication with the server is required.

For an Update of an existing record, the following commands need to be issued using the CICS ECI to the *NACT02* application:

Read with Lock

Displays the existing record data for subsequent modification and prevents other users from updating the record. The response code for Read with Lock needs to be checked to verify that the record is not locked by another user.

Update

Sends the modified record details when completed and releases the record.

For new record creation, the following commands are required:

Enquiry

Checks whether a record already exists. A non-zero response code indicates that no record exists for the specified account number or that the database is off-line.

Lock

Locks the account number that is intended for use in the new record.

Create

Creates the new record with details entered by the user.

The options available to the user have been limited to the following:

Enquiry
Create
Delete
Update

This ensures that unnecessary locks are not performed. Based on the type of command entered, the Visual Basic application determines when to issue a Read with Lock in line with the logic used for this purpose in *NACT02*. *NACT02* uses the checks carried out by *NACT01* (which handles the presentation logic for BMS screens) if any additional functions should be issued for the selected option.

Understanding the CICS External Call Interface (ECI)

The CICS External Call Interface (ECI) is an integral component in the communication between the Visual Basic component and the business application logic. Before going on to look at the two access methods, using the native CICS API and VisualAge Interspace, you may find it helpful to understand more about the ECI. Figure 12-4 shows a high-level overview of the process. The ECI enables a non-CICS application to call a CICS program in a CICS server. Any program that can be called as a subroutine using *EXEC CICS LINK*, and which does not require a CICS terminal, may be accessed by this means. Data is exchanged between the two applications by means of a COMMAREA. The non-CICS application does not issue any CICS calls itself; the CICS commands are only issued by the called program running in the server.

The non-CICS application builds two data areas, then issues the ECI call. The CICS client then sends the request to the CICS server.

The server receives the request, performs any required data translation, and starts a transaction for the ECI request. Any translation of data required is performed in the server. Once the transaction is complete, the CICS server returns the updated COMMAREA to the CICS client. Provided the return code supplied indicates that the call was successful, the updated COMMAREA can then be used.

In the simplest case in our example, the ECI is used to call a single CICS program with simple synchronous calls. Additional options include the use of asynchronous calls and multiple calls within a single unit of work, however, these options are outside the scope of this book.

The ECI is the recommended interface for the development of new client/server applications. Its call structure easily divides the presentation logic (usually in the client) from the business logic in the CICS application (usually in the server), offering application designers maximum flexibility.

Using the ECI

The first of the data areas used by the non-CICS application is used to hold the COMMAREA. The COMMAREA contains all of the data to be passed to the CICS application that is to be called. On completion, the CICS application will return the updated COMMAREA. The maximum size of COMMAREA that can be used is 32,500 bytes; data areas larger than this must be segmented.

The second data area used by the non-CICS application is the ECI parameter block. Parameters passed in this block include items such as:

- The type of ECI call to be made
- The name of the CICS program to be called
- The user ID and password to be used
- The address and length of the COMMAREA
- The return code

It is important that the ECI parameter block is initialized with nulls (binary zeros).

Normally the return code from the CICS application will be contained within the COMMAREA. Additional information will be passed back within the ECI parameter block for system errors and CICS abend codes when the transaction that started the CICS program has ended abnormally.

Initiating the CICS client

For Windows NT, *Start Client* and *Stop Client* options are provided under the CICS Client for Windows NT entry in the Programs List. The CICS client also starts automatically when an application issues the first client call.

Data Conversion Between the CICS Universal Client and CICS Transaction Server

CICS Transaction Server for OS/390 uses an EBCDIC codepage for character data, whereas the CICS Universal Client for Windows NT uses an ASCII codepage. Therefore, the COMMAREAs within an ECI request require data conversion.

The rule for data conversion within CICS is that the conversion occurs on the system that owns the resource. Our sample CICS applications reside on CICS Transaction Server for OS/390, therefore it is CICS Transaction Server for OS/390 that performs the data conversion.

For inbound ECI requests, CICS Transaction Server for OS/390 uses the *DFHCNV* data conversion macro to convert the COMMAREA from ASCII to EBCDIC.

Where individual fields within the COMMAREA are not to be interpreted as having a character data type they will need to have entries giving their offset and length, and details of the data type to be used. By making sure the COMMAREA used by the ECI is entirely character-based, the need for involved entries within the *DFHCNV* macro is removed and the processing overhead significantly reduced.

Accessing Applications on the CICS Server with Standard CICS Object-Oriented Support

The CICS Clients technology provides programming support for procedural or object-oriented programming. This is helpful to the Visual Basic programmer, in that it hides much of the complexity of communication to CICS inside a simple external shell. Extended support is based on the provision of an ECI class library modeling the full function of the ECI in an object-oriented way.

Using the CICS Client Component Object Module (COM) libraries

The COM libraries introduced with IBM CICS Universal Client Version 3.1 greatly simplify linking from Visual Basic applications providing COM classes for the CICS ECI and EPI on Microsoft Windows NT, Windows 95, or Windows 98.

These COM classes can be accessed from Microsoft Visual Basic, from Visual Basic for Applications (which is provided built-in to applications such as Microsoft Excel Version 5.0), and from VBScript.

The sample Visual Basic application makes use of the ECI COM library. Two interfaces are provided for each COM class. The newer of these is the Custom Interface provided for use with Visual Basic, which is much faster than the IDispatch provided to support older Visual Basic applications and VBScript. The sample makes use of the Custom Interface.

The interfaces, their methods, and their parameters can be viewed using the Microsoft Object Viewer, or the Object Browser provided within Visual Basic Version 5.

The COM objects supplied for use with the CICS ECI in the CclECILib library are listed in Table 12-1.

Table 12-1. COM Objects

COM Object	Description
CclOBuf	Buffers data passing to and from CICS
CclOConn	Controls a connection to a CICS server
CclOECI	Provides access to a list of CICS servers configured in the client
CclOFlow	Controls a single interaction with a CICS server program
CclOSecAttr	Provides information about security attributes (passwords)
CclOSecTime	Provides date and time information
CclOUOW	Coordinates a recoverable set of calls to a CICS server

In addition, the COM classes in Table 12-2 are also supplied for use with the objects listed in Table 12-1.

Table 12-2. COM Classes

COM Class	Description
CclConnectStatusCodes	Set of codes to indicate server connection availability.
CclECIExceptionCodes	Set of exception codes for connection failure.
CclFlowCallTypes	Set of call types associated with CclFlow.
CclFlowSyncTypes	Set of CICS interaction types, either synchronous or deferred synchronous. These are the only two types of calls supported with Visual Basic.

Accessing Applications on the CICS Server Using the VisualAge Interspace API

The VisualAge Interspace product minimizes, as far as possible, what the user has to code in order to communicate with a CICS Server application. It provides a simple API that can be used from within a number of different front ends, such as Visual Basic, PowerBuilder, and VisualAge for Java, to link through to CICS and various other middleware services. This API is divided into three layers to provide maximum functionality and flexibility in any distributed environment:

GUI-Enabling Layer (GEL)
> The top layer; provides the Visual Basic developer with a way of invoking middleware services.

Distributed Processing Layer (DPL)
> The middle layer; provides a common API that is not dependent on the underlying middleware.

Distributed Interface Layer (DIL)
> The bottom layer; translates DPL-layer functions into the appropriate middleware API functions.

Each layer is constructed using the layer below it to ensure a consistent programming interface regardless of the underlying implementation. Figure 12-5 illustrates these principles. The online help file provided with VisualAge Interspace is a reference guide to the functions in the top layer.

 The Visual Basic programmer needs to include the VisualAge Interspace modules *dcidpl.bas* and *dcigel.bas* in any Visual Basic Project that needs to link to a CICS server application.

Communications with CICS applications are handled by means of services. VisualAge Interspace also includes a tool, the Service Interface Painter, which simplifies the process of developing and testing these services for specific CICS server

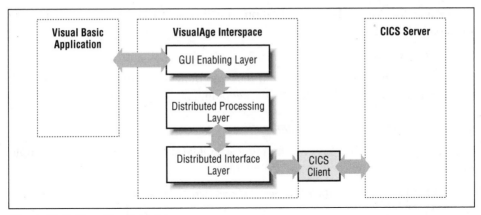

Figure 12-5. VisualAge Interspace

applications. The Service Interface Painter is used to define an application's services, generate code for the application, and test its services. The Interspace functions that invoke services move data back and forth between Visual Basic structures and middleware communication buffers; as a result, a Visual Basic programmer can quickly write Interspace-enabled applications without learning anything about CICS.

Creating the link to the CICS ECI

Provided that the CICS client has been correctly set up, the link to CICS can be established from within the Visual Basic application by means of the Interspace API call:

```
dcifx_init(DEname As String, AppName As String, UserName As String, Password As
String)
```

The options for this command are:

DEname
> The distributed environment being used (in our case CICS).

AppName
> The name of the CICS application being used (if several applications are to be linked to then a generic name can be specified and details of the services to be used included in a catalog file of the same name).

UserName
> The name of the user who connects to the application.

Password
> The user password.

The call initializes the Interspace internal memory structure with service/field information. Based on the specified middleware product, it establishes a connection and allocates a message buffer.

On exiting the Visual Basic application, the link to CICS is dropped using the Interspace API call:

```
dcifx_exit(DEname As String)
```

The call frees any Interspace-allocated message buffers, disconnects from the middleware, and performs Interspace housekeeping.

Communicating with the CICS application

The Interspace call used to send the request COMMAREA to the CICS server application and receive the reply COMMAREA is:

```
receive_<service>_sync(ByRef Request As <service>_request_msg, ByRef Reply As
<service>_reply_msg)
```

Where *<service>* is the name of the Interspace service created to pass information to and from the CICS server application of the same name.

The call invokes a synchronous service, loading the request buffer from the *<service>_request_msg* structure and populating the *<service>_reply_msg* with the received data.

Additional API functions are available but do not fall within the scope of what is required for this sample. For a detailed description of the API calls available, refer to the VisualAge Interspace online help.

The setting up of buffers and the necessary structures required for the CICS ECI is all handled by Interspace and requires no further action on the part of the Visual Basic programmer.

Designing Error Handling

There are standard response codes provided by the *NACT02* and *NACT05* programs that need to be analyzed so that appropriate messages to the user are issued. Distinction needs to be made between what can be regarded as recoverable situations—such as when a record is locked by another user—and non-recoverable situations, where, for example, the CICS system has abended for some reason. Care needs to be taken about the instructions issued to the user so that they know who to contact when there is a serious problem and what information to provide.

However good the error handling is, there is always the possibility that an unforeseen error of some type may occur. For this reason it is advisable to have a panel identification field clearly visible which includes an identification of the particular panel and the version of the application being used. The user can then be asked for this information by the helpdesk, if needed. We have left this as an exercise for the reader to add to the sample code.

VI

The Visual Basic Component

Visual Basic is a Microsoft Windows application development tool that incorporates a variant of the BASIC programming language. New or casual programmers can use it to create simple applications for Windows platforms; more experienced programmers can write more complex, server-based applications.

The building blocks of Visual Basic applications are forms and controls, which are referred to as *objects*. The programmer creates and manipulates objects using a drag-and-drop graphical interface to create a framework for a Visual Basic application. The programmer can then use the programming language to reference and tie these objects together to create a complete application, referred to within Visual Basic as a *project*.

Visual Basic uses interpreter mode during application development and testing. Once testing is complete, compile the application using the Visual Basic native compiler. The end result is executable code optimized for a production environment. Both the Visual Basic application development tool and the optimized generated code run only on Microsoft Windows platforms.

Having created your Visual Basic component, the final stage is to connect it to CICS. This Part contains the following chapters:

- Chapter 12, *Designing the Visual Basic Component*, describes the design of the Graphical User Interface (GUI), and looks at the methods of communicating between Visual Basic and CICS.

- Chapter 13, *Programming the Visual Basic Program*, shows how to create the GUI and set up the linkages between Visual Basic and CICS.

In addition to the usual software, we have used the following in this Part:

- Microsoft Visual Basic Version 6.0
- IBM CICS Universal Clients Version 3.1
- VisualAge Interspace Version 6.0

13

Programming the Visual Basic Program

Having designed the Visual Basic component, now is the time to start programming it. And having programmed it, you need to set up the required configuration so that it can communicate with the CICS application.

Writing the Graphical User Interface

In "Designing the Graphical User Interface" in Chapter 12, we described the functions that would appear in the Log In panel, and the two main user interface screens, the Main Menu and the Account Details form. You can see the full Visual Basic application by looking at the code on the CD that accompanies this book. In this section, we look at how some of the controls on the user interface screens are coded.

Controls used on the Main Menu include:

- Data entry fields for the user to enter information

- List boxes to display the results of a name search, and the request type options

- Push buttons to perform actions

- Keyboard short cuts to enable experienced users to perform actions quicker

- Tab indexes to scroll from one data entry field to another

- The Main Menu also includes two other design elements: the Print control and links to help information (Figure 13-1)

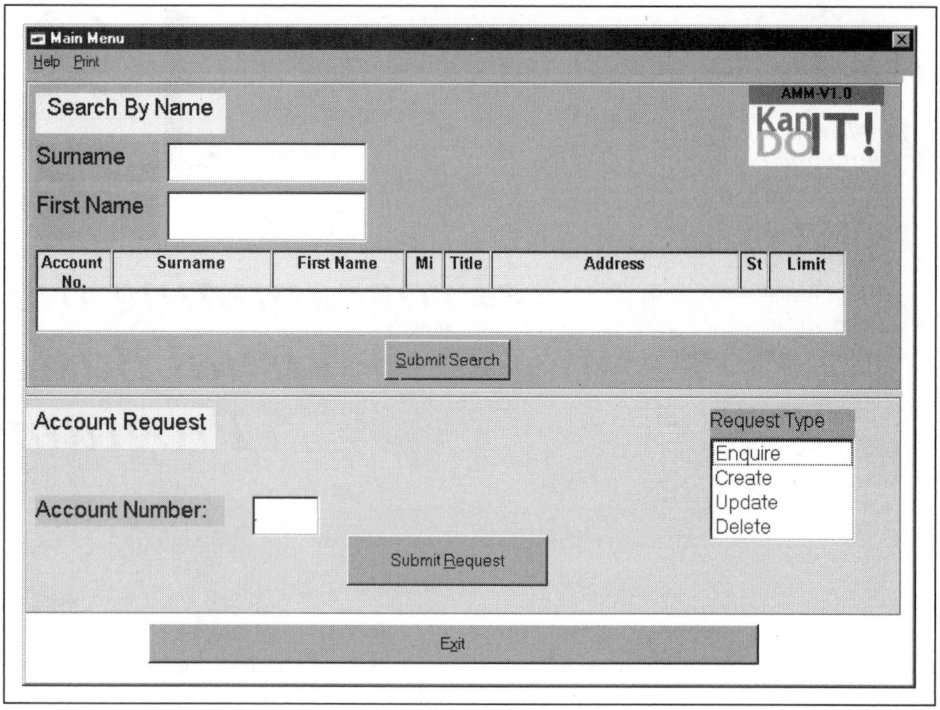

Figure 13-1. The Main Menu

The controls are created in Visual Basic by dragging and dropping objects from a palette onto a design area. You can then change control properties, and write code that is activated when a control is selected. For details of how to create basic controls and change properties, you need to look at the Visual Basic documentation. But let's now look at the code behind the list boxes.

First, let's consider the case where a user wishes to search for a particular account number, and then do an account request based on an entry from the list displayed. Selecting an entry from the resulting list box causes the selected account number to be entered in the Account Number box for the Account Request part of the form. The following code shows the method used:

```
Private Sub ResultList_Click( )
      AccountTxtBox.Text = cabrws_matches(ResultList.ListIndex).Acct
End Sub
```

The available request types for the Account Request are also shown in a list box. When the user selects a request type, the appropriate character is placed in the single character field used within the CICS COMMAREA. The following code shows the method used:

```
Private Sub RequestList_Click()
      'Initial letter of highlighted item is stored in the Request List.
```

```
      ca_request = RequestList.List(RequestList.ListIndex)
   End Sub
```

Figure 13-2 shows the Account Details form.

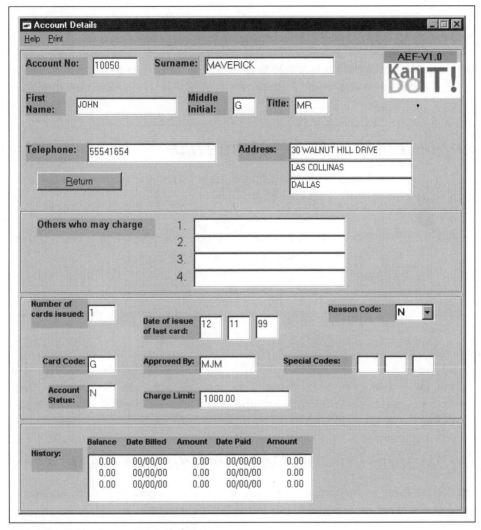

Figure 13-2. The Account Details form

There is one additional control that doesn't appear on the Main Menu: the combo box is used for the reason code, which enables the user to type the code or select it from a list. The selection list is specified as one of the properties of the object. However you still need to write some additional code to check that one of the correct values (in this case, N, L, S, or R) has been entered:

```
If ReasonCodeCombo.Text Like "[!NLSRnlsr]" Then
        Call Guide_msg_box("Please enter valid reason code. Valid values are
```

```
                N,L,S,R", "Help Message")
         ReasonCodeCombo.BackColor = vbWhite
         ReasonCodeCombo.SetFocus
         Exit Sub
     End If
```

Implementing the Print Function

The Print function is set up as a selection on the menu bar. As mentioned in Chapter 17, the Print option uses the **PrintForm** method. The code looks like this:

```
Menu.PrintForm
```

Implementing the Online Help

In "Designing the Online Help" in Chapter 12, we described three types of help text that you might wish to include in the GUI:

Tooltip text

Tooltip text is entered as a property for an object. The text that is entered then appears when the mouse pointer passes over the object.

WhatsThisHelp facility

WhatsThis Help is also defined as a property, but the help information associated with the object is specified in a separate help file that is called when the user requests help.

Help options

Help options, which appear under Help on the menu bar, are specified using the menu editor in Visual Basic. You can create a help file for each help option, and this is invoked when the user clicks on the help option in the menu.

Implementing the Data Validation Code

The Visual Basic component of the sample application contains many additional routines that work behind the scenes in the GUI. These include:

• Routines for checking that alphabetic data has been entered in a field.

• Date format checks.

• Error-handling routines, invoked when incorrect data has been entered.

You can view these routines by looking at the Visual Basic application on the CD that is supplied with this book.

Accessing Applications on the CICS Server

This section describes two methods of handling data with standard CICS object-orientated support through the ECI and secondly using VisualAge InterSpace services.

Handling Data

Let's look at some extracts taken from the Visual Basic Project module, *comsubs. bas*, of our sample application. *Comsubs.bas* is concerned with the connection to the CICS server application by native CICS calls. The data-handling methods used with VisualAge Interspace is discussed "Creating the VisualAge Interspace Service for the NACT02 CICS Server Application" later in this chapter.

The definitions of the Visual Basic GUI data fields used by *NACT05* are shown in Example 13-1.

Example 13-1. Definitions of the Visual Basic GUI Data Fields

```
'structure of Account Browser (NACT05) commarea
Public Const commBRWSlength = 30668 '0 to 30688 total value 30669
' Byte array for Acct Browse CICS COMMAREA
Public cabrws(commBRWSlength) As Byte
Public cabrws_version As String * 3
Public cabrws_request  As String * 1
Public cabrws_response As String * 4
Public cabrws_reason   As String * 4
Public cabrws_function As String * 5
Public cabrws_limit    As String * 4
Public cabrws_found    As String * 4
Public cabrws_more     As String * 4
Public cabrws_matches(80) As AccRecord
```

Note how nested structures contained within the COMMAREA are handled. The COMMAREA definition contains a datatype *AccRecord* whose definition includes a datatype of *PayHistory*. The datatype *AccRecord* is defined as shown in Example 13-2.

Example 13-2. Datatypes for AccRecord

```
Type AccRecord
   Acct        As String * 5      'Account number
   SName       As String * 18     'Last/surname
   FName       As String * 12     'First Name
   Mid         As String * 1      'Middle Initial
   Title       As String * 4      'Title e.g. Mr./Mrs./Dr.
   TelNo       As String * 10     'Telephone Number
   Address1    As String * 24     'Address field 1
```

Example 13-2. Datatypes for AccRecord (continued)

```
Address2        As String * 24    'Address field 2
Address3        As String * 24    'Address field 3
AuthUser1       As String * 32    'Additional Authorised Card User 1
AuthUser2       As String * 32    'Additional Authorised Card User 2
AuthUser3       As String * 32    'Additional Authorised Card User 3
AuthUser4       As String * 32    'Additional Authorised Card User 4
Cards           As String * 1     'Number of cards issued to Customer
Imonth          As String * 2     'Month card issued
Iday            As String * 2     'Day card issued
Iyear           As String * 2     'Year card issued
Reason          As String * 1     'Reason code for card issue
CardCode        As String * 1     'Card status Code e.g. G for Gold
Approver        As String * 3     'Code of Card issue approver
SpecialCode1    As String * 1     'Additional Privilege Code 1
SpecialCode2    As String * 1     'Additional Privilege Code 2
SpecialCode3    As String * 1     'Additional Privilege Code 3
Status          As String * 2     'Account Status
Limit           As String * 8     'Customer Account Credit Limit
History1        As PayHistory     'Payment History first of last three
                                  'months
History2        As PayHistory     'Payment History second of last three
                                  'months
History3        As PayHistory     'Payment History third of last three
                                  'months
End Type
```

PayHistory is itself a data structure of fields of type String. The datatype of String used in the Visual Basic application corresponds to a datatype of CHAR on the OS/390 host. *PayHistory* is defined in Example 13-3.

Example 13-3. Definitions of Pay History Datatype

```
Type PayHistory
  Balance       As String * 8     'Account Balance
  BMonth        As String * 2     'Month
  BDay          As String * 2     'Day
  BYear         As String * 2     'Year
  BAmount       As String * 8     'Amount of Balance
  PMonth        As String * 2     'Payment Month
  PDay          As String * 2     'Payment Day
  PYear         As String * 2     'Payment Year
  PAmount       As String * 8     'Payment Amount
End Type
```

Writing the ECI Component

This section shows extracts from the Visual Basic module *comsubs.bas* that are used to link to the CICS Browser application. The Visual Basic application makes use of the ECI Component Object Module (COM) library supplied with the CICS

Universal Clients Version 3.1. A set of samples is also supplied in the *cicsadp*\
IBM CICS Universal Client\Samples\VB directory.

Making an ECI link call to CICS

The following guidelines will help you make an ECI link call to CICS:

1. Declare and instantiate the objects to be used. This can be done in the *Form_
   Load* subroutine or at some later stage in response to some user action. Note
   that a *CclOECI* must be created first to allow use of the ECI COM class. The
   definitions look like this:

```
Public  ECI As New CclOECI
Private Connect As New CclOConn
Private Flow As New CclOFlow
Private buffer As New CclOBuf
Private UOW As New CclOUOW
```

Using the *CclOUOW* class, a number of link calls can be made to a
CICS server within a single unit of work (UOW). Updates to recoverable resources in the CICS server can then be committed or backed
out by the client program as necessary. An example of UOW use is
where several databases using the same data are to be updated by
different CICS applications. It is important that either all or none are
updated with the new information to keep them in step with one
another. This is integral to the function on mainframe CICS, but this
is an exercise for the programmer on CICS client.

By specifying a null value for the UOW, we are in effect saying that
each link call constitutes a complete unit of work (equivalent to
LINK SYNCONRETURN in the CICS server).

---

2. Set the length of the buffer to the required COMMAREA size for the Browser
   program *NACT05*:

```
buffer.SetLength commBRWSlength
```

3. Provide details of the CICS server to be used. The CICS server name variable
   CICSServer has been left as null, forcing the first entry in the CICS Client initiation file *ctg.ini* to be used. The user ID and password values are those supplied by the user at Log in. Details are supplied using the details method for
   the Connect COM class. Before the Connect COM class can be used it needs
   to be initialized using the details method:

```
Connect.Details CICSServer, Userid, Password
```

4. Build the buffer. This is done automatically, because the required fields for the
   input COMMAREA have already been set within the Data Structure, as
   described in the Data field definitions earlier in this chapter.

5. Move data into the COMMAREA byte array. The parameters used are:

Ca( )

    The COMMAREA byte array

In_str

    The input string to be added to the byte array

Ca_ofs

    The offset in the byte array at which the input string is to be added

Ca_len

    The length of the data (in bytes) to be added

Example 13-4 shows the routine that is used to move data into the COMMAREA byte array.

Example 13-4. Code to Move Data into the Byte Array for COMMAREA

```
Public Sub move_comm(ca() As Byte, in_str As String, ca_ofs As Integer, ca_len As
        Integer)
    Dim st As String
    ' Get the input string
    st = in_str
    While Len(st) < ca_len
        st = st + " "
    Wend
    ' Make sure that the result is not too long
    If Len(st) > ca_len Then
        st = Left(st, ca_len)
    End If
    ' Now, move the data into the COMMAREA array
    For i = 1 To ca_len
        ca(ca_ofs + i - 1) = Asc(Mid(st, i, 1))
    Next
End Sub
```

6. Use the *SetData* for the *CclOBuffer* object to populate the buffer with the contents of the byte array *ca*:

```
buffer.SetData ca
```

7. Now we are ready to make the call to CICS. The Link method takes as parameters the Flow object, the name of the CICS server program to be invoked, the buffer object, and a UOW object. In this example, the UOW object has been defined but not set explicitly. Java initializes it to a null value; this call is not part of a recoverable unit of work:

```
Connect.Link Flow, prog, buffer, UOW
```

8. The updated data contained in the buffer object is stored in the variable *tempca* and then restored to the COMMAREA byte array *ca*:

```
For i = 0 To commlen
        ca(i) = tempca(i)
    Next i
```

9. Finally, the CICS COM objects are deleted:

```
Public Sub deleteECIobjects()
    ' Delete the ECI objects we created
    Set buffer = Nothing
    Set Flow = Nothing
    Set Connect = Nothing
    Set ECI = Nothing
End Sub
```

Handling ECI errors

The recommended way of handling errors with the CICS ECI COM classes is to use the standard Visual Basic *On Error* statement.

The form of the call used in the sample Visual Basic application is shown in the following code extract:

```
' Execute the CICS NACT05 program

    On Error GoTo ErrorHandler
    Connect.Link Flow, prog, buffer, UOW
```

When an error condition occurs, the program logic drops through to the label *ErrorHandler* at the end of the subroutine, or in this case, function. The code below shows how the error information is stored. *CclExceptionCodes* contains details of the possible error exception codes that can be returned from CICS. Each exception code has a number and associated message that can be displayed to the application user. Where an abend has occurred, the value of the error returned is *cclTransaction* (code 13) and the *Abendcode* can be queried and displayed.

Example 13-5 shows the use of the preceding Exit Function statement to stop the error handler code being run as part of the normal flow through the function.

Example 13-5. Code to Stop Error Handling Code Used as Part of the Normal Flow

```
Exit Function
ErrorHandler:
'The connect call failed
'Parse the error number this will work regardless of
'how the ECI objects were Dimmed

Dim RealError As CclECIExceptionCodes
RealError = Err.Number And 65535 - ECI.ErrorOffset
If RealError = cclTransaction Then
    'Transaction abend, so query the Abend code
```

Example 13-5. Code to Stop Error Handling Code Used as Part of the Normal Flow (continued)

```
    If AbendCode = "AEY7" Then
MsgBox "Invalid Userid/Password to execute the CICS Program", , "CICS ECI Error"
    Else
MsgBox "Unable to execute EC01, transaction abend:" + AbendCode, , "CICS ECI Error"
    End If
Else
  MsgBox RealError, , "CICS Error"
  MsgBox Err.Description, , "CICS ECI Error"
End If
rc = RealError
End Function
```

Accessing Applications on the CICS Server with the VisualAge Interspace API

There are a number of methods for using VisualAge Interspace with CICS as a starting point for new CICS applications. We have focused on using a service to communicate using the CICS ECI with the existing CRUD program *NACT02*.

The following steps are required:

1. Use the VisualAge Interspace Service Interface Painter to create the service to link to the CICS server application.

2. Test the service from the painter.

3. Generate the Visual Basic module for the service to be used by the Visual Basic program developer.

4. Incorporate the generated service module together with other required modules into the Visual Basic project.

5. Make the necessary VisualAge Interspace API calls to link to and use the CICS server application.

We now look at each of these steps in more detail in the following sections.

Creating the VisualAge Interspace Service for the NACT02 CICS Server Application

VisualAge Interspace thinks of a service for communicating with an application as providing a request to which it receives a reply. The request is the COMMAREA being sent to the *NACT02* program and the reply is the COMMAREA returned from the *NACT02* program. Figure 13-3 shows the Defaults window.

The *Distributed Environment* for which the new services will be used is CICS. The *Buffer Type* is STRING that corresponds to the datatype of CHAR used for the COMMAREA field definitions used in our COBOL program *NACT02*. The field

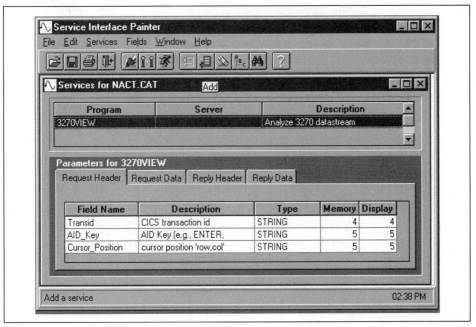

Figure 13-3. VisualAge Interspace Defaults window

definitions and services created are stored in a plain text catalog file that we have chosen to call *NACT* and placed under the Interspace base directory. These are the only default settings we need to concern ourselves with for this example.

In order to set up the COMMAREA for the service we first need to provide Interspace with definitions for fields to be used in the COMMAREA. This can be done in one of two ways:

- Typing the details into the field list

- Using Interspace to extract the field definitions from the relevant COBOL copybook

For more information about the Importing Fields topic, refer to the Interspace online help.

VisualAge Interspace allows for a request header and request data. The request header can be thought of as the fields at the start of the COMMAREA, and the request data as a set of records of the same layout returned at the end of the COMMAREA. We have chosen to split the COMMAREA between the request header and request data but could equally as well have chosen to supply the entire COMMAREA as the request data. The design of VisualAge Interspace is such that it normally expects a set of control character fields at the start of a transmission from the calling application which, amongst other information, gives the number of records of the type specified as request data that are being returned.

There is also an option Suppress Control Fields; this must be set here as the *NACT02* program will not supply or understand these control fields. When set, the Suppress Control Fields option does not send any control data or expect any to be returned from the called application. Interspace assumes that it is to receive one record whose structure is specified by the fields set up in the Request Data. This simplifies the communication with any CICS ECI application.

NACT02 only ever receives one record. If we were to work with a different application that provided a list of records, then there are additional steps which would need to be implemented. VisualAge Interspace uses the idea of what it calls a *composite service* to deal with this type of CICS application. The data area used to hold the records being returned by the CICS application is defined as a single field. This field can then be supplied as the request data to a composite service set up by the user which transforms it into a field array using the record structure detailed in the reply data of the composite service.

Taking a simple case the field *RecordData* returned from a CICS application contains several customer records. This data is supplied as the request data to a composite service. The reply data is defined as consisting of three fields:

- name (a nine-character STRING)
- valuea (a one-character STRING)
- valueb (a one-character STRING)

Data is extracted from *RecordData* using the field structure specified in the reply data for the *composite service*. The process is then repeated on the remaining characters in the string until it is used up, as shown in the following table:

Reply Data Provided from CICS Application	Request Data Supplied to Composite Service	Reply Data from Composite Service
field1 xxxx field2 xxxx RecordData SMITH....12JONES.... 34	RecordData SMITH....12JONES.... 34	name(1) SMITH.... valuea(1) 1 valueb(1) 2 name(2) JONES.... valuea(2) 3 valueb(2) 4

Again, this idea is explained in more detail in the online help provided with Visu-alAge Interspace.

Once the necessary fields have been set up within the Service Interface Painter, you can then create the service itself.

Click on the Add icon to create a new service.

The Add Service panel, as shown in Figure 13-4, is then used to add the fields in the order required for the *NACT02* COMMAREA.

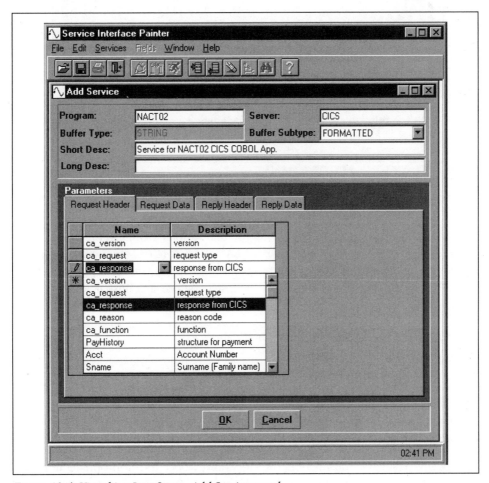

Figure 13-4. VisualAge InterSpace: Add Service panel

Testing the VisualAge Interspace Service

Once the service has been created it can be tested within the painter provided that the CICS client has been set up correctly and the *NACT02* program is accessible. To bring up the Test window, select the *NACT02* service and click on the Test icon; the Test window is shown in Figure 13-5.

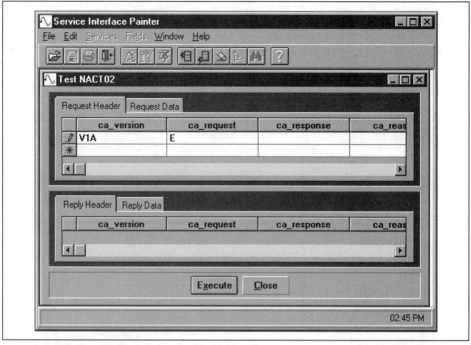

Figure 13-5. VisualAge Interspace: Test Window

You can then add the values required for the various COMMAREA fields. Click *Execute* to send the completed COMMAREA to the *NACT02* program. The Reply Header and Reply Data are returned from the CICS application assuming it is available. This means that the service can be tested before any Visual Basic code is written.

Generating the Visual Basic module for the service

Once the service has been tested and data successfully retrieved, you can generate the required Visual Basic module that will link to *NACT02*:

1. Click on the Generate icon to display the Service Interface Generation window, shown in Figure 13-6.

2. Check the Visual Basic box, if it is not already checked.

3. Specify a suitable destination directory and select the appropriate template from the set provided by VisualAge Interspace. For this synchronous communication with CICS we specify the *vbsync.tpl* (seeFigure 13-6).

4. Click *OK*. This causes the Visual Basic module *NACT02.bas* to be generated in the specified directory:

The module generated contains all the necessary procedures required to communicate with the *NACT02* program, and includes all the relevant data structures.

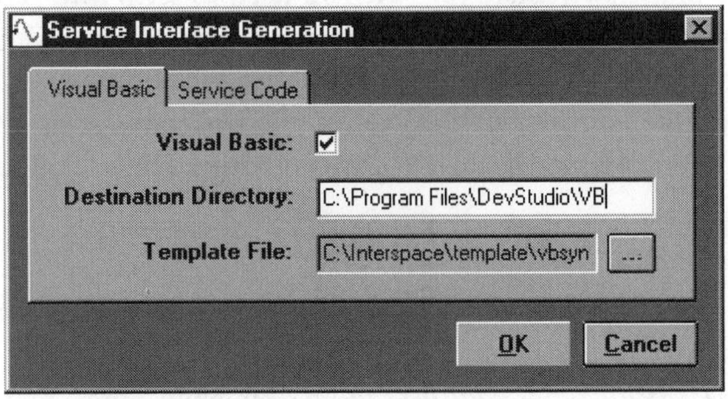

Figure 13-6. VisualAge Interspace: Service Interface Generation

Incorporating the generated service module into the Visual Basic project

To incorporate the service module into Visual Basic:

1. Add the *NACT02.bas* module.

2. Add the required Interspace function modules *DCIDPL.bas* and *DCIGEL.bas*.

Coding the required VisualAge Interspace API calls

Programming steps include:

1. Initialize Interspace to CICS at startup.

2. Create instances of the structures for *NACT02* used to send and receive data.

3. Prepare the COMMAREA fields required to be sent.

4. Issue the Interspace request and receive the reply.

5. Exit Interspace when the program has ended.

These steps are described in more detail below.

Initialize Interspace to CICS at startup. The application name field has been specified as *NACT* rather than *NACT02*. We are making use of the catalog file *nact.cat*, which contains the details of the *NACT02* service and could be used to hold additional services. It is not unusual to keep a large number of services for related applications in the same catalog. The *nact.cat* file needs to be made available to VisualAge Interspace by placing it in the Windows NT path or current directory. The code looks like this:

```
ReturnCode = dcifx_init("CICS", "NACT", Userid, Password)
If ReturnCode = -1 Then
    dcifx_show_error vbCritical, "Interspace Initialization Failed"
    Call endProgram
End If
```

Create instances of the structures for NACT02 used to send and receive data. In order to communicate with the *NACT02* server application, we need to create instances of the request and reply structures that will be used by the Interspace service. These are then accessed from within two separate forms, so we have chosen to add the declaration to the *NACT02.bas* module. The code looks like this:

```
'Create instances of the request message NACT02_request_msg
'and reply message NACT02_reply_msg.
Global NACT02_Request As NACT02_request_msg
Global NACT02_Reply As NACT02_reply_msg
```

Prepare the COMMAREA fields required to be sent. Now we need to set the required COMMAREA fields. The code looks like this:

```
'Set value of version in request service header
NACT02_Request.header.ca_version = "V1A"
'Set value of request type in request Service Header
NACT02_Request.header.ca_request = "E"
'Ensure we can write data into the RequestData
ReDim NACT02_Request.data(1)
'Set value of account number in request data
NACT02_Request.data(1).Acct = "10000"
```

Notice the use of header and data prefixes together with the fields names that were used in the Service Interface Painter service.

Issue the Interspace request and receive the reply. Once the required data has been added to the request COMMAREA we can issue the call to the *NACT02* program through Interspace and check the response. Interspace returns the reply from *NACT02* in the *NACT02_Reply* object structure. The code looks like this:

```
'Issue the relevant call for Interspace to send the request
'to NACT02 and receive the reply
ReturnCode = receive_NACT02_sync(NACT02_Request, NACT02_Reply)
'Check request issued correctly
    If ReturnCode = -1 Then
        dcifx_show_error vbCritical, "Call to the CICS application NACT02 failed
        to complete"
        Exit Sub
    End If
```

Exit Interspace when ending the program. To end communication using Interspace, issue the *dcifx_exit* call for CICS:

```
'Check to see if Interspace was initialized
If CICSOpen = 1 Then
        'Issue call to exit Interspace
        ReturnCode = dcifx_exit("CICS")
        'Check request issued correctly
        If ReturnCode = -1 Then
           dcifx_show_error vbCritical, "Interspace Exit Call Failed"
        End If
    End If
```

Interspace insulates the Visual Basic programmer from needing to know anything about CICS in order to make use of the *NACT02* program. You can use the same Visual Basic application to communicate with several CICS server applications by generating additional service modules using the Service Interface Painter, and then adding them to the project.

Communicating with CICS

In order to communicate with a CICS application on a CICS server machine, you need have an IBM CICS Universal Client on your workstation, and to establish a connection from this client to the CICS server. In the sample application, we use TCP/IP to connect from our CICS client to our CICS for OS/390 server. However, our CICS for OS/390 server makes use of an LU6.2 protocol. Therefore, there is a mismatch between our workstation using TCP/IP and the server's SNA LU6.2 protocol. This requires a translator of some sort to be used to allow the client and server to communicate. Fortunately CICS can handle the necessary translation using the TCP62 driver.

There are two ways to connect your CICS Universal Client to CICS TS on OS/390. You can use TCP62, which we are going to describe, or SNA. Talk to your local SNA specialist if your site uses this connection method.

A Digression About TCP62

TCP62 enables a CICS Universal Client to use TCP/IP to access a CICS Transaction Server. This access is achieved using a product called AnyNet. It is a part of ACF/VTAM for OS/390. On the client workstation, the AnyNet component is provided by IBM Personal Communications for Windows NT, Windows 98, and IBM Personal Communications for OS/2. Don't worry if you think that you don't have this because a cut-down version is shipped with the CICS Universal Client. When you install the latter, just make sure that you select the TCP62 checkbox in the installation wizard. This is how TCP62 works:

1. The CICS Universal Client, using the definition in your *ctg.ini* file, passes data to the AnyNet.

If you have been using earlier versions (before Version 3.1) of the CICS Universal Client, you are probably used to the name *cicscli.ini*. This has been changed to *ctg.ini* in Version 3.1.

2. The AnyNet component on the client workstation uses the domain name suffix with the partner LU name to generate an Internet Protocol (IP) name. The IP address for this name is then determined either from the local IP hosts file or from the Domain Name Server (DNS). Using standard TCP/IP flows, the data is shipped from the TCP/IP component on the workstation to TCP/IP on OS/390.

3. TCP/IP on OS/390 routes the data received from the workstation to the Any-Net component on OS/390.

4. The SNA over TCP/IP feature of AnyNet translates the inbound IP routing information to SNA routing information. The data is passed to VTAM and, in turn, to CICS Transaction Server for OS/390. Figure 13-7 illustrate the interrelations between the various products.

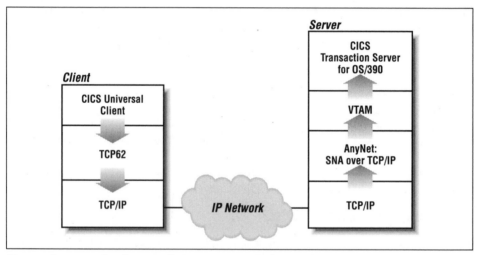

Figure 13-7. Data flow between the CICS Universal Client and CICS TS 1.3

For more information refer to *VTAM AnyNet: Guide to SNA over TCP/IP V4R4 for MVS/ESA*. This manual describes how to configure AnyNet to run on your OS/390 system

That's the end of the digression; now back to the business of configuring the host and client.

Configuring the Application

In order to establish the necessary communication between the CICS client and CICS server you need to:

1. Configure CICS Transaction Server for OS/390 for TCP62

2. Configure VTAM for OS/390

3. Handle data conversion

4. Configure the Windows NT *etc\HOSTS* file on the client

5. Configure the CICS Universal Client

We will now look at these steps in more detail in the following sections.

Configuring CICS Transaction Server for OS/390 for TCP62

In order to use the TCP62 driver from the CICS client, set up the LU6.2 terminal autoinstall on the CICS Transaction Server for OS/390 first:

1. Create a copy of the supplied autoinstall connection and session models and group, CBPS:

```
CEDA COPY CONNECTION(CBPS) GROUP(DFHAI62) TO(CBPS)
CEDA COPY SESSION(CBPS) GROUP(DFHAI62) TO(CBPS)
CEDA EXPAND GROUP(CBPS)
```

Figure 13-8 shows the screen.

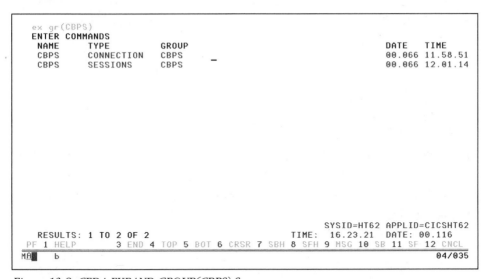

```
 ex gr(CBPS)
 ENTER COMMANDS
   NAME      TYPE          GROUP                          DATE    TIME
   CBPS      CONNECTION    CBPS          _                00.066 11.58.51
   CBPS      SESSIONS      CBPS                            00.066 12.01.14




                                            SYSID=HT62 APPLID=CICSHT62
      RESULTS: 1 TO 2 OF 2               TIME:  16.23.21 DATE: 00.116
   PF 1 HELP        3 END 4 TOP 5 BOT 6 CRSR 7 SBH 8 SFH 9 MSG 10 SB 11 SF 12 CNCL
 MA    b                                                         04/035
```

Figure 13-8. CEDA EXPAND GROUP(CBPS) Screen

Check that the CONNECTION definition has ATTACHSEC set to LOCAL by typing **V** (for VIEW) next to the CONNECTION entry displayed and page down (PF8) to see the ATTACHSEC attributes.

2. Check the SESSION definition. You can modify settings by typing **A** (for ALTER) next to the appropriate entry in the screen. In the session definition:

- — Set MAXIMUM to 8,1 (Maximum eight sessions, one contention winner only).

- — Set MODENAME to either #INTER or IBMRDB (these are present in the default mode table, ISTINCLM, which is known to all VTAMs). What you specify here must be known to VTAM and must match MODENAME in the client *INI* file (*ctg.ini*).

3. Install this GROUP definition:

```
CEDA INSTALL GROUP(CBPS)
```

4. Add the new CBPS group to a list. In order to install your group at CICS startup, add the LIST to the GRPLIST=(...) in the system initialization parameters:

```
CEDA ADD GROUP(CBPS) LIST(locallist)
```

where *locallist* is a unique name for you. If you enter a new name, it is automatically created.

5. Set the terminal autoinstall program to DFHZATDY (default is DFHZATDX, which does not support LU6.2 autoinstall):

```
CEMT SET AUTOINSTALL PROGRAM(DFHZATDY)
```

6. Check that the system initialization parameters are defined as follows:

- — *AIEXIT=DFHZATDY*

- — *ISC=YES*

- — *GRPLST=(DFHLIST,locallst)*

Configuring VTAM for OS/390

Check with your VTAM system programmer before attempting to do the following steps yourself:

1. Ensure that the VTAM APPL definition for CICS has:

```
AUTH=(ACQ,VPACE,PASS),
    VPACING=5,
    PARSESS=YES,
    SONSCIP=NO
```

You must NOT have APPC=YES on the CICS Applid definition. And if you use #INTER as your MODENAME, you do not need MODETAB=MTCICS on the CICS APPL definition. The default is ISTINCLM.

2. Create a major node definition for AnyNet. If this is a new system, the VTAM JCL will probably be in SYS1.PROCLIB(*memberName*), and it uses the *ATCSTR00* startup options member in SYS1.VTAMLST. Example 13-6 shows an example of the definition.

Example 13-6. Sample of VTAM Definition

```
0         1         2         3         4         5         6         7         8
1234567890123456789012345678901234567890123456789012345678901234567890123456789 0
*    TCP62 major node definition
TCP62>>    VBUILD TYPE=TCP,                                                     X
              DNSUFX=domain-suffix-of-TCPIP-in-the-MVS-with-CICS                 X
              PORT=397,                                                          X
              TCPIPJOB=TCPIP
TCP62G    GROUP ISTATUS=ACTIVE
TCP62L    LINE  ISTATUS=ACTIVE
TCP62P    PU    ISTATUS ACTIVE,NETID=VTAM-network-name-of-client-LU
```

> Your system programmer may be using JCL from a different dataset and with a different member name. Find where the *//VTAMLST DD* card points, usually to *SYS1.VTAMLST.* Edit *SYS1.VTAMLST* and create a new member; for example, *TCP62.* In TCP code, the macros are column sensitive.

3. There are two ways that you can use TCP62. The preferred method is to make a dynamic link; this is easier and, by definition, does not need you to define multiple static CDRSC definitions within VTAM. To do this you need to check to see if the parameter DYNLU=YES is set as a startup option for VTAM. DYNLU=YES dynamically allocates CDRSC definitions. For security reasons, this is often turned off at many sites. If this is the case, your VTAM programmer will have to set up a *localLuName* for you. This is entered in the *ctg.ini* file. To check the status of this parameter, locate member ATCSTR00 in SYS1. VTAMLST and check that DYNLU=YES.

4. To check your VTAM to TCP/IP interface settings, enter on a system console:

```
/D NET,ID=TCP62P
```

where Where *TCP62P* is the PU name from the sample JCL shown in Example 13-6. If your system is active, look in your system log and it returns:

```
D NET,ID=TCP62P,E
IST097I DISPLAY ACCEPTED
IST075I NAME = TCP62, TYPE = PU_T2.1 170
IST486I STATUS= ACTIV, DESIRED STATE= ACTIV
```

Handling Data Conversion

The CICS Transaction Server for OS/390 uses an EBCDIC code page whereas the CICS Universal Client for Windows NT uses an ASCII code page. It follows that the COMMAREA supplied within an ECI request requires data conversion. To keep things simple, it is a good idea to arrange all the fields defined within the COMMAREA into datatype CHARACTER on the OS/390 system.

Data conversion is handled by the system that owns the resource being used. It follows that for an ECI request of the type we are using, the CICS Transaction Server for OS/390 is responsible for the data conversion. The CICS-supplied macro DFHCNV is used to perform the conversion.

 If it is not practical for all fields to be CHARACTER type, then the DFHCNV macro must be coded to specify which conversion is necessary for each part of the COMMAREA, and this must be kept up to date as the COMMAREA structure is changed.

Assemble and link edit the sample DFHCNV macro. An extract from the source of a DFHCNV macro is shown in Example 13-7.

Example 13-7. Sample of the DFHCNV Macro

```
        DFHCNV TYPE=INITIAL
* Program: NACT02
*
        DFHCNV TYPE=ENTRY,RTYPE=PC,RNAME=NACT02,USREXIT=NO,           *
            SRVERCP=037,CLINTCP=850
        DFHCNV TYPE=SELECT,OPTION=DEFAULT
        DFHCNV TYPE=FIELD,OFFSET=0,DATATYP=CHARACTER,DATALEN=32767,   *
            LAST=YES
*
* Program: NACT05
*
        DFHCNV TYPE=ENTRY,RTYPE=PC,RNAME=NACT05,USREXIT=NO,           *
            SRVERCP=037,CLINTCP=850
        DFHCNV TYPE=SELECT,OPTION=DEFAULT
        DFHCNV TYPE=FIELD,OFFSET=0,DATATYP=CHARACTER,DATALEN=32767,   *
            LAST=YES                                                  *
        DFHCNV TYPE=FINAL
```

The following parameters are of particular interest:

DFHCNV TYPE=INITIAL

Defines the beginning of the conversion table.

DFHCNV TYPE=ENTRY

You specify an entry for each resource where data conversion is to take place. The entry in Example 13-7 is specific to the sample programs *NACT02* and *NACT05.*

RTYPE=PC

You specify a resource type of PC (Program Call) for a CICS server program that is to be invoked by the ECI.

RNAME=SRVTIME

Specifies the resource name is the CICS server program. There are two files that you have to define in the sample application. They are *NACT02* (the business logic) and *NACT05* (the browse logic).

SRVERCP=037

Specifies the server code page. 037 (U.S. English, EBCDIC) is normally used in the U.S.; 285 (UK, EBCDIC) is normally used in the U.K.

CLINTCP=850

Specifies the client code page, 437 (U.S. English, ASCII) and is normally used in the U.S.; 850 (W. Europe, ASCII) is normally used in Latin-1 countries in Western Europe.

OFFSET=0

Specifies the byte offset in the COMMAREA at which the data conversion should start. *OFFSET=0* specifies the beginning of the COMMAREA.

DATATYP=CHARACTER

Specifies that the data in the COMMAREA is a character field. The sample program uses only uppercase alphanumeric characters.

DATALEN=32767

Specifies the length of the data field to be converted. For variable length fields, specify the maximum possible length (32767).

DFHCNV TYPE=FINAL

Defines the end of the conversion table.

Configuring the Windows NT HOSTS File on the Client

To configure the Windows NT HOSTS file on the client, locate the HOSTS file on NT in: *\WINNT\system32\drivers\etc\hosts* and add an entry such as:

```
# MVSA       (this is a comment line)
n.n.n.n.    lu.netid.domain-suffix
```

The items in this macro are:

n.n.n.n.

The TCP/IP address (for example 195.24.24.292)

lu

The LU name (`applid`) of the CICS region

netid

The VTAM network name of the CICS region. You can find the LU name and the *netid* by entering *D NET,ID=lu,E* on an OS/390 system.

Domain-suffix

The name of your local domain, for example, *hursley.ibm.com*

In this command, LU name and net ID are reversed relative to standard SNA conventions. For the changes to take effect, you need to reboot your Windows NT system.

Configuring the CICS Universal Client

Before you start to configure the CICS Universal Client, you should have the following information:

- The IP address and domain name of an OS/390 system.

- The name of the CICS server. This is a purely arbitrary name but it is as well to decide on a name at this stage and keep to it.

- A description of the CICS server. Again, this is an arbitrary description.

- The protocol to be used. In our case, this will be TCP62 to allow the necessary communication between the client using TCP/IP and the server using LU6.2 protocols.

Either use the CICS Universal Clients configuration tool or locate and edit the client INIT file:

```
\Program Files\ IBM\IBM CICS Universal Client\bin\ctg.ini
```

then code the information as shown in Example 13-8.

Example 13-8. Sample CTG.INI file

```
        SECTION CLIENT = CICSHT61
        CCSID=850    ; Ensures that the correct codepage is used for our ACCT app.
        CPNAME=GBIBMIYA.IYAMT0E0              ; See the VTAM definitions
        CPIPADDRESSMASK=FFFFFE00
        DCECELLDIRECTORY=Y
        DOMAINNAMESUFFIX=HURSLEY.IBM.COM
        ENABLEPOPUPS=Y
        LOADMANAGER=N
        LOGFILE=CICSCLI.LOG
        MAXBUFFERSIZE=32
        MAXREQUESTS=256
        MAXSERVERS=10
        MAXWRAPSIZE=0
        REMOTENODEINACTIVITYPOLLINTERVAL=60
        SRVRETRYINTERVAL=60
        TERMINALEXIT=EXIT
        TRACEFILE=CICSCLI.BIN
        USEOEMCP=N
ENDSECTION
```

Example 13-8. Sample CTG.INI file (continued)

```
SECTION SERVER = cicsadp                      ; Arbitrary name
    DESCRIPTION=TCP62 link to winmvs26    ; Arbitrary description
    LOCALLUNAME=LU62****          ; This uses dynamic generation of an LUname
    LUIPADDRESSMASK=FFFFFE00
    SNAMAXRUSIZE=1024
    SNASESSIONLIMIT=8
    MODENAME=ibmrdb               ;Corresponds to the name in the CICS session
    SNAPACINGSIZE=8               ;Corresponds to CICS MAXIMUM number of SESSIONs
    NETNAME=GBIBMIYA.CICSHT61   ; The VTAM netid and the name of the CICS region
    PROTOCOL=TCP62
    UPPERCASESECURITY=N
    USENPI=N
ENDSECTION

SECTION DRIVER = TCP62
    DRIVERNAME=CCLTCP62
ENDSECTION

SECTION LOADMANAGER
    TYPE=1
    Timeout=60
ENDSECTION
```

 The *CPName* must be the net ID of the client plus some arbitrary mask.

The *CPIPAddressMask* masks out all but the right-most bits which will be set dynamically. This mask should match *LUIPAddressMask*.

The *DomainNameSuffix* is determined by the network systems programmer. Note that this may not be the same as the domain name suffix of the host CICS as specified in the TCPMAJ definition if CICS TS for OS/390 is in a different domain from the client.

For *LocalLUName* you should use 4 asterisks (****) on the right of the mask because the sample autoinstall program uses the last four characters of the *LUNAME* to define the connection name, and this must be unique.

Testing the TCP62 Connection

To check to see if your CICS client TCP62 connection is working, you can start a *cicsterm* session as described in the following procedure. Then either use one of the CICS supplied transaction commands; for example, CEMT or CEDA, or if you are really bold try entering the NACT transaction. The screen will look similar to Figure 13-9.

```
ACCOUNTS MENU

    TO SEARCH BY NAME, ENTER SURNAME AND IF REQUIRED, FIRST NAME

        SURNAME     : _             (1 TO 18 ALPHABETIC CHRS)
        FIRST NAME  :               (1 TO 12 ALPHABETIC CHRS OPTIONAL)

    TO PROCESS AN ACCOUNT, ENTER REQUEST TYPE AND ACCOUNT NUMBER

        REQUEST TYPE:               (D-DISPLAY, A-ADD, M-MODIFY, X-DELETE, P-PRINT)
        ACCOUNT     :               (10000 TO 79999)
        PRINTER ID  :               (1 TO 4 CHARACTERS (REQUIRED FOR PRINT REQUEST))




    ENTER DATA AND PRESS ENTER FOR SEARCH OR ACCOUNT REQUEST OR PRESS CLEAR TO EXIT
  4A           b                                                              05/022
```

Figure 13-9. CICSTERM: The NACT transaction

To start a *cicsterm* session:

1. If the CICS Universal Client has been running, stop the client by selecting *Start → Programs → IBM CICS Universal CICS Client → Stop Client* or at a command prompt by entering:

   ```
   cicscli -x
   ```

2. Start the CICS Client by selecting *Start → Programs → IBM CICS Universal CICS Client → Start Client* or at a command prompt by entering:

   ```
   cicscli -s
   ```

3. To test your connections to the server start a CICS terminal session, either by selecting *Start → Programs → IBM CICS Universal CICS Client → CICS Terminal* or at a command prompt by entering:

   ```
   cicsterm -s=CICSADP
   ```

   where CICSADP is the name of your definition that you created in the *ctg.ini* file. When it is connected to your CICS region a terminal identifier appears at the bottom left of the *cicsterm* window; for example, /AAA.

4. Verify that the connection works by typing *CEMT* in the CICS terminal window and pressing the Enter key (on a CICS terminal, this is the Ctrl key). This starts the CICS Master Terminal program. Alternatively you could enter the transaction identifier of our application (*NACT* in uppercase).

 Many installations put a high level of security on the CEMT transaction, so do not be surprised if you get a message about a security violation.

Running the ACCT Application

To install the application open the *Visual Basic with Interspace Customer Service Application* directory on the CD-ROM and double-click on the setup icon.

What's Next....

Chapter 12, *Designing the Visual Basic Component*, and Chapter 13, *Programming the Visual Basic Program*, described how to get a Visual Basic application working using ECI through a CICS client connection. Part VII describes how to develop a Java application and link two major products, CICS and MQSeries together. Kan-DoIT's managers want the ability to enter an account number and view the details of the account without, in this case, making any changes.

VII

CICS and MQSeries

This Part provides the foundation to integrate our CICS application with another product, in this case, IBM's message queueing product called MQSeries. The reason for doing this is to provide the head office of the KanDoIT company with a way of viewing the customer accounts from a workstation.

Important features of a message queuing product are:

*   Assured and unattended delivery of information
*   Network independence
*   Availability over a range of operating systems and hardware platforms

The IBM MQSeries range of products provides application programming services that enable application programs to communicate with each other using messages and queues. This form of communication is referred to as *commercial messaging*. It provides assured, once-only message delivery. Using MQSeries means that you can separate application programs, so that the program sending a message can continue processing without having to wait for a reply from the receiving programs. If the receiver, or the communication channel to it, is temporarily unavailable, the message can be forwarded at a later time. MQSeries also provides mechanisms for the acknowledgment of messages received and processed.

One of the difficult areas of developing good commercial applications is to ensure that the interfaces between the products are as seamless as possible. To overcome this problem there are two bridge interfaces—MQSeries-CICS bridge and MQSeries-IMS bridge. Obviously we are only concerned with the MQSeries-CICS bridge in this part. There are two ways to use this bridge, the first, that we will be using, is the DPL function that accesses a user's application directly while the other uses a user exit to emulate a 3270 terminal. This part contains the following chapters:

- Chapter 14, *Designing an Application to Use the MQSeries-CICS Bridge.*

- Chapter 15, *Programming the MQSeries-CICS Bridge.*

In addition to the usual software, we have used the following in this part:

- MQSeries for OS/390 Version 2.1

- MQSeries for Windows NT Version 5.1

- Java Development Kit (JDK) 1.2, which includes Swing

14

Designing an Application to Use the MQSeries-CICS Bridge

The application described in this chapter is required for the head office to view a customer account. It makes use of the inquire function provided within the *NACT02* program. The application needs to allow the user to input a customer account number and retrieve the account details. No modifications to the data will be made.

Background to MQSeries

Programs in the MQSeries application suite can be running on different computers, on different operating systems, and at different locations. The applications are written using a common programming interface known as the Message Queue Interface (MQI), so that applications developed on one platform can be ported to others.

Figure 14-1 shows two applications communicate using messages and queues; one application puts a message on a queue, and the other application gets that message from the queue.

Queue Managers

In MQSeries, queues are managed by a component called a queue manager. The queue manager provides messaging services for the applications and processes the MQI calls they issue. The queue manager ensures that messages are put on the correct queue or that they are routed to another queue manager.

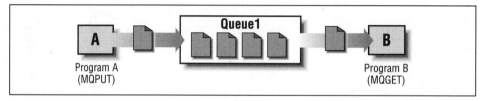

Figure 14-1. MQSeries: Messaging using a single queue manager

Before applications can send any messages, you must create a queue manager and some queues. MQSeries for Windows NT Version 5.1 provides a utility called MQSeries Explorer to help you do this and to create any other MQSeries objects that you need for your applications.

How Applications Identify Themselves to Queue Managers

Any MQSeries application must make a successful connection to a queue manager before it can make any successful MQI calls. When the application successfully makes the connection, the queue manager returns a connection handle. This is an identifier that the application must specify each time it issues an MQI call.

Opening a Queue

Before your application can use a queue for messaging, it must open the queue. If you are putting a message on a queue, your application must open the queue for putting. Similarly, if you are getting a message from a queue, your application must open the queue for getting. You can specify that a queue is opened for both getting and putting, if required. The queue manager returns an object handle if the open request is successful. The application specifies this handle, together with the connection handle, when it issues a put or a get call. This ensures that the request is carried out on the correct queue.

Putting and Getting Messages

When the open request is confirmed, your application can put a message on the queue. To do this, it uses another MQI call on which you have to specify a number of parameters and data structures. These define all the information about the message you are putting, including the message type, its destination, which options are set, and so on. The message data (that is, the application-specific contents of the message your application is sending) is defined in a buffer, which you specify in the MQI call. When the queue manager processes the call, it completes a message descriptor, which contains information that is needed to ensure the message can be delivered properly. The message descriptor is in a format defined by MQSeries; the message data is defined by your application (this is what you put into the message data buffer in your application code). Bear in mind that these values are not only determined by the queue manager but can also be defined in your program.

The program that gets the messages from the queue must first open the queue for getting messages. It must then issue another MQI call to get the message from the queue. On this call, you have to specify which message you want to get. Finally, it has to close the queue.

If your messaging application has only a low volume throughput, you will find the MQPUT1 call useful. It combines open, put, close in one call; thus, saving computer resources.

Messaging Using More Than One Queue Manager

The arrangement in Figure 14-1 is not typical for a one messaging application because both programs are running on the same computer, and connected to the same queue manager. In a commercial application, the putting and getting programs would probably be on different computers, and so be connected to different queue managers.

Figure 14-2 shows how messaging works where the program putting the message and the program getting the message are on the different computers and are connected to different queue managers.

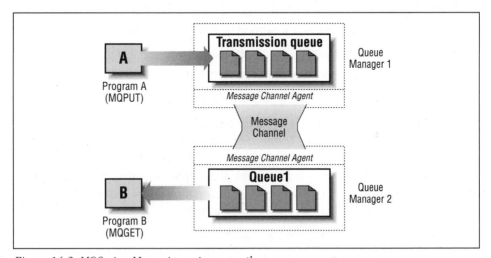

Figure 14-2. MQSeries: Messaging using more than one queue manager

The difference between Figure 14-1 and Figure 14-2 is the addition of a message channel and a transmission queue.

The MQSeries-CICS Bridge

The MQSeries-CICS bridge enables an application, not running in a CICS environment, to run a program or transaction on CICS and get a response back. This non-CICS application can be run from any environment that has access to an MQSeries network that encompasses MQSeries for OS/390.

A program is a CICS program that can be invoked using the *EXEC CICS LINK* command. It must conform to the DPL subset of the CICS API; that is, it must not use CICS terminal or syncpoint facilities. The full list is documented in the *CICS Application Programming Guide*.

A transaction is a CICS transaction designed to run on a 3270 terminal. This transaction can use BMS or Terminal Control (TC) commands. It can be conversational or pseudo-conversational. It is permitted to issue syncpoints.

When To Use the MQSeries-CICS Bridge

The MQSeries-CICS bridge allows an application to run a 3270-based CICS transaction, without knowledge of the 3270 data stream. It uses standard CICS and MQSeries security features and can be configured to authenticate, trust, or ignore the requestor's user ID. Given this flexibility, there are many instances where the MQSeries-CICS bridge can be used:

- To write a new MQSeries application that needs access to logic or data (or both) that reside on your CICS server.

- To enable your Lotus Notes application to run CICS programs.

- To be able to access your CICS applications from:

    — Your MQSeries Java client application

    — A web browser using the MQSeries Internet gateway.

The MQSeries-CICS DPL bridge allows an application to run a single CICS program or a set of CICS programs (often referred to as a unit of work). It caters to the application that waits for a response to come back before it runs the next CICS program (synchronous processing) and to the application that requests one or more CICS programs to run, but doesn't wait for a response (asynchronous processing). To enable the MQSeries-CICS bridge to work:

- MQSeries and CICS must be running in the same OS/390 image.

- The MQSeries-CICS bridge queue is local (same queue manager) as the MQSeries-CICS bridge.

- The reply-to queue can be either local or remote (on a different queue manager).

- The MQSeries-CICS bridge tasks run in the same CICS as the bridge monitor. The user programs can be in the same or a different CICS system.

- The MQSeries CICS adapter is enabled.

Enough about the background; what are the key things that have to be done to use the MQSeries-CICS bridge in the sample application?

The MQSeries queue defined to hold requests for the CICS bridge is not to be used by any other application. Each CICS bridge monitor task started requires its own MQSeries queue to hold requests.

Designing the Graphical User Interface

The main panel for this Java application has to contain all the fields returned in the COMMAREA from the *NACT02* program. The main panel (see Figure 14-3) has a clear separation between the area where data is to be inputted and the fields that are used to hold the information returned from the CICS program. The information returned is itself divided into four areas: top left for customer details, top right for details of others who can charge to the customer's account, bottom left for card details and bottom right for billing history (see *RecordPanel.java* for these details). The four sections are similar to those used with the web component of the Account Details panel output screen described in Chapter 8, *Designing the Web Component.*

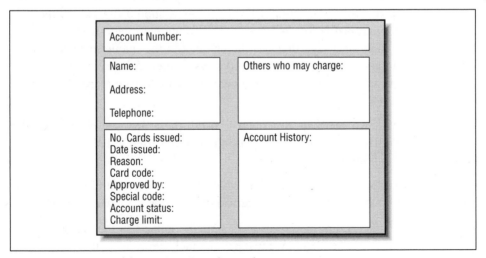

Figure 14-3. Design of the Account Details panel

Designing the Java Application

The steps required within the Java application are as follows:

1. Obtain user input of the required Account Number keyfield

2. Connect to the MQSeries queue manager

3. Open the relevant MQSeries queues to be used

4. Create an MQSeries message containing the NACT02 COMMAREA suitable for use with the MQSeries-CICS DPL bridge

5. Send the message to the appropriate MQSeries for OS/390 queue manager

6. Receive the reply message containing the updated NACT02 COMMAREA

7. Check that the CICS program has not reported any errors

8. Display the relevant information obtained from the COMMAREA

Configuring MQSeries

An MQSeries client is part of an MQSeries product that can be installed on a machine without installing the full queue manager. It is possible to have only an MQSeries client on the machine from which the Java head office application is to run and have all the MQSeries objects that are used defined on the Windows NT server's queue manager. There are advantages and disadvantages to this which are discussed in detail in MQSeries documentation.

We have chosen to have a queue manager set up on our Windows NT Java machine to improve the robustness of the application should the link to the OS/390 machine be unavailable for any reason. The additional queue manager allows messages to be kept until such times as the channel to the queue manager on the OS/390 machine is available. This is referred to as assured delivery. It ensures that the message is received when the channel connecting the queue managers is available and is sent once and once only.

Whichever of the two methods described is used, there are two changes to the Java application that are necessary. They are the libraries used at link-edit time and the channel definitions; see Figure 14-4.

The Java application, in our case, uses an MQI channel to send and receive messages to and from the local queue manager on the Windows NT workstation.

The queue that it is sending messages to is actually defined to the OS/390 queue manager. Messages are sent over a message channel. Reply messages created by the MQSeries-CICS DPL bridge are sent to the reply-to queue on Windows NT queue manager by means of a separate message channel. Separate message

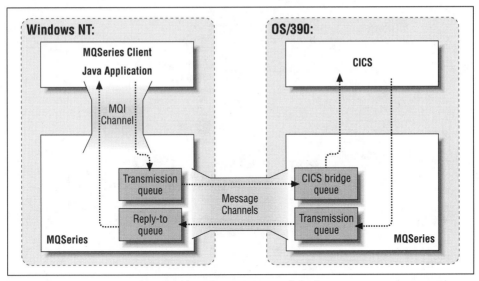

Figure 14-4. Connections between the Java program and the host

channels are required to send and receive messages between queue managers, as message channels only have the ability to send MQSeries messages in one direction.

To process the MQSeries message sent from the Java application and link to/run the CICS program *NACT02*, we make use of the MQSeries-CICS DPL bridge.

Running CICS DPL Programs

The MQSeries message provides the data necessary to run the program. The bridge task builds a COMMAREA from this data, and runs the program using the *EXEC CICS LINK* command. Figure 14-5 shows the sequence taken to process a single message to run a CICS DPL program.

The following describes each step, and explains what takes place:

1. A message with a request to run a CICS program is put on the CICS bridge queue.

2. The CICS bridge monitor task, which is waiting for messages, recognizes that a *start unit of work* message has arrived. This information is contained in the message header in the correlation ID field, which contains a value MQCI_NEW_SESSION.

3. Relevant authentication checks are made, and a CICS DPL bridge task is started with the appropriate authority.

4. The CICS DPL bridge task removes the message from the CICS bridge queue.

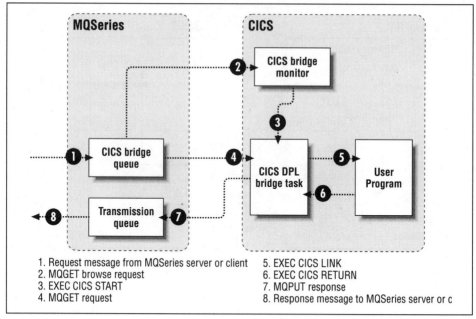

Figure 14-5. Details of the MQSeries-CICS DPL bridge

5. The CICS DPL bridge task builds a COMMAREA from the data in the message and issues an EXEC CICS LINK for the program requested in the message.

6. The program executes and returns the response in the COMMAREA used by the request.

7. The CICS DPL bridge task reads the COMMAREA, creates a message, and puts it on the reply-to queue specified in the request message. All response messages (normal and error, requests and replies) are put to the reply-to queue with default context.

8. A message is returned to the MQSeries server or client.

A unit of work can be just a single-user program, or it can be multiple-user programs. There is no limit to the number of messages you can send to make up a unit of work.

Why Design It This Way?

The same information could have been obtained by setting up a CICS client to server link; so why have we chosen to use an MQSeries method to obtain the data? MQSeries allows applications on disparate platforms to be accessed and used within a single application. An MQSeries message obtains information from our CICS program on OS/390. A separate message can be used to obtain information from a non-CICS application on a different platform such as a credit check application running on an AIX machine. The asynchronous nature of MQSeries messaging means that messages can be sent almost simultaneously to obtain information from several different programs.

This head office application is seen as a first step in a larger process to create new applications that can provide head office with full customer details and statistics in a single view.

Using MQSeries for Java provides us with what is seen as one of the main advantages of Java: *Write once, run anywhere.* The Java application is readily portable and the code and structures reusable. The Java application can be transformed easily into a Java applet or servlet if we wish to make it available as part of a web-based application in the future.

What's Next...

Having introduced the MQSeries-CICS bridge and outlined the design, Chapter 15, *Programming the MQSeries-CICS Bridge*, leads you through the steps that you need to take to create the application and make all the right connections.

15

In this chapter:
- *Building the Java GUI*
- *Coding the Java Application*
- *Setting Up MQSeries and CICS*
- *What's Next*

Programming the MQSeries-CICS Bridge

This chapter describes the process of building the Java GUI and the coding of the application. In addition, it describes the way to set up communication between MQSeries for Windows NT and MQSeries for OS/390.

Building the Java GUI

The Java GUI has been written in Swing, which provides a larger set of components and which can produce more aesthetically pleasing results than the Java Abstract Window Toolkit (AWT). Swing is a subset of Java Version 1.2, which is used to develop GUIs. In particular, the JTable object used in Swing has been used to create the main panel. The JTable for the main panel is set up in *MQClient.java*. Within this class, the menu bar (instance of JMenuBar) and associated controls are created. The data entry area consists of a combination box (instance of JCombo) and a click button (instance of Jbutton) to submit the request. The results are displayed within a panel (instance of JPanel) where a four-section grid layout, as described in "Designing the Graphical User Interface" in Chapter 14, is used. The full source code can be found in the *MQSeries-Java Client* directory on the CD that accompanies this book.

The Java GUI has deliberately been kept simple. The main purpose of this application is to show the mechanism used to obtain data from a CICS program using MQSeries messaging.

 If you want to know more about Swing, refer to either *http://ibm. com/java/jdk/index.html* or *http://java.sun.com.*

Coding the Java Application

There are seven steps that are involved in developing this part of the application:

- Coding the Java application
- Opening the relevant MQSeries queues
- Creating the MQSeries message
- Adding the CICS program name and the COMMAREA fields in the message buffer
- Sending the request message to the bridge queue in MQSeries for OS/390
- Receiving the response message
- Checking for CICS related errors

Coding the Java Application

To provide the connection to an MQSeries queue manager, we have created a Java class *MQCommunicator*. It looks like this:

```
public class MQCommunicator {.......}
```

The full code is on the accompanying CD in the directory called *\mqseries-java client\MQCommunicator.class*.

MQSeries provides a number of Java classes, which we can access on Windows NT by importing the package *com.ibm.mq.**. In order to make a connection to the relevant queue manager we need to supply the following information:

- The IP address of the host machine on which the OS/390 queue manager that we are going to use is located
- The name of the Windows NT queue manager
- The name of the MQI channel that makes the connection from the MQSeries client to the Windows NT queue manager (named in the previous bullet)
- The request queue where we put the MQSeries message containing details of the customer account number
- The reply-to queue onto which we get the response message containing the customer details supplied by the *NACT02* application

The code looks like this:

```
// Setup MQ object

MQComms=newMQCommunictaor(hostname,qManager,channel,requestQueue,replyQueue);
```

Using the MQSeries supplied environment class *MQEnvironment*, we set the variables for the host name, queue manager, and the communications port to use:

```
MQEnvironment.hostname = hostname;          // ARG#1
MQEnvironment.channel  = channel;           // ARG#2
MQEnvironment.port = 1414;                  // Hard code port
```

The communications port in this case has the system default value of 1414. When no value is set for the port, this value will normally be assumed. This is important if you are using more than one port.

Connection to the selected queue manager is then made by creating an instance of the MQSeries supplied object *MQQueueManager*.

```
qMgr = new MQQueueManager(qManager);
```

Opening the Relevant MQSeries Queues

Once we have established the connection, we can open the MQSeries queues for use. *requestQueue* and *replyQueue* are instances of the MQSeries supplied object *MQQueue*.

To enable the request queue so that we can place messages on it, we set the relevant open option:

```
openOptions = MQC.MQOO_OUTPUT ;             // Open queue to perform MQPUTs
```

This information is then supplied with the open request:

```
requestQueue = qMgr.accessQueue(aRequestQueue, openOptions,
              null,          // queue manager on which the queue is defined
              null,          // no dynamic queue name
              null);         // no alternate user id
```

The use of null for the queue manager name denotes that the queue is defined to the queue manager to which this *MQQueueManager* object is connected.

Similarly, we enable the reply-to queue so that we can get the response message:

```
openOptions = MQC.MQOO_INPUT_AS_Q_DEF ;
replyQueue = qMgr.accessQueue(aReplyQueue, openOptions,
              null,          // queue manager on which the queue is defined
              null,          // no dynamic queue name
              null);         // no alternate user id
```

We have used some MQSeries constants in the previous examples such as *MQC.MQOO_OUTPUT....* There are a number of such constants defined by MQSeries which are similar across the different platforms supported by MQSeries. All Java versions of these classes are prefixed by MQC. The *MQOO* indicates that this is an open option. *MQMT* would indicate a message type option.

Creating the MQSeries Message

To create an instance of the MQSeries object *MQMessage:*

```
sendMessage = new MQMessage();
```

Default values for the message can be used for most of the message options. The following changes need to be made:

- Set message type to request message:

```
sendMessage.messageType = MQC.MQMT_REQUEST;
```

- Set details of the queue to which the response message will be sent:

```
sendMessage.replyToQueueName = replyQueue;
```

Add the COMMAREA fields to the message buffer:

```
MQMessage.WriteString
        .
Add COMMAREA structure
```

Under certain circumstances, the message format required for the MQSeries CICS DPL bridge contains an additional structure compared with standard MQSeries messages.

For our simple example (which only starts one program), this MQCIH structure is not required. The MQCIH is required when you want to do one of the following:

- Run a 3270 transaction
- Run the bridge with AUTH=VERIFY_*
- Include more than one program in a unit of work

The MQCIH header is placed at the start of the message buffer.

Adding the CICS Program Name and COMMAREA Fields to the Message Buffer

The contents of the request COMMAREA for this application always contain the same supplied values apart from the customer account number keyfield. We have chosen to store the COMMAREA fields before the customer account number keyfield in the string *bufferFront*. The fields following the customer account number keyfield are stored in the string *bufferEnd*.

The *bufferFront* string is composed as follows:

```
bufferFront = "NACT02" +    // Program name
        "V1A"+              // Version
        "E"+                // Request type
        "    "+             //
        "    "+
        "    "
```

We need to supply the remainder of the COMMAREA after the customer account number. It consists of only spaces. As a result, *bufferEnd* is a string of 378 spaces.

These values are now used to create the message buffer string:

```
String buffer = new String(bufferFront + customerNumber + bufferEnd);
```

The *customerNumber* field is a 5-character string holding the customer account number value.

This is then written to the MQSeries message instance *sendMessage:*

```
sendMessage.writeString(buffer);
```

Sending the Request Message to the Bridge Queue on MQSeries for OS/390

MQSeries provides an object to specify options for the message being put onto a queue. In most cases the default options are acceptable. We create an instance of this *MQPutMessageOptions* object *pmo:*

```
// Specify the message options...(default)
MQPutMessageOptions pmo = new MQPutMessageOptions();
```

The message can now be placed on the appropriate queue:

```
requestQueue.put(sendMessage, pmo);
```

Receiving the Response Message.

The response message is recognized by its correlation ID (*CorrelId*), which matches the original message ID (*msgId*) passed with the request message. The application copies the global: message ID of the request message into the correlation ID of a new *MQMessage* object, in this case, the response message.

In a similar way to which we built the request message, we first create an instance of the MQSeries object *MQGetMessageOptions*, which is used to set the options for getting the response message:

```
MQGetMessageOptions gmo = new MQGetMessageOptions();
```

You can modify the default values of this new instance *gmo* as follows:

1. Specify that you will wait for the message if it is not already on the reply-to queue. Also that the incoming message should be converted to the correct CCSID for your machine if required:

```
gmo.options = MQC.MQGMO_WAIT   MQC.MQGMO_CONVERT;
```

2. Specify the length of wait as 300 seconds:

```
gmo.waitInterval = 300000;
```

We already have the required MQSeries message object in the instance *StoredMessage* which is supplied as the parameter *replyMessage*. The code to get the message is:

```
ReplyQueue.get(replyMessage,gmo);
```

We have omitted error trapping from the code fragments to help with clarity. It is worth mentioning that if there is an error response to the DPL request message, it will contain an *MQCIH* (even if one was not present in the request message) and associated error text.

Checking for CICS-Related Errors

The COMMAREA returned by *NACT02* within the response message contains a response code and reason code. These need to be checked in order to determine whether the request to retrieve the customer details was successful or whether some error was encountered. For a non-zero return code, the following need to be checked:

- No record exists for the customer account number supplied.

- The record is currently not accessible. This occurs if a lock has been put on the record where updating is in progress.

- The data supplied to CICS contains an error.

- The CICS system has abended for some reason.

- Some other CICS-related error has occurred. This is a catchall and details of the EXEC Interface Block (EIB) values EIBRESP and EIBRESP2 are provided in the *CICSresponseCode* and *CICSreasonCode* fields, as shown in Example 15-1,which is an example of the coding involved in checking whether the record exists or is locked.

Example 15-1. Sample Code for CICS-Related Errors

```
//informUser("Message received!");
//print("Message is: "+messageReturned);
//Check that inquire has been successful
CICSresponseCode = messageReturned.substring(12,16);
print(">CICS response code" +CICSresponseCode+"#");

CICSreasonCode=messageReturned.substring(16,20);
print(">CICS reason code" + CICSreasonCode+"#");
if (CICSresponseCOde.equals("0000")){
    //Strip off the fields preceding the customer record
    customerDetails = messageReturned.substring(25,408);
    AccountRecord retrieved=new AccountRecord(customerDetails);
```

Example 15-1. Sample Code for CICS-Related Errors (continued)

```
        displayRecord(retreived);
        return;
    }
//No valid record to display so clear fields
clearDisplay();
        //Check out error response returned by CICS
        if(CICSresponseCode.equals("0013")){
            informUser("No record can be found for the custimer number given.")
            return;
        }
        if(CICSresponseCode.equals("LOCK")){
            informUser("The requested record is currently unavailable, possibly being
                updated."
                        + "\nPlease try again later.");
          return;
        }
        if(CICSresponseCode.equals("ABND")){
            informUser("Please inform the systems administrator the the CICS system has"
                +"\nabnormally ended with code" + CICSreasonCode + "Severe Error");
            return;
        }
        if((CICSresponseCode.equals("FRMT")) & (CICSreasonCode.equals("LENE")){
            informUser("Please inform the systems administrator that the call to the CICS
                program" + "\nhas failed due to an error in the length of the data
                supplied.");
        }
        if((CICSresponseCode.equals("FRMT")) & (CICSreasonCode.equals("REQE"))){
            informUser("Please inform the systems administrator that the call to the CICS
                program + "\nhas failed due to an error in the type of request made.");
        }
        informUser("Please inform the systems administrator that the call to the CICS
                program + "\nhas failed with the following error" + "\
                nEIBRESP="CICSresponseCode+"EIBRESP2=" CICSreasonCode);
    }finally{
            enableDisableListitems(true);
    }
```

Displaying the Relevant Information

The next step is to create *retrieved*, a new instance of *AccountRecord* and pass the appropriate portion of the response message string as a parameter. The constructor class for this instance of *AccountRecord* uses the supplied string held in *customerDetails* to construct the various fields that make up the customer information returned within the COMMAREA from the *NACT02* program. The basic method is to assign substrings based on position to the various declared fields of the *AccountRecord* structure. A *getfieldname* method is provided for each record field so that the fields can be easily retrieved by other Java classes. The code looks like:

```
    AccountRecord retrieved = new AccountRecord(customerDetails);
```

The MQClient method *displayRecord* can then be used to populate the various fields displayed on our main panel:

```
displayRecord(retrieved);
```

Setting Up MQSeries and CICS

There are six steps that you need to do to set up the MQSeries-CICS bridge:

- Define MQSeries for Windows NT
- Start MQSeries for Windows NT
- Set up MQSeries for OS/390
- Start the sender channel to OS/390
- Set up CICS to use the MQSeries-CICS bridge on OS/390
- Start the MQSeries-CICS bridge on OS/390

Define MQSeries for Windows NT

Before you start, we have included a series of files on the CD that create and start all the queue manager, queues, and channels that you need on MQSeries for Windows NT. Of course, you have to edit the files so that the IP address, queue, and channel names are appropriate. The first three steps are found in \ *MQSeries-Java Client\MQSeries Client* directory.

There are a number of standard definitions supplied by MQSeries that can be used to quickly set up the relevant required MQSeries objects. There may well be a suitable MQSeries set up on your machine that can be modified to enable communications with the CICS system.

Before you start, you need to know the IP address of the OS/390 machine you intend to communicate with, the name of the queue manager on that machine, and the name of the message channels that will be used to send messages to and from that machine.

The commands can be entered from a command prompt. Alternatively, MQSeries for Windows NT Version 5.1 supplies a Graphical User Interface, known as MQSeries Explorer, that can be used. To start MQSeries Explorer select *Start*, *Programs*, *IBM MQSeries*, and *MQSeries Explorer*. When you've defined the queues and queue managers, you'll see the following screen shown in Figure 15-1.

Alternatively, you can use the following command files that we have provided on the CD-ROM. To do this:

1. Copy the MQSeries-Java Client directory from the CD to a suitable directory on your workstation.

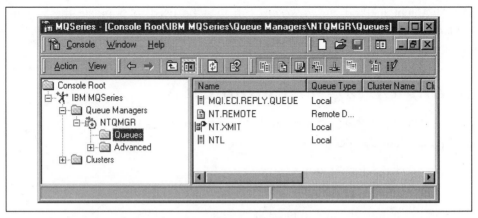

Figure 15-1. MQSeries for Windows NT: MQSeries Explorer showing queues

2. Edit the file *cicsadp\MQSeries-Java Client\MQSeriesClient\1. Start MQSeries.
cmd* so that the queue manager name is correct for your system. Then run the
command file. This stops any existing queue manager that has the same name
as the one you have chosen. It then deletes the queue manager before creating and starting your new queue manager.

3. Edit the file *cicsadp\MQSeries-Java Client\MQSeriesClient\admvs.DEF* to add
the IP address of your OS/390 system.

4. Run the command file called *cicsadp\MQSeries-Java Client\MQSeriesClient\2.
Load MQ for MVS Definitions.cmd;* this defines the queue and channel names
for your MQSeries for Windows NT server as they are defined in *admvs.DEF.*

5. Run the command file *cicsadp\MQSeries-Java Client\MQSeriesClient\3.* Start
SevicesMVS.cmd; this starts the queue manager and the sender channel.

You can also enter the commands from a command prompt, which if you are
using MQSeries from other platforms, you will have to:

1. Start MQSeries on Windows NT, if it not already running. Open the Control
Panel, and select *Services*, highlight *MQSeries,* and select *Start.*

2. Set up a default queue manager called NTQMGR:

crtmqm -q NTQMGR

3. Start the queue manager:

strmqm

4. Set up the various MQSeries objects required such as queues, channels, and
their identifiers. The following commands are contained in a definitions file
MQSeries-Java Client\MQSeries Client\admvs.def and build on the standard
definitions supplied by MQSeries for Windows NT. You need to edit the name
of the queue manager on your OS/390 machine (it is called MQQ1 in the following example) and CONNAME to be the IP address of your host machine.

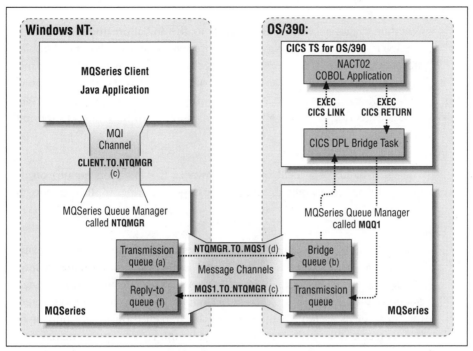

Figure 15-2. Queue Manager, Channel, and Queue names for the sample application

The transmission queue

The transmission queue is used to hold data to be sent on the message channel NTQMGR.TO.MQQ1 to your OS/390 machine, see (a) on Figure 15-2.

```
DEFINE QLOCAL('NT.XMIT') REPLACE +
          TRIGDATA(NTQMGR.TO.MQQ1) +
          TRIGGER   +
          INITQ(SYSTEM.CHANNEL.INITQ) +
          USAGE(XMITQ)
```

QLOCAL(q-name)

A local queue is one that is owned by the queue manager to which it is being defined. *q-name* is the local name of the queue (NT.XMIT). This is required. The name must not be the same as any other queue name (of whatever queue type) currently defined on this queue manager (unless *REPLACE* is specified).

TRIGDATA

The data that is inserted in the trigger message. The maximum length of the string is 64 bytes. For a transmission queue on AIX, HP-UX, OS/2 Warp, OS/400, Sun Solaris, or Windows NT, you can use this parameter to specify the name of the channel to be started.

NOTRIGGER and TRIGGER

> Whether trigger messages are written to the initiation queue (named by the INITQ attribute) to trigger the application (named by the *PROCESS* attribute), *NOTRIGGER* means that triggering is not active, and trigger messages are not written to the initiation queue. This is the default supplied with MQSeries, but your installation might have changed it. *TRIGGER* means triggering is active, and trigger messages can be written to the initiation queue.

INITQ

> The local name of a local queue (known as the initiation queue) on this queue manager, to which trigger messages relating to this queue are written.

USAGE

> Queue usage can be either *NORMAL* where the queue is not a transmission queue, or *XMITQ* where the queue is a transmission queue. A transmission queue is used to hold messages that are destined for a remote queue manager. When an application puts a message to a remote queue, the message is stored on the appropriate transmission queue until it has been successfully transmitted and stored by the remote queue manager.

Remote definition of the CICS bridge queue

This is the remote definition of the CICS bridge queue, SYSTEM.CICS.BRIDGE. QUEUE, on the OS/390 machine's queue manager (MQQ1); see (b) on Figure 15-2. The code looks like this:

```
DEFINE QREMOTE('NT.REMOTE') REPLACE +
    RNAME('SYSTEM.CICS.BRIDGE.QUEUE') +
    RQMNAME('MQQ1') +
    XMITQ('NT.XMIT')
```

QREMOTE(string)

> A remote queue is one that is owned by another queue manager that application processes connected to this queue manager need to access. This is required.

RNAME(string)

> The name of remote queue. This is the local name of the queue as defined on the queue manager specified by *RQMNAME*. If this definition is used for a local definition of a remote queue, *RNAME* must not be blank when the open occurs.

RQMNAME(string)

> The name of the remote queue manager on which the queue *RNAME* is defined. If an application opens the local definition of a remote queue, *RQMNAME* must not be blank or the name of the local queue manager. When the open occurs, if XMITQ is blank, there must be a local queue of this name, which is to be used as the transmission queue.

XMITQ(string)

The name of the transmission queue to be used for forwarding messages to the remote queue, for either a remote queue or for a queue-manager alias definition. If *XMITQ* is blank, a queue with the same name as *RQMNAME* is used instead as the transmission queue.

The MQI channel

This defines the MQI channel, CLIENT.TO.NTQMGR, used to send messages between the MQSeries client and MQSeries server on your Windows NT machine; see (c) on Figure 15-2. The definition looks like this:

```
DEFINE CHANNEL('CLIENT.TO.NTQMGR') CHLTYPE(SVRCONN) TRPTYPE(TCP) +
    MCAUSER(' ')
```

CHLTYPE

This specifies the channel type and is required. It must follow immediately after the (channel-name) parameter on all platforms except OS/390. There are various options, but the ones that we use in this sample are *SVRCONN* (Server-connection channel), *SDR* (Sender channel), and *RCVR* (Receiver channel).

TRPTYPE

This specifies the transport type to be used.

MCAUSER

This specifies the message channel agent user identifier. If it is blank, the message channel agent uses its default user identifier.

The message channel (Sender)

This defines the Windows NT message channel, NTQMGR.TO.MQQ1, used to send messages to the queue manager MQQ1 on your OS/390 machine; see (d) on Figure 15-2. The definition looks like this:

```
DEFINE CHANNEL('NTQMGR.TO.MQQ1') CHLTYPE(SDR) TRPTYPE(TCP) +
    XMITQ('NT.XMIT') +
    CONNAME('<<Your IP Address>>') +
    MCAUSER(' ') REPLACE
```

CONNAME

This specifies the IP address of the host machine.

The other options are described as for the other definitions.

The message channel (Receiver)

This defines the message channel, MQQ1.TO.NTQMGR, used to receive messages from the queue manager, MQQ1, on your OS/390 machine; see (e) on Figure 15-2. The definition looks like this:

```
DEFINE CHANNEL('MQQ1.TO.NTQMGR') +
    CHLTYPE(RCVR) +
    TRPTYPE(TCP) +
    SEQWRAP(999999999) +
    MCAUSER(' ') REPLACE
```

SEQWRAP

When this value is reached, sequence numbers wrap to start again at 1. This value is non-negotiable and must match in both the local and remote channel definitions.

The reply-to queue

This defines the queue used to receive response messages from our OS/390 machine; see (f) on Figure 15-2. The definition looks like this:

```
DEFINE QLOCAL('MQI.ECI.REPLY.QUEUE') REPLACE +
    DEFPSIST(YES) +
    SHARE
```

DEFPSIST

This specifies the message persistence to be used when applications specify the MQPER_PERSISTENCE_AS_Q_DEF option. There are two options: *NO*, which specifies that messages on this queue are lost across a restart of the queue manager. This is the default supplied with MQSeries, but your installation might have changed it. *YES* specifies that messages on this queue survive a queue manager restart.

Starting MQSeries for Windows NT

These definitions can be implemented using the following command. The results and any error messages are written to *admvs.out*:

```
runmqsc "< admvs.def > admvs.out"
```

1. Start the channel listener on the default port 1414:

```
start runmqlsr -t TCP -p 1414
```

2. Start the message channel to queue manager MQQ1 on your OS/390 machine:

```
start runmqchl -m NTQMGR -c NTQMGR.TO.MQQ1
```

Provided there have been no errors in establishing the channel connections, the Windows NT machine now has all the required definitions to send and receive messages from the queue manager MQQ1 on the OS/390 machine.

Error messages relating to the channel can normally be found in an error log *Amqerrnn.log* where *nn* is a number such as "01". A typical directory for this log file is:

```
C:\mqm\qmgrs\NTQMGR\errors
```

At this point you will have all the definitions ready on your Windows NT system and now need a similar set of definitions on MQSeries for OS/390.

Setting Up MQSeries for OS/390

Setting up MQSeries and its definition to CICS on the OS/390 server machine would normally be handled by a system programmer who has been assigned that responsibility. The full details of setting up your MQSeries server can be found in the *MQSeries for OS/390: System Management Guide.*

Assuming that MQSeries has been installed and a queue manager set up, the following shows the steps that the system programmer would have to undertake to allow the MQSeries-CICS DPL bridge to work:

Defining MQSeries to CICS

Two install groups are supplied by MQSeries for this purpose: CSQCKB and CSQCAT1. CSQ4CKBC and CSQ4B100 are the member names in your partitioned data sets (PDS).

Preparing to run the MQSeries-CICS bridge

Before you can run the MQSeries-CICS bridge you must ensure that your OS/390 system has both the CICS and MQSeries components installed.

Setting Up CICS To Use the MQSeries-CICS Bridge

You need to define the following CICS bridge transactions and programs using the resource definition utilities DFHCSDUP and CSQ4CKBC as input:

Program or Transaction	Description
CKBR	Bridge monitor transaction
CSQCBR00	Bridge monitor program
CKBP	Bridge ProgramLink transaction
CSQCBP00	Bridge ProgramLink program
CSQCBP10	Bridge ProgramLink abend handler program
CSQCBTX	Bridge error messages

Add the group CSQCKB to your start-up group list.

The CICS bridge uses CICS temporary storage IDs with the prefix CKB. You should make sure these are not recoverable.

By default, your CICS DPL programs run under transaction code CKBP. You need to change the TASKDATALOC attribute if you are going to run 24-bit programs. If you wish to run your programs under different transaction codes, you need to install copies of the definition of CKBP, changing the transaction name to the ones of your choice.

DPL bridge transactions must not be routed to a remote system.

Defining MQSeries for OS/390 Objects

The most straightforward way to define queues and channels on OS/390 is to have a PDS member with all the definitions in it and include it in the *CSQINP2* DD concatenation of the startup job. For the purposes of this book we are using option 6 from ISPF so that we can step through and describe each of the definitions.

We need to define two queues, a local queue as our transmission queue and a remote queue. In addition, we need to define both the *SENDER* and *RECEIVER* channels:

1. Log on to your OS/390 system, enter ISPF, select option 6.

2. On the command line enter *CSQOREXX*. The screen shown in Figure 15-3 appears.

```
                    IBM MQSeries for OS/390 - Main Menu

     Complete fields. Then press Enter.

        Action . . . . . . . . 1        1. Display    5. Perform
                                        2. Define     6. Start
                                        3. Alter      7. Stop
                                        4. Delete

        Object type  . . . . . _____    +
        Name . . . . . . . . . _____
        Like . . . . . . . . . _____

        Connect to queue
        manager  . . . . . . :
        Target queue manager :
        Response wait time . : 30    seconds

     (C) Copyright IBM Corporation 1993,1999. All rights reserved.




     Command ===> _____
      F1=Help        F2=Split     F3=Exit      F4=Prompt    F6=QueueMgr  F9=Swap
     F10=Messages F12=Cancel
    MA▇    b                                                         05/026
```

Figure 15-3. MQSeries for OS/390 Main Menu

3. Press PF6 to enter the name of your queue manager for the Target queue manager; for example, MQQ1 (see Figure 15-4). Leave the Response wait-time entry as 30 seconds; this is probably a realistic time for the purposes of most samples. Press Enter to save your entries and return to the original screen.

4. On the original screen, you can enter the Object type. The first definition that we make is the name of the transmission queue on OS/390. This is called NTQMGR in Figure 15-2. If you are following the sample, enter *QLOCAL* for

```
                       IBM MQSeries for OS/390 - Main Menu
   Complete fields. Then press Enter.
  ┌────────────────────────────────────────────────────────────────────────┐
  │                          Change the Queue Manager                        │
  │  Make changes and press Enter.                                           │
  │                                                                          │
  │    Connect to queue                                                      │
  │    manager . . . . . . . MQQ1                                            │
  │                                                                          │
  │    Target queue manager . MQQ1_____   │
  │                                                                          │
  │    Response wait time . . 30   5 - 999 seconds                           │
  │                                                                          │
  │    F1=Help     F2=Split     F9=Swap     F12=Cancel                       │
  └────────────────────────────────────────────────────────────────────────┘
   (C) Copyright IBM Corporation 1993,1999. All rights reserved.



       Command ===> _____
        F1=Help        F2=Split      F3=Exit       F4=Prompt     F6=QueueMgr   F9=Swap
       F10=Messages F12=Cancel
      MA█   b                                                         12/032
```

Figure 15-4. MQSeries for OS/390: Changing the queue manager

the object type and *NTQMGR* for the Name. Select option 2 to define your
queue and press Enter. On Figure 15-5, change Usage to X to show that this is
a transmission queue. If you want to see the remainder of the options, press
PF8, however, for our sample you don't need to change anything else.

```
                           Define a Local Queue
   Complete fields, then press F8 for further fields, or Enter to define queue.
                                                              More:     +

   Queue name  . . . . . . . . . NTQMGR
   Description . . . . . . . . . _____
                                 _____

   Put enabled . . . . . . . . . Y   Y=Yes,N=No
   Get enabled . . . . . . . . . Y   Y=Yes,N=No
   Usage . . . . . . . . . . . . N   N=Normal,X=XmitQ
   Storage class . . . . . . . . DEFAULT








   CSQ0040I Object named NTQMGR of type QUEUE already exists.
   Command ===> _____
    F1=Help        F2=Split      F3=Exit       F7=Bkwd       F8=Fwd        F9=Swap
   F10=Messages F12=Cancel
  MA█   b                                                         07/032
```

Figure 15-5. MQSeries for OS/390: Defining a local queue

F4 provides you with a prompt that lists all the objects that you can enter. They are grouped as queue objects, channel objects, cluster objects, and other objects.

You need to define a transmission queue and a receiver channel on OS/390 so that you can send data to your Windows NT system:

The transmission queue

The transmission queue is used to hold data to be sent on the message channel MQQ1.TO.NTQMGR to your Windows NT machine. This is called *NTQMGR* and has Usage option set to X to denote that it is used as a transmission queue.

Defining The RECEIVER channel (NTQMGR.TO.MQQ1)

The definition of the message channel NTQMGR.TO.MQQ1 is used to send messages from your Windows NT machine to the queue manager MQQ1 on your OS/390 machine. From the ISPF screen enter *CHLRECEIVER* and the name of the channel (see Figure 15-6). The name must match the name used for the sender channel of your MQSeries for Windows NT server.

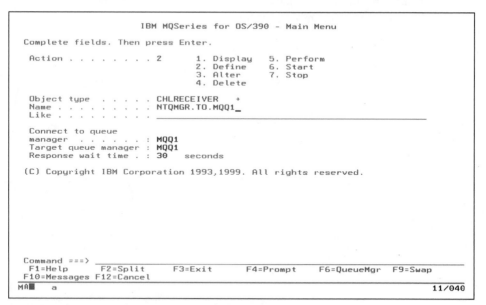

Figure 15-6. MQSeries for OS/390: Defining the RECEIVER channel

The SENDER channel (MQQ1.TO.NTQMGR)

The definition of the message channel MQQ1.TO.NTQMGR is used to send messages to the reply-to queue on the Windows NT machine from the queue manager, *MQQ1*, on your OS/390 machine. From the ISPF screen enter CHLSENDER and the name of the channel. Change the Transport type to T for TCP/IP and for the Connection name enter the IP address of your MQSeries for Windows NT server together with the port number (MQSeries listens on port number 1414 by default). Finally, enter the name of your transmission queue (see Figure 15-7). The name must match the name used for the receiver channel of your MQSeries for Windows NT server.

```
                        Define a Sender Channel
     Complete fields, then press F8 for further fields, or Enter to define channel.

                                                          More:     +

     Channel name  . . . . . . . .  MQQ1.TO.NTQMGR
     Description . . . . . . . . . . Channel from OS/390 to NT Server
                                     _____
     Transport type  . . . . . . .  T   L=LU6.2,T=TCP/IP
     Connection name . . . . . . .  9.20.30.2(1414)
     LU6.2 mode name . . . . . . .  _____
     LU6.2 TP name . . . . . . . .  _____

     Transmission queue  . . . . .  NTQMGR










     Command ===> _____
      F1=Help       F2=Split     F3=Exit     F7=Bkwd     F8=Fwd     F9=Swap
     F10=Messages F12=Cancel
    MA█   a                                                      07/032
```

Figure 15-7. MQSeries for OS/390: Defining the SENDER Channel

Defining the remote queue (MQI.ECI.REPLY.QUEUE)

The remote definition of the queue is used to receive response messages from our OS/390 machine. Here you define the queue name, the remote name, remote queue manager and the transmission queue (see Figure 15-8).

Defining a local queue for the bridge queue

The bridge queue is used in the transfer of messages from MQSeries to the CICS DPL bridge task. For the sample application we have defined a local queue as *SYSTEM.CICS.BRIDGE.QUEUE*. To define a local queue press PF4 from the main menu and select action 2. Press PF12 to return to the main menu. Enter the name of your local queue, select option 3 to alter the definition and then PF8 to find the attributes as shown in Figure 15-9. You must set the following attributes:

SHARE (Permit shared access)

This ensures that both the CICS-bridge monitor and the CICS DPL bridge tasks can read the bridge queue.

```
------------------------------------------------------------------
                       Define a Remote Queue
  Complete fields, then press F8 for further fields, or Enter to define queue.

                                                       More:     +

  Queue name  . . . . . . . . . MQ.ECI.REPLY.QUEUE
  Description . . . . . . . . . Remote queue definition for
                                reply queue on queue manager

  Put enabled . . . . . . . . . Y   Y=Yes,N=No
  Default persistence . . . . . N   Y=Yes,N=No
  Default priority  . . . . . . 0   0 - 9
  Remote name . . . . . . . . . MQ.ECI.REPLY.QUEUE_____
  Remote queue manager  . . . . NTQMGR_____
  Transmission queue  . . . . . NTQMGR_____




  CSQO040I Object named MQ.ECI.REPLY.QUEUE of type QUEUE already exists.
  Command ===>
   F1=Help      F2=Split    F3=Exit      F7=Bkwd      F8=Fwd       F9=Swap
  F10=Messages F12=Cancel
  MA█     a                                                       16/038
------------------------------------------------------------------
```

Figure 15-8. MQSeries for OS/390: Defining the Remote Queue

MSGDLVSQ (Message delivering sequence)
> Messages are processed in First in, First out (*FIFO*) sequence. The alternative is priority sequence.

If recovery is required, you need to define the following:

DEFPSIST (Default persistence)(YES)
> Set messages as persistent on the queue by default if recovery is required.

HARDENBO (Harden Backout counter)
> If *DEFPSIST*(YES) is set, set *HARDENBO* to ensure messages are not reprocessed erroneously after an emergency restart.

Starting Your Channel

Finally, return to the main menu and select option 6 to start the *SENDER* Channel. Enter *CHLSENDER* as the object type and the name of your sender channel MQQ1. TO.NTQMGR. Now press Enter.

Connecting to MQSeries from Your CICS Region

Having started the MQSeries channels, you now have to start the MQSeries-CICS bridge monitor from your CICS region:

1. Log on to your CICS region and enter transaction *CKQC* if you are authorized to do so, or ask your systems administrator. Figure 15-10 shows the screen.

```
                        Alter a Local Queue
     Press F7 or F8 to see other fields, or Enter to alter queue.

                                                          More:   - +
     Default persistence . . . . . Y   Y=Yes,N=No
     Default priority  . . . . . . 0   0 - 9
     Message delivery sequence . . F   P=Priority,F=FIFO
     Permit shared access  . . . . Y   Y=Yes,N=No
     Default share option  . . . . E   E=Exclusive,S=Shared
     Index type  . . . . . . . . . N   N=None,M=MsgId,C=CorrelId,T=MsgToken
     Maximum queue depth . . . . . 999999999  0 - 999999999
     Maximum message length  . . . 4194304    0 - 104857600
     Retention interval  . . . . . 999999999  0 - 999999999 hours

     Cluster name  . . . . . . . . _____
     Cluster namelist name . . . . _____
     Default bind  . . . . . . . . O   O=Open,N=Notfixed




     Command ===> _____
      F1=Help      F2=Split      F3=Exit      F6=Clusinfo  F7=Bkwd      F8=Fwd
      F9=Swap     F10=Messages F12=Cancel
     MA█      a                                                  15/032
```

Figure 15-9. MQSeries for OS/390: Alter the bridge queue

```
     _  Connection       CKTI       Task
     -----------------------------------------------------------------------
     CKQCM0     IBM MQSeries for OS/390 - CICS adapter control initial panel

     Select menu bar item using Tab key. Then press Enter.


     #           #    ########   ##########
     ##         ##  ###      ### ##       ##
     ###       ### ##         ## ##                           ##
     ####     #### ##         ## ######      #####   ## ####     #####   ######
     ## ##   ## ## ##         ##       ###### #    # #####  ## #    # #
     ##  ## ##  ## ##         ## ##   ###### ####### ##      ## ####### #######
     ##   ###   ## ###      ### ## ##   ## #      ##    ## #           #
     ##    #    ##  ########  ## ########## #####   ##      ## #####  ######

                                                            for OS/390


     (C) Copyright IBM Corporation 1993, 1999. All rights reserved.


     F1=Help  F3=Exit
```

Figure 15-10. MQSeries for OS/390: CICS adapter control initial panel

2. With the cursor under Connection, press Enter. Figure 15-11 shows you that option 4 has been highlighted, which shows that your MQSeries system is already running. If it was not running, option 1 would be displayed inviting you to start the connection to MQSeries.

3. Check that you are connected to your queue manager by pressing Enter. Figure 15-12 shows the name of your CICS region and that you are connected to a queue manager called MQQ1. If you are not connected, return to the

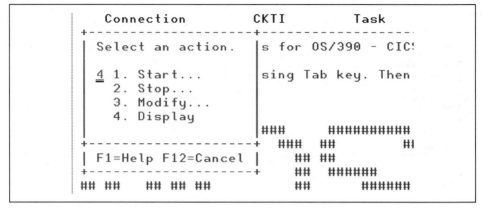

Figure 15-11. MQSeries for OS/390: The Connection pulldown

previous screen and enter option 1 to start the connection. We don't need to go into the details of the INITQ (initiation queue) in this book; instead, we start the CICS to MQSeries connection manually.

```
_CKQCM2                    Display Connection panel

Read connection information. Then press F12 to cancel.

   CICS Applid =  CICSHT62  Connection Status = Connected        QMgr name= MQQ1
   Trace No.   = 001        Tracing           = On               API Exit = Off
   Initiation Queue Name = CICS01.INITQ
-------------------------- S T A T I S T I C S -------------------------------
Number of in-flight tasks =   0            Total No. of API calls =          1
Number of running CKTI    =   0
        APIs and flows analysis                   Syncpoint          Recovery
--------------------------------------     ------------------     ---------------
Run OK             0   MQINQ          0     Tasks          2     Indoubt        0
Futile             0   MQSET          0     Backout        0     UnResol        0
MQOPEN             1   ------ Flows ------   Commit         0     Commit         0
MQCLOSE            0   Calls          4     S-Phase        0     Backout        0
MQGET              0   SyncComp       3     2-Phase        0
 GETWAIT           0   SuspReqd       0     -------------------------------------
MQPUT              0   MsgWait        0     InitTCBs  8 StrtTCBs  8 BusyTCBs  0
MQPUT1             0   Switched       3




  F1=Help  F12=Cancel  Enter=Refresh
MA    b                                                                  01/001
```

Figure 15-12. MQSeries for OS/390: Display Connection panel

Starting the CICS Bridge

The following guidelines will help you start the CICS bridge:

1. Return to your CICS region and enter the transaction *CKBR* to start your CICS bridge monitor. However, this locks your terminal for as long as the CICS bridge monitor is running. If you have forgotten where the CICS bridge monitor fits into this scene, look back at Figure 14-5.

Alternatively, you can enter *CECI START TRANSACTION(CKBR)*, which runs the transaction independently of your terminal. To check if the transaction is running, enter *CEMT INQUIRE TASK*.

Any transaction that starts with a C is an IBM-supplied transaction. Since they control the CICS system you may not be authorized to use them. You may have to ask your system administrator to issue the command for you.

Starting the Listener on OS/390

You may have to stop and restart the listener to be sure that the application works. To do this:

1. Go to the IBM MQSeries for OS/390 Main Menu (using *CSQOREXX*).

2. For the object type enter SYSTEM and select 7 to stop the listener or 6 to start the listener. The important thing here is to ensure that the port number of your sender channel on Windows NT matches the port number that your OS/390 systems is listening on. You can redefine the port number just before you start the listener as shown in Figure 15-13.

```
                            Start a System Function

    Select function type, complete fields, then press Enter to start system
    function.

    Function type  . . . . . . . 3       1. Channel initiator
                                          2. Channel listener for LU6.2
                                          3. Channel listener for TCP/IP

    Channel initiator
        Parameter module name . . _____
        JCL substitution   . . . . _____
                                    _____

    Listener for LU6.2
        LU name . . . . . . . . . . _____

    Listener for TCP/IP
        Port number . . . . . . . 3235_




    Command ===> _____
    F1=Help        F2=Split      F3=Exit       F9=Swap     F10=Messages F12=Cancel
```

Figure 15-13. MQSeries for OS/390: Start a System Function

To check that OS/390 is listening on the same port number that the Windows NT Sender channel, choose option 1 from the MQSeries for OS/390 Main Menu and enter *SYSTEM* for the Object type. On the "Display a System Function" screen, select option 1 for distributed queueing; the next screen shows you the port number that your system is using, as shown in Figure 15-14.

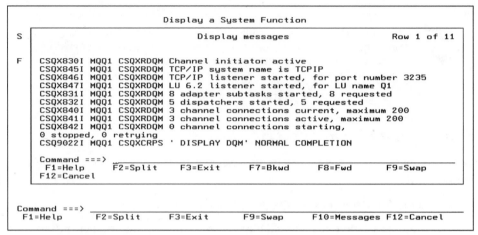

Figure 15-14. MQSeries for OS/390: Display a System Function

Running the Application for the Workstation

The following guidlines will help you run the application for the workstation:

1. Copy the files from the CD directory called *MQSeries-Java Client* to your workstation.

2. Change directory to the MQSeries Client and edit the *admvs.def* file to refer to the queue manager on MQSeries for OS/390. Also edit CONNAME and change the IP address.

3. If you have changed the names of any variable, you need to check the three command (.*cmd*) files and edit them accordingly.

4. Run each of the three command (.*cmd*) files:

    a. *Start MQSeries*

    b. *Load MQ for MVS definitions*

    c. *Start ServicesMVS*

5. Change to the directory called *MQSeries-Java Clients* and run *4.Client*. This starts the MQClient Java program (see Figure 15-15).

Troubleshooting

Table 15-1 lists the ways of checking errors that may occur when you are trying to make the connections between CICS and MQSeries and Windows NT and OS/390.

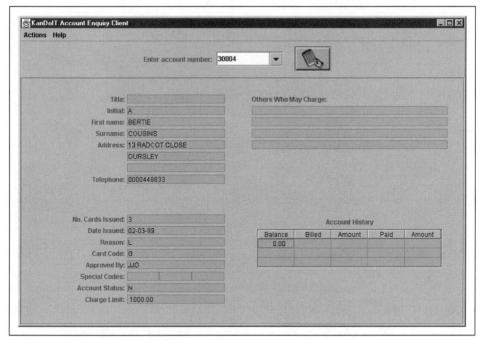

Figure 15-15. Input screen of MQSeries-Java client

Table 15-1. Troubleshooting Chart

Task	Action
Check that the sender and receiver channels are running.	Use MQSeries Explorer on Windows NT to check the status of the channels. If the sender channel is not running, right-click and select Start. If the receiver channel is not running, go to OS/390 and start the sender channel there.
Is the Bridge Monitor running?	From your CICS for OS/390 system, enter *CEMT INQUIRE TASK*. If CKBR does not appear in the list, start the transaction by entering *CECI START TRANSACTION(CKBR)*.
Check that the port and connection name are the same in both systems.	Use the MQSeries Explorer to check the the port number that the sender channel is using. Check the setting for SYSTEM object and select the display option to see the port number that OS/390 is listening on.

What's Next...

At the end of this exercise you should be able to run the MQSeries client and enter account numbers to get back the details of the customer accounts. The main concept that you should understand is the way the the queues and channels interrelate between MQSeries for OS/390 and MQSeries for Windows NT. Secondly, you should have an understanding of the way that CICS and MQSeries interact on an OS/390 system.

VIII

Debugging

This Part, which consists of Chapter 16, *Debugging in CICS*, describes some of the tools that you can use to debug your programs. If you are new to CICS programming, you may find the section using the CICS-supplied transaction, CEDF, of particular use as it describes a walk-through of a CICS program.

16

Debugging in CICS

Even the best programs tend to have the occasional bug in them. Fortunately, CICS includes several tools and aids to help you debug online applications. This chapter contains brief details of some of the CICS-supplied transactions that are most commonly used. You'll find details of the CEMT transaction in the *CICS Supplied Transactions* manual and extensive details about CEBR, CECI, and CEDF are in the *CICS Application Programming Guide.*

Two of these transactions (*CEDF* and *CEDX*) enable you to use the Execution Diagnostic Facility (EDF); it allows you to inspect and change variables that your application gives and receives from CICS. This is described in detail in "EDF: Execution Diagnostic Facility." Within your organization there are likely to be other debugging aids available, for example, line-by-line source debuggers for finding pure application errors, especially during development, rather than that result of passing bad data to CICS; this information should be readily available from other development and technical team members.

When carrying out problem determination, it is worth noting details of actions taken and results obtained in a log to provide information to other people that you may need to consult. For a simple fault, debugging a failure may involve nothing more than reading the error message and checking the program source. For a really obscure error, you may have to use a whole battery of tools, including the processing of dumps and traces.

Let's consider what happens when a transaction abend occurs. A *snapshot* of all related areas of storage at that moment in time is output to a data set as a transaction dump. You can then run a batch job to format the dump. One of the areas in the dump contains the contents of the trace table (if it was switched on), which is a wraparound table of limited size that contains *footprints* of all the logical steps as they occurred.

In certain cases, if additional information is required, an auxiliary trace can be run. This again outputs footprints of the logical steps that occurred during that time to a data set. As with the dump, a batch job has to be run to format the trace.

The dump and trace data sets are usually defined to CICS in pairs, known as A and B, which are set to operate in a switching mode like the trace table. You can switch the current data set to the *other* one in order to process data just captured.

Many installations use third-party vendor products for dump and trace analysis. They eliminate the need to run formatting jobs. Before attempting to use these tools, check with your CICS system programmer for information about company's supported tools.

You'll find details of how to switch data sets in the description of the CICS Master Terminal (CEMT) transaction.

In order to use any CICS transactions or other tools, you will need the appropriate access and authority. This can vary according to the technical set-up and the CICS systems that you are working with. Check with your CICS system programmer for information about your company's practices.

CICS-Supplied Transactions

Here we describe a number of the transactions that are designed to help you manage CICS regions dynamically. We have included those that can help you understand what is happening in your CICS system and to help you resolve any problems. They are listed in the following table and described later:

Transaction	Function
CEMT	CICS Master Terminal transaction
CMAC	CICS Messaging and Codes transaction
CETR	CICS Trace transaction
CEBR	CICS Queue Browse transaction
CECI	CICS Execution Command-level Interpreter
CEDF and CEDX	CICS Execution Diagnostic Facility (EDF)

CEMT

This transaction provides many facilities, one of which enables you to inquire on the status of CICS resources, such as a file. The returned status will indicate the state that resource is in, for example, when it was disabled.

You start the transaction by entering *CEMT* on your screen. You are then prompted to enter one of the options returned. Suppose you entered Inquire (ing). You would then be prompted to enter a resource from the list returned. If you already know all of the required information, you can enter the details in a single command:

```
CEMT INQUIRE FILE(AC*)
```

Lowercase characters are converted to uppercase where applicable. The output of the command is shown in Figure 16-1.

```
inq file(AC*)
STATUS:   RESULTS - OVERTYPE TO MODIFY
 Fil(ACCTFIL ) Vsa Clo Ena Rea Upd Add      Del      Sha
         Dsn( CICSTS21.ACCTFILE                          )
 Fil(ACCTNAM ) Vsa Clo Ena Rea          Bro           Sha
         Dsn( CICSTS21.ACCTNAME                          )
 Fil(ACINUSE ) Vsa Clo Ena Rea Upd Add Bro Del      Sha
         Dsn( CICSTS21.ACTINUSE                          )
```

Figure 16-1. CEMT inquire file(AC*)

CEMT can also be used for processing dumps or traces. In this case you need to use the Set option to switch the relevant data set (A to B or vice versa), to ensure that the next dump or trace is output to the other one. This allows data on the previous data set to be selected, formatted, or processed in any other way.

When you're running an auxiliary trace, the *CEMT* transaction also provides an easy way to stop it:

```
CEMT SET AUXTRACE STOP
```

A full description of CEMT is found in the *CICS Supplied Transactions* manual.

CMAC

When given an abend code or message number, this transaction returns message information. To use the CMAC transaction:

1. Add the DFHCMAC group on the CICS system definition (CSD) file to your initialization list (DFHLIST).

2. Add the dataset name of the CICS messages file to the definition of the DFHCMACD file within the DFHCMAC group.

3. Install the DFHCMAC group.

You can start the transaction by entering:

CMAC

This returns a screen where you can, for example, enter a common abend code such as ASRA, or enter a message number DFHxxxx, where xxxx is the message number. Figure 16-2 shows the screen that appears when you have entered *ASRA*.

```
 _        ASRA


          EXPLANATION:  The task has terminated abnormally because
          of a program check.

          SYSTEM ACTION:  The task is abnormally terminated and CICS
          issues either message DFHAP0001 or DFHSR0001.  Message
          DFHSR0622 may also be issued.

          USER RESPONSE:  Refer to the description of the associated
          message or messages to determine and correct the cause of
          the program check.

          MODULE:  DFHSRP
```

Figure 16-2. ASRA abend information

The information returned depends on how the transaction was started, and whether more information is required or just basic message information.

For a full list of all the CICS messages and codes, see *CICS Messages and Codes* manual, which is on the CD-ROM.

CETR

This transaction is used to control tracing activities within CICS, for example, when an auxiliary trace is required.

If you enter *CETR*, the values of the current system are displayed, as shown in Figure 16-3. Various transaction, terminal, and component options are displayed, and you then can set and control the required trace activities.

You'll find more information on how to use trace as an aid to problem determination, including details of the format of the trace entries, in the *CICS Problem Determination Guide*, which is on the CD-ROM.

CEBR

This transaction enables you to browse and delete CICS temporary-storage queues and CICS transient data queries.

To display the queue called TEMPTS, you would enter *CEBR TEMPTS*. The format of the command is:

CEBR Temporary_Storage_Queue

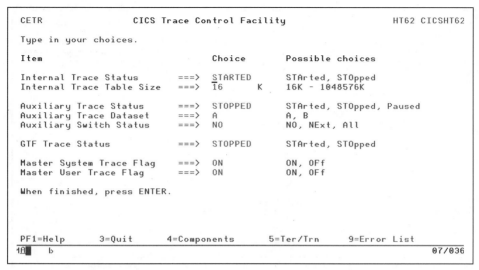

```
  CETR                    CICS Trace Control Facility              HT62 CICSHT62

  Type in your choices.

  Item                              Choice        Possible choices

  Internal Trace Status      ===>   STARTED       STArted, STOpped
  Internal Trace Table Size  ===>   16      K     16K - 1048576K

  Auxiliary Trace Status     ===>   STOPPED       STArted, STOpped, Paused
  Auxiliary Trace Dataset    ===>   A             A, B
  Auxiliary Switch Status    ===>   NO            NO, NExt, All

  GTF Trace Status           ===>   STOPPED       STArted, STOpped

  Master System Trace Flag   ===>   ON            ON, OFf
  Master User Trace Flag     ===>   ON            ON, OFf

  When finished, press ENTER.



  PF1=Help      3=Quit      4=Components      5=Ter/Trn      9=Error List
  1A          b                                                    07/036
```

Figure 16-3. CETR screen

Where *Temporary_Storage_Queue* is the name of your temporary-storage queue. As well as using the PF key options, you can also enter the following commands:

column nn

> Shifts (left or right) to column number *nn*

line nn

> Moves to the record number immediately before number *nn*

A sample of the display returned is shown in Figure 16-4.

There is more information in the *CICS Application Programming Guide,* which is on the CD-ROM.

CECI

You can use the command-level interpreter (CECI) transaction to check the syntax of CICS commands and process these commands interactively on a 3270 screen. *CECI* allows you to follow through most of the commands to execution and display the results. It also provides you with a reference to the syntax, as a whole, of the CICS command-level application programming and system programming interfaces.

CECI interacts with your test system to allow you to create or delete test data, temporary storage queues, or to deliberately introduce wrong data to test out error logic. You can use *CECI* to repair corrupted database records on your production system.

To start the command-level interpreter using our sample, enter:

```
CECI RECEIVE MAP ('ACCTMNU') MAPSET('NACTSET') TERMINAL
```

```
CEBR  TSQ TEMPTS           SYSID HT62 REC    1 OF      0   COL    1 OF   0
ENTER COMMAND ===>  _
      ************************* TOP OF QUEUE  *******************************
      ************************* BOTTOM OF QUEUE *****************************










TS QUEUE TEMPTS            DOES NOT EXIST
PF1 : HELP                 PF2 : SWITCH HEX/CHAR    PF3 : TERMINATE BROWSE
PF4 : VIEW TOP             PF5 : VIEW BOTTOM        PF6 : REPEAT LAST FIND
PF7 : SCROLL BACK HALF     PF8 : SCROLL FORWARD HALF PF9 : UNDEFINED
PF10: SCROLL BACK FULL     PF11: SCROLL FORWARD FULL PF12: UNDEFINED
MA   b                                  A                          02/022
```

Figure 16-4. Sample CEBR screen

CICS responds (see Figure 16-5) with a display of the command, its associated functions and options of the *EXEC CICS RECEIVE MAP* command.

```
RECEIVE MAP('ACCTMNU') MAPSET('NACTSET') TERMINAL  _
STATUS:  ABOUT TO EXECUTE COMMAND                    NAME=
 EXEC CICS  RECeive Map( 'ACCTMNU' )
  < Set() | INTo() >              .
  < MAPSet( 'NACTSET' ) >
  < From() < Length() > < MAPPingdev() < AId() > < Cursor() > > | Terminal
    < ASis > < INPartn() > >














PF 1 HELP 2 HEX 3 END 4 EIB 5 VAR 6 USER 7 SBH 8 SFH 9 MSG 10 SB 11 SF
MA   b                                                            01/053
```

Figure 16-5. Typical CECI display for the command syntax check

If you leave the command out and just enter CECI, you get a list of all the possible commands.

If you use the transaction CECS, the interpreter simply checks your command for correct syntax. Using CECI, you have the option of executing your command once the syntax is correct. For full details about CECI and CECS, see the *CICS Application Programming Guide*.

CEDF and CEDX

These transactions enable you to use the CICS Execution Diagnostic Facility (EDF) to test application programs associated with transactions.

CEDX

CEDX is used with programs associated with non-terminal transactions and *CEDF* with those associated with transactions initiated from a terminal.

Transactions can be started using one of the following commands:

```
CEDF tttt,ON
CEDX tran,ON
```

Similarly transactions can be stopped using one of the following commands:

```
CEDF tttt,OFF
CEDX tran,OFF
```

where *tttt* is the terminal ID and *tran* is the transaction ID.

The next section gives an example or the EDF process.

EDF: Execution Diagnostic Facility

The Execution Diagnostic Facility, EDF, is a useful tool for debugging and testing application programs associated with transactions. This section covers the following topics:

- Interception points
- EDF displays
- Other information displayed
- Useful techniques with EDF
- EDF options
- Examples of EDF displays

Full details of EDF are supplied in the *CICS Application Programming Guide.*

Interception Points

When using the Execution Diagnostic Facility with a transaction, EDF intercepts the program at the following points:

- Program initiation (just before the program gets control)
- Just before the execution of each CICS command
- Just after the execution of each CICS command (except *ABEND, XCTL,* and *RETURN*)
- Program termination

- At normal task termination

- When an abend occurs

- At abnormal task termination

EDF Displays

EDF interrupts program execution with a display consisting of a header and the main body of the display. The header contains:

- Transaction ID

- Program name

- The number of the task currently executing within CICS

- A display number within EDF

- Under 'STATUS', the reason for the interception by EDF

The header is followed by the main body display, which contains a variety of information depending on the interception point being processed; for example:

ABOUT TO EXECUTE COMMAND
    Details of the command about to be executed including keywords, options, and argument values along with information to identify the command type and offset in the program.

COMMAND EXECUTION COMPLETE
    Details as for the above item along with the result (response code).

The display is completed with the list of Enter and PF key options available at this time.

Other Information Displayed

Depending on the PF key options available on an EDF display, additional information can be displayed. The choices include:

- Looking at the EIB display

- Checking working storage for the program being executed

- Stepping back through up to ten previous EDF displays

- Examining the contents of a temporary-storage queue

The EIB in the EDF display is the Exec Interface Block, as described in the *CICS Application Programming Reference*.

Useful Techniques with EDF

Various changes can be applied in the EDF displays; for example, to enable the logical flow of the program to be changed to test error handling, or correct the field value to enable the program to work correctly. For example, you can:

• Suppress the execution of a command

• Change argument values

• Change the response code after execution of a command

• Alter data areas within working storage

• Suppress EDF displays

• Set Stop conditions to suppress displays until a certain command or error occurs

EDF Options

The PF keys and the Enter key enable you to use the EDF options. The most useful ones include:

Continue

Press the Enter key to continue. If you have made changes to the current display, it is redisplayed with the applied changes; otherwise, EDF continues to the next interception point.

Current Display

Occasionally, pressing the Enter key shows the current display. If you have made changes to the current display, it is redisplayed with the applied changes; otherwise, EDF returns to the last command interception point display.

Previous Display and Next Display

Use the *Previous Display* and *Next Display* options to navigate through up to ten command display screens.

Working Storage

Once the program is initiated, you can use the *Working Storage* option, together with other options such as *Scroll Forward*, to display the contents of the working storage and to change data if required. From this display, other options become available, such as browsing temporary storage.

Switch HEX/CHAR

On the command displays, you can use this option to switch between hexadecimal and character form in the presentation of data in the display.

Getting Started

To run CEDF at the same terminal that you are testing, simply enter *CEDF* and you will get the message *THIS TERMINAL: EDF MODE ON*. Now enter the name of your transaction; for example, *NACT*, and you will get a screen similar to Figure 16-6. Press the Enter key to step through the transaction.

If you are using two terminals, you enter *CEDF tttt* at one, where *tttt* is the name of the second terminal. Then you run your transaction on the second terminal.

Examples of EDF Displays

The remainder of this chapter shows the following debugging screens:

- Program Initiation with EIB
- About to Execute Command
- Command Execution Complete
- Working Storage
- Task Termination

Program Initiation with EIB

In Figure 16-6 you can see the three parts that make up the EDF display during program initiation.

1. The first part shows a header, the name of the transaction you entered, *NACT*, the name of the program, *NACT01*, and the name of your CICS region, CICSHT62.

2. The second part consists of the main body of the display, which contains a variety of information depending on the interception point being processed. In this example, it is the EIB contents in character form.

3. The third part consists of the list of Enter and PF key options available at this time.

```
      _TRANSACTION: NACT PROGRAM: NACT01   TASK: 000014 6 APPLID: CICSHT62 DISPLAY:  00─┐
      ─ STATUS:  PROGRAM INITIATION
2────────EIBTIME    = 120300
         EIBDATE    = 0100117
         EIBTRNID   = 'NACT'
         EIBTASKN   = 146
         EIBTRMID   = 'TC30'

         EIBCPOSN   = 4
         EIBCALEN   = 0
         EIBAID     = X'7D'                                    AT X'002000EA'
         EIBFN      = X'0000'                                  AT X'002000EB'
         EIBRCODE   = X'000000000000'                          AT X'002000ED'
         EIBDS      = '........'
    +    EIBREQID   = '........'



3──  ENTER:  CONTINUE
     PF1 : UNDEFINED           PF2 : SWITCH HEX/CHAR    PF3 : END EDF SESSION
     PF4 : SUPPRESS DISPLAYS   PF5 : WORKING STORAGE    PF6 : USER DISPLAY
     PF7 : SCROLL BACK         PF8 : SCROLL FORWARD     PF9 : STOP CONDITIONS
     PF10: PREVIOUS DISPLAY    PF11: EIB DISPLAY        PF12: UNDEFINED
     MA    b                                                      01/001
```

Figure 16-6. CEDF program-initiation screen

About to Execute Command

You can see in Figure 16-7 that the parts that make up the display that occur when EDF is *about to execute* a command, in this case, *EXEC CICS ASSIGN*.

1. The first part shows a header, the name of the transaction you entered, *NACT*, the name of the program, *NACT01*, and the name of your CICS region, in this case, CICSHT62.

2. The second part shows the status: *About to Execute command*.

3. The third part is the command and the value of the variables that you have defined for your CICS command.

4. The fourth part shows where the program is being executed. It shows the Offset address, the Line number where the EXEC statement was in the original source, and the EIBFN function reference.

5. The fifth part consists of the list of Enter and PF key options available at this time.

Command Execution Complete

You can see in Figure 16-8 that the parts that make up the display that occurs when EDF is in *Command Execution Complete state*:

1. The first part shows a header, the name of the transaction you entered, *NACT*, the name of the program, *NACT01*, and the name of your CICS region, in this case, CICSHT62.

2. The second part shows the status: *Command Execution Complete*.

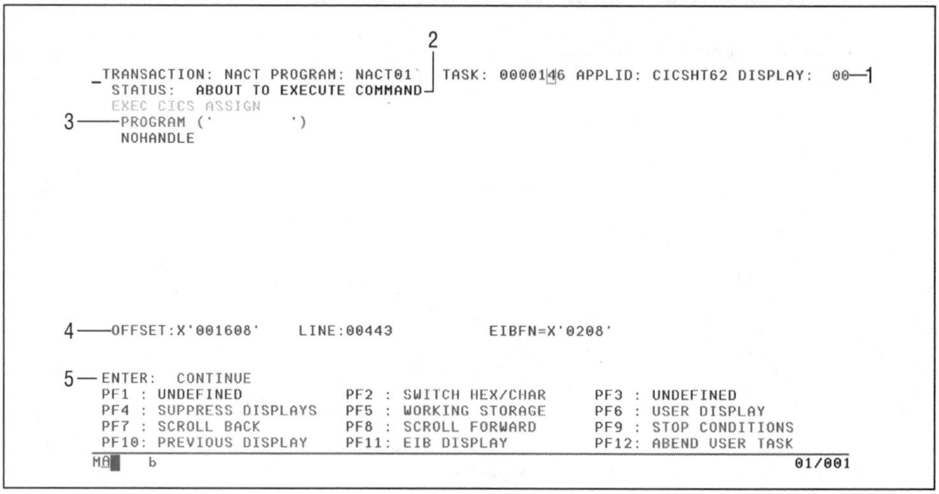

```
                                           2
       _TRANSACTION: NACT PROGRAM: NACT01 | TASK: 000014̶6 APPLID: CICSHT62 DISPLAY:  00—1
        STATUS:  ABOUT TO EXECUTE COMMAND—
         EXEC CICS ASSIGN
   3———PROGRAM ('        ')
         NOHANDLE




   4———OFFSET:X'001608'    LINE:00443           EIBFN=X'0208'


   5—ENTER:  CONTINUE
       PF1 : UNDEFINED          PF2 : SWITCH HEX/CHAR      PF3 : UNDEFINED
       PF4 : SUPPRESS DISPLAYS  PF5 : WORKING STORAGE      PF6 : USER DISPLAY
       PF7 : SCROLL BACK        PF8 : SCROLL FORWARD       PF9 : STOP CONDITIONS
       PF10: PREVIOUS DISPLAY   PF11: EIB DISPLAY          PF12: ABEND USER TASK
      MA▌   b                                                           01/001
```

Figure 16-7. CEDF: About to Execute command screen

3. The third part is the value returned by CICS to your request for *EXEC CICS ASSIGN* program.

4. The fourth part shows where the program is being executed. It shows the Offset number, the Line number where the *EXEC* statement was in the original source, and the EIBFN reference.

5. The fifth part consists of the list of Enter and PF key options available at this time.

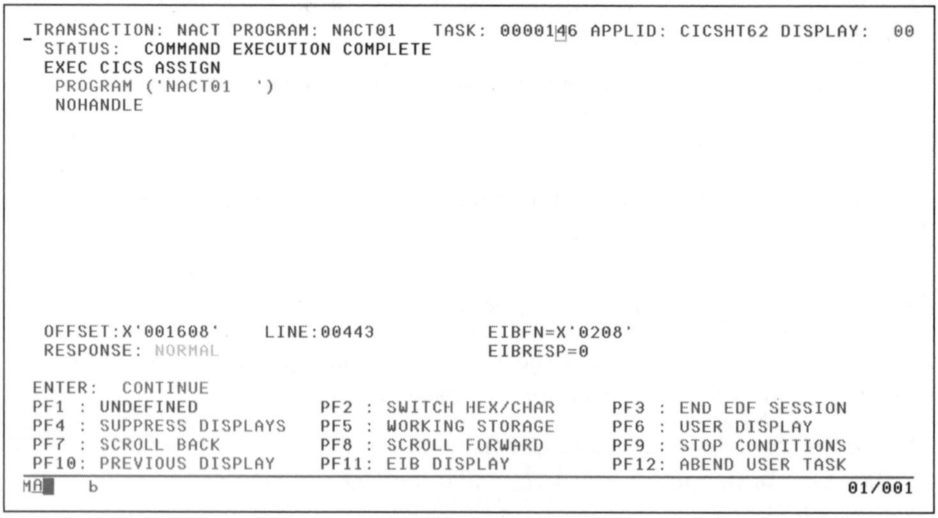

```
   _TRANSACTION: NACT PROGRAM: NACT01   TASK: 000014̶6 APPLID: CICSHT62 DISPLAY:   00
    STATUS:  COMMAND EXECUTION COMPLETE
    EXEC CICS ASSIGN
      PROGRAM ('NACT01 ')
      NOHANDLE




    OFFSET:X'001608'   LINE:00443            EIBFN=X'0208'
    RESPONSE: NORMAL                         EIBRESP=0

   ENTER:  CONTINUE
   PF1 : UNDEFINED          PF2 : SWITCH HEX/CHAR      PF3 : END EDF SESSION
   PF4 : SUPPRESS DISPLAYS  PF5 : WORKING STORAGE      PF6 : USER DISPLAY
   PF7 : SCROLL BACK        PF8 : SCROLL FORWARD       PF9 : STOP CONDITIONS
   PF10: PREVIOUS DISPLAY   PF11: EIB DISPLAY          PF12: ABEND USER TASK
  MA▌   b                                                           01/001
```

Figure 16-8. Command Execution Complete screen

Command Sequence for the Browse

Each command has an *About to Execute Command* screen and a *Command Execution Complete* screen. As you step through the screens you will see the flow of the program, which is as follows:

1. Figures 16-7 and 16-8 show the passing of control to the 3270 presentation logic program (*NACT01*) with *EXEC CICS ASSIGN*.

2. *EXEC CICS HANDLE ABEND* references our error handing program (*NACT04*) just in case things go wrong.

3. If you entered a valid name into the surname (last name) field of your Accounts Menu screen, the next command to appear when you press Enter will be *EXEC CICS RECEIVE MAP*. Figure 16-9 shows the last name (surname) you entered in the *INTO* field after command execution is complete.

```
_TRANSACTION: NACT PROGRAM: NACT01   TASK: 0000165 APPLID: CICSHT62 DISPLAY:  00
 STATUS:  COMMAND EXECUTION COMPLETE
 EXEC CICS RECEIVE MAP
   MAP ('ACCTMNU')
   INTO ('..............HORSWILL            ...........................'...)
   MAPSET ('NACTSET')
   TERMINAL
   NOHANDLE




   OFFSET:X'001CA8'    LINE:00625          EIBFN=X'1802'
   RESPONSE: NORMAL                        EIBRESP=0

 ENTER:   CONTINUE
 PF1 : UNDEFINED          PF2 : SWITCH HEX/CHAR      PF3 : END EDF SESSION
 PF4 : SUPPRESS DISPLAYS  PF5 : WORKING STORAGE      PF6 : USER DISPLAY
 PF7 : SCROLL BACK        PF8 : SCROLL FORWARD       PF9 : STOP CONDITIONS
 PF10: PREVIOUS DISPLAY   PF11: EIB DISPLAY          PF12: ABEND USER TASK
MA    b                                                              01/001
```

Figure 16-9. Part of the EXEC CICS RECEIVE MAP screen

4. Having received the map, the next command is an *EXEC CICS LINK* to the browse program (*NACT05*) (see Figure 16-10).

5. The next screens take you through the program initiation for *NACT05*, which, of course, include *EXEC CICS ASSIGN* and *EXEC CICS HANDLE ABEND* commands in the same way as the *NACT01* program.

6. *EXEC CICS STARTBR* (see Figure 16-11) starts the business of trying to find a matching record and, can follow the commands through the *READNEXT* until no further match is found when the *ENDBR* command is issued.

```
_TRANSACTION: NACT PROGRAM: NACT01    TASK: 000016̲5 APPLID: CICSHT62 DISPLAY:   00
 STATUS:  ABOUT TO EXECUTE COMMAND
 EXEC CICS LINK PROGRAM
  PROGRAM ('NACT05 ')
  COMMAREA ('V1AB0000000000000000000600000000      HORSWILL                   '...)
  LENGTH (30669)
  NOHANDLE




    OFFSET:X'0044D2'    LINE:02246              EIBFN=X'0E02'


 ENTER:  CONTINUE
 PF1 : UNDEFINED             PF2 : SWITCH HEX/CHAR    PF3 : UNDEFINED
 PF4 : SUPPRESS DISPLAYS     PF5 : WORKING STORAGE    PF6 : USER DISPLAY
 PF7 : SCROLL BACK           PF8 : SCROLL FORWARD     PF9 : STOP CONDITIONS
 PF10: PREVIOUS DISPLAY      PF11: EIB DISPLAY        PF12: ABEND USER TASK
 MA̲    b                                                              01/001
```

Figure 16-10. Part of EXEC CICS LINK screen

```
_TRANSACTION: NACT PROGRAM: NACT05    TASK: 000016̲5 APPLID: CICSHT62 DISPLAY:   00
 STATUS:  ABOUT TO EXECUTE COMMAND
 EXEC CICS STARTBR
  FILE ('ACCTNAM ')
  RIDFLD ('HORSWILL           HORSWILL.....................................'...)
  REQID (0)
  GTEQ
  NOHANDLE




    OFFSET:X'000D10'    LINE:00382              EIBFN=X'060C'


 ENTER:  CONTINUE
 PF1 : UNDEFINED             PF2 : SWITCH HEX/CHAR    PF3 : UNDEFINED
 PF4 : SUPPRESS DISPLAYS     PF5 : WORKING STORAGE    PF6 : USER DISPLAY
 PF7 : SCROLL BACK           PF8 : SCROLL FORWARD     PF9 : STOP CONDITIONS
 PF10: PREVIOUS DISPLAY      PF11: EIB DISPLAY        PF12: ABEND USER TASK
 MA̲    b                                                              01/001
```

Figure 16-11. Part of EXEC CICS STARTBR screen

7. Having done its job, the *NACT05* program closes and returns control to the
   NACT01 program using an *EXEC CICS RETURN* command. In Figure 16-12 you
   can see the data in the COMMAREA that is being returned. Finally, the program (*NACT01*) issues an *EXEC CICS SEND MAP* to display the data on the
   screen. If you look back at the screen where you issued the original NACT
   transaction, you should see the results of your inquiry. The Task Termination
   screen (Figure 16-14) will appear and you can close your EDF session by
   entering "No" when prompted.

```
_TRANSACTION: NACT PROGRAM: NACT01   TASK: 000016⃞5 APPLID: CICSHT62 DISPLAY:  00
 _ STATUS:  COMMAND EXECUTION COMPLETE
  EXEC CICS LINK PROGRAM
   PROGRAM ('NACT05  ')
   COMMAREA ('V1AB0000000000000000006000100001000006HORSWILL        JOHN    '...)
   LENGTH (30669)
   NOHANDLE




     OFFSET:X'0044D2'   LINE:02246         EIBFN=X'0E08'
     RESPONSE: NORMAL                      EIBRESP=0

  ENTER:   CONTINUE
  PF1 :  UNDEFINED           PF2 : SWITCH HEX/CHAR     PF3 : END EDF SESSION
  PF4 : SUPPRESS DISPLAYS    PF5 : WORKING STORAGE     PF6 : USER DISPLAY
  PF7 : SCROLL BACK          PF8 : SCROLL FORWARD      PF9 : STOP CONDITIONS
  PF10: PREVIOUS DISPLAY     PF11: EIB DISPLAY         PF12: ABEND USER TASK
 MA▆    b                                                           01/001
```

Figure 16-12. Part of EXEC CICS LINK screen

Working Storage

From the Command Execution Complete screen (Figure 16-8), press PF5 to show the working storage. Working storage is one of a number of functions that you can view to help you diagnose your problem. Use PF6 for user display and PF11 for EIB display. Figure 16-13 shows the parts that make up the display that occur when EDF displays the working storage of the program:

- The first part shows a header, the name of the transaction you entered, *NACT,* the name of the program, *NACT01,* and the name of your CICS region, in this case, *CICSHT62.*

- The second part shows the starting address in working storage.

- The third part addresses on the left center HEX values of storage. On the right is the readable/EBCDIC value of storage.

- The fourth part consists of the list of Enter and PF key options available at this time.

Task Termination

Figure 16-14 shows the parts that make up the display that occurs when EDF terminates the task:

- The first part shows a header, the name of the transaction entered, *NACT,* the name of the program, *NACT01,* and the name of your CICS region, in this case, CICSHT62.

```
TRANSACTION: NACT PROGRAM: NACT01     TASK: 0000165 APPLID: CICSHT62 DISPLAY:   00
  ADDRESS: 1140AC10                      WORKING STORAGE
1140AC10   000000    D5C1C3E3 F0F16060 60606060 60E6D6D9    NACT01-------WOR
1140AC20   000010    D2C9D5C7 40E2E3D6 D9C1C7C5 40404040    KING STORAGE
1140AC30   000020    D5C1C3E3 E3C3F3F0 F0F0F0F0 F1F6F540    NACTTC300000165
1140AC40   000030    114035C8 40E2E4D9 D5C1C3E3 F0F14040    . .H SURNACT01
1140AC50   000040    D5C1C3E3 F0F24040 D5C1C3E3 F0F34040    NACT02   NACT03
1140AC60   000050    D5C1C3E3 F0F44040 D5C1C3E3 F0F54040    NACT04   NACT05
1140AC70   000060    40404040 00000000 00000000 00000007
1140AC80   000070    0000E85C C1C3C3E3 40404040 E2E4D9D5    ..Y*ACCT     SURN
1140AC90   000080    C1D4C540 40404040 4040C6C9 D9E2E340    AME         FIRST
1140ACA0   000090    4040D4C9 4040E3E3 D3404040 C1C4C4D9      MI  TTL    ADDR
1140ACB0   0000A0    C5E2E240 40404040 40404040 40404040    ESS
1140ACC0   0000B0    40404040 4040E2E3 40404040 4040D3C9          ST      LI
1140ACD0   0000C0    D4C9E340 40404040 40404040 40404040    MIT
1140ACE0   0000D0    40404040 40404040 40404040 40404040
1140ACF0   0000E0    40404040 40404040 40404040 40404040
1140AD00   0000F0    40404040 40404040 40404040 40404040

ENTER:  CURRENT DISPLAY
PF1 : UNDEFINED              PF2 : BROWSE TEMP STORAGE PF3 : UNDEFINED
PF4 : EIB DISPLAY           PF5 : INVOKE CECI         PF6 : USER DISPLAY
PF7 : SCROLL BACK HALF      PF8 : SCROLL FORWARD HALF PF9 : UNDEFINED
PF10: SCROLL BACK FULL      PF11: SCROLL FORWARD FULL PF12: REMEMBER DISPLAY
MA   b                                                              02/012
```

Figure 16-13. CEDF: Working Storage screen

- The second part shows the status: *Task Termination.*

- The third part shows the option to continue EDF or not.

- The fourth part consists of the list of Enter and PF key options available.

CICS defaults the reply at Task Termination to Yes, so if you want to end your debugging session, you need to overtype the *YES* with *NO* and press Enter.

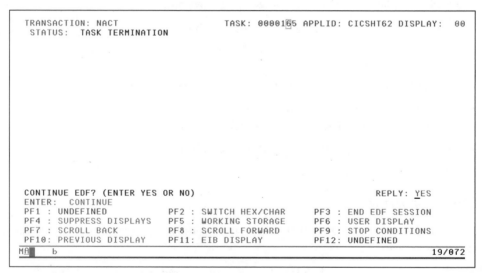

```
TRANSACTION: NACT                    TASK: 0000165 APPLID: CICSHT62 DISPLAY:   00
  STATUS:  TASK TERMINATION












CONTINUE EDF? (ENTER YES OR NO)                              REPLY: YES
ENTER:  CONTINUE
PF1 : UNDEFINED            PF2 : SWITCH HEX/CHAR      PF3 : END EDF SESSION
PF4 : SUPPRESS DISPLAYS    PF5 : WORKING STORAGE      PF6 : USER DISPLAY
PF7 : SCROLL BACK          PF8 : SCROLL FORWARD       PF9 : STOP CONDITIONS
PF10: PREVIOUS DISPLAY     PF11: EIB DISPLAY          PF12: UNDEFINED
MA   b                                                              19/072
```

Figure 16-14. CEDF: Task Termination screen

Summary

You have seen some of the tools that support CICS and help you to track down a problem. CEDF facility has shown how you can follow the path of an application program where it interacts with CICS and allowed you to inspect and change the variables that the application passed to and received from CICS.

IX

Appendices

The two appendices provide information to help you use the CD that accompanies this book:

- Appendix A describes what you need to do to get the sample application running on your mainframe (OS/390) system. Information about developing and configuring each of the components is contained in their respective programming chapters.

- Appendix B provides an outline of the directories that are on the CD-ROM in order to help you find the files that we describe in this book.

A

Configuring Your CICS for OS/390 Environment

Up until now we have described the individual components in the KanDoIT business application. This appendix explains how to configure your CICS region on OS/390 so that you can run the sample application. The CD-ROM that accompanies this book contains both compiled code and source code.

The COBOL code has been compiled and is ready to run with CICS TS for OS/390 Version 1.3 and Language Environment (LE) for OS/390 2.8. If you are running any earlier version of CICS or LE you need to compile the source files that are provided.

This chapter is solely concerned with the installation of the compiled sample code.

Before you start to use the application you need to check the systems requirements in "Getting Ready."

The COBOL business logic is the core of the sample and is mandatory if you are to use any of the presentation interfaces. Installing the COBOL code supplied includes the 3270 interface so you will be able to use the application (see "Configuring the COBOL Component"). The other options for the presentation logic are:

- The CORBA Server and the web component as described in "Configuring the CICS Java Component" and "Programming the Web Component" in Chapter 9.

- The customer services frontend using Visual Basic as described in "Accessing Applications on the CICS Server" in Chapter 13.

- The MQSeries-CICS bridge as described in "Setting Up MQSeries and CICS" in Chapter 15.

You will find a complete list of the programs that are provided on the CD-ROM in Appendix B.

Getting Ready

Before you can install the complete sample program you need:

- A Windows desktop system with a 3270 emulator such as IBM Personal Communications (PCOMM).

- Ability to log on to TSO on an OS/390 system.

- Ability to log on to a CICS region.

- Authority to update the program libraries of that CICS region from your TSO ID, or if not, access to someone else who can update the libraries for you.

- Authority on that CICS region to issue resource definition *DEFINE* and *ALTER* commands, or if not, access to someone else who will issue the commands for you.

- Check your local site procedures to ensure that you have all the necessary software installed.

Using the CD-ROM

Insert the CD-ROM into your workstation CD-ROM drive. This brings up the welcome panel and gives you four options:

- Configuring CICS on OS/390

- Configuring the CORBA server and web frontend

- Configuring the Customer Services (Visual Basic) frontend

- Configuring the Head Office (MQSeries) demonstration program

These options need not be invoked all together and can be invoked on different workstations at different times.

You can also browse the CD-ROM directly to read and copy the source code for all parts of the application. Appendix B lists the files on the CD-ROM.

Getting the Data from the CD-ROM

You need to upload the following files from the directories shown:

File(s)	Directory
cicsadp.loa and *cicsadp.cor*	\cicsadp\Cobol Application\Tso\loadlib
cicsadp.csd	\cicsadp\Cobol Application\Tso\csddefs
cicsadp.jcl	\cicsadp\Cobol Application\Tso\vsam_jcl
cicsadp.cpy	\cicsadp\Cobol Application\Tso\copybook
cicsadp.txt	\cicsadp\Cobol Application\Tso\vsam_data
cicsadp.mac and *cicsadp.src*	\cicsadp\Cobol Application\Tso\source

Uploading the Files

There are many tools that you can use to upload the files from the CD-ROM to your OS/390 system. Whichever tool you use, you should be sure that you can define the process to transfer files:

- As binary

- Fixed record length of 80

- With a file extension of **.seq* when they are received on your mainframe.

If you miss any of these attributes, then when you receive the file into the datasets you will probably receive a message describing the files as invalid or something similar.

We will describe two methods that you can use to upload the load modules to the host. The first uses File Control Protocol (FTP) and doesn't require any additional software other than that which comes with TCP/IP. Secondly, we describe how to use IBM Personal Communications (PCOMM) product. Other tools that you can use include WS_FTP_Pro and a SNA Server 3270 applet.

Example A-1 shows the FTP commands that you can use. The most important line is *bin fixed 80* and the filename extension that includes the *.seq* at the end. When you have completed this process, you can go directly to the receive commands shown in Example A-3.

Example A-1. Procedure for Using FTP to Upload the Files

```
FTP hostname
userid Your_userid
pwd Your_password
bin fixed 80
put cicsadp.loa cicsadp.loaseq
put cicsadp.cor cicsadp.corseq
put cicsadp.src cicsadp.srcseq
put cicsadp.jcl cicsadp.jclseq
put cicsadp.txt cicsadp.txtseq
put cicsadp.csd cicsadp.csdseq
put cicsadp.cpy cicsadp.cpyseq
put cicsadp.mac cicsadp.macseq
quit
```

If you are using Personal Communications (PCOMM) to upload the files, first set up the transfer type of *loadlib* before you initiate the send. To do this, use the *Setup → Define Transfer Types* option from the *Transfer* menu bar pull-down and create the *loadlib* type (with the *ASCII, CRLF,* and *Append* checkboxes all unselected), the *Fixed* radio button selected and the *LRECL* set to 80. See Figure A-1.

Select the *Send File to Host* option from the *Transfer* menu of your PCOMM host session, specify the PC filename, host filename, and transfer type, as shown in

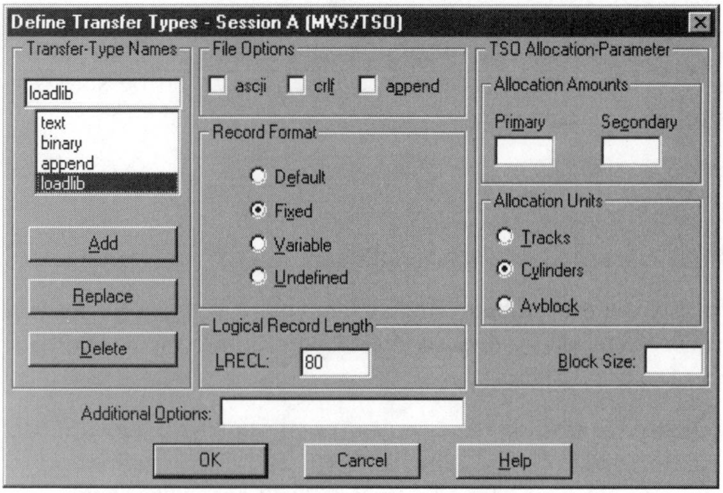

Figure A-1. Personal Communications: Define Transfer Types panel

Example A-2. Once you have completed this process, you can proceed to the receive process described in Example A-3.

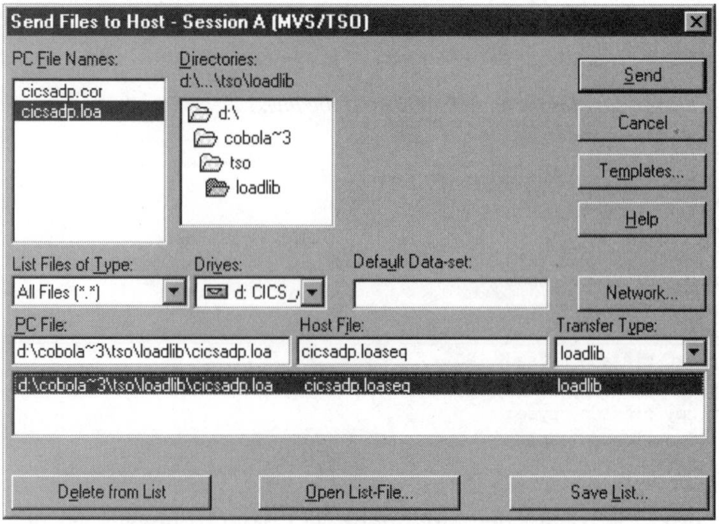

Figure A-2. Personal Communications: Send Files to Host panel

Example A-2. Procedure for Using PCOMM to Upload the Files

```
PC File:        cicsadp.loa
Host File:      cicsadp.loaseq
Transfer Type:  loadlib

PC File:        cicsadp.cor
```

Example A-2. Procedure for Using PCOMM to Upload the Files (continued)

```
Host File:       cicsadp.corseq
Transfer Type:   loadlib

PC File:         cicsadp.src
Host File:       cicsadp.srcseq
Transfer Type:   loadlib

PC File:         cicsadp.mac
Host File:       cicsadp.macseq
Transfer Type:   loadlib

PC File:         cicsadp.jcl
Host File:       cicsadp.jclseq
Transfer Type:   loadlib

PC File:         cicsadp.txt
Host File:       cicsadp.txtseq
Transfer Type:   loadlib

PC File:         cicsadp.csd
Host File:       cicsadp.csdseq
Transfer Type:   loadlib

PC File:         cicsadp.cpy
Host File:       cicsadp.cpyseq
Transfer Type:   loadlib
```

Receiving the data sets

Logon to your TSO system to receive the data sets. Issue the commands in Example A-3 to unload the sequential files into TSO partitioned data sets.

Example A-3. Receiving the Files into Your Data Sets

```
receive indsname(cicsadp.loaseq)
dsn('CICSTS130.CICSADP.LOADLIB')   (when prompted for a dataset)

receive indsname(cicsadp.corseq)
dsn('CICSTS130.CICSADP.CORLIB')    (when prompted for a dataset)

receive indsname(cicsadp.macseq)
dsn('CICSTS130.CICSADP.COBSRCE')   (when prompted for a dataset)

receive indsname(cicsadp.srcseq)
dsn('CICSTS130.CICSADP.COBSRCE')   (when prompted for a dataset)

receive indsname(cicsadp.jclseq)
dsn('CICSTS130.CICSADP.JCLLIB')    (when prompted for a dataset)

receive indsname(cicsadp.txtseq)
dsn('CICSTS130.CICSADP.VSAMDATA')  (when prompted for a dataset)
```

Example A-3. Receiving the Files into Your Data Sets (continued)

```
receive indsname(cicsadp.csdseq)
dsn('CICSTS130.CICSADP.CSDDEFS')    (when prompted for a dataset)

receive indsname(cicsadp.cpyseq)
dsn('CICSTS130.CICSADP.COBCOPY')    (when prompted for a dataset)
```

Where the high-level qualifier used in the examples, it is called *CICSTS130. CICSADP.NAME.* This is only a suggestion and you should follow the guidelines for your site. Opening any of these datasets shows you the files that have been received.

---

cicsadp.txt will be copied into a Sequential Data Set (SDS). Specify a new data set name so that you don't conflict with any existing data sets.

cicsadp.cor will be copied into a Partitioned Data Set Extended (PDSE).

All the other files are copied into Partioned Data Sets (PDS).

Configuring the COBOL Component

This section describes which files to copy to the CICS program libraries and how to configure CICS to use the files. You may not have the authority to perform some if these steps, where this is the case please ask the appropriate person at your site for assistance.

Setting up the VSAM File

Using the following guidelines to set up the VSAM file:

1. Edit the sample VSAM file in JCLLIB:

    a. Add a job card at the beginning.

    b. Enter the appropriate High Level Qualifiers for correct data file *CICSADP. DATA.*

    c. Enter the input file name for the repro job to load the VSAM DATA into ACCTFILE.

2. Run the JCL; this creates three VSAM files of the form:

    — *high.level.qualifer.ACCTFILE*

— *high.level.qualifier.ACCTNAIX* with the path *high.level.qualifier.ACCTNAME*

— *high.level.qualifier.ACTINUSE*

Setting Up and Installing the CICS Resource Definitions

The following guidelines will help you set up and install the CICS resource definitions:

1. Edit the supplied CSD definitions file. If you followed our conventions, it is the data set in the PDS called *CICSTS130.CICSADP.CSDDEFS*. The CICS files in group CICS0ADP (*ACCTFIL*, *ACCTNAM*, and *ACINUSE*) need to be updated to point to the dataset names. For example:

— *high.level.qualifer.*ACCTFILE

— *high.level.qualifier.*ACCTNAME

— *high.level.qualifier.*ACTINUSE

2. Update your CSD with the definitions contained in your file. This probably means asking someone at your site with the right authorization to run the DFHCSDUP job.

 If you intend using the CORBA option later, add a further DD statement to your DFHCSDUP job using CICSJADP as input. You can run this at the same time.

---

3. Enter ADD GROUP(CICS0ADP) LIST(*YourGroupList*) where *YourGroupList* is specified in your GRPLIST system initialization parameter (SIP) in your CICS startup job.

4. If you do a warm start of your CICS region, this new definition will not be recognized.

5. If you are cold starting CICS, the definitions that you have added to your CSD-DEFS job are automatically installed. On the other hand, it is more likely that you will be warm starting CICS, in which case you should logon to your CICS region and install the CICS0ADP group (or your self-defined group) using:

```
CEDA INSTALL GROUP(CICS0ADP)
CEDA INSTALL GROUP(CICSJADP)
```

You should see these resource definitions shown in Figure A-3.

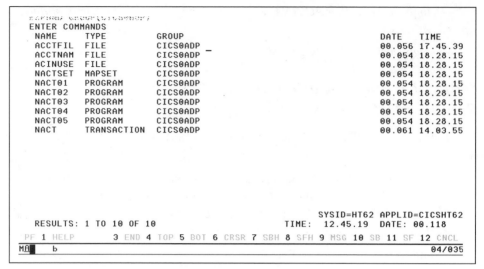

```
EXPAND GROUP(CICS0ADP)
ENTER COMMANDS
  NAME      TYPE         GROUP                             DATE    TIME
  ACCTFIL   FILE         CICS0ADP  _                       00.056  17.45.39
  ACCTNAM   FILE         CICS0ADP                          00.054  18.28.15
  ACINUSE   FILE         CICS0ADP                          00.054  18.28.15
  NACTSET   MAPSET       CICS0ADP                          00.054  18.28.15
  NACT01    PROGRAM      CICS0ADP                          00.054  18.28.15
  NACT02    PROGRAM      CICS0ADP                          00.054  18.28.15
  NACT03    PROGRAM      CICS0ADP                          00.054  18.28.15
  NACT04    PROGRAM      CICS0ADP                          00.054  18.28.15
  NACT05    PROGRAM      CICS0ADP                          00.054  18.28.15
  NACT      TRANSACTION  CICS0ADP                          00.061  14.03.55




                                             SYSID=HT62 APPLID=CICSHT62
  RESULTS: 1 TO 10 OF 10               TIME:  12.45.19  DATE: 00.118
 PF 1 HELP        3 END 4 TOP 5 BOT 6 CRSR 7 SBH 8 SFH 9 MSG 10 SB 11 SF 12 CNCL
MA    b                                                            04/035
```

Figure A-3. CEDA EXPAND GROUP(CICS0ADP) screen

Running the Application

1. Edit your CICS startup JCL to add the loadlibrary containing the load module into the DFHRPL concatenation. The statement looks like this:

```
DFHRPL DD DISP=SHR,DSN=High.Level.qualifier.Loadlib
       DD DISP=SHR,DSN=High.Level.qualifier.Corlib
```

2. Start CICS and logon to your CICS region from a 3270 emulation screen or a 3270 monitor.

3. Issue the transaction *NACT.* You should now be running the application. Figure A-4 shows the screen that you see.

So far you have the main COBOL application running and you will be using this as the backend application to run the remaining parts of the sample application.

A check should be performed to ensure that the resource names associated with the NACT transaction do not conflict with the resources already in use. If so, you will have to change the CICS programs and resources to use another prefix and recompile the programs.

```
ACCOUNTS MENU

   TO SEARCH BY NAME, ENTER SURNAME AND IF REQUIRED, FIRST NAME

      SURNAME    : _               (1 TO 18 ALPHABETIC CHRS)
      FIRST NAME :                 (1 TO 12 ALPHABETIC CHRS OPTIONAL)

   TO PROCESS AN ACCOUNT, ENTER REQUEST TYPE AND ACCOUNT NUMBER

      REQUEST TYPE:               (D-DISPLAY, A-ADD, M-MODIFY, X-DELETE, P-PRINT)
      ACCOUNT    :                (10000 TO 79999)
      PRINTER ID :                (1 TO 4 CHARACTERS (REQUIRED FOR PRINT REQUEST))









   ENTER DATA AND PRESS ENTER FOR SEARCH OR ACCOUNT REQUEST OR PRESS CLEAR TO EXIT
 MA    b                                                              05/022
```

Figure A-4. Accounts Menu from a 3270 screen

Configuring the CICS Java Component

To find out more about configuring the CICS Java component, see Part III. These instructions describe the steps that you need to carry out to set your CICS TS for OS/390 system.

As this is a client/server setup, you also need to configure the client sample code, as explained in the instructions that relate to Part IV, *The Web Component.* It is also assumed you have successfully installed and have running the COBOL application, which is invoked by starting the *NACT* transaction.

 PDSEs (Partition Data Set Extended) must be defined to hold the CICS Java programs and resource files you have built. You must use PDSE libraries (not PDS ones) so that you can create long-name aliases in addition to the eight-character primary member name. At run time, CICS searches the PDSE directories for the long name to obtain the corresponding short name. In the sample application we describe in the book, the long name is *accountObject.*

Defining Your CICS Resources

Before you startup or log on to your CICS region, you need to check your CICS startup JCL and also some system initialization parameters as follows:

- Edit the DFHRPL concatenation of your CICS startup JCL. Add the loadlibrary containing the location of the Java DLLs (you may have already done this), add the location of your SDJLOAD library and also the HPJ build library. Clearly these will be different from ours, but to give you an idea, an example of the statement looks like this:

```
DFHRPL DD DISP=SHR,DSN=Corlib                        (location of Java dlls)
       DD DISP=SHR,DSN=High.Level.qualifier.SDFJLOAD
       DD DISP=SHR,DSN=HPJ.BUILD.TST1015P.LOAD
```

- Check that your system initialization parameters include the following settings:

    — *MXT=075,SEC=NO* (increase max tasks)

    — *RLS=YES* (invoke RLS support, if enabled)

    — *TCPIP=YES* (add TCPIP support)

    The maximum number of tasks should be set to at least 75, if it isn't already set much higher.

If your installation is not using Record Level Sharing (RLS) and you add it to your CICS TS 1.3 system initialization parameters, when you try to run the NACT transaction, you will receive an abend in *NACT01* and a DFHFC0541 message.

The COBOL application installation process should have installed the group CICS-JADP, which contains resource definitions for the CORBA Server sample. In addition to those definitions you also need to add a definiton for both *TCPIPSERVICE* and *REQUESTMODEL* togther with the associated transactions *CIOF* and *ACTO*. They are defined and installed using *CEDA*, into a group called CICSJADP:

TCPIPSERVICE

Configures a port to listen for incoming IIOP requests. For IIOP requests, the transaction ID must be set to *CIOR*. When requests are made to the specified port, *CIOR* is attached and started. We are not using Secure Sockets Layer (SSL), and the socket remains open at all times.

a. Logon to your CICS region and enter:

```
CEDA EXPAND GROUP(CICSJADP)
```

Figure A-5 shows you the screen that contains all the definitions that you need in the group, CICSJADP. Enter *A* alongside the PRMTCPIP entry to view and, if necessary to change the values.

b. Figure A-6 shows you the values that you could enter for the *TCPIPSERVICE* called PRMTCPIP.

```
   EXPAND GROUP(CICSJADP)
   ENTER COMMANDS
     NAME       TYPE         GROUP                       DATE   TIME
     ZSRV02     PROGRAM      CICSJADP  _                  00.062 18.01.39
     ACTO       TRANSACTION  CICSJADP                     00.062 18.01.39
     CIOF       TRANSACTION  CICSJADP                     00.062 18.01.39
     ACCTRM     REQUESTMODEL CICSJADP                     00.062 18.01.39
     DEFAULT    REQUESTMODEL CICSJADP                     00.062 18.01.39
     PRMTCPIP   TCPIPSERVICE CICSJADP                     00.074 16.45.16




                                                 SYSID=HT62 APPLID=CICSHT62
     RESULTS: 1 TO 6 OF 6                  TIME:  13.39.15  DATE: 00.117
   PF 1 HELP       3 END 4 TOP 5 BOT 6 CRSR 7 SBH 8 SFH 9 MSG 10 SB 11 SF 12 CNCL
   MA  b                                                          04/035
```

Figure A-5. CEDA EXPAND GROUP(CICSJADP) screen

```
   Alter TCPIPSERVICE (PRMTCPIP) GROUP (CICSJADP)_
   OVERTYPE TO MODIFY                              CICS RELEASE = 0530
    CEDA  ALter TCpipservice( PRMTCPIP )
     TCpipservice    : PRMTCPIP
     Group           : CICSJADP
     Description  ==> CICS ADP book sample
     Urm          ==>
     Portnumber   ==> 32662              1-32767
     Certificate  ==>
     STatus       ==> Open               Open | Closed
     SSl          ==> No                 Yes | No | Clientauth
     TRansaction  ==> CIOR
     Backlog      ==> 00005              0-32767
     TSqprefix    ==>
     Ipaddress    ==>
     SOcketclose  ==> No                 No | 0-240000 (HHMMSS)



                                                 SYSID=HT62 APPLID=CICSHT62
     ALTER SUCCESSFUL                      TIME:  15.05.28  DATE: 00.139
   PF 1 HELP 2 COM 3 END        6 CRSR 7 SBH 8 SFH 9 MSG 10 SB 11 SF 12 CNCL
   MA  b                                                          04/035
```

Figure A-6. CEDA VIEW TCPIPSERVICE(PRMTCPIP)

If you need to change the port number, overtype the port number as shown in Figure A-6 and hit the Enter key. Before you can re-install this resource you will have to close the previous port. To do this enter:

`CEMT INQUIRE TCPIPSERVICE(PRMTCPIP)`

Figure A-7 shows the list of the resource definitons. Overtype *Ope* with *Clo* to close the port. Now you can re-install the *TCPIPSERVICE* resource definition using *CEDA*.

```
INQUIRE TCPIPSERVICE(PRMTCPIP)
 STATUS:   RESULTS - OVERTYPE TO MODIFY
  Tcpips(PRMTCPIP) Bac( 00005 ) Con(0000) Por(32662)      Ope
     Tra(CIOR)                  Ipa(9.20.101.6    )                Wai




                                         SYSID=HT62 APPLID=CICSHT62
     RESPONSE: NORMAL                 TIME:  13.47.28  DATE: 04.26.00
  PF 1 HELP        3 END      5 VAR      7 SBH 8 SFH 9 MSG 10 SB 11 SF
 MA    b                                                      01/034
```

Figure A-7. CEMT INQUIRE TCPIPSERVICE(PRMTCPIP) screen

Make a note now of the port you are using and the hostname (or IP address) as this will be needed in the set up for Part IV, *The Web Component* to generate the *genfac.ior* file used by the CORBA client to locate the remote object in CICS. The IPA value in Figure A-8 shows you the IP address that you are using.

REQUESTMODEL

Defines the pattern for the remote object and its exposed interface and methods. In this case, we're specifying that any method (by using a * wildcard) in the *accountObject* module in the interface AccountInterface will run under transaction *ACTO*.

OMG definitions are case sensitive and must match those in the IDL.

Similarly for the Generic Factory, we set up a default *REQUESTMODEL,* which runs under the default transaction of *CIOF*.

For each *REQUESTMODEL* we need to define corresponding transactions, *ACTO* and *CIOF*.

```
 Alter REQUESTMODEL (ACCTRM) GROUP (CICSJADP)
 OVERTYPE TO MODIFY                              CICS RELEASE = 0530
  CEDA  ALter Requestmodel( ACCTRM   )
   Requestmodel    : ACCTRM
   Group           : CICSJADP
   Description   ==> Account Object for CICS Primer
   OMGModule     ==> accountObject
   OMGInterface  ==> AccountInterface*
   OMGOperation  ==> *
   Transid       ==> ACTO




                                        SYSID=HT62 APPLID=CICSHT62
   ALTER SUCCESSFUL                 TIME:  15.13.32  DATE: 00.139
 PF  1 HELP 2 COM 3 END         6 CRSR 7 SBH 8 SFH 9 MSG 10 SB 11 SF 12 CNCL
MA▌    b                             A                        06/022
```

Figure A-8. CEDA ALTER REQUESTMODEL (ACCTRM) screen

```
 Alter REQUESTMODEL (DEFAULT) GROUP (CICSJADP)_
 OVERTYPE TO MODIFY                              CICS RELEASE = 0530
  CEDA  ALter Requestmodel( DEFAULT  )
   Requestmodel    : DEFAULT
   Group           : CICSJADP
   Description   ==> Generic factory
   OMGModule     ==> org::omg::CosLifeCycle
   OMGInterface  ==> GenericFactory
   OMGOperation  ==> *
   Transid       ==> CIOF




                                        SYSID=HT62 APPLID=CICSHT62
   ALTER SUCCESSFUL                 TIME:  15.15.42  DATE: 00.139
 PF  1 HELP 2 COM 3 END        6 CRSR 7 SBH 8 SFH 9 MSG 10 SB 11 SF 12 CNCL
MA▌    b                                                      04/035
```

Figure A-9. CEDA DEFINE REQUESTMODEL (DEFAULT) screen

The program for IIOP requests is always *DFHIIOPA* (only transaction ID, group, description and program were specified, all other parameters left at default values).

Finally, you need to install a CICS-supplied group DFH£EXCI if it isn't already installed. To do this enter:

```
CEDA INSTALL GROUP(DFH£EXCI)
```

```
 OBJECT CHARACTERISTICS                               CICS RELEASE = 0530
  CEDA  View TRANSaction( ACTO )
   TRANSaction    : ACTO
   Group          : CICSJADP
   DEscription    : TRAN FOR ACCOUNTOBJECT IIOP REQUESTS
   PROGram        : DFHIIOPA
   TWasize        : 00000              0-32767
   PROFile        : DFHCICST
   PArtitionset   :
   STAtus         : Enabled            Enabled | Disabled
   PRIMedsize     : 00000              0-65520
   TASKDATALoc    : Below              Below | Any
   TASKDATAKey    : User               User | Cics
   STOrageclear   : No                 No | Yes
   RUnaway        : System             System | 0 | 500-2700000
   SHutdown       : Disabled           Disabled | Enabled
   ISolate        : Yes                Yes | No
   Brexit         :
 + REMOTE ATTRIBUTES

                                          SYSID=HT62 APPLID=CICSHT62

 PF 1 HELP 2 COM 3 END          6 CRSR 7 SBH 8 SFH 9 MSG 10 SB 11 SF 12 CNCL
 MA█   b                                                          01/003
```

Figure A-10. CEDA DEFINE TRANSACTION screen

```
 OBJECT CHARACTERISTICS                               CICS RELEASE = 0530
  CEDA  View TRANSaction( CIOF )
   TRANSaction    : CIOF
   Group          : CICSJADP
   DEscription    : CICS Generic factory started by CIOR
   PROGram        : DFHIIOPA
   TWasize        : 00000              0-32767
   PROFile        : DFHCICST
   PArtitionset   :
   STAtus         : Enabled            Enabled | Disabled
   PRIMedsize     : 00000              0-65520
   TASKDATALoc    : Any                Below | Any
   TASKDATAKey    : User               User | Cics
   STOrageclear   : No                 No | Yes
   RUnaway        : System             System | 0 | 500-2700000
   SHutdown       : Enabled            Disabled | Enabled
   ISolate        : Yes                Yes | No
   Brexit         :
 + REMOTE ATTRIBUTES

                                          SYSID=HT62 APPLID=CICSHT62

 PF 1 HELP 2 COM 3 END          6 CRSR 7 SBH 8 SFH 9 MSG 10 SB 11 SF 12 CNCL
 MA█   b                                                          01/003
```

Figure A-11. CEDA ALTER TRANSACTION screen

Setting Up CICS Java on OS/390

Deit your CICS Startup JCL as follows:

Add the loadlibrary containing the load module into the DFHRPL concatenation. The statement looks like this:

```
DFHRPL DD DISP=SHR,DSN=High.Level.qualifier.Loadlib
       DD DISP=SHR,DSN=High.Level.qualifier.Corlib
SYSIN  DD *
DB2CONN=YES                        (Connect to DB2)
```

```
MXT=75,SEC=NO                    (Increased max tasks)
RLS=YES                          (Invoke RLS support, if enabled)
TCPIP=YES                        (Add TCPIP support)

DFHRPL DD DISP=SHR,DSN=CICSTS130.CICSADP.CORLIB     (location of Java dlls)
       DD DISP=SHR,DSN=CICSTS130.CICS530.SDFJLOAD
       DD DISP=SHR,DSN=CICSTS130.CICS530.SDFHLOAD
       DD DISP=SHR,DSN=HPJ.BUILD.TST1015P.LOAD
```

Using the PDF Files for the CICS Main Library

The pdf files of the CICS library for CICS TS for OS/390 Version 1.3 are provided on the CD-ROM. To use it you need to have an Adobe Reader installed. This is provided on the CD-ROM as *\cicsadp\pdfs\adobe\rs405eng.exe*. This installs the Adobe Reader Version 4.0.5, which includes search facilities. To download the latest version of the Adobe Reader, visit their web site at *http://www.adobe.com*.

To access the CICS TS 1.3 library:

1. Start Adobe Reader.

2. Change directory to the *\cicsadp\pdfs\cicsts* directory on the CD-ROM. Select and open the pdf file called *CICStart.pdf*.

B

List of CD-ROM Files

The sample that is described in this book is a simplified application that dynamically creates, reads, updates, and deletes customer records. It is based on a COBOL application that has been written as a two-tier structure of business and presentation logic. This permits the flexibility of a variety of frontends to the business logic. The application shows a web-based frontend using a Java ORB approach with IIOP, a second web-based frontend ECI to link to Business logic, an interface to allow messaging through the facilities of MQSeries, as well as the traditional 3270 frontend.

The sample is implemented as a set of COBOL programs, copybooks, BMS maps, and mapsets. These are supplied in both source code and are also compiled for use with CICS TS V1.3 in an LE environment. In addition to the COBOL programs the code is provided for the Java ORB and Web, HTML pages, and the code for Parts 6 and 7.

Files Used by the COBOL Application

Table B-1. Files Used by the COBOL Application

File	Description
Loadlib	
nact01.cobol	This is the load module for the program that provides the frontend interface (presentation logic) for 3270 terminals as part of the sample application. It is the first program executed when the transaction NACT is run.
nact02.cobol	This is the load module for the program, which provides the Create, Read, Update, Delete (CRUD) functions of the sample application. It is designed to be *LINK*ed to in order to allow any number of frontends to use its services.

Table B-1. Files Used by the COBOL Application (continued)

File	Description
nact03.cobol	This is the load module for the program, which provides the convenience print function as part of the sample application.
nact04.cobol	This is the load module for the program, which provides the error and ABEND handling logic for the sample application.
nact05.cobol	This is the load module for the program, which provides the Name Search (Browse) function for the sample application. It is designed to be *LINK*ed to in order to allow any number of frontends to use its services.
nactset.map	This is the assembled module for the maps used by the *Designing & Programming CICS Applications* book sample application.
RDO	
cics0adp.txt	These are the CICS Resource Definitions, which must be installed for the COBOL Application to run.
cicsjadp.txt	These are the CICS Resource Definitions, which must be installed for the Web Component to run.
Sample_JCL	
csdupdte.jcl	This is sample JCL to update a CSD with the resource definitions for the sample application.
vsam.jcl	This is sample JCL to *DELETE/REDEFINE/SETUP* for the sample VSAM datasets.
Source	
naccbrws.cobcopy	This COBOL Copybook is the linkage COMMAREAs version of the interface to the Browse (*NACT05*) program.
nacccrud.cobcopy	This COBOL Copybook is the linkage COMMAREAs version of the interface to the CRUD (Create, Read, Update, and Delete) *NACT02* program.
naccerrh.cobcopy	This COBOL Copybook is the linkage COMMAREAs version of the interface to the Error Handler (*NACT04*) program.
nacctrec.cobcopy	This COBOL Copybook is the linkage COMMAREAs version of the Account record layout.
nact01.cobol	This is the source file for the program, which provides the frontend interface (presentation logic) for 3270 terminals as part of the sample application. It is the first program executed when the transaction NACT is run.
nact02.cobol	This is the source file for the program, which provides the CRUD functions of the sample application. It is designed to be *LINK*ed to in order to allow any number of frontends to use its services
nact03.cobol	This is the source file for the program, which provides the convenience print function as part of the sample application.
nact04.cobol	This is the source file for the program, which provides the error and abend handling logic for the sample application.

Table B-1. Files Used by the COBOL Application (continued)

File	Description
nact05.cobol	This is the source file for the program, which provides the Name Search (Browse) function for the sample application. It is designed to be *LINK*ed to in order to allow any number of frontends to use its services.
nacset.dsect	This is the *DSECT* file for the maps used by the sample application.
nactset.map	This is the source file for the maps used by the sample application.
nacwbrws.cobcopy	This COBOL Copybook is the working storage version of the interface to the Browse (*NACT05*) program.
nacwcrud.cobcopy	This COBOL Copybook is the working storage version of the interface to the CRUD (*NACT02*) program.
nacwerrh.cobcopy	This COBOL Copybook is the working storage version of the interface to the Error Handler (*NACT04*) program
nacwlits.cobcopy	This COBOL Copybook is used in working storage and contains a number of commonly used variables, which are static while the application is running, but may be changed at a later date. These include, transaction names, program names, filenames, system traps, and abends.
nacwlock.cobcopy	This COBOL Copybook is used in working storage and contains a description of the logical locking ("in use") record. It is only used in the CRUD (*NACT02*) program but could, theoretically, be used in some other program.
nacwtrec.cobcopy	This COBOL Copybook is the working storage version of the Account record layout.
Data	
cicsadp.txt	The file contains the data to be placed in the sample VSAM file.

Glossary

The following terms are used in this book. Other terms used in CICS can be found in the *CICS Glossary* that is in PDF format on the CD. The IBM Dictionary of Computing at *http://www.networking.ibm.com/nsg/nsgmain.htm* provides a long list of computer terms, as well.

abend

Abnormal end of task.

ACID properties

The term, coined by Haerder and Reuter (1983), and used by Jim Gray and Andreas Reuter to denote the properties of a transaction:

Atomicity

A transaction's changes to the state (of resources) are atomic: either all happen or none happen.

Consistency

A transaction is a correct transformation of the state. The actions taken as a group do not violate any of the integrity constraints associated with the state.

Durability

After a transaction completes successfully (commits), its changes to the state survives failures.

Isolation

Even though transactions execute concurrently, they appear to be serialized. In other words, it appears to each transaction that any other transaction executed either before it, or after it.

In CICS, the ACID properties apply to a unit of work (UOW). See also *unit of work.*

applet

An application program, written in the Java programming language, that can be retrieved from a web server and executed by a web browser. Compare with servlet.

basic mapping support (BMS)

An interface between CICS and application programs that formats input and output display data and routes multiple-page output messages without regard for control characters used by various terminals.

BMS

See basic mapping support.

business application

An application that transacts the business of a company—that is, an application that performs business transactions on behalf of the company.

business logic

The code that implements a business application.

business operations application

See business application.

CAD

Computer-aided design.

channel

See message channel.

CICS

See Customer Information Control System.

CICS Transaction Gateway (CTG)

This provides a comprehensive set of Java-based web server facilities for access to CICS applications from a web browser.

CICS-value data area

A CICS value on INQUIRE and SET commands, specifically those that refer to resource status or definitions. See the *CICS System Programming Reference* for more information.

CICS Web Interface (CWI)

A collection of CICS resources supporting direct access to CICS transaction processing services from web browsers.

class

In object-oriented design or programming, a model or template that can be instantiated to create objects with a common definition and, therefore, common properties, operations, and behavior. An object is an instance of a class.

client

A computer system or process that requests a service of another computer system or process that is typically referred to as a server. Multiple clients may share access to a common server.

client/server

A distributed application design model in which the frontend transaction (the one that initiates the conversation) is called the client and controls the course of the conversation. The server receives a request from the client, processes it, and returns the results.

COBOL

Common business-oriented language. An English-like programming language designed for business data processing applications.

COMMAREA

See communication area.

Common Object Request Broker Architecture (CORBA)

An architectural standard proposed by the Object Management Group (OMG), an industry standards organization for creating object descriptions that are portable among programming languages and execution platforms.

communication area (COMMAREA)

A CICS area that is used to pass data between tasks that communicate with a given terminal. The area can also be used to pass data between programs within a task. A CICS program typically populates it with data accessed from files or databases.

component tracing

Tracing facility provided by CICS to trace transactions through the CICS components, and through user programs.

constructor

A special class method that has the same name as the class and is used to construct and possibly initialize objects of its class type.

conversational

(1) Pertaining to a program or a system that carries on a dialog with a terminal user, alternately receiving and transmitting data. (2) Pertaining to an SNA conversation or a dialog between two programs.

CORBA

See Common Object Request Broker Architecture.

CORBA services

Services that specify the standard interfaces of the OMG object services.

CRUD

Create, Read, Update, and Delete.

CTG

See CICS Transaction Gateway.

Customer Information Control System (CICS)

A General-purpose data communication system (or online transaction processing system). An online system controller and some batch utilities that are capable of supporting a network of many terminals. The CICS family of products provides a range of application platforms on many operating system platforms, including OS/390, MVS/ESA, MVS/XA, MVS/370, VSE/ESA, DOS/VS, OS/2, System/400, and System/6000.

CVDA

See CICS-value data area.

CWI

See CICS Web Interface.

Database 2 (DB2)

A relational database management system in which data is presented to the user in the form of tables. It can be accessed by CICS application programs issuing SQL requests.

DB2

See Database 2.

e-Business

(1) The transaction of business over an electronic medium such as the Internet. (2) Any organization (for example, commercial, industrial, nonprofit, educational, or governmental) that transacts its business over an electronic medium such as the Internet. An e-business combines the resources of traditional information systems with the vast reach of an electronic medium such as the Internet (including the World Wide Web, intranets, and extranets); it connects critical business systems directly to critical business constituencies—customers, employees, and suppliers. The key to becoming an e-business is building a transaction-based web site in which all core business processes (especially all processes that require a dynamic and interactive flow of information) are put online to improve service, cut costs, and sell products.

e-Commerce

The subset of e-business that involves the exchange of money for goods or services purchased over an electronic medium such as the Internet.

EBCDIC

Extended binary-coded decimal interchange code.

ECI

See external call interface.

EDF

See execution diagnostic facility.

end user

Anyone using CICS to do a job, usually by interacting with an application program (transaction) by means of a terminal.

Enterprise ToolKit for OS/390 (ET/390)

This is supplied with VisualAge for Java Integrated Development Environment (IDE) to develop Java applications to run in the OS/390 UNIX or CICS for OS/390 environments.

EXCI

See external CICS interface.

ET/390

See Enterprise ToolKit for OS/390.

execution diagnostic facility (EDF)

A facility used for testing application programs interactively online, without making any modifications to the source program or to the program preparation procedure. The facility intercepts execution of the program at various points and displays information about the program at these points. Also displayed are any screens sent by the user program, so that the user of EDF can converse with the application program during testing just as a user would do on the production system.

external call interface (ECI)

A CICS facility that allows a calling program to call a CICS program as though it had been linked to (using the *LINK* facility) by another CICS program.

external CICS interface (EXCI)

A CICS application programming interface that helps to make CICS applications more easily accessible from non-CICS environments. It enables a non-CICS program (a client program) running in OS/390 to call a program (a server program) running in a CICS Transaction Server region and to pass and receive data by means of a communication area. The CICS program is invoked as if linked to by another CICS program. For programming information about EXCI, see the *External CICS Interface User's Guide*.

Extended binary-coded decimal interchange code

A coded character set of 256 8-bit characters.

FIFO

First in, first out.

file transfer protocol (FTP)

In the Internet suite of protocols, an application layer protocol that uses TCP and Telnet services to transfer bulk-data files between machines or hosts.

firewall

A firewall is a software configuration that prevents unauthorized traffic between a trusted network and an untrusted network.

FTP

See file transfer protocol.

graphical user interface (GUI)

A type of computer interface consisting of a visual metaphor of a real-world scene, often of a desktop. Within that scene are icons, representing actual objects, that the user can access and manipulate with a pointing device.

GUI

See graphical user interface.

HTML

See hypertext markup language.

HTTP

See hypertext transfer protocol.

HyperText Markup Language (HTML)

A markup language that is specified by an SGML document type definition (DTD) and is understood by all web servers. It was designed primarily to support the online display of textual and graphical information that includes hypertext links.

Hypertext Transfer Protocol (HTTP)

In the Internet suite of protocols, the protocol that is used to transfer and display hypertext documents.

IDE

See Integrated Development Environment.

IDL

See interface definition language.

IIOP

See Internet Inter-ORB Protocol.

inheritance

(1) A mechanism by which an object class can use the attributes, relationships, and methods defined in more abstract classes related to it (its base

classes). (2) An object-orientated programming technique that allows you to use existing classes as bases for creating other objects.

initiation queue

A local queue on which the queue manager puts trigger messages.

Integrated Development Environment (IDE)

In VisualAge for Java, a set of windows that provide the user with access to development tools.

Interactive System Productivity Facility (ISPF)

An IBM licensed program that serves as a full screen editor and dialog manager. It is used for writing application programs and provides a means of generating standard screen panels and interactive dialogues between the application programmer and terminal user.

interface

Hardware, software or both, that links systems, programs, or devices.

interface definition language (IDL)

A contractual, neutral, and declarative language that specifies an object's boundaries and its interfaces. IDL provides operating system independent and programming language independent interfaces to all services and components that reside on a CORBA bus.

Internet

A wide area network connecting thousands of disparate networks in industry, education, government, and research. The Internet network uses TCP/IP as the standard for transmitting information.

Internet Inter-ORB Protocol (IIOP)

An object-oriented protocol that makes it possible for distributed programs written in different programming languages to communicate over the Internet. An industry standard protocol that defines how General Inter-ORB Protocol messages are exchanged over a TCP/IP network.

interoperable object reference (IOR)

A string that keeps information about the type and key of an object and the communications profiles needed to contact the object server and locate the object. An IOR is represented through a String instance by a process known as *stringification.*

intranet

A private network that integrates Internet standards and applications (such as web browsers) with an organization's existing computer networking infrastructure.

IOR

See interoperable object reference.

ISPF

See Interactive System Productivity Facility.

Java

An object-oriented programming language for portable interpretive code that supports interaction among remote objects. Java was developed and specified by Sun Microsystems, Inc.

JavaBeans

A platform-independent, software component technology for building reusable Java components called *beans*. Once built, these beans can be made available for use by other software engineers or can be used in Java applications. Also, using JavaBeans, software engineers can manipulate and assemble beans in a graphical drag-and-drop development environment.

JCL

See Job Control Language.

Job Control Language (JCL)

Control language used to describe a job and its requirements to an operating system; for example, OS/390.

KSDS

See Key Sequenced Data Set.

LAN

See local area network.

line of business application

See business application.

local area network (LAN)

A computer network located on a user's premises within a limited geographical area. Communication within a local area network is not subject to external regulations; however, communication across the LAN boundary may be subject to some form of regulation.

local queue

A queue that belongs to the local queue manager. A local queue can contain a list of messages waiting to be processed. Contrast with remote queue.

local queue manager

The queue manager to which a program is connected and that provides message queueing services to the program. Queue managers to which a program is not connected are called remote queue managers, even if they are running on the same system as the program.

mainframe

A computer, usually in a computer center, with extensive capabilities and resources to which other computers may be connected so that they can share facilities.

MCI

See message channel interface.

message

(1) In message queuing applications, a communication sent between two programs. (2) In system programming, information intended for the terminal operator or system administrator.

message channel

In distributed message queuing, a mechanism for moving messages from one queue manager to another. A message channel comprises two message channel agents (a sender at one end and a receiver at the other end) and a communication link. Contrast with MQI channel.

message channel interface (MCI)

The MQSeries interface to which customer- or vendor-written programs that transmit messages between an MQSeries queue manager and another messaging system must conform. A part of the MQSeries Framework.

message queue interface (MQI)

The programming interface provided by the MQSeries queue managers. This programming interface allows application programs to access message queueing services.

method

(1) A fragment of Java code within a class that can be invoked and passed a set of parameters to perform a specific class. (2) An implementation of an operation. Code that can be executed to perform a specific request. Methods associated with an object can be structured into one or more programs

MQI

See message queue interface.

MQI channel

Connects an MQSeries client to a queue manager on a server system, and transfers only MQI calls and responses in a bidirectional manner. Contract with message channel.

MQSeries

The IBM MQSeries family, which provides an open, scalable, industrial-strength messaging and information infrastructure, enabling enterprises and beyond to integrate business processes.

middleware

A vague term that refers to the software between an application program and the lower-level platform functions.

network

(1) An interconnected group of nodes. (2) The assembly of equipment through which connections are made between work stations.

object

(1) A collection of data and methods that operate on that data, which together represent a logical entity in the system. In object-orientated programming, objects are grouped into classes that share common definitions and methods. Each object in the class is said to be an instance of the class. (2) An instance of an object class consisting of attributes, a data structure, and operational methods. It can represent a person, thing, event, or concept. Each instance has the same properties, attributes, and methods as other instances of the object class, although it has unique values assigned to its attributes. (3) In MQSeries, an object in a queue manager, a queue, a process definition, a channel, a namelist, or a storage class (OS/390).

Object Management Group (OMG)

A consortium of vendors that defines standards pertaining to object-orientated distributed systems. The OMG is responsible for defining CORBA, CORBA services, and CORBA facilities in accordance with the Object Management Architecture.

object-oriented programming

A programming approach based on the concepts of data abstraction and inheritance. Unlike procedural programming languages, object-orientated programming concentrates on those data objects that constitute the problem and how they are manipulated, and not on how something is accomplished.

Object Request Broker (ORB)

A CORBA term designating the means by which objects transparently make requests and receive responses from other objects, whether local or remote.

ORB

See Object Request Broker.

PC

See personal computer.

personal computer (PC)

(1) A microcomputer primarily intended for stand-alone use by an individual. (2) A desk-top, floor-standing, or portable microcomputer that usually consists of a system unit, a display monitor, a keyboard, one or more diskette drives, internal fixed-disk storage, and an optional printer. PCs are designed

primarily to give independent computing power to a single user and are inexpensively priced for purchase by individuals or small businesses.

proxy object

An object on the client side that has the same interface as the server object it represents. Instead of having the actual method implementation, its methods communicate with an ORB.

pseudo-conversational

A type of CICS application design that appears to the user as a continuous conversation, but that consists internally of multiple tasks—also called *transaction-oriented programming*.

queue

An MQSeries object. Message queueing applications can put messages on, and get messages from, a queue. A queue is owned and maintained by the queue manager. Local queues can contain a list of messages waiting to be processed. Queues of other types cannot contain messages; they point to other queues, or can be used as models for dynamic queues.

queue manager

(1) A system program that provides queuing services to applications. It provides an application programming interface so that programs can create and access messages on the queues that the queue manager owns. See local queue manager and remote queue manager. (2) An MQSeries object that defines the attributes of a particular queue manager.

receiver channel

In message queueing, a channel that responds to a sender channel, takes messages form communication link, and puts them on a local queue.

remote queue

A remote queue is a local definition of a queue on a remote queue manager. A program opens a remote queue, the put goes on an XMITQ. Contrast with local queue.

remote queue manager

To a program, a queue manager that is not the one to which the program is connected.

reply-to queue

The name of a queue to which the program that issued an *MQPUT* call wants a reply message or report message sent.

sender channel

In message queueing, a channel that initiates transfers, removes messages from a transmission queue, and sends them over a communication link to a receiver or requester channel.

server

(1) A functional unit that provides shared services to clients over a network; for example, a file server, a print server, a mail server. (2) In TCP/IP, a system in a network that handles the requests of a system at another site, called a client-server.

servlet

An application program, written in the Java programming language, that is executed on a web server.

SIT

See system initialization table.

skeleton

The object-interface-specific ORB component that assists an object adaptor in passing requests to particular methods.

SNA

See Systems Network Architecture.

stringification

The process of converting a reference to the CORBA server object to and/or from a string representation of an IOR. Once an object reference has been stringified, it can be used by other applications to obtain a reference to the remote object.

stub

A local procedure corresponding to a single operation that invokes the operation when called.

synchronous

(1) Pertaining to an event that happens, exists, or arises at precisely the same time as another event. (2) Pertaining to an operation that occurs regularly or predictably with regard to the occurrence of a specified event in another process; for example, the calling of an input/output routine that receives control at a precoded location in a program. Contrast with asynchronous.

syncpoint

A logical point in the execution of an application program where the changes made to the databases by the program are consistent and complete and can be committed to the database.

system initialization table (SIT)

A table containing the parameters used by CICS on start up.

Systems Network Architecture (SNA)

A description of logical structures, formats, protocols, and operational sequences for transmitting information units through, and controlling the configuration and operation of, networks. The structure of SNA allows the end users to be independent of, and unaffected by, the specific structures used for information exchange.

task

(1) A unit of work for the processor; therefore the basic multiprogramming unit under the control program. (2) Under CICS, the execution of a transaction for a particular user. Contrast with transaction.

TCP/IP

See Transmission Control Protocol/Internet Protocol (TCP/IP).

Transmission Control Protocol/Internet Protocol (TCP/IP)

A set of communication protocols that support peer-to-peer connectivity functions for both local and wide area networks.

transaction

A transaction can be regarded as a unit of processing (consisting of one or more application programs) initiated by a single request. A transaction may require the initiation of one or more tasks for its execution.

unit of work (UOW)

A sequence of processing actions (database changes, for example) that must be completed before any of the individual actions performed by a transaction can be regarded as committed. After changes are committed (by successful completion of the UOW and recording of the syncpoint on the system log), they become durable, and are not backed out in the event of a subsequent failure of the task or system.

The beginning and end of the sequence may be marked by:

- Start and end of transaction, when there are no intervening syncpoints
- Start of task and a syncpoint
- A syncpoint and end of task
- Two syncpoints

Thus a UOW is completed when a transaction issues an explicit syncpoint request, or when CICS takes an implicit syncpoint at the end of the transaction. In the absence of user syncpoints explicitly taken within the transaction, the entire transaction is one UOW.

Unix operating system

An operating system developed by Bell Laboratories that features multiprogramming in a multi-user environment. The Unix operating system was originally developed for use on minicomputers but has been adapted for mainframes and microcomputers. (Trademark of AT&T Bell Laboratories.)

UOW

See unit of work.

VSAM

See Virtual Storage Access Method.

VTAM

See Virtual Telecommunications Access Method.

Virtual Storage Access Method (VSAM)

An access method for direct or sequential processing of fixed and variable-length records on direct access devices. The records in a VSAM data set or file can be organized in logical sequence by a key field (key sequence), in the physical sequence in which they are written on the data set or file (entry-sequence), or by relative-record number.

Virtual Telecommunications Access Method (VTAM)

IBM software that controls communication and the flow of data in an SNA network by providing the SNA application programming interfaces and SNA networking functions. An SNA network includes subarea networking, Advanced Peer-to-Peer Networking (APPN), and High-Performance Routing (HPR). Beginning with Release 5 of the OS/390 operating system, the VTAM for MVS/ESA function was included in Communications Server for OS/390; this function is called Communications Server for OS/390 - SNA Services.

Suggestions for Further Reading

Here are the URLs of links that will help you to keep up-to-date with events in the CICS world:

http://www.software.ibm.com/ts/cics
> The CICS home page on the internet; a good starting point giving an overview and links to many developer sites, case studies, and other sites.

http://www.software.ibm.com/ts/cics/library/ts390
> The site for the CICS TS/390 Newsletter.

http://www.s390.ibm.com/ads
> The site for the IBM S/390 Application Development Solutions.

http://www.redbooks.ibm.com/
> Redbooks are produced by small teams of IBM professionals to provide specialist books based on first hand experience for people implementing IBM solutions. *The redbooks listed in this bibliography can be found at this site.*

http://www.ibm.com/developer/java/
> The IBM site for Java. It provides valuable information about Servletes, XML as well as all things Java. A really good resource.

http://www.omg.org/
> The site for the Object Management Group (OMG). The OMG was formed to create a component-based software marketplace by hastening the introduction of standardized object software. The OMG is responsible for the establishment of worldwide standards for CORBA.

http://java.sun.com
> The Sun Java web site.

Here is a brief list of some books that you might find helpful:

Deborin E., Ekstedt A., Gardner A., and Verbestel N., *CICS Transaction Server for OS/390: Web Interface and 3270 Bridge*. IBM International Technical Support Organization, 444 pages (SG24-5243). This book is particularly useful if you want to develop your MQSeries CICS application based on the sample that we described in Part VII of this book. Part 2 gives an overview of the Bridge Exit as well as describing how to write your own exit. It is illustrated using a number of samples. It also describes how to use the CICS Web Interface (CWI).

Deborin E., Irmer F., Lux A., Verbestel N., and Weiand D., *Java Application Development for CICS: Base Services and CORBA Client Support*, IBM International Technical Support Organization, 436 pages (SG24-5275). A practical and very complete book that supports and amplifies the information introduced in Parts 3 and 4.

De Simoni G., Thrum, D., and Wall S., *Accessing CICS Business Applications from the World Wide Web*, Prentice Hall, 234 pages. This provides a discussion about TCP/IP, sockets, security that extends the discussion in this book. It also provides further examples.

Hollingshead A., Kawanami M., Moffat I., Walls J., Goodall C., and Nagel H., *Revealed! CICS Transaction Gateway with More CICS Clients Unmasked*, IBM International Technical Support Organization, 407 pages (SG24-5277). The best single source to get your CICS Client running especially for the TCP62 connection.

Wakelin P., Song X., Robins T., Kaputin J., and Nagel H., *Revealed! Architecting Web Access to CICS*. IBM International Technical Support Organization, 321 pages (SG24-5466). This recent book (May 1999) outlines the options that are available to access the CICS from the World Wide Web. Part 3 descrines the CICS Transaction Gateway (CTG) that provides an alternative way to develop the Visual Basic application described in Part VI of this book.

This is a list of the CICS manuals that are referred to in this book. They are all found in PDF format on the CD that accompanies this book.

CICS Application Programming Guide (SC33-1687)
    This gives you more details of the languages that are supported by CICS and BMS maps.

CICS Application Programming Reference (SC33-1688)
    This is the definitive reference to all the CICS Application Program Interface commands.

CICS External Interfaces Guide (SC33-1944)

This book describes how you can make the CICS transaction processing services of CISC TS for OS/390 available to a variety of external users.

CICS Supplied Transactions (SC33-1686)

These transactions are used in the Debugging chapter. They allow you to manage the definitions of resources dynamically.

CICS System Programming Reference (SC33-1689)

This is the definitive reference to all the CICS *INQUIRE* and *SET* commands.

CICS Messages and Codes (SC33-1694)

This lists all the messages and codes that are generated from CICS.

CICS Problem Determination Guide (SC33-1693)
CICS Recovery and Restart Guide (SC33-1698)

These are referred to in the Debugging chapter

Two books from MQSeries Library are:

MQSeries System Management Guide (SC34-5374)

This has a chapter which describes the MQSeries-CICS Bridge.

MQSeries Application Programming Guide (SC34-0807)

This book describes how to write an MQSeries-CICS bridge application.

Index

About the Author

John Horswill is a member of IBM's CICS User Technololgy team at IBM in Hursley Park, U.K. He has been involved in delivering information on various platforms, including OS/390, AIX, Solaris, Digital Unix, HP, and Windows NT, for the past 11 years. Before joining IBM, he worked in Further Education in England for many years. He graduated from London University and completed an M.Sc. in Applied Cell Science and Virology at Brunel University before turning his attention to computing. If you can't find him in his office or working from home, he is probably in his garden or hopefully "at the top of a mountain on a clear day."

Andy Krasun graduated from Oxford University, U.K. with a B.A. degree in Mathematics and, not wishing to start work, studied for an M.Sc. in Numerical Analysis at Dundee University in Scotland. He currently works in the CICS Strategy group and has been in and around CICS since it arrived in Hursley, England in 1975. He is a well-known speaker at User Groups around the world, talking on CICS Application Design and Development. When time permits, he is thinking about writing up his thesis for an M.Sc. at Oxford University in Software Engineering, sailing on a square rigger somewhere in the English Channel, or skiing in France.

Here are some links to the Hursley home pages that give a better idea of the IBM CICS Development team:

Hursley home page
> *http://www.hursley.ibm.com/*

IBM CICS Development team
> *http://www.hursley.ibm.com/devt_groups.html*

IBM Hursley
> *http://www.hursley.ibm.com/about_hursley.html*

Colophon

Our look is the result of reader comments, our own experimentation, and feedback from distribution channels. Distinctive covers complement our distinctive approach to technical topics, breathing personality and life into potentially dry subjects.

The animal on the cover of *Designing and Programming CICS Applications* is a gyr falcon. The gyr falcon has been characterized as a "heavily built bird." Hailing from Northern Canada, it inhabits the open tundra areas, but can be seen as far south as the United States/Canadian border. The gyr falcon's plumage varies from white to gray, depending on its region. This bird of prey's diet consists mainly of small rodents and other birds.

The black gyr falcon is popular in Europe, and over generations has been crossed with the peregrine hawk to produce the gyr/peregrine. The male, which is smaller than the female, is known as an excellent game hawk, while the female is noted for her precise hunting abilities.

Maureen Dempsey was the production editor and copyeditor for *Designing and Programming CICS Applications*. Norma Emory was the proofreader. Sarah Jane Shangraw and Madeleine Newell provided quality control. Brenda Miller wrote the index.

Edie Freedman designed the cover of this book, based on a series of her own design. The cover image is a 19th-century engraving from the Dover Pictorial Archive. Emma Colby produced the cover layout with QuarkXPress 4.1 using Adobe's ITC Garamond font.

Alicia Cech and David Futato designed the interior layout based on a series design by Nancy Priest. Mike Sierra implemented the design in FrameMaker 5.5.6. The text and heading fonts are ITC Garamond Light and Garamond Book. The illustrations that appear in the book were produced by Robert Romano and Rhon Porter using Macromedia FreeHand 8 and Adobe Photoshop 5. This colophon was written by Maureen Dempsey.

Whenever possible, our books use RepKover™, a durable and flexible lay-flat binding. If the page count exceeds RepKover's limit, perfect binding is used.

How to stay in touch with O'Reilly

1. Visit Our Award-Winning Web Site

http://www.oreilly.com/

★ "Top 100 Sites on the Web" —*PC Magazine*
★ "Top 5% Web sites" —*Point Communications*
★ "3-Star site" —*The McKinley Group*

Our web site contains a library of comprehensive product information (including book excerpts and tables of contents), downloadable software, background articles, interviews with technology leaders, links to relevant sites, book cover art, and more. File us in your Bookmarks or Hotlist!

2. Join Our Email Mailing Lists

New Product Releases

To receive automatic email with brief descriptions of all new O'Reilly products as they are released, send email to:
listproc@online.oreilly.com
Put the following information in the first line of your message (*not* in the Subject field):
subscribe oreilly-news

O'Reilly Events

If you'd also like us to send information about trade show events, special promotions, and other O'Reilly events, send email to:
listproc@online.oreilly.com
Put the following information in the first line of your message (*not* in the Subject field):
subscribe oreilly-events

3. Get Examples from Our Books via FTP

There are two ways to access an archive of example files from our books:

Regular FTP

- ftp to:
  ftp.oreilly.com
  (login: anonymous
  password: your email address)
- Point your web browser to:
  ftp://ftp.oreilly.com/

FTPMAIL

- Send an email message to:
  ftpmail@online.oreilly.com
  (Write "help" in the message body)

4. Contact Us via Email

order@oreilly.com
To place a book or software order online. Good for North American and international customers.

subscriptions@oreilly.com
To place an order for any of our newsletters or periodicals.

books@oreilly.com
General questions about any of our books.

software@oreilly.com
For general questions and product information about our software. Check out O'Reilly Software Online at **http://software.oreilly.com/** for software and technical support information. Registered O'Reilly software users send your questions to: **website-support@oreilly.com**

cs@oreilly.com
For answers to problems regarding your order or our products.

booktech@oreilly.com
For book content technical questions or corrections.

proposals@oreilly.com
To submit new book or software proposals to our editors and product managers.

international@oreilly.com
For information about our international distributors or translation queries. For a list of our distributors outside of North America check out:
http://www.oreilly.com/www/order/country.html

5. Work with Us

Check out our website for current employment opportunites:
www.jobs@oreilly.com
Click on "Work with Us"

O'Reilly & Associates, Inc.
101 Morris Street, Sebastopol, CA 95472 USA
TEL   707-829-0515 or 800-998-9938
           (6am to 5pm PST)
FAX   707-829-0104

International Distributors

UK, EUROPE, MIDDLE EAST AND AFRICA (EXCEPT FRANCE, GERMANY, AUSTRIA, SWITZERLAND, LUXEMBOURG, LIECHTENSTEIN, AND EASTERN EUROPE)

INQUIRIES
O'Reilly UK Limited
4 Castle Street
Farnham
Surrey, GU9 7HS
United Kingdom
Telephone: 44-1252-711776
Fax: 44-1252-734211
Email: josette@oreilly.com

ORDERS
Wiley Distribution Services Ltd.
1 Oldlands Way
Bognor Regis
West Sussex PO22 9SA
United Kingdom
Telephone: 44-1243-779777
Fax: 44-1243-820250
Email: cs-books@wiley.co.uk

FRANCE

INQUIRIES
Éditions O'Reilly
18 rue Séguier
75006 Paris, France
Tel: 33-1-40-51-52-30
Fax: 33-1-40-51-52-31
Email: france@editions-oreilly.fr

ORDERS
GEODIF
61, Bd Saint-Germain
75240 Paris Cedex 05, France
Tel: 33-1-44-41-46-16 (French books)
Tel: 33-1-44-41-11-87 (English books)
Fax: 33-1-44-41-11-44
Email: distribution@eyrolles.com

GERMANY, SWITZERLAND, AUSTRIA, EASTERN EUROPE, LUXEMBOURG, AND LIECHTENSTEIN

INQUIRIES & ORDERS
O'Reilly Verlag
Balthasarstr. 81
D-50670 Köln
Germany
Telephone: 49-221-973160-91
Fax: 49-221-973160-8
Email: anfragen@oreilly.de (inquiries)
Email: order@oreilly.de (orders)

CANADA (FRENCH LANGUAGE BOOKS)

Les Éditions Flammarion ltée
375, Avenue Laurier Ouest
Montréal (Québec) H2V 2K3
Tel: 00-1-514-277-8807
Fax: 00-1-514-278-2085
Email: info@flammarion.qc.ca

HONG KONG

City Discount Subscription Service, Ltd.
Unit D, 3rd Floor, Yan's Tower
27 Wong Chuk Hang Road
Aberdeen, Hong Kong
Tel: 852-2580-3539
Fax: 852-2580-6463
Email: citydis@ppn.com.hk

KOREA

Hanbit Media, Inc.
Chungmu Bldg. 201
Yonnam-dong 568-33
Mapo-gu
Seoul, Korea
Tel: 822-325-0397
Fax: 822-325-9697
Email: hant93@chollian.dacom.co.kr

PHILIPPINES

Global Publishing
G/F Benavides Garden
1186 Benavides Street
Manila, Philippines
Tel: 632-254-8949/637-252-2582
Fax: 632-734-5060/632-252-2733
Email: globalp@pacific.net.ph

TAIWAN

O'Reilly Taiwan
No. 3, Lane 131
Hang-Chow South Road
Section 1, Taipei, Taiwan
Tel: 886-2-23968990
Fax: 886-2-23968916
Email: taiwan@oreilly.com

CHINA

O'Reilly Beijing
Room 2410
160, FuXingMenNeiDaJie
XiCheng District
Beijing, China PR 100031
Tel: 86-10-66412305
Fax: 86-10-86631007
Email: beijing@oreilly.com

INDIA

Computer Bookshop (India) Pvt. Ltd.
190 Dr. D.N. Road, Fort
Bombay 400 001 India
Tel: 91-22-207-0989
Fax: 91-22-262-3551
Email: cbsbom@giasbm01.vsnl.net.in

JAPAN

O'Reilly Japan, Inc.
Kiyoshige Building 2F
12-Bancho, Sanei-cho
Shinjuku-ku
Tokyo 160-0008 Japan
Tel: 81-3-3356-5227
Fax: 81-3-3356-5261
Email: japan@oreilly.com

ALL OTHER ASIAN COUNTRIES

O'Reilly & Associates, Inc.
101 Morris Street
Sebastopol, CA 95472 USA
Tel: 707-829-0515
Fax: 707-829-0104
Email: order@oreilly.com

AUSTRALIA

Woodslane Pty., Ltd.
7/5 Vuko Place
Warriewood NSW 2102
Australia
Tel: 61-2-9970-5111
Fax: 61-2-9970-5002
Email: info@woodslane.com.au

NEW ZEALAND

Woodslane New Zealand, Ltd.
21 Cooks Street (P.O. Box 575)
Waganui, New Zealand
Tel: 64-6-347-6543
Fax: 64-6-345-4840
Email: info@woodslane.com.au

LATIN AMERICA

McGraw-Hill Interamericana
Editores, S.A. de C.V.
Cedro No. 512
Col. Atlampa
06450, Mexico, D.F.
Tel: 52-5-547-6777
Fax: 52-5-547-3336
Email: mcgraw-hill@infosel.net.mx

O'REILLY®

TO ORDER: **800-998-9938** • **order@oreilly.com** • **http://www.oreilly.com/**
OUR PRODUCTS ARE AVAILABLE AT A BOOKSTORE OR SOFTWARE STORE NEAR YOU.
FOR INFORMATION: **800-998-9938** • **707-829-0515** • **info@oreilly.com**

O'REILLY®

O'Reilly & Associates, Inc.
101 Morris Street
Sebastopol, CA 95472-9902
1-800-998-9938

Visit us online at:
www.oreilly.com
order@oreilly.com

O'REILLY WOULD LIKE TO HEAR FROM YOU

Which book did this card come from?

_____

Where did you buy this book?
- ❏ Bookstore
- ❏ Direct from O'Reilly
- ❏ Bundled with hardware/software
- ❏ Computer Store
- ❏ Class/seminar
- ❏ Other _____

What operating system do you use?
- ❏ UNIX
- ❏ Windows NT
- ❏ Macintosh
- ❏ PC(Windows/DOS)
- ❏ Other _____

What is your job description?
- ❏ System Administrator
- ❏ Network Administrator
- ❏ Web Developer
- ❏ Programmer
- ❏ Educator/Teacher
- ❏ Other _____

❏ Please send me O'Reilly's catalog, containing a complete listing of O'Reilly books and software.

Name _____ Company/Organization _____

Address _____

City _____ State _____ Zip/Postal Code _____ Country _____

Telephone _____ Internet or other email address (specify network) _____

Nineteenth century wood engraving
of a bear from the O'Reilly &
Associates Nutshell Handbook®
Using & Managing UUCP.

BUSINESS REPLY MAIL
FIRST CLASS MAIL   PERMIT NO. 80   SEBASTOPOL, CA

Postage will be paid by addressee

O'Reilly & Associates, Inc.
101 Morris Street
Sebastopol, CA 95472-9902